MARKETS AND MANUFACTURE
IN EARLY INDUSTRIAL EUROPE

MARKETS AND MANUFACTURE IN EARLY INDUSTRIAL EUROPE

Edited by Maxine Berg

London and New York

First published 1991
by Routledge
11 New Fetter Lane, London EC4P 4EE

Simultaneously published in the USA and Canada
by Routledge
a division of Routledge, Chapman and Hall, Inc.
29 West 35th Street, New York, NY 10001

Phototypeset by Input Typesetting Ltd, London

Printed in Great Britain by T.J. Press (Padstow) Ltd, Padstow,
Cornwall

British Library Cataloguing in Publication Data
Markets and manufacture in early industrial Europe.
   1. Europe. Industrialization, history
   I. Berg, Maxine
   338.094

Library of Congress Cataloging in Publication Data
Markets and manufacture in early industrial Europe / edited by Maxine
   Berg.
        p. cm.
     Includes bibliographical references.
      1. Europe—Industries—History—18th century. 2. Europe—
   Industries—History—19th century. 3. Europe—Manufactures—
   History—18th century. 4. Europe—Manufactures—History—19th
   century. I. Berg, Maxine.
   HC240.M247   1991
   338.094—dc20   90–32515

   ISBN 0–415–03720–4

In memory of Franklin Mendels 7 August 1943–10 April 1988

CONTENTS

CONTENTS

TABLES

FIGURE AND MAPS

FIGURE

MAPS

PREFACE

This book presents new research on the early phases of industrialization in eighteenth and nineteenth-century Europe. Its framework derives from recent debates on proto-industrialization, but it takes up new directions in that debate, and brings to bear new approaches to the economic history of the period.

The collection focuses on the commercial relations, marketing structures and development of consumption which accompanied early industrial expansion. It looks at the international matrix of early industrialization, dwelling on themes of trade, state policy and mercantile and urban networks. The papers in the collection, moreover, are not concerned simply to describe trade patterns and policies, but to examine the relationship between these and aspects of industrial structure and work organization.

While a good deal of recent research in eighteenth and early nineteenth-century economic and social history has been concerned with industrial and work organization, there has been little attempt to connect this to changes in market structures and the emergence of a consumer culture in Europe at the time. Yet recent sociological discussion of specialized and mass markets (the so-called 'flexible specialization') and recent historical research on the 'material culture' of the early modern period have pushed the question of the market to the forefront of new historical research.

The market discussed in these papers is not the abstraction of the economists, but the market as an institution which interacted with other social institutions of early industrial manufacture. Hence the papers discuss the structures of the market, state and urban economic policies, guild responses to national and international trade, the design and style of products for particular markets, and the relation of particular market structures to old and new social institutions and work practices. These aspects of the market are discussed in depth over a number of European countries – Britain, France, Spain, Ireland and Sweden, through the early years of growth or decline in the eighteenth and nineteenth centuries.

Some of the problems raised in examining the relation between market expansion and institutional structures illustrate the confrontation between, as well as the connection with, commercial expansion and custom. Both are apparent in municipal government and guild rules, and also in work codes and practices relating to gender roles, in debtor relations and in agrarian and community structures.

The papers collected together here provide a comparative range, seeking connections between the market and early industrial work experiences in different settings. They also provide solid and substantial information on actual marketing mechanisms and structures. The book raises key questions about the commercial side of early industrial communities – the nature of marketing, the role and meaning of consumption, and state and municipal initiatives and controls. These areas are very much in the forefront of new directions of research on early industrialization, and are developed in this book to complement earlier research on production, technology and labour.

The collection is the culmination of a series of workshops and a conference which I organized together with Professor John Davis from 1985 to 1989. These were the ESRC and Warwick Workshops on Early Industrial Communities. The workshops took the debate on proto-industrialization as their starting point, and moved discussion towards the wider social and economic dimensions of early industrial expansion, as well as looking in depth at the experiences of different regions across Europe. I would like to thank those who came from many different countries to participate in one or more of these workshops. I would also like to thank Leonore Davidoff and Geoff Crossick who organized one of the workshops at the University of Essex, Leonard Schwarz for organizing one at the University of Birmingham, Charles Saumarez-Smith and John Styles who held one at the Victoria and Albert Museum, and Professor Christopher Smout who held one at the University of St Andrews. Professor John Davis provided much of the ground level organization for the International Conference on Commerce and Custom in Early Industrial Europe which took place at the

University of Warwick in 1987. Most of the papers in this volume are drawn from that conference. Funding for the workshops and conference were provided by Warwick University, the Nuffield Foundation and the ESRC.

Historical research is best nourished in discussion and debate with other historians. The participants of these workshops provided my context for a long time, and many of them still do. I would especially like to thank Pat Hudson and Michael Sonenscher for making the Industrial Revolution and artisan industry the talk of good friends. And I am ever grateful to John Robertson for keeping my Industrial Revolution a provincial and European, and not a narrowly English and national, event.

My interest in the early phases of industrialization was sparked by the work of Sidney Pollard, E. L. Jones, Franklin Mendels and Hans Medick. Franklin Mendels attended the first workshop and the conference on Commerce and Custom. His analytical and wide ranging research and provocative discussion of it stimulated a major international debate on proto-industrialization. Many disagreed with him, but all were impressed with his dynamism. His early and untimely death was a great loss to economic and social historians, and this book is therefore dedicated to him.

Maxine Berg
April 1990

Part I
INTRODUCTION

1

MARKETS, TRADE AND EUROPEAN MANUFACTURE

Maxine Berg

A new interest in consumption and commercial expansion has been a characteristic of recent writing in economic and social history. But this interest has thus far been separated off from studies of economic growth during the Industrial Revolution. Economic growth in that key period has been considered almost entirely in the light of estimates of productivity change in selected industrial sectors and in agriculture, and it has been explained by changes in resource usage and technology.[1] The approach to industrialization has been dominated by supply side considerations, while factors affecting demand have been pushed into the background. The once fashionable focus on dramatic increases in foreign trade, and the steady expansion of the home market[2] have been dropped in favour of estimates of increases in output.

Recently, however, market structures and consumption patterns have returned to the historical agenda. Historians of the early phases of industrialization are now examining the market structures and policies which provided the context for industrial growth, and they have turned to the expenditure patterns, fashion and tastes, and the impact of new commercial structures on customary practices. *Markets and Manufacture in Early Industrial Europe* brings together a set of papers focused on commerce and its institutions in the creation of manufacturing communities. The book develops several themes of state policy, urbanization, marketing and mercantile organization, the role of women as a labour force and as consumers, and the impact of commercial expansion on local customary and community practices, artisan landholding and artisan credit and debt. The papers in this collection are the culmination of a long series of workshops and a conference on early industrial communities. While the early workshops in the series

3

were occupied with proto-industrialization, discussions relating to later workshops and to these papers have ranged far beyond this literature.

The book is divided into six sections. Section I provides an introduction to the book, and a survey of European markets and trade during the eighteenth century in relation to manufacturing. Section II discusses *The Market and the State*, examining issues of region versus nation state, and the impact of national economic policies. Section III, *Markets, Merchants and Middlemen*, looks at the organization of the market through agents, marketing networks and the diffusion of fashion. Section IV, *Markets and Urban Manufacture*, examines the general relationship of urban and rural industrialization and the special role played by urban institutions. The special experience of Birmingham is highlighted. Section V, *Market Production and Women's Work*, examines the way production for the market affected women's access to apprenticeship in England, and their labour force status in France. Section VI, *Market Structures and Social Institutions*, raises issues of access to markets and older social institutions such as landholding arrangements. Community practices affecting the organization of work were also practices which affected consumption and the market. Truck payments, embezzlement, debt and tavern life marked the interface of the market and the community.

PROTO-INDUSTRIALIZATION AT ITS LIMIT

The theory of proto-industrialization was developed in its simplest form by E. L. Jones, Franklin Mendels, and Medick, Schlumbohm and Kriedte.[3] It provided an integrated perspective on the European economy in the period just prior to industrialization, combining in a novel way the agricultural, industrial, mercantile and demographic change of that phase of capitalist development. In doing so it provided a new type of explanation of the source of industrial growth in a region.

Proto-industrialization was defined as the phase of the wide proliferation of rural domestic manufacture, a phase made distinctive by three factors. The essential features of proto-industrialization as these theorists identified them were: (1) economic and social symbiosis between agriculture and industry across the seasons; (2) industry co-ordinated by urban merchants; (3) industry dependent on distant markets. These factors distinguished

4

proto-industrialization from other forms of industrial organization and entailed the emergence of a distinct and dynamic socio-economic system. Proto-industrialization was also a distinctively regional phenomenon. Within any single region, proto-industrialization was based on a functional interrelationship between merchant capital, involved in the putting-out system, and the family economy.

The theory of proto-industrialization has been the subject of extensive debate and criticism. Empirical work using the hypothesis has elaborated a much more complex picture of the environments favourable to manufacturing. Research on the demographic conditions, agrarian and agricultural context and social and institutional framework of proto-industrialization has dramatically complicated our understanding of its preconditions.[4]Other research has focused on the success rates of the transition of a proto-industrial area into a region of more fully developed industrialism. Contrary to the original hypothesis, success rates were found to be poor and difficult to predict. Research on the actual experiences of individual regions constituted a challenge to unilinear approaches.[5] The emphasis of much work on the early phases of industrialization has, as a result, shifted away from development models, demography and agriculture towards the impact of social institutions and industrial and labour organization. But little serious consideration has yet been given to a major part of the framework of proto-industrialization – markets, merchant capital and the urban economy.

COMMERCE AND MARKETS

Medick, Kriedte and Schlumbohm first located the rise of proto-industrial occupations within the context of the commercial revolutions of the sixteenth and seventeenth centuries. A major contributory factor was, they argued, the emergence of a world system, especially the new colonialism with its plantation economy and slave trade. A new export base was the engine of growth for the first mass produced consumer industries. Yet in the debate on proto-industrialization little attention has been directed at the role and structure of the market. The traditionally-accepted division, between production in rural areas and commercial and market transactions in urban areas has not been challenged. This rural/

urban dichotomy has falsely separated production from consumption and trade.

The emphasis of most work on proto-industrialization has gone, by definition, to the rural economy. This entailed a definite neglect of the urban economy and urban manufactures in the same period. To some extent, such an emphasis was justified by the preoccupation of earlier historians with either agriculture or the urban and factory phases of industrialization. Certainly, in terms of numbers, rural putting out was much the most significant form that industry took in the period just prior to full industrialization. Nevertheless, the urban economy did play an important role even *vis à vis* rural manufacture. And urban manufactures were themselves significant and experienced variety and change in their organizational structures over the seventeenth and eighteenth centuries.

Systematic formulations of the role of urban and commercial networks have recently been offered by Jan de Vries, Paul Hohenberg, E. A. Wrigley and Paul Bairoch.[6] This work has assessed the commercial and even the producer role of the city in the early industrial period. It has charted patterns of urban growth and decline, assessing these in particular relation to the proto-industrial period. There is, these studies suggest, a real need to study the commercial and financial functions of urban areas as well as their own manufacturing. How dependent were these on national and international economic cycles, and how closely were they related to the surrounding countryside? The debate on proto-industrialization should have brought the commercial and the industrial, the rural and the urban together. Instead it divided them further. Proto-industrialization, and demographic and agrarian history have once again been compartmentalized from a separate urban history.

The need to relate the city to the early phases of industrialization in Europe may, at first sight, appear to need justification. Paul Bairoch has argued that the city played little part in unleashing the Industrial Revolution, or in the first stages of its diffusion to the rest of Europe. There were no traditional cities, especially large ones, among those regions in which the Industrial Revolution developed. The sectors which provided the driving force behind the Industrial Revolution were located if not entirely in rural districts, then in regions with only very small towns. Furthermore, those countries in which industrialization developed soonest were almost all initially little urbanized, while those which lagged were much more heavily urbanized.[7] But the relationship between urban and industrial development was more complex than the co-existence or not of cities and industry.

Jan de Vries in his highly original and important work, *European Urbanization 1500–1800*[8], points out the far-reaching effects of the pull of proto-industrialization on both urban and rural society. Proto-industrialization, in contrast to the production of rural handicrafts for local markets, required the commercial organization of a region, and that commercial organization was generally conducted from cities. The rise of proto-industrialization was to a large extent a consequence of city-centred investment. Rural locations attracted labour and capital from the cities, but the investors or co-ordinators were usually urban. With proto-industrialization, urban industrial employment was frequently undermined, but urban commercial and service functions were strengthened.

De Vries makes proto-industrialization the crucial link between the pre-industrial agrarian world and the growth of large cities in the nineteenth century. The smaller cities of Europe as a whole in the seventeenth and eighteenth centuries experienced decline, and the main reason for this was the transfer of industrial production to the countryside. But this development, in turn, could only have occurred because of the prior achievement of an urban system with a hierarchy of cities and towns. Thus the city's function in the process of proto-industrialization and general economic growth has to be seen in a broad regional context.

De Vries also analyses the timing of these processes. Between 1600 and 1750 a large proportion of Europe's cities with 5,000 or more inhabitants stagnated, as did thousands of smaller cities. The period 1750–1800 was a time of net urbanization across Europe, but it is notable that this urbanization was the result of the growth of smaller cities and the development of new cities rather than the growth of the traditional big urban centres and metropolises. This new urban growth was a growth from below, and the early stages of the Industrial Revolution were played out in such small cities and rural locations. Smaller cities with resource-based industries like metallurgy grew, while rural areas grown thick with proto-industrial textile production became industrial cities. Between 1750 and 1800 about 200 cities were added to the number of European towns with between 5,000 and 10,000 inhabitants. Thus we see the urban foundations within the region for proto-industrial growth, and the significance of the growth of the smaller urban areas in the crucial period between 1750 and 1800.

The regional interrelationship of town and country emphasized by De Vries was modelled by Paul Hohenberg in Hohenberg and Lees, *The Making of Urban Europe*.[9] The model delineated some of the macroeconomic relations between town and country, in particular integrating movements in income distribution with demographic change.

Rather than looking at production costs as the determining factor in the spread of proto-industrialization, Hohenberg emphasized demand. The model related incomes, and with this demand in the towns, to conditions in the countryside. Incomes in the towns, he points out, were based largely on property, that is, rents. The expansion or decline of towns in a region was thus related, via property incomes, to conditions in the countryside. The model, in motion, showed that periods of favourable harvest might stimulate economic activity and population growth. This expansion would be shared by urban capitalists and merchants via profits. When rural producers eventually met diminishing returns, higher grain prices and lower discretionary incomes would follow. These would hurt rural manufacturers. But, for a time, alongside this rural malaise, property incomes would remain buoyant due to high Ricardian rents, and urban employment and manufacture would thrive. The crisis in the countryside would eventually hit rents, due to the onset of demographic crisis and, with this, the urban boom would end.

This very schematic model is useful for pointing out the reasons for alternating phases of urban and rural strength in manufacturing. And it produces reasons based not on the traditional factor of costs, but rather on demand and income distribution. The model points out that, within the proto-industrial framework, towns could prosper in a variety of ways: they could concentrate on trade; they could be centres of direct production, that is, proto-industrial cities; or they could administer the collection of the surplus and organize its consumption.

Though urban industry rose and waned in the manner described by de Vries, and in relationship to the countryside in the way delineated by Hohenberg, it is also true that some urban industries resisted decline or flourished, counter to the prevailing trend. Crises could reaffirm dominance, or lead to the displacement of one leader by another.

These recent studies of urbanization have considered the framework of proto-industrial activity and the rural economy. They have avoided false assumptions of rural-urban dichotomies. The results of this research, in the case of British development, are spelled out by Wrigley, who links structural and demographic change in the eighteenth century to proto-industrial activity. He argues that there was a major fall in the proportion of the rural labour force engaged in agricultural occupations, complemented by a turning to rural *industrial* occupations including mining. The bulk of England's remarkable rise in population, he argues, emerged from the part which made its living outside agriculture. And he finds that an explanation of English agricultural improvement may lie in the rapid and uninterrupted growth in the urban sector of the economy which provided a great stimulus to agricultural and commercial improvement, and also fostered a major expansion of rural employment outside agriculture.

De Vries found that European industry developed in the late seventeenth and early eighteenth centuries in smaller cities and rural locations at a time when large cities and traditional urban centres were stagnating. This was followed by an urban resurgence in the later eighteenth century. But in England, Wrigley argues, there was no such urban decline in the early modern period; rural and urban industry developed together.[10]

Other countries too departed from the overall averages. Bairoch has pointed out that while four out of ten European cities stagnated or declined in population between 1500 and 1700, these ratios differed widely between countries. In Spain, it was 7 out of 10, Italy 5 out of 10, and in Belgium and Germany a little more than 4 out 10. But in the UK and the Netherlands, it was less than 2 out 10. Italy and Spain, therefore, accounted between them for 45 per cent of European cities suffering decline.[11]

Several of the papers in this collection take up the theme of urban institutions, marketing and industry. Hohenberg develops his model to incorporate the impact of the municipal authorities; Berg looks at industry and its organization in a large early manufacturing town, Birmingham; Thomson and Torras look at the impact of economic policy and trading monopolies, the diasporas, on large-scale urban manufactures; Kusamitsu and Collins disentangle the marketing and capital networks between urban centres and rural manufacturing outlets.

FLEXIBLE SPECIALIZATION

The new emphasis entailed in these works on the commercial organization of proto-industrialization, and the relationship of the rural economy to the cities and towns of its region raises the issue of demand.

The recent analysis of early industrialization reflects that of economic history more generally – emphasis on supply side considerations of labour supply, wage differentials, capital costs and the supply of materials. But the role of consumption and the special characteristics of the market have rarely been considered. Consumption and the special characteristics of the market have, however, been given a special place in a separate though related historical debate on flexible specialization.

Recent sociological literature on what is now known as 'flexible specialization' has looked to the heritage of craft industry, and related its history to flexible markets. It asserts the existence of a choice of technologies, related in turn to product choices. It thus calls for new attention to consumption and design.[12]

It is argued, for instance, that regional differences in tastes and markets in early modern France in the eighteenth and nineteenth centuries accommodated an expansion of the market for manufactured goods without homogenizing it. The demand for manufactured goods arose from regionally based groups of nobles and commoners, and tastes and markets differed from region to region. Guild standards of quality continued to maintain a hold, and the country was specializing from the eighteenth century in the production of a wide range of high quality goods. Even in the nineteenth century, the railways did not lead to the creation of mass markets but were used to make the flexible production capacities of the districts more accessible to the whole country. In Great Britain, by contrast, mass urban markets for cheap consumer goods emerged early. This tendency was fuelled by a high rate of urbanization and population increase. Colonial markets demanded a limited range of similar goods. A significant amount of diversity still prevailed, however, throughout the United Kingdom; provincial tastes differed and an abundance of skilled labour underpinned a long tradition of artisan production.

Flexible production techniques held sway through a large part of the nineteenth century in the production of silk textiles in Lyon, printed cottons in Alsace, ribbons, hardware, special steels and luxury engineering in St Etienne, hardware in Birmingham, and cutlery and edge tools in Sheffield and Solingen. In these regions, manufacturing units were mainly small, that is with less than fifty workers, their workforces were skilled, machinery multi-purpose and products varied. Even larger firms were more like a collection of artisanal workshops under one roof than the organizational innovation represented by the factory system.

The big contrast was with the United States, where the imposition of standardized tastes entailed mass production techniques. There labour was in short supply and a tradition of guild organization and standards was missing. Employers had the motive to invent labour-saving machinery and customers were ready to buy standardized goods. This difference in consumption patterns allowed for the rapid development of mass mechanized and large-scale production.[13]

The idea of 'flexible specialization' as a concept of alternative production organization, contrasted with hierarchically organized, factory-centred mass production, attractive as it may be, is open to serious objections of definition. The Japanese innovations of the 1960s demonstrated that assembly line factories could be used more flexibly than they had been in most western countries, and that assembly industries created opportunities of connecting large-, medium- and small-scale enterprises. New computer-controlled equipment could produce a greater variety of output, but it could not 'restore an economic system based on redeployable productive resources and low fixed costs'.[14]

The historical examples were also questionable, and open to other interpretations. The artisan clothiers of the Yorkshire woollen industry were successful for a long time, that is until the last quarter of the nineteenth century, but they were broken by changes in the market and competitive pressures in the industry, by the centralization of finance and the disappearance of community and artisan values, which had previously fostered the self-exploitation of family labour.[15] Harmonious class relations in Birmingham and highly skilled independent artisans in Sheffield owed more to historical myth than reality.[16] And Philadelphia's flexible and specialized textile industry was fundamentally a story of a great turnover of firms.[17]

The research based on the underlying idea of the significance of different national and regional consumption patterns is, however, important in raising the issue, developed in several of the papers in this book, especially those of Pollard, Collins, Kusamitsu, and Berg, of the relation of types of national and international markets to the emergence and retention of specific industrial structures.

CONSUMPTION, THE PRODUCT AND DISTRIBUTION

The concepts of both proto-industrialization and flexible specializ-ation have raised the need for economic historians to consider the types of product consumed, how the market and thus the product and its design were decided, and how the networks of distribution affected this. But until very recently there was little research on consumption, apart from a few very general pieces asserting its significance. This research discussed the role of the home market (A. H. John, D. C. Eversley, N. McKendrick, W. A. Cole),[18] and related this in turn back to agriculture.

Recent reassessments of economic growth in the eighteenth cen-tury, summarized by Crafts, attribute most of the growth that did take place to changes in agricultural productivity which reached their most significant levels in the seventeenth and early eighteenth centuries.[19] There is a long tradition of belief in a special connec-tion between increases in agricultural productivity and the devel-opment of the home market for manufactured commodities. Gilboy[20] first argued that rising real wages created new wants. This association was continued by A. H. John, who argued that lower food prices in 1730–50 led to surpluses for wage earners. These surpluses were in turn spent on domestic manufactured commodities, and stimulated innovation in the industrial period. Eversley then developed this analysis, arguing that the momentum continued until 1780, and also encompassed a middle-class market.

This traditional connection between wage increases and the development of the home market has recently been challenged. O'Brien has argued that only 6 per cent of the increment to expenditure on manufactures between 1700 and 1800 was due to higher wages paid to workers released through increases in agricul-tural productivity. In addition, there was only a small shift in terms of trade between agriculture and industry in the long period of stable prices between 1650 and 1750. This may have raised expenditures on industrial goods by between 3 and 8 per cent.

In general, then, agriculture's contribution towards widening the domestic market for industrial expansion was slight. As O'Brien concludes:

> Although most of the increment to industrial output was certainly sold on the home market, it is difficult to see increased agricultural productivity as the primary source behind the growth of domestic purchasing power for manufactures.[21]

The most recent research by R. A. C. Allen indicates that agricultural demand for manufactures was quiescent in the eighteenth century. Exports, non-agricultural investment and consumption by the bourgeoisie provided the principal markets for industrial output. Agriculture did not, therefore, provide the home market for the Industrial Revolution. Allen demonstrates that real wages and returns to farm capital were static from the seventeenth century to the nineteenth; the numbers of farmers and labourers fell, and their spending power diminished with this. The gains from improvements in agriculture accrued instead to landlords as higher rents; the gentry and aristocracy then spent on servants, stately homes and custom-made handicrafts, not on mass produced commodities.[22] The markets for the new industrial commodities were provided in the first instance from bourgeois consumption and the demands of the non-agricultural sector; and in the second instance by exports. It is, therefore, important to go on to examine the middle-class market, fashion and urban demand.

CONSUMPTION AND FASHION

Changing tastes in the eighteenth-century middle classes were fostered by international trade. Jones has argued that there was a new passion for oriental designs brought by maritime expansion, and that the French, in particular, dominated European culture and dictated fashion. Both of these influences were reinforced by urbanization and the growth of London. The new fashions for calico-printed fabrics and chinoiserie were particularly important in creating demand in the cotton industry and the small metal trades; new calico-printing techniques and the invention of japanning were direct results. The markets for such goods expanded rapidly, fostered by prosperity among the middle classes and the class of small tradesmen. The development of retailing through shops and commercial travellers promoted a national market for those goods.

At one level demand for the new manufactured commodities of the eighteenth century was determined by fashion. There were social hierarchies of fashion. Manufacturers took advantage of existing demand to release the potentialities of latent demand. Boulton and Watt, for example, sought out wealthy customers – the 'legislators of taste'. Then Boulton made goods accessible in price and place of sale to a mass market. 'It would not be worth my while to make for three countries only; but I find it well worth my while to make for all the world.'[23]

Boulton made commemorative issues of goods for royal birthdays, and sent new patterns to members of the aristocracy. He then produced a similar commodity in a variety of materials accessible to all levels of society. The classic example was the shoe buckle. The 'gradations of society' were codified in a whole 'protocol of shoe buckles made in every size and every material from diamonds to paste, from gold to pinchbeck'.[24]

> The variety of the great will ever be affecting new modes, in order to increase that notice to which it thinks itself exclusively entitled. The lower ranks will imitate them as soon as they have discovered the innovation.[25]

But the theory of emulation can only explain a portion of eighteenth-century consumption patterns. Equally important was the place of consumer expenditure in cementing social connections and family relationships. Aristocratic consumption frequently had dynastic motivations, while that of the gentry and middle classes conveyed protocol and a sense of belonging as well as the stability of family connections.[26] Furthermore, studies of fashion and consumerism in the eighteenth century have been confined for the most part to the gentry and the wealthier tradesmen. The consumption of the bulk of the middle ranks and of wage earners is not included. We have to turn to recent studies of probate inventories to discover more about the consumption habits of a broader spectrum of the population. This research indicates an overall increase in the ownership of all household goods during the first part of the eighteenth century. Kitchen and china ware, clocks, pictures, mirrors and curtains became more common everywhere. Patterns of consumption of household goods do not, however, coincide directly with other economic indicators. During the period

1715–25, for example, imports of tea and coffee rose rapidly, but imports of china, pottery, printed goods, paper and beer remained steady. Changes in national income, and even in wage trends, were not automatically reflected in the frequencies of ownership of household goods.[27]

EUROPEAN AND INTERNAL PATTERNS OF TRADE

The other major source of markets for the manufacturing sector was trade. The patterns of English trade over the sixteenth to the eighteenth centuries have been described many times before. These need to be put together with patterns of European trade at the time, and both related to the fortunes of the manufacturing sector.

The geographical distribution of European trade

Home demand always provided by far the most significant part of the market for the new manufactures. For the period 1700/10 to 1780/90 the home market absorbed 92 to 95 per cent of total output; foreign demand was responsible for only 5 to 9 per cent of the increase in England's total product. But the role of foreign demand grew sharply thereafter, so that between the 1780s and the 1860s it absorbed 30 per cent of UK additional output; in the period 1783–1803 the incremental ratio of exports to national product was as high as 40 per cent. From the end of the American War of Independence to the first years of the nineteenth century exports were a powerful engine of growth.[28] This is not to say, however, that external demand provided an exogenous cause of the Industrial Revolution. The main growth of Britain's industrial exports from 1790 to 1870 was underpinned by falling relative costs and prices. But the rapid expansion in trade earlier in the eighteenth century was more closely tied to the entry of the re-export trade in exotic commodities and the rise in population in England's 'free trade zone' of England, Wales, Scotland, Ireland and the colonies in North America and the West Indies.[29]

In the years of commercial expansion from 1769 to 1800 population rose rapidly in Europe. The fastest growing populations were Scandinavia, England, Belgium and Portugal. France's population rose at 0.23 per cent per annum, with the highest rates of growth in the south and the east. Italy's population grew fastest in the south, increasing 80 per cent between 1700 and 1800, 50 per cent in the north and 20 per cent in the central region. Spain's population rose 44 per cent; Catalonia's tripled and Valencia's doubled. This population was also more urbanized by later in the century; 7.6 per cent of Europe's population lived in cities of over 10,000 in 1600; 10 per cent in 1800.[30]

European trade with Asia, Africa and the Americas grew rapidly from the seventeenth century. The flow of bullion and the silver trade integrated Asia and Europe. Asian goods – spices, coffee, tea, indigo, silk and cotton textiles – flowed west, interacting with the flow of new colonial products from the Americas. Export surpluses in Asia, the Baltic and the Levant were met by inter-European trade. French and Dutch export surpluses with Spain facilitated bullion supplies to maintain the Asian trade. Only the Americas constituted an important early industrial export market. The African market took only firearms and linen; the Asian virtually nothing. But colonial staples from the Americas and Asia stimulated profitable processing and finishing industries – sugar refining, tobacco processing and calico printing – the fundamental industries underpinning the re-export trade.[31] This trade in colonial staples was the primary stimulus to urban growth throughout the seventeenth and eighteenth centuries. The populations of Marseilles and Bordeaux doubled; that of Nantes tripled. Glasgow, Bristol and Liverpool grew from towns of between 2,000 and 11,000 inhabitants to major cities of 77,000, 64,000 and 30,000 respectively.[32]

Most of Europe's foreign trade in the period, however, was conducted within its own frontiers. Britain was the major exception, for it underwent a dramatic change over the eighteenth century, abandoning the European dominance of its markets. The distribution of trade within and outside Europe changed dramatically over the course of the eighteenth century. The share of English exports going to Europe fell from 82 per cent in 1700/1 to 40 per cent in 1772/3; the share going to America rose from 10 per cent in 1700/1 to 37 per cent in 1772/3.[33] But in the late seventeenth and early eighteenth centuries, the main focus of English trade was Europe, not the periphery. England expanded its markets in the Mediterranean in the late seventeenth century – markets centred on the Levant trade based on broadcloth exports and raw silk imports from Turkey.[34] A substantial proportion of total imports in both France and England were accounted for by industrial raw materials. In France, these made up more than one-third of imports in the early eighteenth century, but 49 per cent by the end, with textile raw materials accounting for 70 per cent of these industrial raw materials. In England, raw materials accounted for 35 per cent of total imports in the early eighteenth century, but 50 per cent by its end.

While trade with the Mediterranean was important to England in the early commercial period, this declined over the eighteenth century. The Mediterranean was dominated by the trade in spices and luxuries from the Orient. But it was clear from the early eighteenth century that Italy had failed to move to the New Draperies, and had turned to the import of finished goods and services and the export of raw materials. In Spain, the transatlantic trade declined. The share of eastern central Europe in the international trading system also fell in parallel with the expansion of the transatlantic trade. But regions on the North Sea and the Baltic were developing a new trade in products for mass consumption. The Netherlands experienced an industrial revival in the late seventeenth century. Leiden's woollen industry revived, and it also took charge of the profitable finishing stages in other textiles: it bleached German, French and Flemish linen and prepared Italian silk. Sugar refineries and tobacco processing were also major industries until overtaken by England in the eighteenth century. Dutch export industries in the late seventeenth century were widely celebrated for their technical virtuosity. As pointed out by Jonathon Israel, Holland at this time was the exhibition centre for textile machinery, copper stills, presses, saws, shipbuilding innovations and scientific and consumer novelties from microscopes, firefighting engines and street lights to food-processing machinery. But these were export industries writ large, and based on quality, specialization and technical innovation. With the onset of industrial mercantilism in the rest of Europe in the early eighteenth century, this industrial base crumbled. It seems at one level that there was a close interdependence between Dutch commerce and industry. Dutch industry specialized in the finishing processes in the commodities she stockpiled for world trade – for example, dyeing, bleaching and printing with the cloth, dyestuffs and chemicals she traded.[35] But within the new protectionist framework of the eighteenth century European economies, divisions between trade and manufacture took hold. In England, free trade policies were espoused in the one sphere; protection of domestic markets in the other. The relative success of one sphere or the other in influencing economic policy determined the future course of growth. In England in 1700 domestic manufacturers had legislation passed against the import of Persian, Indian and Chinese silks and cottons; in Holland the merchants and financiers held sway, but in newly protected world markets their trade-dependent manufactures declined.[36]

English exports

English trade in the first instance was dominated by commerce rather than industry. Between 1660 and 1701 the re-export trade grew from negligible proportions to one-third of total exports. It was this trade that provided the basis for the wealth of the merchant classes. The eighteenth century opened with a period of growth followed in 1722–4 by a slump after the South Sea Bubble, and another depression in the early 1750s. There was another major commercial crisis between 1772 and 1774, but good years on either side.[37]

The course of English export growth over the eighteenth century was, however, closely related to trade policies in Britain and in Europe. Exports of English goods to southern Europe grew by only 50 per cent; those to northern Europe fell as these areas became increasingly protectionist. Meanwhile, however, exports to England's dependencies (North America, the West Indies, West Africa and the East Indies) rose sevenfold between 1699–1701 and 1772–4 from only 18.8 per cent of total English exports to 59.6 per cent of these exports.[38]

Woollens and worsteds accounted for most of English exports in the eighteenth century, but their role and growth were already diminishing by this time relative to other commodities. Up to the 1760s exports of woollens and worsteds grew at 0.9 per cent per year as against 1.6 per cent for total English exports. There was a more rapid rise in exports of linens, cottons, metals, metal manufactures and coal. The share of woollens in total exports fell from 70 per cent in 1700–9 to 44 per cent in 1760–9. There was a widening in the base of the British export trade from the seventeenth century: exports of pig iron doubled between 1760 and 1788 and increased fourfold between 1788 and 1806.[39] All the main British industries, in fact, contributed to the increasing ratio of exports to national income up to the 1780s. This broadly based export trade was overtaken from the 1780s until the end of the

Napoleonic Wars by a dramatically increasing foreign trade sector, but one based narrowly on cotton textiles. For most of the early nineteenth century, trade returned to its broad base, and the incremental ratio of exports to output fell, with the home market absorbing much of the additional production.[40]

Most of England's woollen exports (92 per cent) in the first half of the eighteenth century went to the rest of Europe. There was, during this period, a decline in these exports to several European countries, offset for a time by a rapid increase in exports to Spain and Portugal. The trend to industrial self-sufficiency in many European countries was paralleled in Britain. The Scottish and Irish linen industries were developed, and by the 1770s supplied most of the requirements of England and the colonies. The result for Germany and Holland was a 50 per cent reduction in their linen markets in Britain. England's trade with Europe became more concerned over the eighteenth century with the impact of industrial raw materials, especially from the Baltic and the Mediterranean. The dynamic element in the export trade passed to exports to the colonies. There was a rapid rise in the West African demand for English exports in the 1740s, and a new shift in exports to Asia with military establishments in Bengal and the Madras. Further export markets were developed in Ireland, and while privileged markets in the American colonies were disjointed with the War of Independence, exports resumed rapidly thereafter.

The growth in foreign trade before 1780 has been succinctly summarized by Jacob Price to be the result of three related phenomena: (1) growing demand in Britain for exotic products and for European industrial raw materials; (2) increasing demand in northern and western Europe for British re-exports of exotic products; (3) rising demand by the American colonies for British manufactures and re-exports. All of these parts were interdependent. Domestic industries needed imported raw materials. These were paid for by re-exports of exotic commodities from the American colonies and Asia. Slaves were bought in Africa with Birmingham ware and Mediterranean and Asian commodities. Linen was exported to America from Bohemia, Westphalia, Ulster and Fife. All of this was co-ordinated by merchants in the long-distance trade in London, Bristol, Liverpool and Glasgow.[41]

From the end of the eighteenth century, the transformation of the English cotton and metal industries was recasting the trade connections and industrial specialisms of Europe. In Pollard's view, industrialization now took on a European framework, and complex regional interrelationships of trade and specialization were developed. British yarn fed German looms; British iron German metal goods. Lancashire and Yorkshire concentrated on coarse quality manufactured goods, the French on high quality fabrics; the British on pig iron, the French and Germans on finished metal goods.[42]

MARKET ORGANIZATION AND WORK ORGANIZATION

The organization of international and internal markets is relatively unknown, apart from the study of individual industries and regions. We cannot assume that the organization of these markets simply developed in a rational and cohesive response to the growth of trade. First, there is a need to look at the creation and effects of distributive networks. Were these markets controlled, as in much of the English woollen industry, by metropolitan merchants, the Blackwell Hall factors? Alternatively, were there systems of free marketing, after the example of the Leeds cloth hall? Were markets controlled from outside the region, as in the Irish sewing outwork described in this volume by Collins? Or were they controlled by guilds, as in the trading diasporas in Spain described by Torras? What were the networks of middlemen, and why do many manufacturers move away from the use of agents to direct marketing, as for example among the cotton merchant manufacturers investigated by Kusamitsu and the Birmingham manufacturers examined by Berg? What were the avenues for introducing new products into European markets, and what were the sources for new patterns and designs?

The transport and retailing of commodities was also important in establishing the extent of a national market or of cohesive regional economies. Construction of the canal systems in England was based on regions, which for a time became more distinct, specialized and separated off from each other than they had been previously. Where canal systems did connect regions, it was frequently with ports and led out to connections with the international economy, rather than to national markets connected via London.[43] But the metropolis was still vitally important in setting the parameters on markets. It was the centre of mass consumption and set the fashion and tastes for the whole country. Marketing outlets in London, whether organized through agents or through warehousing and retailing owned and directed by individual provincial manufacturers, were vital to the survival of most provincial producers. Many small producers, as in the Birmingham small metal trades, relied on the larger firms for their national and international marketing outlets.

There is considerable debate on the significance of national markets in the early industrial period. Braudel, for example, believes that though Holland had a commercial revolution, and Spain an extensive colonial trade, neither country moved on to an Industrial Revolution because both lacked a purely national market.[44] In France, a divide prevailed between 'trading France' and 'territorial France'; the one a 'slim ribbon of precocious development', the other a 'landlocked mass marked by frequent poverty' of subdivided peasant agriculture and stagnant industry. The English, by contrast, ruled their economy from London. Before the canal networks, goods were dispatched by road or the coastal shipping routes to London, only to be redispatched to the provinces. There were, of course, exceptions. Defoe noted that the Manchester men and the Yorkshire and Coventry manufacturers carried their goods themselves. Wedgwood and Boulton were other celebrated exceptions. Wedgwood sold and advertised his products by setting up warehouses and showrooms in the main centres and using agents in foreign markets. Boulton also quickly abandoned commercial merchants and used his own marketing specialists at home and abroad. But this was a novelty, for the usual circuit was from provincial manufacturer to London factor or warehouse keeper, who then sold to a London shopkeeper or export merchant, or to a wholesaler who redistributed it back to the regions for retailing.[45]

It was not until the later eighteenth century with trade, industrial development and the new canal networks, that the provincial manufacturing centres and ports (Liverpool, Bristol and Glasgow) developed themselves, and established new regional strongholds.[46] Furthermore, as research based on 'flexible specialization' has emphasized, different regions tended to specialize in different products, suitable to specific types of market.[47] The methods and the types of product developed in a successfully expanding region could also come to influence the methods of an entire sector.[48]

THE COMMERCE AND CUSTOM OF EARLY MANUFACTURE

Market organization must also be related to social institutions, notably institutions of gender roles and training and of agrarian and community structures. To what extent did commercial and market expansion affect the gender basis of work and with this the social status accorded to men and women? The dramatic expansion of women's work in proto-industrial occupations has been related to agrarian and demographic change by Snell and Levine, and to the division of labour and technical change by Medick and Berg.[49] But issues of status and training are closely bound up with the kinds of changes wrought in social institutions by commercial expansion. In the case of the status accorded to women's work and the training given for it, whatever the new demand for labour, there appears, according to the papers by Gullickson and Simonton in this book, to have been very little fundamental change.

Social institutions bound up in community and agrarian structure were either totally changed by market expansion, or if they were retained, affected market structures themselves. Enclosure in the East Midlands in the eighteenth century destroyed a whole range of retail trades and manufactures.[50] The retention of small holding in the West Riding woollen industry, by contrast, created a base there for an open marketing system and direct retailing by artisans. Landholding institutions and the access of small artisans to land protected their independence and with this their direct access to the market. Hudson's paper in the book uses two contrasting communities to demonstrate this connection between artisanship and small holding. Extending and adapting customary practices within a new more competitive and commercial framework created marketing opportunities. Artisan initiative and direct marketing thus integrated commercial and customary arrangements to create new forms of market orientated production.

Other community institutions of status and social connection were transformed with the market into new industrial consumption patterns. Drinking and the social life centred on the café and the tavern reflected status divisions between masters and labourers and between men and women. These connections between work, status and consumption are outlined in the book in essays on the role of women by Gullickson and on Swedish artisans by Magnusson. The social institutions of work also received a new market connotation in truck payments, embezzlement and debt, as illuminated in the case of Swedish metalworkers by Magnusson.

Markets, both home and international, regional and national, provided the indispensable framework for the expansion and reorganization of manufacturing in early industrial Europe. Market institutions in the form of state policies, merchanting and retailing, and credit and debt arrangements within trades also transformed the social institutions of the production process at the heart of manufacturing. Markets and manufacture, commerce and the changing customs of production were the fundamental dualities of the European economy in the early industrial period.

NOTES

1 See N. F. R. Crafts, *British Economic Growth during the Industrial Revolution*, Oxford, 1985; E. A. Wrigley, *Continuity, Chance and Change*, Cambridge, 1988.

2 E. J. Hobsbawm, *Industry and Empire*, Harmondsworth, 1985; A. H. John, 'The Home market and economic growth', *Journal of Economic History*, 24, 1965.

3 F. Mendels, 'Proto-industrialization: the first phase of the industrialization process', *Journal of Economic History*, 32, 1972; E. L. Jones, 'Agricultural origins of industry', *Past and Present*, no. 40, 1968; P. Kriedte, H. Medick and J. Schlumbohm, *Industrialization before Industrialization. Rural Industry in the Genesis of Capitalism*, Cambridge, 1981.

4 For summaries of these critiques and empirical literature see D. C. Coleman, 'Proto-industrialization: a concept too many', *Economic History Review*, 36, 1983; M. Berg, P. Hudson and M. Sonnenscher, *Manufacture in Town and Country Before the Factory*, Cambridge, 1983; R. B. Houston and K. D. M. Snell, 'Proto-industrialization? Cottage industry, social change and the Industrial Revolution', *Historical Journal*, 27, 2, 1984.

5 See F. Mendels and P. Deyon, 'Proto-industrialization: theory and reality', *8th International Congress of Economic History*, Section A–2, Proto-industrialization, Budapest, 1982.

6 J. de Vries, *European Urbanization 1500–1800*, London, 1985; P. Hohenberg and L. Lees, *The Making of Urban Europe, 1000–1950*, Cambridge, Mass., 1985; E. A. Wrigley, *People, Cities and Wealth: The Transformation of Traditional Societies*, Oxford, 1987; Paul Bairoch, *Cities and Economic Development*, London, 1988.

7 Bairoch, op. cit., 503, 504.

8 Jan de Vries, op. cit; P. Hohenberg and L. Lees, op cit., chap. 4.

9 Hohenberg and Lees, op. cit.

10 E. A. Wrigley, op. cit.

11 Bairoch, op. cit., 185.

12 See C. Sabel and J. Zeitlin, 'Historical alternatives to mass production: politics, markets and technology in nineteenth-century industrialization', *Past and Present*, 108, 1985.

13 The above paragraphs summarize the arguments in Sabel and Zeitlin, op. cit.

14 See K. Williams, T. Cutler, J. Williams and C. Haslam, 'The end of mass production?', *Economy and Society*, 6,3, 422, 433.

15 See P. Hudson, 'The emergence of the factory in Yorkshire: some thoughts on the "Two Roads to Industrialization" ', History Workshop Conference, unpublished paper, Manchester, 1983.

16 See M. Berg, *The Age of Manufactures*, London, 1985, chap. 12; C. Behagg, 'Myths of cohesion', *Social History*, 11, 1986 and *Politics and Production in the early Nineteenth Century*, London, 1990; G. I. H. Lloyd, *The Cutlery Trade*, London, 1913, 191–7.

17 P. Scranton, *Propriety Capitalism: The Textile Manufacture at Philadelphia, 1800–1885*, Cambridge, 1983. For a more general critique of the historical case see D. Landes, 'Small is beautiful. Small is beautiful?', Fondazione ASSE, Instituto per la Storia dell Umbria Contemporanea, *Piccola e Grande Impresa: un Problem Storico*, Milan, 1987.

18 A. H. John, 'Agricultural productivity and Economic Growth', D. C. Eversley, 'The home market and economic growth in England' in E. L. Jones and G. Mingay, *Land, Labour and Population in the Industrial Revolution*, London, 1967; N. McKendrick, 'Home demand and economic growth: a new view of women and children in the Industrial Revolution' in N. McKendrick (ed.), *Historical Perspectives. Studies in English Thought and Society*, Cambridge, 1974; W. A. Cole, 'Factors in demand' in R. Floud and D. McCloskey (eds), *The Economic History of Britain since 1700*, I, *1700–1860*, Cambridge, 1981.

19 Crafts, op. cit. See also Wrigley, *Continuity*, op. cit., chap. 2; M. Overton, *Agricultural Revolution in England: The Transformation of the Rural Economy, 1500–1830*, Cambridge, forthcoming; R. A. C. Allen, 'The growth of labour productivity in early modern English agriculture', *Explorations in Economic History*, 25, 1988 and *Enclosure and the Yeoman*, Oxford, forthcoming.

20 E. Gilboy, 'Demand as a factor in the Industrial Revolution' in R. M. Hartwell (ed.), *The Causes of the Industrial Revolution*, London, 1967, 121–38.

21 P. K. O'Brien, 'Agriculture and the home market', *English Historical Review*, 1985, 773–9.

22 R. A. C. Allen 'The Agrarian Revolution and the Yeoman', Oxford, forthcoming 1991.

23 Quoted in N. McKendrick. J. Brewer and J. H. Plumb, *The Birth of a Consumer Society*, London, 1983, 77.

24 E. H. Robinson, 'Matthew Boulton and Josiah Wedgwood: apostles of fashion' in R. P. T. Davenport-Hines and J. Liebenau, *Business in the Age of Reason*, London, 1987.

25 ibid.

26 See Mary Douglas and B. Isherwood, *The World of Goods: Towards an*

24

Anthropology of Consumption, Harmondsworth, 1980; Helen Clifford, 'A study of an eighteenth-century goldsmithing business with reference to the Garrod ledgers 1760–1776', PhD thesis, London, 1989; Amanda Vickery, 'Women and the world of goods: a Lancashire consumer and her possessions, 1751–1781' in John Brewer and Roy Porter (eds), *Consumption and the World of Things*, London, forthcoming 1991.

27 L. Weatherill, *Consumer Behaviour and Material Culture in Britain, 1660–1760*, London, 1988.

28 F. Crouzet, 'Towards an export economy: British exports during the Industrial Revolution', *Explorations in Economic History*, 17, 1980, 65, 69, 81.

29 J. Price, 'What did merchants do? Reflections on British overseas trade, 1660–1790', *Journal of Economic History*, 49, June 1989, 269–70.

30 J. Goodman and K. Honeyman, *Gainful Pursuits. The Making of Industrial Europe 1600–1914*, London, 1988, 24, 25.

31 ibid., 53, 56.

32 ibid., 57.

33 Crouzet, op. cit., 69.

34 R. Davis, 'England and the Mediterranean, 1570–1670' in F. J. Fisher, *Essays in the Economic and Social History of Tudor and Stuart England*, Cambridge, 1961.

35 Jonathan I. Israel, *Dutch Primacy in World Trade 1585–1740*, Oxford, 1989, 356–7, 386, 409.

36 P. Kriedte, *Peasants, Landlords and Merchant Capitalists*, Leamington Spa, 1980, 90.

37 Davis, op. cit., 93.

38 Price, op. cit., 274.

39 Crouzet, op. cit., 87.

40 ibid., 90–2.

41 Price, op. cit., 277–8.

42 S. Pollard, 'Industrialization and the European economy', *Economic History Review*, 26, November 1973, 641, 643 and *Peaceful Conquest*, Oxford, 1981.

43 P. Hudson, *Regions and Industries. A Perspective on the Industrial Revolution*, Cambridge, 1989, esp. chap. 1, 'The regional perspective', 15.

44 F. Braudel, *Civilization and Capitalism* (English transl.), London, 1984, vol. 3, 297.

45 ibid., 366.

46 ibid., 375. See also Hudson, *Regions*, op. cit., chap. 1.

47 Sabel and Zeitlin, op. cit., 133–76.

48 Hudson, *Regions*, op. cit., 29.

49 See K. D. M. Snell, *Annals of the Labouring Poor: Social Change and Agrarian England 1600–1900*, Cambridge, 1985; David Levine, *Reproducing Families: The Political Economy of English Population History*, Cambridge 1987; Hans Medick, 'The proto-industrial 'family economy', *Social History*, October 1976; Maxine Berg, 'Women's work and mechanization in the early phases of industrialization', in Patrick Joyce (ed.), *The Historical Meanings of Words*, Cambridge, 1987.

50 J. M. Martyn, 'Village traders and the emergence of a proletariat in South Warwickshire 1750–1851', *Agricultural Historical Review*, 32, 2, 1984.

Part II

THE MARKET AND THE STATE

2

REGIONAL MARKETS AND NATIONAL DEVELOPMENT

Sidney Pollard

I

It will be widely, even if not universally, agreed that the debate on proto-industrialization since its emergence in the literature[1] has served to focus attention on a significant phenomenon which, though known,[2] was properly integrated neither into the historical literature nor into the historical theories covering the period. At the same time the term, and some of the ideas associated with it, have found less than universal approbation. While this is, perhaps, to be expected with every new concept, some of the objections have been rather more than the irritated reaction of the old against the innovations of the young.[3]

In trying to steer a middle course between the two extremes, we may begin with some of the positive contributions which the debate has made since Mendels launched his concept in public in 1972. He found an immediate echo not least because the consciences of many of us had been stirred repeatedly, if ineffectually, by the cavalier treatment which a system referred to, usually rather clumsily, as the domestic or 'putting-out system' (with an occasional nod towards the more elegant German '*Verlag-system*') had received in our history books. Descriptive history and theory both tended to dismiss it as a hybrid, as something lying between a recognized economic structure based on handicraft and guilds, on the one side, and an equally legitimate factory system on the other, as something, in other words, which had no right of existence on its own, but marked a transition.[4] From the handicraft age it had kept the domestic workshop and individual control over timing, hours and speed of work; it anticipated factory capitalism by the large capital, the large-scale ordering and the impersonal market. The fact that the transition lasted a good few hundred years and had, on the continent perhaps even more than in Great Britain, brought forth astonishing industrial, technical and artistic achievements, was noted from time to time but did not lead to a change of stance.

It would be unfair to suggest that examples of domestic industry were not often described; on the contrary, contemporaries and later historians delighted in relating details of this or that industry and its organizational structure. But by failing to see it as part of a viable and logical system, they failed to recognize its variety, its social and geographical implications and its power of survival. What was emphasized above all was its failure to stand up to the superior factory system.

Besides simply establishing 'proto-industrialization' as something worthy of study in its own right, the new view also rightly stressed its link to a world market.[5] This need not necessarily mean an actual market a long way away; some domestic industry worked for markets within easy reach. What it did mean was that the market was not necessarily confined to an easily accessible vicinity, but could range beyond a region's or even the country's boundaries, over many far-away areas simultaneously, and that it could switch from one area to another as opportunities arose or were closed. Localized production has therefore become part of what in some theories was called commercial capitalism or the commercial revolution, in which large-scale capital accumulations were used in an innovative way, but applied essentially to trading and not yet to production.

This 'world' market had at least two, linked, properties that were to be significant. Producers and sellers operating in it had to meet the competition of other producers, and while competition had not been unknown before, it had taken place within a stable and geographically limited environment. Now producers were forced to be alert and to be knowledgeable about things going on elsewhere, and at the least to question the tendency of many producing regions to believe that it was precisely their local tradition, specialism, style or quality that the world was waiting for and was willing to pay for, which had imposed an immobilism on everyone concerned with local production in the past. It was the last phase of a system in which goods were defined, and named, by the town or region in which they were produced.[6]

But, simultaneously, 'world' markets also meant the opportunity to expand, to find new, better or more regular demand conditions. This marked a shift, to be characteristic and significant in the early phases of industrialization in the classic sense, towards problems of improving production and lowering costs, since sales at falling prices in an expanding world would take care of themselves. The world of proto-industrialization was therefore an active, competing, shifting and dangerous world, compared with the relative stability assumed in the world of guild or estate production.

Third, and here is to be the emphasis of this paper, proto-industry was essentially regional, bunched in well-defined geographical concentrations, in which it either formed a major, if not the major source of income of the population, or at least the major by-employment for an agrarian population to provide the rents or servile dues which were technically paid for the use of land, but were calculated on the yields of industry. Typically, proto-industrial employers sought out rural families with spare time on their hands, in periods left unused by the rhythm of the agricultural year, such as the winter months, and this, in turn, was regionally determined. Thus the location of the English woollen industry, according to Coleman, depended on 'families of unemployed workers rather than on local wool'.[7] In Prussia and some other German states, the spare time of the numerous and poverty-stricken soldiers and their families was used,[8] so that the location tended to be the garrison towns. Essentially, therefore, previously idle labour was used, a classic example of the 'vent for surplus'.[9]

Proto-industry as a regional phenomenon was so much taken for granted that it required no particular mention; the nation state in this connection has been called an 'anachronism'.[10] On the other hand, many were the arguments as to why a particular industry had settled in one area or region rather than another, and why its boundaries ran in a particular way. My own interest has hitherto lain in the regional character of the Industrial Revolution, which had certain features that cannot be applied to other phases of economic development. The unspoken assumption of geographical concentration and specialization, based on pragmatic familiarity with the data, has now also been carried over into the proto-industrial debate. However, it should be stressed that, unlike the key regions of the classical Industrial Revolution, the regions housing the proto-industrial concentrations could be of very varying size and structure: cities or small towns, large regions amounting to whole provinces or narrow valleys, densely populated or thinly rural.

Against these merits of the proto-industrialization classification, at least two major lines of criticism have been voiced. The first is that the concept, in the sense of attempting to unify and make sense out of a series of very different phenomena, has so far failed to identify the mechanism of relationship with the major breakthrough into the factory system which followed. We do not seem to be able to tell why some regions with flourishing domestic industries converted to the machine-factory stage while others, or perhaps most, failed to do so and went under or survived simultaneously with the factory system.[11] The problem is not solved by maintaining that the proto-industry was there in its own right and did not have to explain the system which followed, for the problem is one of the inner dynamic of the system itself. Why were some sectors of it mobile and progressive, and others fixed and conservative? What can an improved understanding of its inner laws of motion tell us about the nature of its demise? This is a subject to which I shall return later.

It is the very merit of the new concept, by calling attention to a widespread and significant system of industrial market activity which had previously been rather neglected, that has led to the second line of criticism: namely, that it concentrates on only one of the organizational forms in which industry operated in the long period of the run-up to the Industrial Revolutions of the eighteenth/nineteenth centuries in Europe. This may be a more damaging critique, for it may imply that the new approach focuses on the wrong characteristic in seeking to describe and explain a period of general technical and industrial progress.

Proto-industry, as treated in the debate, was largely limited to three types of industry: textiles, small iron and steel articles, and some composite articles, like clocks, watches or dolls. Even here there were considerable differences in detail which throw some doubt on the decision to group all of them together. Thus in watch-making, the division of labour consisted in the specialized production of parts, each household or village responsible for some part which would ultimately be combined into one set of products in the manufacture of which they had all collaborated.[12] In textiles, by contrast, specialization normally meant that each household or village produced different types, qualities or forms of textiles in competition, as it were, with the others.

As a matter of fact, much the largest numbers of industrial workers were found in this type of industry: in the age before what Rostow has called the 'age of mass consumption', textiles represented the most important manufacture altogether. Thus in Bohemia at the end of the eighteenth century, 84 per cent of those employed in manufacturing and 17.5 per cent of the total population were employed in textiles, in Flanders it was 22 per cent of the total population and in Prussia, 83 per cent of those in manufacturing, while in Ulster one-quarter were connected with linen.[13] To that extent, it was right to focus attention on the practices current in the production of textiles. Nevertheless, the domestic system was not the only form of industrial organization, nor possibly the most significant in the general dynamic of European progress.

Simultaneously, and to some extent as part of the same development, there also arose different forms of manufactories or 'proto-factories' as key elements in the industrial scene and carriers of progress and change. At least three forms can be distinguished though they tend to merge into each other and in the past have not always been kept clearly apart.

One form consisted of pulling together, under one roof, relatively large numbers of workers doing much the same – and possibly showing much the same skills – as those employed outside in their own homes in proto-industry proper. Numerous examples of this form of employment could be found, especially among spinners and weavers in various parts of Europe.[14] It involved the employer in providing the capital for the building and possibly for the equipment, and in paying for supervision. But it gave him the advantages of quality control and the protection of material from embezzlement, especially in the case of valuable goods;[15] organization in feudal or semi-servile conditions, as in Russia or Bohemia;[16] or saving costs of transport and distribution. Although the work was the same and occurred simultaneously and in direct competition with proto-industry, it did not necessarily lead to any of the assumed consequences of the latter in the social, familial or demographic sphere.

A second type was the centralized workshop as found frequently in the dyeing, shearing or printing of textiles, but also in the earlier stages, as in scribbling mills. Apart from quality control and the ability to react quickly to new orders, the major reason for this form of organization was that the minimum technical size of unit simply precluded domestic or cottage-type organization.[17] Where guild restrictions did not prevent it, these workshops would be in larger towns, such as Norwich.[18]

Technical needs also accounted for a third type which had no connection with any outside 'proto-industrial' sector whatever. Among the industries managed in this form were paper-making and printing, glass-making and salt and chemical works, potteries and iron foundries, and the production of luxury goods like gobelins, coaches, fine furniture and porcelain. Some of these were of very great significance for the future.[19]

Additionally, we find craftsmen working away from home, under one roof, jointly using power or heat paid for by themselves, as in the cutlery, tools or small arms industries, who should perhaps form a category of their own.[20] And, finally, there existed large units with complex organization and considerable accumulations of capital, which could no longer be described as manufactories. Among them were coal and metal mines, shipyards and large porter breweries, as well as some large, if temporary, building enterprises.[21] We must also, for some purpose, add enterprises in the field of transport, like ships or canal companies, which obeyed different rules of organization again.

These enterprises might not only be among the most significant in the industrial context of their day, instrumental in determining the economic strength and possibly political power of their countries, but they might also be responsible for the success or failure of the proto-industrial sector itself. To put it another way, these were not later stages of development but simultaneous ones, intimately and necessarily meshing into the market world of the domestic weavers or nail-makers. The access by the latter to their markets, the forms of transport, the method of production of tools and machinery, advertising, sampling, information, and the purchasing power and application of the product by the buyer could depend significantly on developments in the non-proto-industrial sector. Therefore, when I now turn to a consideration of the regional factor in the period immediately before the Industrial Revolution, I shall be unable to keep to the purely proto-industrial sector as a separate category. It would not, except in a local social context, have had much sense then, and it would not make much sense now.

II

Industry, in the age before industrialization, tended to be regionally concentrated. There were exceptions, of isolated works, and the regions could be of different size and nature, yet the normal regional concentration was evident and significant. In the context of the later, more advanced economic development, the key element of this was the existence of one or more 'base' (or export) industries – a specialization which provided for a degree of homogeneity within, and structural differentiation against neighbouring areas outside.[22] Behind this lay two groups of factors, resources and economies of scale, or, put differently, the effects of nature and the effects of society, causes that were permanent and those that were historical.

Resources are frequently taken for granted: they are stable, and they have been there a long time. But it is a mistake to neglect them in any account of the development of the European economy. Before the present-day skills of transmuting almost all substances into others, and whisking them across the world at next to no cost, resources were indispensable. We shall go seriously wrong if we do not start with them.

Mineral resources were the most obvious. Before industrialization many of our major industrial regions, including Saxony, Wallonian Belgium, Cornwall and the southern Urals derived a major part of their existence and significance from their mineral treasures.[23] Minerals are important not only because they inevitably fix the location of an industrious population and thus form the core of an industrial region, but because, almost inevitably in that period, their working tended constantly to create situations in which great rewards beckon just out of reach of existing technology. New seams or lodes, at greater depth than current methods could tap, or at the risk of drowning by water, of collapsing rock or of lethal gas, were a constant challenge to the enterprising: these formed a most favourable context for innovation and improvement. It was in continental mines, from the sixteenth century onwards, that some of the most complex machinery of the age was first employed; it was in British mines that the steam engine, the iron rail and ultimately the railway, besides many other innovations in technology, in capital organization and in labour management were first employed. Mining engineers were among the best-trained scientists on the continent, and among the most rational planners in Britain.[24]

Apart from mineral wealth there were agricultural, replaceable resources, including flax, wool and timber on which industrial regions might depend. Fields of flax, grazing grounds for sheep and forests are more dispersed than metal or coal mines, and the links to the manufacturing concentrations are not always as close. Moreover, textile fibres may be valuable enough to permit their transport over a distance. Nevertheless, textile concentrations, especially of woollens and linens, were generally based originally on local or regional supply and, once established, on the pulling power of the existing industrial region to draw the raw material from farther afield. By its very nature a proto-industrial region, making use of a rural, even part-time labour force, tends to be more dispersed than a mineral working one, except for the central workshops and the warehouses and sales offices, which may be highly concentrated.

In general, the industrialization of a region was often accompanied by a marked improvement in agricultural technique. Nevertheless, it was normally associated with the need to import food and the conversion of neighbouring regions to agricultural specialization and possible deindustrialization.[25] On the other hand, specialization in agrarian exports could itself lead to regional economic development.[26]

A third significant resource is water: as a source of power, as a means of transport, and for cleaning, scouring or otherwise working materials.[27] The number of water mills in existence, and the skill with which, on important rivers, every loss of height of the water level was exploited to generate motive power is often underrated by an age which had come to depend on more 'man-made' sources of energy. Water transport, including the downriver floating of timber or other produce, has kept its economic significance rather longer than water power.

A fourth resource is manpower. This refers not so much to labour's skill or willingness to work, which should be accounted part of the historical background of regional concentration, but the surplus given by a disproportion between the land and the people it has to bear. The link between poor agricultural soil and industrial concentration has often been remarked and is both plausible and empirically verifiable in many cases. It has to be seen in a dynamic setting, based on population increase, and is not unconnected with the historically given systems of landholding and inheritance. Where, as in Saxony, or Ravensberg, or southern Ireland, the number of agricultural holdings cannot be increased while population increases, the additional population (though not necessarily the same persons), will be pushed into the poorest, landless class. There it forms a ready-made recruiting ground for industrial employment; or, indeed, it will be driven to starve or to emigrate, as in Ireland. Within a region, as in the canton of Zurich or in Lancashire, industry settles in the less fertile part and draws the whole of the regional population surplus to itself.[28]

Location may also be counted as a resource though in this case it is even more evident than in the case of other resources that it is not so much the purely geographical element which is decisive, but the fact that historical changes have occurred to turn location along a transport route or within easy access to markets into a significant advantage.[29] The centres round large capital, residential or garrison cities are obvious cases in point,[30] as were the industries springing up in the Dutch provinces in the golden age of Dutch wealth and high consumption.

By the same token, resource-based regions run the risk of decline as their resource gives out, or the market to which it was geared begins to decline. Cases of decline will be discussed below, but we might note here that the decline of three of the most spectacularly successful industrial regions of the early British Industrial Revolution – Shropshire, North Wales and Cornwall[31] – may in their different ways be traced back to the giving out of their resource wealth.

III

The causes for the regional concentrations of industry which may be termed social or historical have been frequently discussed, and therefore need not be described in any detail here. They may mostly be subsumed under two headings: action by the state and external economies.[32]

The industries of the day might perhaps be weak and backward by the standards of the later factory age, but they were valued greatly by the state beyond their share of the total national income, for they were the mobile, the expanding and the disposable element.

The rural sector was largely self-supporting, needing little and providing little for what Braudel has called the capitalist areas of the economy.[33] Rulers might value their agrarian population as a source of cannon fodder, and the ruling classes depended on it as a source of their rent income, but in an age of absolutism and mercantilism they had their eye on the industrial and mercantile sectors when it was a question of active support for political reasons.

Essentially this was because industries were reckoned to be sources of not only economic but also of military and, ultimately, of political power. Industrial self-sufficiency thus became a reasonable aim for countries craving great power status, as well as for others trying to imitate them on a smaller scale. The industrial history of the age is intimately linked with economic policies by states, provinces and cities pursuing such aims.

The economic policies actually maintained by governments are difficult to summarize. They were complex, variegated and sometimes contradictory.[34] Not even their aims were necessarily always internally compatible. Moreover, if we accept industrial concentrations to be mainly regional phenomena, we shall credit the state with less influence than is commonly supposed since in spite of all it did, industrial regions were far more like industrial regions abroad than like their neighbours in their own countries. Or, in other words, industrial structure derived from evident economic necessity more than from political decision. For our purposes we may limit the consideration of state actions to two aspects: the freeing from ancient shackles, and direct encouragement by protection, subsidization and other means.

By our period, guild restrictions were widely seen as hampering and inhibiting. Proto-industry, indeed, had itself often sought a rural setting in order to escape control by urban guilds; and generally, enlightened states like France or like Austria under Joseph II deliberately set out to limit the power of urban guilds on a national basis, where they were not whittled down in detail. Yet the effects of guild regulation were not always negative, even under the new conditions. Quality control and guarantee, systems of training and the fair distribution of scarce materials might at times be valuable, even in the new age, under existing uncertainties. On the whole the western European state was, in this regard, on the side of the angels.

It was otherwise in the field of direct support and subsidy. There were many forms: royal manufactures, privileged manufactures, subsidized manufactures. Typically, they were fostered in order to introduce a new industry not previously known in the realm or to ensure supplies in times of war.[35] Though often producing goods of the highest quality or of artistic excellence, and in some cases representing springboards for later advance, they were yet, economically speaking, remarkably unsuccessful overall.

The causes for this are many and varied, and can only be hinted at here. Almost by definition, these privileged enterprises were not there to supply a real need – or else private enterprise would have met it – but to fulfil a preconceived notion of what resources a state should possess. They were therefore generally too large: top heavy, with too many courtiers and officials, and with buildings that were too grand and too costly. Corruption and favouritism were inevitable under such conditions. As for management, the choice went at best to technical competence; but this was but seldom combined with business ability.[36]

Once a business was established without regard to the market, but with royal favour, it quickly found that survival depended on further favours, further subsidies, monopolies or protective tariffs. Many of these firms formed classic examples of what economists nowadays call 'rent-seeking': making an income not by contributing to national production and output, but by transferring to themselves incomes already generated elsewhere.[37] Meanwhile the large, privileged firm sat across the path of others who might have developed things on their own, had they been given the chance.

From one point of view, it might be said that the age lacked a bureaucracy able and incorruptible enough to run industries as demanded by current policies. But, at the same time, most industries were, if they had stayed at their optimum size, too small to carry a bureaucracy. There were therefore good technical reasons why, in this age, progress had to depend on private, individual enterprise, in which the entrepreneur took risks largely with his own capital.

But, equally fairly, it might be said that the direction and aims of state policy as a whole were wrong, quite irrespective of the means available to achieve them. Enterprises of this kind, whether merely privileged or directly subsidized, tended to aim at a fixed market and at a fixed technology. Development was seized at a certain point in time and held fast there, both by the heavy capital usually invested at a single stroke, and by the tendency of privileged and protected entrepreneurs to shun experiment. What should, in a period of change, have been centres of progress and adaptation became centres of stagnation and blockage for others. Bureaucrats, in any case, are much better at making for a certain aim than at pioneering beyond it.

If, not unexpectedly, the initiative of the state tended to help, at best, to reach a certain level rather than to create an industrial structure that would remain progressive, it had the same clear tendency to fix things the way they were on a regional basis. Regional planning, except perhaps in the filling up of empty agricultural territories, was not in fashion. Support and privilege almost invariably meant supporting and strengthening things where they were already.[38]

The levying of protective tariffs in order to support home industry, and even more the direct subsidy paid to manufacturers, tended to tax the poor in order to benefit the rich, and to tax the backward regions in order to enhance the lead of the advanced ones. State action, if indeed it had any positive effect whatever, tended to confirm the regional structure of industry.[39] In the search for the reasons why some regions survived and others did not, the role of the state should not be omitted.

If we now turn to the second factor, external economies, we find one important element to have been access to the market itself. Distant markets were not easily reached or held, given the then-available means of transport and communication.[40] Capital, risk-taking, long-term commitment and a great deal of knowledge were a necessity. These, in turn, required a minimal flow of goods.

Anyone entering a trade in its established region had such links at his disposal at once, and by his own contribution helped to strengthen and possibly cheapen them by spreading them over a larger turnover. Information on market changes, on new regulations, taxes or changing fashions would also reach the existing centres first. Buyers, similarly, would naturally turn there for their supplies. At the same time, the lush market of the capital city called forth significant proto-industrial and industrial concentrations around it in almost every European country.[41]

A similar advantage would accrue in the buying in of raw materials, intermediate products such as dyes, and even consumer goods for the industrial population. The established region would enjoy a bonus in efficiency and price as well as choice. Last, but not least, it will have built up a credit structure geared to the need of that particular industry, with bankers and merchants in a position to have informed opinions on the creditworthiness of the clients. Regional differences in credit and interest rates have survived into the modern epoch.[42]

In the industrial sphere itself, local know-how would be uniquely available to any newcomer within the region, knowledge which would not be found outside.[43] Long-term capital would be more easily provided in a region where everyone knew and took for granted the particular ways of the region's leading industry – quite apart from the chance of inserting oneself into the credit network by skilfully paying late and dunning early. Above all, if entrepreneurship is the scarcest of all resources, entrepreneurs or capitalists in the sense of Schumpeter or Braudel, respectively, will hardly be needed within the region, since management is largely routine, whereas a high degree of entrepreneurship will be needed outside it.

Possibly the most powerful factor in favour of the established region is the availability of skilled or knowledgeable workers, with their resources of local information, technique and practice.[44] This refers not only to the workers to be employed directly, but to those in ancillary and complementary tasks. Nothing is more instructive here than the remarkable, and at times hilarious, account provided by Professor J. R. Harris in a recent number of the *Journal of European Economic History* of the attempts of a group of Birmingham workers and managers under Michael Alcock to introduce some Birmingham trades into France.[45] A region is normally the storehouse not just of one skill, but of a range of complementary skills, built up laboriously over a long period and not easily replicated. Of interest in this context is also the differentiation and specialization *within* industrial regions.[46]

Against this, the problems of establishing a rival firm outside the existing regional concentration must appear overwhelming and hardly a rational proposition, unless some very exceptional circumstances apply.[47] The snowball effect strengthening the existing concentrations will, in a period of general expansion, have little to fear from threats from outside.

IV

The issue which has, perhaps more than any other, dominated the literature on proto-industrial regions is their ultimate fate. Some survived for a considerable time, even into the twentieth century.

Others transformed themselves into centres of modern large-scale industry. Still others lost their industrial character and became deindustrialized. What, then, determined the future fate of proto- and other pre-factory industrial regions? There were always numerous particular causes, associated with particular resources and changes in the geographical environment. Beyond this, how- ever, there is a need to try and establish causes which might have more general application.

Before doing so, it might be worthwhile to look briefly at an alternative explanation altogether. This is not so much concerned with the success or otherwise of proto-industrial regions in adapt- ing to mass production methods, but sets out to show that there was no intrinsic advantage in the mass production organization of industry to begin with (though later it won through by a momen- tum of its own). According to this view, history might easily have taken a different course, with smaller-scale industry, characterized by 'flexible specialization'[48] expanding output just as effectively as the mass production units in the nineteenth and earlier twentieth centuries, until it re-emerged, as it has allegedly done again in the modern period, as a viable and in some ways preferable alterna- tive.

It may readily be conceded that there were costs associated with the large-scale factory: heavy capital investment, costs of management and supervision, and problems of accounting and profit calculation,[49] and that therefore the factory or other large- scale unit would be adopted only if its productivity gain was large enough to outweigh these additional costs. In the event, the cost advantages of large-scale operations were so overwhelming that they defeated all previous systems of industrial organization in one industry after another.

By denying this, the defenders of the superiority of small-scale 'flexible specialization' tend to confuse core and periphery. It is true, and has always been understood, that mass production will frequently need individualized service or adaptation at the level of the consumer. Thus motor cars, produced by the million, need local repair garages, and cloth, woven in huge factories, has (some- times) to be fitted by the handicraft tailor. But not only does technical progress consist in ever minimizing that last personal fitting; it is only through the cheapening of the earlier mass pro- duction stages that the consumer can be supplied at all, able to afford a motor car or a new suit of clothes. Again, if we grant that the small-scale unit takes the strain of fluctuations,[50] its role is not that of supplanting the large efficient plant but of supplementing it, making it more economical still. Similarly, the high-class, luxury end of some industries which, quite rightly, can be described as still working by adaptable specialization, may exist only because of the social wealth created by the conveyor belt.

There is here something of the dialectic of personal service. A poor society has many personal servants; as it becomes richer, and wages rise, these disappear as they can no longer be afforded; but as society becomes richer still, they emerge once more with the growing surplus in every household, in the form of a rapidly growing service sector. The industrial sector on which this development is based shrinks in terms of manpower and relative capital investment, but it is still the vital foundation of the expanding tertiary superstructure. Small-scale, perhaps rural industry – to return to our theme – may seem more attractive to the nostalgic historian, but it cannot begin to match the productivity of mass scale in the key sectors: textiles, iron- and steel-making, coal mining, railway transport, shipbuilding, shipping, gas works and electric power stations, to name but a few.

Let us return to the survival of proto-industrial regions. We might begin by considering that, in a changing world, nothing lasts forever, neither resources not the demand for them. Many of the natural resources which formed the *raison d'être* of an industrial region in the first place might give out: copper in the Lake District, iron ore in Shropshire, lead in Derbyshire. On the other hand, and usually simultaneously in a world full of alternatives and new discoveries, new sources may be developed which are cheaper, even if the older mines still have some metal in them. The region is then threatened. It might still use its skills, or possibly its resources in fuel such as coal to draw the metal from elsewhere to smelt it or work it up, but this clearly forms a less secure foundation, beside losing the spin-offs of the mining activity itself.[51]

This may also apply to agrarian resources. Timber may have been used up, or replaced by cheaper imports from richer forests. Similarly, the wool-growing regions of Germany and England were, in the middle of the nineteenth century, replaced by Australian wool-growing regions, which might affect the locational advantages of woollen textile manufacturing.

Markets will not last for ever either. Fashions may change, as Bradford worsted-makers discovered towards the end of the nineteenth century, when their specialism was made valueless,[52] or new materials may come in to undermine the markets of the old, like cottons in the case of light woollens and linens, or artificial fibres today. Matters are made worse by the tendency for the region to believe that the loss will be temporary, and hang on, in spite of falling incomes. Precisely because of its earlier success the specialist region will be among the last to let go of the old and adopt the new, by which time it may well be too late.[53]

Thus a specialized region which, as we have seen, may accumulate numerous advantages in one period, may by this very fact be handicapped in the next. It is a common experience in economic history that what was once progressive ultimately becomes a fetter – and this is also true of a developed, specialized industrial region. By being highly advantaged, it also becomes highly vulnerable. There are, to begin with, the well-known problems of high wages, high costs of living, overcrowding and monopolizing tendencies, the kinds of problems summarized by the inverted 'U'-curve of regional specialization.[54] But above all, in our period, there is the staying power of the erstwhile success and competitive advantage of one method or material or product. Pride, conservatism, self-satisfaction, misplaced hopes, misunderstood market signals all combine to derive from earlier success a reluctance to change, and to lead to loss of market and momentum when change becomes necessary. The economic strength of a region is tested, in the end, not in a stable but in a dynamic situation.

How, then, do some manage to survive into a new age? Among several causes I would like to emphasize one which has emerged clearly from our discussion so far. It is the chance of an alternative when the original base disappears.

I have earlier referred to the three Industrial Revolution regions which declined when their resource base disappeared.[55] Compare with them the industrial regions of the classic Industrial Revolution and later, which survived and expanded. Glasgow and the Clyde valley, for example, enjoyed a well-known sequence of linen-tobacco-coal-cotton-iron-engineering, steel and shipbuilding. Several of these disappeared completely in due course, but the Clyde region did not. Similarly, consider the North-East region: coal with salt, glass and chemicals, then iron, followed by steel, shipbuilding and engineering. Or the Lancashire industrial region: wool or linen, then cotton, coal, chemicals, metals, iron, engineering. Again, some of these gave out, but the region lived on. Similar examples of what Meade has called the 'economics of conglomeration'[56] may be culled from the continental experience.[57]

Some of the advantages accruing to a region which I noted earlier will apply *a fortiori* if several industries are hitched together. To some extent they will support each other directly, such as textile machinery-making or chemical dye works in the case of Lancashire cotton. But they will also spread the cost of complementary services and overheads, or indeed make them economically possible: banking, merchanting and brokerage services, roads, canals and harbours, schools and technical colleges.[58]

In the pre-factory age, such multiple industrial complexes were less frequent, and perhaps technically less significant. But they were not unknown, if we bear in mind that the proto-industry was not the only one in existence. Thus in the complex built up on Tyneside on the basis of cheap coal, including salt works, glass works, chemical works and ultimately also engineering, together with an elaborate system of loading facilities, shipping, credit and monopoly organization, all by the middle of the eighteenth century, we have a many-faceted structure that would survive, at least as long as the coal was there. Or consider the mixed metal and hardware trades of Birmingham and the Black Country, and to a lesser extent the example of Sheffield where, in the one case, nails, tools, chains, small arms, non-ferrous metal goods and a whole range of 'toys' supported each other, yet also offered a kind of insurance if one trade should give out. Sheffield with its steel, cutlery, tools and silverware also had a most varied potential, quite apart from the coal both there and in the Black Country.[59] The mixed industrial regions round capital cities such as Paris, Vienna and Berlin furnish other examples of salvation by variety.

If an alternative is difficult to prepare for, favourable preconditions for the next stage might help. Both Lancashire and the West Riding of Yorkshire, in addition to their vital water power, also had coal as well as iron to ease their way into the next stage when the time was ripe. The same was true of the lesser textile districts of the English Midlands.

By contrast, the typical textile region on the continent, with its labour scattered over a rural area dovetailed into the agrarian system either within its region or with the neighbouring region, centred on a town with no economic resources beside serving that region as market and credit centre, faced an entirely different task when its market was undermined by a new fabric or by a technical revolution elsewhere. There was, almost by definition, no wholly alternative industrial employment on offer: there was no iron, no coal, no non-ferrous metal or timber, and still less were there any local skills to attract industrial jobs away from the regions where these were found.[60] I think we should also make a distinction here, too often neglected in the literature, between a regional industry which merely forms the by-employment of a population still largely engaged in agriculture, and one which has become the main employment of an important part of the inhabitants. We should also study more carefully the transition from one to the other,[61] though this is not the place for it. Whereas the former could more easily revert to agriculture or an alternative domestic industry, in the latter case the decline of the base industry would have more drastic social consequences.

Particularly where rural industry had been a main employment, the tendency was, as we have seen, for a number of reasons to try and hang on to the tried and tested methods and products. Even if there should be local enterprise enough to introduce revolutionary changes, the very strength of the region will work against them, for it will then concern itself with the social consequences of technological unemployment: the Silesian weavers rebelled, and in Flanders there was a concensus that machines would not help to keep the rural workers in employment.[62] The cards are stacked against the one-industry region.

V

In attempting to draw some conclusions, I am only too well aware that there is a great danger here of circular reasoning. By stressing the regional form of pre-factory industry all over Europe, it has not been too difficult to arrive at the conclusion that the changing shape of industry in Europe, and the differential developments, have explanations which are to a large extent regional. The fate of an industry has become not merely the fate of workers and capitalists, but the fate of a region as a whole dependent upon it.

Similarly, by stressing flexibility rather than temporary strength something akin to a tautology has emerged. Those regions adapt themselves to changing circumstances which are best at adapting themselves to change.

Yet at least one new theorem has been added. Taking for granted the tendency of those who are good at doing one thing to be reluctant to do something else, we can add at least one element to the survival chances of a specialist industrial region in an age of change: that is the alternatives available, within the region, should the local basic industry be forced to shrink.[63] Geographical proximity, and the network of social, economic, financial and educational institutions thus play a very different part than would emerge if we had looked at industrial history on a national basis only.

What is on offer here is not a complete explanation of the different future facing industry in different regions before the classical industrialization,[64] but merely one element, though it may be an important element. It tends to confirm the thesis that no full understanding of the economic development of Europe is possible without close attention to the geographical, and in particular the regional context.

NOTES

1 F. Mendels, 'Proto-industrialization: the first phase of the industrialization process', *Journal of Economic History* 32, 1972, 241–61 and 'Proto-industrialization: theory and reality?', *8th International Economic History Congress*, Budapest, 1982, 'A' Themes, 69–107; P. Kriedte, H. Medick and J. Schlumbohm, *Industrialization before Industrialization*, Cambridge, 1981.

2 E.g. P. Hudson, 'Proto-industrialization: the case of the West Riding', *History Workshop*, 12, 1981, 53–4, note 2; M. Berg, P. Hudson and M. Sonenscher, *Manufacture in Town and Country Before the Factory*, Cambridge, 1983, Introduction, 1–2, and M. Berg, 'Political economy and the principle of manufacture', ibid.; J. Thirsk, 'Industries in the countryside' in F. J. Fisher (ed.), *Essays in the Economic and Social History of Tudor and Stuart England*, Cambridge, 1961; H. Kellenbenz, 'Ländliches Gewerbe und bäuerliches Unternehmertum', *2nd Economic History Conference, Aix-en-Provence*, Paris, 1965, 377–429; E. Tarlé, *L'industrie dans les campagnes en France à la fin de l'ancien régime*, Paris, 1910; H. Freudenberger and F. Redlich, 'The industrial development of Europe: reality, symbols, images', *Kyklos*, 17, 1964, 380; H. Kellenbenz, 'Rural industries in the west from the end of the Middle Ages to the eighteenth century' in P. Earle (ed.), *Essays in European Economic History 1500–1800*, Oxford, 1974, 45–88.

3 D. C. Coleman, 'Proto-industrialization: a concept too many', *Economic History Review*, 2nd series, 36, 1983, 435–48; R. Houston and K. D. M. Snell, 'Proto-industrialization?', *Historical Journal*, 27, 1984, 473–92.

4 E.g. G. Unwin, Introduction to G. W. Daniels, *The Early English Cotton Industry*, Manchester, 1920, xx: 'This almost universally diffused domestic manufacture, organized for the supply of distant markets,

SIDNEY POLLARD

represents a phase of industrial development historically intermediate between the "handicraft system" of the medieval city and the factory system of the nineteenth century.'

5 F.-W. Henning found the following manufactured exports per head in the early nineteenth century (in Talers):

West Prussia	0.11
East Prussia, Pomerania	0.2
Bavaria	0.25
Bohemia	2
Electoral Saxony	3
County of Ravensberg	10
Duchy of Berg	over 11

'Die Wirtschaftsstruktur mitteleuropäischer Gebiete an der Wende zum 19. Jahrhundert unter besonderer Berücksichtigung des gewerblichen Betriebes' in W. Fischer (ed.), *Beiträge zu Wirtschaftswachstum und Wirtschaftsstruktur im 16. und 19. Jahrhundert*, Berlin, 1971, 118; also see L. A. Clarkson, *The Pre-Industrial Economy in England 1500–1750*, London, 1971, 95; Berg, Hudson and Sonenscher, op. cit., 16; P. Steinbach, 'Zur Diskussion über den Begriff der "Region" – eine Grundsatzfrage der modernen Landesgeschichte', *Hessisches Jahrbuch für Landesgeschichte*, 31, 1981, 198–200.

6 This is discussed, in relation to the 'New Draperies', by D. C. Coleman, 'An innovation and its diffusion: the "New Draperies" ', *Economic History Review*, 2nd series, 22, London, 1969, 417–29 and *The Economy of England 1450–1750*, London, 1977, 79–81; B. A. Holderness, *Pre-Industrial England. Economy and Society from 1500–1750*, London, 1976, 91–2; C. Wilson, 'Cloth production and international competition in the seventeenth century', *Economic History Review*, 2nd series, 13, 1960–1, 209–21; F. Mendels, 'Agriculture and peasant industries in eighteenth-century Flanders' in W. N. Parker and E. L. Jones (eds), *European Peasants and their Markets*, Princeton, 1975, 183–4.

7 Coleman, op. cit., 78. Also Mendels, 'The first phase' op. cit.; Clarkson, op. cit., 77–8; E. J. T. Collins, 'Labour, supply and demand in European agriculture 1800–1880' in E. L. Jones and S. J. Woolf, *Agrarian Change and Economic Development*, 1969, London, 66; Wolfgang Mager, 'Protoindustrialisierung und agrarisch-heimgewerbliche Verflechtung in Ravensberg während der frühen Neuzeit', *Geschichte und Gesellschaft*, 8, Göttingen, 1982, 441–3; F. Mendels, 'Seasons and regions in agriculture during the process of industrialization' in S. Pollard, (ed.), *Region und Industrialisierung*, Göttingen, 1980, 177–95, also 'Les temps de l'industrie et les temps de l'agriculture', *Revue du Nord*, 63, Lille, 1981, 21–33; P. Laslett, *The World We Have Lost*, London, 1971 edn, 17; J. de Vries, *The Economy of Europe in an Age of Crisis 1600–1750*, London, 1976, 105.

8 H. Krüger, *Zur Geschichte der Manufaktur und der Manufakturarbeiter in Preussen*, Berlin (East), 1958, 201, 278–84.

9 Kriedte, Medick and Schlumbohm, op. cit., 57; R. E. Caves, 'Vent for surplus models of trade and growth' in R. E. Baldwin (ed.), *Trade,*

Growth and the Balance of Payments, Middleton, Conn., 1976; S. L. Engerman, 'Douglas C. North's *The Economic Growth of the United States 1790–1860* revisited', *Social Science History*, 1, 1977, 249.

10 F. Mendels, 'Theory and reality' op. cit., 77; also see P. Deyon, 'L'enjeu des discussions autour du concept de "proto-industrialisation" ', *Revue du Nord*, 61, 1979, 11.

11 Freudeneberger and Redlich, op. cit., 379; O. Büsch, 'Das Gewerbe in der Wirtschaft des Raumes Berlin-Brandenburg 1800–1850' in his *Untersuchungen zur Geschichte der frühen Industrialisierung vornehmlich im Wirtschaftsraum Berlin/Brandenburg*, Berlin, 1971; L. A. Clarkson, *Proto-Industrialization: the First Phase of Industrialization*, London, 1985, chap. 3; W. Mager, 'Protoindustrialisierung und Protoindustrie. Vom Nutzen und Nachteil zweier Konzepte', *Geschichte und Gesellschaft*, 14, 1988, 301–2.

12 E.g. D. S. Landes, *Revolution in Time. Clocks and the Making of the Modern World*, Cambridge, Mass. 1983, 263 *passim;* R. Forberger, *Die Manufaktur in Sachsen*, Berlin (East), 1958, 202–3.

13 A. Klima, 'The beginnings of the machine-building industry in the Czech lands in the first half of the 19th century', *Journal of European Economic History*, 4, 1975, 49–50 and 'Probleme der Proto-Industrie in Böhmen zur Zeit Maria Theresias', Österreichische Akademie der Wissenschaften, *Österreich im Europa der Aufklärung*, Vienna, 1985, 174; Krüger, *Manufakturen*, op. cit., 156; Mendels, 'Agriculture', op. cit., 179. Also see M. Berg, *The Age of Manufactures 1700–1820*, London, 1985, 199 *passim;* Clarkson, Proto-Industrialization, op. cit., 18.

14 M. Dobb, *Studies in the Development of Capitalism*, London, 1947, 138; A. Klima, 'Die Manufaktur in Böhmen', *Scripta Mercaturiae*, 13, 1979, 7; Krüger, *Manufakturen*, op. cit., 174–5, 206.

15 J. Styles, 'Embezzlement, industry and the law in England 1500–1800' in Berg, Hudson and Sonenscher, op. cit., 173–210.

16 A. Klima, 'Die Textilmanufaktur im Böhmen des 18. Jahrhunderts', *Historica*, 15, 1967, 129; also his 'Manufakturen', op. cit., 7 and 'Probleme', op. cit., 173; Krüger, *Manufakturen*, op. cit., 59 *passim*, 193; Houston and Snell, 'Proto-Industrialization', op. cit., 476; Robert Millward, 'The early stages of European industrialization: economic organization under serfdom', *Explorations in Economic History*, 21, 1984, 406–28; Kriedte, Medick and Schlumbohm, op. cit. (German edn, 1977), 198, 262.

17 Dobb, *Studies*, op. cit., 144; Berg, *Age of Manufactures*, op. cit., 89; Krüger, *Manufakturen*, op. cit., 183 ff., 198, 206; S. D. Chapman and S. Chassagne, *European Textile Printers*, London, 1981; Forberger, *Manufaktur*, op. cit., 173–7, 199–200; D. C. Coleman, *Economy*, op. cit., 171; Herbert Kisch, 'Growth deterrents of a medieval heritage: the Aachen area woollen trades before 1790', *Journal of Economic History*, 24, 1964, 531; P. Hudson, *The Genesis of Industrial Capital*, Cambridge, 1986, 33–6; also her 'From manor to mill: the West Riding in transition' in Berg, Hudson and Sonenscher, op. cit., 133–6.

18 J. Thirsk, 'The farming regions of England' in her *The Agrarian History of England and Wales*, vol.4, *1500–1640*, Cambridge, 1967, 45; C. Wilson,

England's Apprenticeship 1603–1763, London, 1965, 190–1; G. L. Gullickson, 'Agriculture and cottage industry: redefining the causes of proto-industrialization', *Journal of Economic History*, 43, 1983, 845; Forberger, *Manufaktur*, op. cit., 265; U. Priestley, ' "The Fabric of Stuffs": the Norwich textile industry *c.* 1650–1750', *Textile History*, 16, 1985, 183–210.

19 Holderness, *Pre-Industrial England*, op cit. 84; Clarkson, *Pre-Industrial Economy*, op. cit., 83; C. Wilson, *Apprenticeship*, op. cit., 302–10; Dobb, *Studies*, op. cit., 139–40; Forberger, *Manufaktur*, op. cit., 179 *passim;* J. U. Nef, 'The Industrial Revolution reconsidered', *Journal of Economic History*, 3, 1943, 21; A. Klima, 'Glassmaking industry and trade in Bohemia in the XVIIth and XVIIIth centuries', *Journal of European Economic and Social History*, 13, 1984, 499–520; A. Raistrick and E. Allen, 'The South Yorkshire ironmasters (1690–1750)', *Economic History Review*, 8, 1937–8, 173–4; C. K. Hyde, 'The adoption of coke smelting by the British iron industry 1709–1790', *Explorations in Economic History*, 10, 1972–3, 397–418 and *Technological Change and the British Iron Industry 1700–1870*, Princeton, 1977, esp. 15–6, 31, 64, 118; Büsch, 'Gewerbe', op. cit., 10–11; Freudenberger and Redlich, op. cit., 374, 379 ff.; K. Takahashi, 'A contribution to the discussion' in R. Hilton (ed.), *The Transition from Feudalism to Capitalism*, London, 1976, 113; A. Paulinyi, 'Die Betriebsform im Eisenhüttenwesen sur Zeit der frühen Industrialisierung in Ungarn' in W. Fischer, *Beiträge*, op. cit., 215–37; M. W. Flinn, 'The growth of the English iron industry 1660–1760', *Economic History Review*, 2nd series, 11 1958–9, 144–53.

20 Freudenberger and Redlich, op. cit., 394; Holderness, *Pre-Industrial England*, op. cit., 108; Berg, *Age of Manufactures*, op. cit., 75, 265, 274–83; T. S. Ashton, 'The domestic system in the early Lancashire tool trade', *Economic History*, 1, 1926–9, 132, 138–9; G. C. Allen, 'Methods of industrial organization in the West Midlands, 1860–1927', ibid.; G. I. H. Lloyd, *The Cutlery Trades*, London, 1913.

21 Freudenberger and Redlich, op. cit., 374; P. Mathias, 'Agriculture and the brewing and distilling industries in the eighteenth century' in E. L. Jones (ed.), *Agriculture and Economic Growth in England 1650–1815*, London, 1967, 81, 83 and *The Brewing Industry in England 1700–1830*, Cambridge, 1959; Coleman, *Economy of England*, op. cit., 168.

22 Douglass C. North, 'Location theory and regional economic growth', *Journal of Political Economy*, 63, 1955, 243–58; H. Kiesewetter, 'Erklärungshypothesen zur regionalen Industrialisierung in Deutschland im 19. Jahrhundert', *Vierteljahrschrift für Sozial- und Wirtschaftsgeschichte*, 67, 1980, 320; T. Pierenkemper and R. H. Tilly, 'Regionale Differenzierung in Deutschland als Schwerpunkt wirtschaftshistorischer Forschung' in R. Fremdling and R. H. Tilly (eds), *Industrialisierung und Raum*, Stuttgart, 1979, 18; R. H. Dumke, 'Intra-German Trade in 1837 and regional economic development', *Vierteljahrschrift für Sozial- und Wirtschaftsgeschichte*, 64, 1977, 469–70; W. Isard, *Methods of Regional Analysis: An Introduction to Regional Science*, Cambridge, Mass., 1973 edn., 190 ff.; S. L. Engerman, 'Douglass C. North . . . Revisited', op. cit., 249; J. R. Meyer, 'Regional economics: a survey', *American Eco-*

nomic Review, 53, 1963, 19–54; G. Adelmann, 'Zur regionalen Differenzierung der Baumwoll- und Seidenverarbeitung . . . 1846–1907', in H. Pohl (ed.), *Gewerbe und Industrielandschaften vom Spät-mittelalter bis ins 20. Jahrhundert, Vierteljahrschrift für Sozial- und Wirtschafts-geschichte*, Beiheft 78, Stuttgart, 1986, 285; F. B. Tipton, Jnr, *Regional Variations in the Economic Development of Germany During the Nineteenth Century*, Middleton, Conn., 1976, esp. 10–11, 144; F. Buttler, K. Gerlach and P. Lippmann, *Grundlagen der Regionalökonomie*, Reinbek, 1977, 29, 58; H. W. Broude, 'The significance of regional studies for the elaboration of national economic history', *Journal of Economic History*, 20, 1960, 588–96; H. Hesse, 'Die Entwicklung der regionalen Einkommensdifferenzen im Wachstumsprozess der deutschen Wirtschaft vor 1913' in W. Fischer (ed.), *Beiträge*, op. cit., 262–4.

23 E.g. W. Feldenkirchen, 'Zum Einfluss der Standortfaktoren auf die Eisen und Stahlindustrie des Ruhrgebietes (bis 1914)' in F. Blaich (ed.), *Entwicklungsprobleme einer Region: Das Beispiel Rheinland und Westfalen im 19. Jahrhundert*, Berlin, 1981, 47–88; W. Isard, 'Some locational factors in the iron and steel industry since the early nineteenth century', *Journal of Political Economy*, 56, 1948, 203–17; M. Hau, 'Energiekosten und Industrialisierung der französischen Regionen von der Mitte des 19. Jahrhunderts bis zum ersten Weltkrieg' in S. Pollard, *Region und Industrialisierung*, op. cit., 239–53; L. Bergeron, 'Kapital und Industrialisierung in Lothringen vom Ende des 18. bis zum Beginn des 20. Jahrhunderts', ibid., 130.

24 M. W. Flinn, *The History of the British Coal Industry*, vol. 2, *The Industrial Revolution 1700–1830*, Oxford, 1984; A. R. Griffin, *The British Coalmining Industry. Retrospect and Prospect*, Hartington, 1977.

25 There is a large literature. See, *inter alia*, Kriedte, Medick and Schlumbohm, op. cit., 69 ff.; Berg, Hudson and Sonenscher, op. cit., 21 ff.; F. Mendels, 'Agriculture and peasant industries', op. cit., 186; R. Braun, 'Proto-industrialization and demographic changes in the canton of Zürich' in C. Tilly (ed.), *Historical Studies of Changing Fertility*, Princeton, 1978, 289–334 and 'Proto-industrialization: theory and reality', op. cit., 76; E. L. Jones, 'Agricultural origins of industry', *Past and Present*, 40, 1968, 58–71 and 'Agriculture and economic growth in England, 1660–1750: agricultural change' in his *Agriculture and Economic Growth*, op. cit., 152–71; E. L. Jones and S. J. Woolf, 'The historical role of agrarian change in economic development' in their *Agrarian Change*, op. cit., 13; P. K. O'Brien, 'Agriculture and the Industrial Revolution', *Economic History Review*, 2nd series, 30, 1977, 166–81; F. Baltzarek, 'Zu den regionalen Ansätzen der frühen Industrialisierung in Europa' in H. Knittler (ed.), *Wirtschafts- und Sozialhistorische Beiträge. Festschrift für Alfred Hoffman*, Vienna, 1979, 339–40; E. A. Wrigley, 'Urban growth and agricultural change: England and the continent in the early modern period', *Journal of Interdisciplinary History*, 15, 1985, 683–728; J. de Vries, 'The population and economy of the pre-industrial Netherlands', ibid., 667; H. Kiesewetter, 'Erklärungshypothesen', op. cit., 316–18; Mager, 'Protoindustrialisierung', op. cit., 472–3; Berg, *Age of Manufacture*, op. cit., 92 ff.; R. Lee, 'Regionale Differenzierung

im Bevölkerungswachstum Deutschlands im frühen neunzehnten Jahrhundert' in Fremdling and Tilly, op. cit., 192–227; R. H. Dumke, 'Intra-German trade', op. cit., 472–3, 487–8.

26 Dumke, op. cit.; K. Borchardt, 'Regionale Wachstumsdifferenzierung in Deutschland im 19. Jahrhundert unter besonderer Berücksichtigung des West-Ost Gefälles', in W. Abel *et al.* (eds), *Wirtschaft, Geschichte und Wirtschaftsgeschichte*, Stuttgart, 1966, esp. 337–9; F. Bateman and T. Weiss, 'Comparative regional development in ante-bellum manufacturing', *Journal of Economic History*, 35, 1975, 188; D. C. North, 'Location theory', *Scandinavian Economic History Review*, 30/1, 1982, issue on proto-industrialization in Scandinavia, esp. 22, 69.

27 E.g. Bergeron, 'Kapital und Industrialisierung', op. cit., 130; Forberger, *Manufaktur*, op. cit., 137–46.

28 R. Braun, 'Proto-industrialization', op. cit.,; Mager, 'Proto-industrialisierung', op. cit., 468; J. D. Chambers, *Population, Economy and Society in Pre-Industrial England*, London, 1972, 132–3, 136; J. Thirsk, 'The farming regions of England', op. cit., 132–3; J. Mokyr, *Why Ireland Starved*, London, 1983; D. A. Farnie, *The English Cotton Industry and the World Market 1815–1896*, Oxford, 1979, 46 *passim*.

29 E.g. Feldenkirchen, 'Einfluss der Standortfaktoren', op. cit., 80–2; J. G. Lambooy, *Economie en Ruimte*, Assen, 1975, 4 *passim*.

30 See note 41.

31 A. H. Dodd, *The Industrial Revolution in North Wales*, Cardiff, 1933; B. Trinder, *The Industrial Revolution in Shropshire*, London and Chichester, 1973; J. Rowe, *Cornwall in the Age of the Industrial Revolution*, Liverpool, 1953.

32 For an interesting attempt to create a theoretical framework for the way in which the local bunching of firms leads to external economies, see G. J. Stigler, 'The division of labour is limited by the extent of the market', *Journal of Political Economy*, 59, 1951, 185–93.

33 F. Braudel, *Capitalism and Material Life 1400–1800*, New York, 1973.

34 E.g. H. Kiesewetter, 'Staat und Regionale Industrialisierung. Württemberg und Sachsen im 19. Jahrhundert' in Kiesewetter and Fremdling, op. cit., 108–32; Tipton, *Regional Variations*, op. cit., 14, 69; M. Barkhausen, 'Government control and free enterprise in West Germany and the Low Countries in the eighteenth century' in Earle, *Essays*, op. cit., 212–73.

35 Forberger, *Manufaktur*, op. cit., 236 ff.; Klima, 'Textilmanufaktur', op. cit., 155 ff.; Kiesewetter, 'Staat', op. cit., *passim*.

36 S. Pollard, *The Genesis of Modern Management*, London, 1965, 12–24.

37 A. O. Krueger, 'The political economy of the rent-seeking society', *American Economic Review*, 65, 1974, 291–303; Y. Barzel, 'Transaction costs', *Zeitschrift für die gesamte Staatswissenschaft*, 141, 1985, 4–20; G. Tullock, 'The cost of transfers;, *Kyklos*, 24, 1971, 629–43; T. L. Anderson and P. J. Hill, 'Institutional change through the Supreme Court and the rise of transfer activity' in R. L. Ransom, R. Sutch and G. M. Walton, *Explorations in the New Economic History. Essays in Honor of Douglass C. North*, New York, 1982, 193–212.

38 Forberger, *Manufaktur*, op. cit., 265–85; R. Tilly, *Financial Institutions*

and the Industrialization of the Rhineland 1815–1870, Madison, 1966, 138; Kriedte, Medick and Schlumbohm, op. cit., 289; Kiesewetter, 'Erklärungshypothesen', op. cit., 328–9; A. Klima, 'Probleme der Leibeigenschaft in Böhmen', *Vierteljahrschrift für Sozial- und Wirtschaftsgeschichte*, 62, 1975, 224–5; W. Fischer, *Wirtschaft und Gesellschaft im Zeitalter der Industrialisierung*, Göttingen, 1972, 473; Tipton, *Regional Variations*, op. cit., 69.

39 Tipton, *Regional Variations*, op. cit., 113; Kiesewetter, 'Erklärungshypothesen', op. cit., 326; G. R. Hawke and J. P. P. Higgins, 'Transport and social overhead capital' in R. Floud and D. McCloskey (eds), *The Economic History of Britain Since 1700*, vol.1, *1700–1860*, Cambridge, 1981, 251; W. K. Hutchinson, 'Import substitution, structural change and regional growth in the United States: the northeast 1870–1910', *Journal of Economic History*, 45, 1985, 319–25; H. S. Seidenfus, 'Was erwartet die Nationalökonomie von einer regionalen Wirtschaftsgeschichte?' in F. Blaich (ed.), *Entwicklungsprobleme einer Region. Das Beispiel Rheinland und Westfalen im 19. Jahrhundert*, Berlin, 1981, 150–1; E. Schremmer, 'Föderativer Staatsverbund, öffentliche Finanzen und Industrialisierung in Deutschland' in Kiesewetter und Fremdling, op. cit., 8; R. Fremdling, 'Der Einfluss der Handels- und Zollpolitik auf die wallonische und rheinisch-westfälische Eisenindustrie', ibid., 72–102.

40 Feldenkirchen, 'Einfluss', op. cit., 65; Forberger, *Manufaktur*, op. cit., 299; J. Reulecke, 'Nachzügler und Pionier zugleich: das Bergische Land und der Beginn der Industrialisierung in Deutschland' in Pollard, *Region und Industrialisierung*, op. cit., 59; C. Tilly and R. Tilly, 'Agenda for European economic history in the 1970s', *Journal of Economic History*, 31, 1971, 189; H. Kisch, 'The textile industries in Silesia and the Rhineland: a comparative study in industrialization', ibid., 19, 1959, 555 ff.; M. Hall (ed.), *Made in New York*, Cambridge, Mass., 1963.

41 Krueger, *Manufakturen*, op. cit., 267–8, 447; F. Baltzarek, 'Zu den regionalen Ansätzen', op. cit., 339 and 'Finanzplatz Wien – die innerstaatliche und internationale Stellung in historischer Perspektive', *Quartalshefte der Girozentrale*, 15, 1980, 11–63; V. Bacskai (ed.), *Bürgertum und bürgerliche Entwicklung in Mittel- und Osteuropa*, 2 vols, Budapest, 1986, 155–61, 166–7, 177, 241–4, 253–4, 549–63; O. Büsch, *Das Gewerbe in der Wirtschaft des Raumes Berlin/Brandenburg 1800–1850*, Berlin, 1970 and *Industrialisierung und Gewerbe im Raum Berlin/Brandenburg 1800–1850*, Berlin, 1969.

42 H. Rockoff, 'Regional interest rates and bank failures, 1870–1914', *Explorations in Economic History*, 14, 1977, 90–5; W. Isard, *Methods of Regional Analysis*, op. cit., 144–78; L. Davis, 'The capital markets and industrial concentration in the US and UK, a comparative study', *Economic History Review*, 2nd series, 19, 1966, 260; M. Miles, 'The money market in the early Industrial Revolution: the evidence for West Riding attorneys', *Business History*, 23, 1981, 127–46; B. L. Anderson, 'Provincial aspects of the financial revolution of the eighteenth century', ibid., 11, 1969, and 'The attorney and the early capital market in Lancashire' in F. Crouzet (ed.), *Capital Formation in the*

Industrial Revolution, London, 1972, 223–55; R. Sylla, *The American Capital Market 1846–1917*, New York, 1975; C. Iversen, *Aspects of the Theory of International Capital Markets*, Copenhagen, 1835; repr. New York, 1967, 114–15; D. F. Good, 'Financial integration in late nineteenth-century Austria', *Journal of Economic History*, 37, 1977, 894; H. I. Halsey, 'The choice between high-pressure and low-pressure steam power in America in the early nineteenth century', ibid., 41, 1981, 724; G. Smiley, 'Regional variations in bank loan rates in the interwar years', ibid., 888–901.

43 E.g. J. Reulecke, 'Nachzügler', op. cit., 57; H. Kisch 'Textile industries', op. cit., 555 ff.; P. Dudzik, 'Die Prägung regionaler Industrialisierung durch das Unternehmerverhalten in der Baumwollindustrie des Elsass und der Schweiz im 19. Jahrhundert' in H. Kiesewetter and R. Fremdling (eds), *Staat, Region und Industrialisierung*, Ostfildern, 1985, 222–36.

44 J. R. Meyer, 'Regional economics', op. cit., 43–4; Tipton, *Regional Variations*, op. cit., 12–13; E. H. Hunt, 'Industrialization and regional inequality: wages in Britain, 1760–1914', *Journal of Economic History*, 46, 1986, 955.

45 J. R. Harris, 'Michael Alcock and the transfer of Birmingham technology to France before the Revolution', *Journal of European Economic History*, 15, 1986, 7–57.

46 P. Hudson, 'Proto-industrialization', op. cit. and 'From manor to mill: the West Riding in transition' in Berg, Hudson and Sonnenscher, op. cit., 124–44; A. Rogers, 'Industrialization and the local community' in Pollard, *Region und Industrialisierung*, op. cit., 196–211; T. Pierenkemper, 'Regionale Differenzierung im östlichen Ruhrgebiet 1850–1887' in Fremdling and Tilly, op. cit., 165–88.

47 F. Baltzarek, 'Zu den regionalen Ansätzen', op. cit., 352; Dumke, 'Intra-German trade', op. cit., 471–2.

48 C. Sabel and J. Zeitlin, 'Historical alternatives to mass production: politics, markets and technology in nineteenth-century industrialization', *Past and Present*, 108, 1985, 133–76.

49 Pollard, *Genesis*, op. cit., 10–24.

50 S. Berger and M. J. Piore, *Dualism and Discontinuity in Industrial Societies*, Cambridge, 1980, esp. 23–5, 37, 47, 62 f.

51 See note 31. Also Baltzarek, 'Zu den regionalen Ansätzen', op. cit., 340; Kriedte, Medick and Schlumbohm, op. cit., 297.

52 D. T. Jenkins and K. G. Ponting, *The British Wool Textile Industry 1770–1914*, London, 1982, 262–5; E. M. Sigsworth and J. M. Blackman, 'The woollen and worsted industries' in D. H. Aldcroft (ed.), *The Development of British Industry and Foreign Competition, 1875–1914*, London, 1968, 142.

53 Kriedte, Medick and Schlumbohm, op. cit., 292 ff.; P. K. O'Brien, 'Do we have a typology for the study of European industrialization in the XIXth century?', *Journal of European Economic History*, 15, 1986, 300; L. Magnusson and M. Isacson, 'Proto-industrialization in Sweden', *Scandinavian Economic History Review*, 30, 1982, 75–6; Berg, *Age of Manufactures*, op. cit., 113–5; Berg, Hudson and Sonenscher, op. cit., 81 ff.;

Baltzarek, 'Zu den regionalen Ansätzen', op. cit., 350; Dumke, 'Intra-German trade', op. cit., 474–5; C. Wilson, *England's Apprenticeship*, op. cit., 290–1, 294; Tilly and Tilly, op. cit., 189; J. Mooser, 'Der Weg vom proto-industriellen zum fabrik-industriellen Gewerbe in Ravensberg, 1830–1914' in K. Düwell and W. Köllmann (eds), *Rheinland-Westfalen im Industriezeitalter*, vol.1, *Von der Entstehung der Provinzen bis zur Reichsgründung*, Wuppertal, 1983, 75–6; E. Harder-Gersdorff, 'Leinen-Regionen im Vorfeld und im Verlauf der Industrialisierung (1780–1914)' in Pohl (ed.), *Gewerbe- und Industrielandschaften*, op. cit., 203, 215, 231; C. Lis and H. Soly, *Poverty and Capitalism in Pre-Industrial Europe*, Brighton, 1982, 148–59; C. P. Kindleberger, 'Germany's overtaking of England,' *Economic Response. Comparative Studies in Trade, Finance and Growth*, Cambridge, Mass, 1978, 210.

54 J. G. Williamson, 'Regional inequality and the process of national development', *Economic Development and Cultural Change* 13/4, Part II, July 1965, 3–84; Dumke, 'Intra-German trade', op. cit., 469; R. Fremdling, T. Pierenkemper and R. Tilly, 'Regionale Differenzierung in Deutschland als Schwerpunkt wirtschaftshistorischer Forschung' in Fremdling and Tilly, op. cit. 19 ff.; T. J. Orsagh, 'The probable geographical distribution of German income 1882–1963', *Zeitschrift für die gesamte Staatswissenschaft*, 124, 1968, 290–1; G. Tichy, *A Sketch of a Probabilistic Modification of the Product-Cycle Hypothesis to Explain the Problems of Old Industrial Areas*, University of Graz, Department of Economics, Research memo. no. 8401, cyclost. 1984; J. de Vries, 'Regional economic inequality in the Netherlands since 1600' in P. Bairoch and M. Lévy-Leboyer (eds). *Disparities in Economic Development Since the Industrial Revolution*, London, 1981, 189–98; H. Freudenberger and G. Mensch, 'Regional differences, differential development and generative economic growth', ibid., 201; J. Söderberg, 'Regional economic disparity and dynamics 1840–1914: a comparison between France, Great Britain, Prussia and Sweden', *Journal of European Economic History*, 14, 1985, 273–96; Hesse, 'Entwicklung', op. cit., 265–8.

55 See note 32 above.

56 J. E. Meade, *The Theory of International Economic Policy*, vol. 2, *Trade and Welfare*, 1964, 1st edn 1955, 258 *passim*. Also see W. Isard, *Introduction to Regional Science*, Englewood Cliffs, New Jersey, 1975, chap. 6, and *Methods of Regional Analysis*, op. cit., 375–7; Kiesewetter, 'Erklärungshypothesen', op. cit., 322.

57 W. Fischer, *Wirtschaft und Gesellschaft*, op. cit., 469 *passim;* P. Jeannin, 'La protoindustrialisation: développement ou impasse?', *Annales ESC*, 35, 1980, 62; Mooser, op. cit., 79 ff.

58 Jeannin, op. cit., 62; Baltzarek, 'Zu den regionalen Ansätzen', op. cit., 337, 355; Bergeron, 'Kapital und Industrialisierung', op. cit., 132–3; P. Cayez, 'Industrielle und regionale Entwicklung im 19. Jahrhundert am Beispiel Lyons' in Pollard, *Region und Industrialisierung*, op. cit., 118, K. Megerle, 'Varianten eines Industrialisierungstyps' in Kiesewetter and Fremdling, op. cit., 146–7.

59 Lloyd, *Cutlery Trades*, op. cit., G. C. Allen, *The Industrial Development of*

SIDNEY POLLARD

Birmingham and the Black Country 1860–1927, London, 1929; N. McCord, *North-East England. An Economic and Social History*, London, 1979.

60 Baltzarek, 'Zu den regionalen Ansätzen', op. cit., 346; Kisch, 'The textile industries', op. cit., 554. For Northern Ireland, see B. Collins, 'Proto-industrialization and pre-Famine emigration', *Social History*, 1, 1982, 127–46.

61 Clarkson, *Pre-Industrial Economy*, op. cit., 80; F.-W. Henning, 'Wirtschaftsstruktur', op. cit., 139; Freudenberger and Redlich, op. cit., 377–8; F. Mendels, 'Agriculture and peasant industries', op. cit., 180; E. Schremmer, 'The textile industry in south Germany 1750 to 1850. Some causes for the technical backwardness', *Textile History*, 7, 1976, 61–2 and 'Proto-industrialization: a step towards industrialization?', *Journal of European Economic History*, 10, 1981, 661; O. Hornby and E. Oxenbøll, 'Proto-industrialization before industrialization: the Danish case', *Scandinavian Economic History Review*, 30, 1982, 17–18; E. Hovland, H. W. Nordvik, S. Tveite, 'Proto-industrialization in Norway 1750–1850: fact or fiction?', ibid., 53; A. Hofmann, 'Zur Problematik der agrarischen Nebengewerbe und der Reagrarisierung' in H. Kellenbenz (ed.), *Agrarisches Nebengewerbe und Formen der Reagrarisierung im Spätmittelalter und 19/20 Jahrhundert*, Stuttgart, 1975, 30–2.

62 S. Pollard, *Peaceful Conquest. The Industrialization of Europe 1760–1970*, Oxford, 1981, 92; Lis and Soly, op. cit., 157; Berg, *Age of Manufactures*, op. cit., 122 ff.; F.-W Henning, 'Der Einfluss der Industrialisierung des Textilgewerbes in Deutschland im 19. Jahrhundert auf die Einkommensmöglichkeiten in den ländlichen Gebieten' in Kellenbenz, *Nebengewerbe*, op. cit., 167; M. Bergman, 'The potato blight in the Netherlands and its social consequences', *International Review of Social History*, 12, 1967.

63 Also see Buttler, Gerlach and Liepmann, op. cit., 87; Deyon, 'L'enjeu', op. cit., 9; Jeannin, 'La proto-industrialisation', op. cit., 62; Mendels, 'Proto-industrialization: theory or reality?', op. cit., 89–91; Kisch, 'Textile industries', op. cit., 554.

64 See Houston and Snell, op. cit., 388–91; Berg, *Age of Manufactures*, op. cit., 113 *passim*.

3

STATE INTERVENTION IN THE CATALAN CALICO-PRINTING INDUSTRY IN THE EIGHTEENTH CENTURY*

J. K. J. Thomson

The development of a European calico-printing industry in the late seventeenth and eighteenth centuries has been judged one of the most important of the period's economic changes. The grounds for the verdict include the following. The establishment of the industry represented the first step in the introduction of the cotton industry to Europe. The concentrated, large-scale organization of production which was to characterize the industry made it a principal agent for the early diffusion of 'manufactures'. The complex dyeing and bleaching processes developed for calico-printing served as a principal channel for creating links between technology and science. The industry's expansion stimulated design both in so far as it occasioned a contact between European and Oriental artistic traditions and also in that its mass market probably made it the principal instrument in the diffusion of new design principles. The value and international character of the trade in both printed and unprinted calicoes occasioned close links between calico trading and merchant banking. It has even been argued that the varied character of development of the industry in different countries partly conditioned the later industrialization process.[1]

Calico-printing was clearly an industry whose rapid expansion provides an excellent illustration of the force of two of the sources of change whose analysis is the concern of this book: the growth during the period leading up to the Industrial Revolution of a larger and socially more heterogeneous consumer market in Europe and the development of more intense links with non-European areas. In connection with the former, the success of printed calicoes was explicable both in terms of their technical superiority over

57

other types of light textiles – they combined colourfulness and lively designs with durability and washability – and in those of their cheapness, which assured ready sales even in areas in which the purchase and wearing of calicoes was illegal and subject to some risk.[2] The non-European links included not only the provision of raw materials – both raw and spun cotton, dyestuffs, gums for thickening mordants, etc. – but also the industry's basic technique – the use of mordants to achieve colour fastness and varied colouring effects – as well as the just-mentioned stimulus to design. Perhaps the greatest contribution of the non-European area, however, was the initial one of providing a vast supply of printed calicoes which served to stimulate a mass demand for the new product. It is this influence which is highlighted by Jan de Vries. The 'demonstration effect' of these and other non-western imports, he points out, served to stimulate the development of import-substituting industries in Europe. It is his grounds for speculating that 'the European economy . . . gained more from its non-western imports than from the colonial export markets it acquired'.[3]

If, though, the development of calico-printing reflects what are central themes of this book, some of the characteristics of the new industry provide contrasts with other industries which have been studied in recent years and also to some of the case-studies included in this collection. It was predominantly an urban industry and this separates it from the majority of examples which have informed the proto-industrialization discussion. It was an industry whose development was sudden and particularly rapid. What has just been said about import substitution provides the principal explanation for this: distribution networks and a mass market were built up prior to its establishment and the new industry was able to take these over to produce immediately on a large scale. Certainly it provides a sharp contrast with, for example, the experience of the Igualada clothier Torelló, described by Jaume Torras, the *preliminary* for whose expansion of production involved a gradual, laborious and costly creation of a marketing network. It was an industry whose organization of production, as already noted, took the form, principally, of concentrated manufactures. This undoubtedly distinguishes it from the majority of industrial activity in this period, characterized still by the predominance of the domestic production unit.

The factors which determined scale and production unit were also different from those applying in some other industries. Certainly landholding patterns, crucial, as Pat Hudson has shown, both in this volume and elsewhere, in the determination of diverging industrial structures in the Yorkshire woollen industry, were of no relevance to an urban industry. The principal influences seem to have been technical – the complexity of the printing and bleaching processes provided the possibility of considerable economies of scale and made necessary an emphasis on quality control favouring concentrated production. Finally it was an industry much influenced by actions of the state. The threat which its growth posed for established manufacturing interests, the relatively low level of value added which it gave rise to, its generation of imports, its contribution to the eliminating of sumptuary distinctions – these were the principal factors which contributed, in a mercantile age, to its being burdened by a series of restrictions in different European countries. In the case of this industry at least – and here there might be a slight difference in interpretation from Sidney Pollard's neighbouring chapter – diverging national economic policies both determined the geography of the industry's diffusion as well as giving rise to, it will be the argument of this chapter, different types of enterprise.[4]

It is principally on this last factor, state intervention, in the Spanish industry, and in particular in the industry of Barcelona, that this chapter is focused. Barcelona represents a suitable case-study both from the point of view of Spain – nearly all of Spanish calico-printing was concentrated in the city – and of that of Europe, for it contained what was probably the largest concentration of calico-printing anywhere by the 1780s.[5] An additional advantage is that the nature of the industry's relationship to the state was complex and varied over time, thus providing a basis for discussing a range of issues concerning the state/industry connection. I would emphasize, though, that this study is by no means a complete survey of this question. Its focus is principally on the early years of the industry's development, up to about 1760. Other periods have been well studied by Catalan historians, although there is certainly more work which needs to be carried out in this area.[6]

The chapter is divided into five sections. In the first, a European panorama is given by identifying the different categories of national response to the new industry. In a second, the Spanish response is analysed and compared to that elsewhere. In a third, an additional facet of the Spanish government's policy, the granting of *franquicias* (literally concessions) to individual manufactures, is documented and explained. In the fourth and fifth sections, arguments are presented that the policies described influenced respectively industrial structure and the type of entrepreneurs who took up production. Finally, in a conclusion, it is argued that though these policies were only enforced for a short period, their long-term consequences were considerable.

DIFFERENT RESPONSES TO CALICOES IN EUROPE

There has been little systematic comparison of different governmental reactions to calico-printing, despite the importance of the issue. The yardstick for comparisons, in so far as they have been made, has tended to be the degree to which reactions favoured the development of the industry and the later growth of cotton manufacturing. Four types of response are indentifiable – an optimal one, of a type to benefit both the growth of calico-printing and cotton manufacturing; a neutral one, which favoured calico-printing but occasioned less stimulus to cotton manufacture; a negative one, which damaged the prospects of both industries; and finally a mixed one, designed to be favourable but using forms of intervention liable to prejudice some of the useful effects achieved. Britain's reaction corresponds to the first category, that of the Dutch republic and a number of central European states, including Switzerland, to the second, that of France to the third and those of a number of more backward European states, whose response to the industry came at a later date, to the fourth.

The British reaction, though judged the most beneficial, was, in fact, far from the most liberal. With its large woollen industry and its developing silk industry (which, being concentrated in London, was strategically situated for exercising pressure on Parliament), Britain possessed strong vested interests opposed to its calico-printing industry (which was centred in London too, and had been established in the 1670s) as well as to the importing of calicoes from India. The imports and the new industry also had a strong protector – the East India Company – but from the late 1680s a series of discriminatory taxes and restrictions attest to the greater weight of the influence of the manufacturing interests. Duties and excise taxes were imposed in 1685, 1690, 1712 and 1714, in 1700 the import of printed calicoes was prohibited and in 1721 the sale, purchase or wearing of all printed cloth containing cotton, with

the exception of fustians, muslins, neckcloths and blue dyed calicoes, were banned. How it was that such apparently discriminatory measures actually came to favour calico-printing and other
manufactures is to be explained by the existence of loopholes which
were probably negotiated by interested parties. Thus, though the
sale of printed calicoes or 'any stuff made of cotton or mixed
therewith' was banned by the 1721 act, that of printed linens and
fustians was permitted and the industry continued to enjoy the
protection from foreign competition which it had been granted in
1700.

The 1721 measure thus confirmed the printers in their possession
of a large and expanding domestic market as well as giving a
new stimulus to the already protected linen industries of Ireland,
Scotland and, increasingly, England, and to the Lancashire-based
production of fustians (a generic term for a range of coarse, twilled,
cotton stuffs). In addition, the printing of calicoes for export
remained unrestricted and this both provided additional markets
and the stimulus of competing with Indian goods – a stimulus
which provoked a steady improvement in the quality of the English
product. Thus each of the measures which were designed principally to protect the woollen and silk manufacturing interests had,
in fact, served to stimulate the progress of the two rival industries
of calico-printing and cotton manufacture. The irony has not
escaped historians. As Paul Mantoux notes, referring to the 1700
import ban: 'It was that very industry (wool) which, by its blind
passion for monopoly, stirred up that competition which it tried
to kill a few years later.'[7]

Areas included in the second category of governmental response
imposed no restrictions on calico-printing of any kind. This liberal
reaction permitted a proliferation of calico-printing concerns in
and around Amsterdam – where some one hundred print-shops
operated between 1675 and 1750[8] – and in a string of German and
Swiss towns, principally Bremen, Frankfurt, Hamburg, Neuchâtel,
Lausanne, Geneva and Basel. There was a particularly dense concentration in the Swiss area. Figures for the years 1760–2 record
the existence of some 33 manufactures for the last four towns listed
and in 1750 the small principality of Neuchâtel alone, with its
50,000 inhabitants, was printing 160,000 pieces of calico a year.[9]
The extent of this concentration was related to state policy towards
calico-printing – not that of the Swiss cantons, however, but of
their powerful French neighbour. The total ban on its calico-

printing industry (which will be described in greater detail below), in conjunction with the contemporaneous Revocation of the Edict of Nantes, caused the French printers (many of whom were Protestants) to move their concerns to adjacent zones, and principally to the Swiss area, whence they could supply the French and central European markets – French bans on the sale and wearing of calicoes, unlike those on the actual processes of printing, were never effectively enforced. A French industry in exile thereby established itself, much of which was to return to France after 1759 when the ban on calico-printing was removed.[10]

The dual encouragement provided by liberalism and the extremes of French policy led to progress in the quality as well as the quantity of production and Switzerland rivalled England in the technological leadership of the industry. The liberalism, though, was not confined to the permissive attitude towards calico-printing. The import of unprinted calicoes was also allowed with the consequence that, unlike in Britain, the local linen and cotton manufacturing industries were not forced into import substitution to supply the printers. The neighbouring textile industry was certainly stimulated, and particularly during the years 1744–63 when war and political instability affected deliveries of Indian calicoes – during the 1750s, for example, 60 per cent of the printing of the large Fabrique Neuve de Cortaillod of Neuchâtel, studied by Pierre Caspard, was done on Swiss cloth[11] – but such local production was at no stage in the eighteenth century of a quality to rival the Indian imports. The continued importance of the Indian link is illustrated by the dominant place in the industry occupied by powerful merchant families, such as the Pourtalès, who had succeeded in cornering a large share of the Indian imports.[12] As Julia Mann concludes, 'In Holland, Switzerland and Germany . . . there was no interference with the use of Indian calicoes, and it was only when they were bad or dear that home-manufactured cloth could compete.'[13]

The extent of France's self-inflicted damage from its rejection of the trade can be judged both by the fact that it was for Marseilles in 1648 that there exists evidence for the first European attempts at calico-printing and also that the industry banned in 1686 was already a large one, France being the first country in which it achieved significant geographical diffusion.[14] The severity of the treatment of the industry is partly explicable in terms of the inflexibility of Colbertism and the priority given within this system to wool and silk, but it owed something, too, to the relative weakness of the French East India Company – imports of printed calicoes to France were largely handled by the Dutch and English companies and so it had less incentive to protect the trade. The ban was total and persistent: between 1686 and 1759 the import, domestic manufacturing, sale and wearing of printed calicoes was forbidden in repeated statutes and ordinances – two statutes, eighty ordinances and even more administrative orders, according to Heckscher.[15] As has just been noted, it was in the restricting of manufacturing that the measures were most effectively enforced. There can be no doubt that both calico-printing and the development of cotton manufacturing suffered as a consequence and that there were other damaging results too.

A succession of historians has commented on the harm done. Without the ban, Depître noted, 'Les progrès de la filature et du tissage du coton eussent été sans doute, comme le prouve l'exemple de la Suisse, accelerés', and he cited Roland de la Platière's judgement concerning the continued inferiority of French printing in 1790 – 'notre industrie n'égale point la Suisse' – despite the rapid post-1759 growth in the industry. 'In France,' Julia Mann concluded, 'printing was not permitted until 1759 and the backwardness of the French cotton manufactures may be partly attributed to its lack of this stimulus in the earlier stages.' Even after 1759 the stimulus was not maximized, as it had been in England, as the import of Indian calicoes in the white continued to be permitted until 1785 and these, according to Lévy Leboyer, accounted for some 80 per cent of the cloth printed in France at this date. The French industry's most recent historian, Serge Chassagne, emphasizes the lack of a link between the rapidly imported post-1759 enterprises and the areas in which they were established – an enclave-type relationship was established – and the shortness of the calico-printing 'era' in France compared to elsewhere, 'The "cycle" . . . scarcely lasted more than half a century,' he writes. A major chance had been lost.[16]

A statement of Chapman and Chassagne provides a good introduction to the fourth category. 'In the second half of the eighteenth century,' they write, 'autocratic regimes of central and eastern Europe contrived to attract calico-printing to their countries.'[17] The grounds for the now principally positive approach towards the new industry were the general European acceptance of the product by this stage and the lack in such areas of strong opposing vested interests in other textile industries. By the mid-eighteenth century, indeed, calico-printing appeared as another basic industry, alongside wool and silk production, which needed to be introduced within any mercantilist import-substituting programme; and it did indeed make its appearance in these parts of Europe contemporaneously with that of these other industries. The 'interventionism', whose possible negative economic repercussions make this fourth category a 'mixed' one in assessing the favourableness of state policy towards the industry, took the forms of the conferring of privileges, the founding of royal manufactures, the granting of monopolies, subsidies and loans and, in the Russian case, the provision of serf labour. The grounds for this interventionism were the 'backwardness' of these areas, a 'backwardness' which included the predominance of corporative economic structures. In these circumstances concessions had to be granted both to attract entrepreneurs into the industry and to provide a legal basis for production. The possible negative repercussions of such policies can be imagined. They contributed to an uncompetitive environment and the policy of granting concessions from, rather than reforming, the corporative system created a situation of yet greater institutional complexity unlikely to favour industrial expansion. Gerschenkron has expressed well the predicament faced by rulers in such areas. The use of state power to induce development might achieve short-term successes but these were likely to be at the expense of those market forces whose development was providing the basis of expansion in Western Europe.[18]

THE RESPONSE IN SPAIN

Spain's geographical position, well placed for contact with all the major trades of seventeenth-century Europe, her penetration by foreign capital and her long tradition of importing manufactured goods make it reasonable to assume, though evidence is lacking, an early introduction to printed calicoes. Barcelona by the 1690s was already importing large quantities. J. Fontana, comparing the city's trade between 1664/5 and 1695/6, notes that a new item, 27,000 metres of painted or printed calicoes, had appeared among imports at the second dates.[19] Their source? Fontana suggests Italy. They had arrived from there together with other textiles. Italy, however, was not a significant centre of calico-printing and so the provenance was more likely to have been either Marseilles, excluded from the French ban on calico printing in 1686, with a substantial printing industry and the regular port of call for Catalan ships returning from Italy, or northern Europe: both the Dutch republic and England traded extensively with Italy and the free port of Leghorn, in particular, was used by English traders as a Mediterranean distribution centre for their exports.[20] It was there that Barcelona supplied itself with Baltic wheat, carried by English shippers,[21] and it seems highly probably that they also brought woollen cloth from England and printed calicoes re-exported from London.

The import of printed calicoes must have damaged the domestic silk and woollen industries in Spain in the same way as such industries were harmed elsewhere. Restrictions on the trade, however, were introduced late. This initial lack of legislative reaction is not surprising – Spain was hardly in a position to exercise an independent commercial policy in the period before and during the Spanish War of Succession – and, besides, as the cases of England and France reveal, it required strong woollen and silk industries, capable of demonstrating direct links between calico imports and industrial crisis, to oppose those merchant groups interested in the calico importing trade and to galvanize governments into action.

The Peace of Utrecht was thus the necessary preliminary for developing government policy towards calico-printing, as it was for other aspects of the new Bourbon dynasty's industrial policy. In 1717 a royal decree forbade the introduction and sale in Spain of silks and other textiles proceeding from Asia and China and a further measure of 1718 extended the restriction to the use of such materials (which was to cease during 1719).

More, of course, was involved than the peace. Vicens Vives raises the possibility that the 1717 measure was introduced at the request of Andalucian traders concerned at the clandestine introduction of Oriental textiles on galleons from Manila[23] but, at a more profound level of causation, the ban clearly forms part of the Colbertian-inspired plans of Philip V and his advisers to give priority to the domestic economy and its protected American trading area over the international trading interests which had effectively been fostered in the previous century. Vilar writes of 'an undeniable improvement in the protection of national interests in face of foreign interests'. The emancipation was assisted by political and economic events which disrupted the previously dominant international networks within which the Spanish economy had fitted: Portugal, whose capital Lisbon had been a principal centre linking Spain to the Atlantic trades, was effectively closed to Spanish merchants by a 1717 ban on their main export, eau-de-vie, and retaliatory prohibitions on the import of cocoa and sugar; French influences were gradually excluded from royal counsels; the creation of a tobacco monopoly domesticated the tobacco trade; everywhere in Europe the international economy was in retreat until the 1730s. The chance factor of plague at Marseilles and other Mediterranean ports in 1715 and, above all, after 1720 increased yet more the dislocation as well as introducing a necessary thoroughness in the control and searching of ships for health reasons which was to be of value later in the prevention of calico smuggling. As Vilar writes again, 'In the memory of contemporaries the years 1720–1725, following the Mediterranean plagues, marked the time when Spain appeared the most difficult of access, best protected.'[24]

In 1728 the ban on the import of printed calicoes was extended to European imitations and from this year greater determination was shown in the enforcement of the calico restrictions, visits of all retail and wholesale outlets for calicoes being carried out in 1730 and 1732 in order to identify and register all stocks of imported goods for a controlled liquidation.[25] The extension of the import prohibition is probably explicable in terms of the growing technical ability of the English and Dutch industries – and their tendency to concentrate on the Spanish and American markets in view of the prohibitions being enforced within Britain and France. Figures for the 1720s show that the textile imports of the English and Dutch East India companies reached the highest levels recorded in the century during these years, and London's calico re-exports increased rapidly after the 1721 prohibition.[26] A likely eventual destiny for some of these re-exports was Spain and Spanish America, reported Europe's best textile market in the late seventeenth century.[27]

If the precise details of the Spanish legislation are compared with those of Britain and France an immediate contrast is apparent. In the latter countries, as has been noted above, the import, printing, sale and wearing of calicoes were all restricted (though in the British case, it has been noted, there were important concessions allowing printing on linens and fustians), but in Spain no restrictions were placed on domestic calico-printing or on the use of domestically produced calicoes. Nor was it purely the lack of a calico-printing industry (in contrast to Britain and France) which accounts for the omission. This is suggested both by the exemption of raw and spun cotton from the 1728 import ban – a concession clearly designed to encourage a domestic cotton industry – and a statement made in 1730 by the Catalan intendant Sartine that it was not the royal intention that the restrictions contained in the edict should extend to 'painted linens, nor cloth woven from cotton imported from Malta . . . which had been made and manufactured in these kingdoms . . . it being the royal desire of His Majesty that his vassals should decide to involve themselves in all sorts of manufactures'.[28] The Spanish legislative response to the industry thus included an explicit commitment to the encouragement of import substitution which was lacking in, and indeed was the reverse of the intentions of, its British and French equivalents.

The national monopoly given to the nascent Spanish industry was not kept intact throughout the eighteenth century. There were some vacillations. The first of these was very early in the industry's development: between November 1742 and December 1743 (the first manufactures had been founded between 1736 and 1737) the ban on the import of calicoes was temporarily replaced by a 30 per cent import due. The second coincided with the accession of Charles III and was to last longer. A royal decree of 15 May 1760 withdrew all restrictions on linen and calico imports, imposing instead a 20 per cent tariff for an experimental period of ten years. Strong pressure was exercised against this liberalization of the trade by Barcelona printers and consequently protection was gradually restored. On 8 July 1768 the ban on the import of printed linens and handkerchiefs was reintroduced, another meas-ure of 19 January 1770 extended the prohibition to various other types of cotton cloth and the Pragmatic Sanction of 24 June 1770 restored full protection by forbidding the import of any sort of cotton cloth or muslin. A measure of 1802 extended the range of prohibition to include spun cotton thereby conferring, as a contemporary commented, the 'ultimate perfection' to the protec-tive system.[29]

The role of the state in the development of the Catalan calico-printing industry has been the subject of dispute among Spanish historians. On the one hand there has been a tendency to contrast the predominantly private basis on which the new industry developed with the practice followed, particularly in Castile, of founding royal manufactures, with substantial state investment, to promote the woollen industry. Carrera Pujal provides an example of such an approach. 'The undoubtable is', he wrote, 'that in Catalonia the cotton industry was established on the basis of a derisory protection if the comparison is made with the abundant privileges and subsidies which were given to a series of commercial companies established in Castile and Aragon'.[30] On the other hand, the positive elements in the legislation have been emphasized. Vázquez de Prada, for example, writes of the royal decrees of 1717, 1718, and 1728 establishing 'a solid platform' for the growth of the industry, and of the privileged access to the American market, which free trade legislation of 1778 permitted, favouring 'the Catalan industry extraordinarily . . . it being the only one in the country in a position to export massively'.[31]

A relating of the Spanish case to the European panorama provided in the previous section should assist in adjudicating between these different points of view. It is clear from what has already been said that it belongs primarily to the fourth category – Britain's case, we have noted, was one of unconscious fostering of the industry, those of Holland, Switzerland and various cities of central Germany represented a free trading response, France's was one of unquestionable rejection, whereas the Spanish record of providing direct encouragement to the industry is consistent with the type of reaction which was shown to have categorized more backward parts of Europe. Such a classification would tend to vindicate the type of interpretation put forward by Vázquez de Prada, but it should be emphasized that the Spanish case would not appear to represent an extreme version of this fourth category. The policy of granting *franquicias* to Catalan calico-printing concerns is going to be described in the next section of this chapter but it can already be noted that it represented a fairly mild form of interventionism, involving only minor fiscal and legal privileges. The Barcelona industry was founded predominantly by free merchants. Catalan historians are thus right in pointing out that there was a contrast with the state-funded royal cloth manufactures founded in Castile. Curiously the contrast even extends to the calico-printing and cotton industry. While the Catalan industry was founded primarily on the basis of free enterprise, the introduction of the industry to Castile was entrusted to a state manufacture, founded in Avila in 1788 with the assistance of imported, English and later Catalan expertise.[32]

This contrast in policies to the same industry in different regions rather than necessarily representing an injustice is a useful illustration of the existence of economic dualism in Spain, a dualism which resulted in different forms of interventionism. Thus Spain rather than fitting comfortably into our fourth category, virtually requires a category of its own, one which would take into account a variety in policy induced by the fact of regional inequality.

It was a dualism which occasioned particularly severe political problems in so far as it was the backward partner which exercised political power. It is this factor which would seem to be the principal explanation for what is another unusual characteristic of the Spanish response to the new industry – its indecisiveness. This has been noted above with respect to the variations in the policy towards protection, and it is emphasized too by Joseph-Maria Delgado who has shown that, after 1770, a bias was exercised in industrial policy favouring industries which were compatible with part-time employment in agriculture – not the case of the calico-printing and developing cotton industries.[33] The early history of the industry provides additional evidence of indecision. Not only, as has been noted, was total protection withdrawn from the industry during the years 1742–3 but there are also signs of hesitancy concerning the policy of granting *franquicias*. These were limited to a single manufacture up to 1746, that of Estevan Canals, and there has been some speculation as to why the requests of a similar manufacture, that of Bernat Glòria, for a privilege were turned down.[34] That the grounds for the refusal were principally political emerges from the brief explanations given for royal responses to requests for privileges made from other parts of Spain during these years – 'I will grant these *franquicias* when these manufactures are established in the interior of the kingdom while I do not consider it be of service to me when they are founded on the coasts' it was noted against one made in 1741.[35] Clearly royal concern existed about the concentration of new enterprises in the peripheral zones of the peninsula.

That the central government was having some reservations about providing backing for industrial expansion in Catalonia during these years is also suggested by the parallel failure to provide support for a Junta de Comercio Terrestre y Marítimo founded in 1735 in Barcelona. This body was established to act as a local agency for the Junta General de Moneda y Comercio and the principal grounds for neither providing it with funds nor

adequately defining its sphere of jurisdiction was clearly a reluctance at this stage to give any institutional recognition to a re-
emerging Catalan bourgeoisie, but the closeness of this consideration to the hesitations about calico-printing is demonstrable both
by the nature of the principal purpose which the Junta saw itself
as designed to fulfil – Jaume de Duran, its director, had argued
for its establishment in 1732 in terms of the role which it would
play in 'the re-establishment of the depressed commerce of the
Principality of Catalonia' and the 're-establishment of manufactures' – and also by the fact that several of the ministers of the
Junta were actually involved in founding manufactures. Glòria, as
well as one of his partners, Pere Gecseli, were in this position
with respect to calico-printing and Duran was involved in the
manufacture of fine cloth in Sabadell and, like Glòria, had his
request for *franquicias* rebuffed in 1741. The linking of the indecision concerning the calico-printing industry with that towards
the granting of an institutional base to the Catalan bourgeoisie is
further supported by the fact that the two questions were settled
within a few years of each other. Between 1746 and 1748 not only
were Canals's calico-printing *franquicias* extended for a further five
years and Glòria (finally) and two others, Campins and Guàrdia,
granted privileges in the new industry but the first negotiations
were initiated for the foundation of the Real Campañia de Barcelona, negotiations which achieved success with the royal decree of
4 May 1755. This company grouped Barcelona's leading merchants and its receipt of royal sanction has been judged as representing the first stage in the restoration of its autonomous commercial institutions.[36]

THE POLICY OF GRANTING *FRANQUICIAS*

The response in Barcelona to the opportunity for import substitution offered by the decree of 1728 was prompt. Bernat Glòria,
whom we have encountered in the previous section, was to claim
that he made his first calico-printing trials in this very year,[37] and
there is indirect evidence of attempts at printing in the early
1730s.[38] The first definite evidence of the new industry is provided
by two notarial contracts registered in 1736, one setting up a
company 'for working in indianas' between Jacinto Esteva, ex-
cord-maker, who described himself as a 'manufacturer of indianas'
and two glass-makers, Geronimo Aranyo and Josep Sala, and the

other recording an agreement between this newly founded company and one Joan Benet Huvet, a Marseillais calico-printer.[39] This concern ceased to produce in 1737 but was rapidly replaced by two others: those of Antoni Serra, Estevan Canals and Bonaventure Canet (1737) and Bernat Glòria and associates (1738).[40]

These Barcelona merchants and artisans initially established their new enterprises without direct royal support.[41] Such support was, though, clearly anticipated: thus an article of the first company's terms of association stated that 'whatever privilege the king at some stage deigns to concede' should be the joint property of all three associates.[42] Samples of what must have been this concern's production reached the court during 1737 in support of a request for privilege[43] and the requests for *franquicias* of Serra (on behalf of the company in which he was collaborating with Canals and Canet) and Glòria, to which reference was made in the previous section of this chapter, were made during 1738.[44] The full commitment of the government to the new industry, which, it was the argument of the last section, appears to have been delayed until 1746, was sustained into the 1750s – a further five privileges for manufactures were granted between 1749 and 1752 (to Sebastià Salomó and Francesc de Clota (1749), Gregoria French (1750), Joan Pongem (1751) and Josep Canaleta (1752)).[45] Further individual privileges were granted during the 1750s and 1760s, a royal decree generalizing concessions to all manufacturers not being extended to the principality because of what was believe to be its advantageous fiscal situation over the rest of Spain.[46]

If requests for *franquicias* were made, and granted with increasing readiness, it was because calico-printers and crown stood in need of each other. The characteristics of their respective needs can be assessed from the negotiations for and contents of the *franquicias*. Using these sources principally, first royal aims and then those of calico-printers will be summarized.

The principal royal wish was to increase the number of manufactures in Spain. This was so much common knowledge that Bernat Glòria, in a request to the intendant for a concession of land for establishing bleaching fields, did not feel the need to stress it, 'leaving to avoid verbosity, to the learned comprehension of your Excellency the utility which comes to royal interests and public utility from the establishment of manufactures in these kingdoms'.[47] Royal interests and public utility were to be benefited in a range of ways. First, imports of foreign manufactures would be diminished, checking on outflow of bullion: royal concern over this question is revealed by a letter to intendent Sartine in connection with Jacinto Esteva's request for privilege which not only demanded information about the new calico-printing concern but also an investigation into the circumstances 'which are being exploited in order to inundate the Principality as it is being with such goods' (referring to imported printed calicoes).[48] Second, employment would be provided and the general level of national prosperity increased: in the *franquicias* granted to Jaume Campins the manufacture's achieving 'the employment of various and burdensome poor who lived idle and unsuitable for other manufactures' is mentioned[49] and in those conceded to Francesc Bosca, to support his linen manufacturing in Gerona, the employment of one thousand men and women, the restoration to Gerona of its 'ancient trade' and the renting and rebuilding of seven houses are all mentioned as proof of his having promoted the manufacture 'for the good of the "patria" '.[50] Third, the price of printed calicoes was to be lowered from that of the imported article, benefiting consumers: Serra's *franquicias* specified selling prices 'more moderate than those at which the foreign articles were selling'. The emphasis on increasing national production is further illustrated by stipulations that a minimum number of looms was to be maintained in action – twelve were required of Serra and his associates in 1739 and a commitment recorded to increase this figure by 'those which they could in the future'[51] and Guàrdia in 1748 committed himself to using sixty-six looms.[52] Renewal of *franquicias*, which were generally granted for four years, was eased if evidence could be provided of increased productive capacity, judged principally in terms of number of looms.

If Spain up to this period had not succeeded generally in developing competitive manufactures a principal reason for this, it was realized, was technological – a failure to incorporate the latest advances in manufacturing techniques. The achievement of technical progress was also thus a principal royal concern. This too is revealed by the terms of *franquicias*: both the introduction of new techniques by, generally, employing foreign workers and the ensuring that these techniques had been passed on to Spanish hands are mentioned. In the case of the Serra privilege, the local subdelegate of the Junta General de Comercio y Moneda, Francisco de Montero, when inspecting the manufacture, had met one

Pedro Genus, of Swiss nationality, a subject capable of painting any colour on the cloths, and engrave all sorts of designs,
and decorations for printing . . . with a certain secret, which
he has revealed already to the associates in the manufacture
to safeguard in it, in the case of any eventuality, so special
a perquisite for quality.[53]

Guàrdia, too, it is stated in the report following a similar inspec-
tion, employed a 'skilful painter' who had passed on his skill, and
in Campins's privilege his manufacture's success at printing 'with
the same brilliance and permanence of colours as in Holland and
other parts of the globe and in achieving the up to now unfound
permanence of what they call Blauets' is recorded.[54] It was
expected that the skills introduced and learned within these calico-
printing concerns would later be diffused to other manufactures.
The director of the Canals manufacture was later to refer to his
concern as the 'mother of the others',[55] a statement which implies
that the role which had been expected of his employer's manufacture had been fulfilled.

The nature of the concessions which were granted in the *franquicias* to the calico-printers fall into three categories: the virtually
essential, for legal or technical reasons; those which conferred fiscal
or other advantages; and those which brought honour. Several
of the concessions bridge these categories. Essential, or virtually
essential, were the permissions to buy land or property to establish
manufactures, the restrictions on neighbouring building and irri-
gation which would (on account of shade or dirtying water supplies) cause harm to the bleaching process, the permission to
import prohibited raw materials and a concession relating to guild
restrictions: permission to sell the finished product despite guilds'
sales monopolies. Part essential and part advantage were the provision of a degree of legal immunity – jurisdiction over calico-
printers' concerns was transferred to the Barcelona subdelegate of
the Junta General de Comercio y Moneda – the exemption of the
manufactures' owners, managers and workers from recruitment
and certain other national duties which might disrupt their manufacturing activities, the right to participate in, and benefit from
(by receiving a share of fines), the controlling of the illegal import-
ation of printed calicoes and the granting of coercive powers in
connection with debtors and the retention of skilled workers. Pure
advantage were the permissions to import raw materials either free,

or at lower rates of import duty, and the granting of reductions in sales tax. The right to carry arms, granted in several *franquicias*, fulfilled a need – roads were dangerous, cloth in bleaching fields liable to theft – but also brought honour: that this was the case is revealed by the opposition of noble groups to this concession.[56] Purely honorific was the right to place the royal coat of arms on the principal manufacturing buildings, sales warehouses and cloth produced.[57]

By aggregating these individual concessions, the following picture of the calico-printers' situation, and of the nature of their requirements from the state, can be built up. Spain was a predominantly corporative society in which the development of a market economy was restricted by guilds and honour was dependent on a range of non-monetary considerations. Its government was interventionist, both economically, restricting imports and the free circulation of goods, and politically, imposing military and other physical obligations on the population. Law and order were not totally established, nor was commercial jurisdiction fully organized. In such circumstances the calico-printers, who were involving themselves in a large and potentially risky investment, required: first, to be assured of their definite legal right to carry out their business and that social consideration would be conferred to their activities (this was provided by the royal status given to their concerns); second, to be released from aspects of economic and political interventionism which would have prevented the efficient running of their concerns; third, some assurance that they would receive special legal protection in view of the novelty and complexity of both the commercial and technical sides of their businesses; and fourth, some direct encouragement in the form of fiscal privileges.

THE INFLUENCE OF THE STATE ON SCALE AND ORGANIZATION OF PRODUCTION

The importance of the role of the calico-printing industry for the emergence of large scale, concentrated manufactures in Europe was mentioned in the introduction to this chapter. The table opposite, which summarizes evidence concerning the size of manufactures in the principal centres of the industry, serves to confirm this point.

Table 3.1 Average size (in terms of labour forces) of calico-printing
concerns in various centres at various dates

Centre	Year	No. of manufs		Total labour	Average labour
Augsburg	1790–1800	9		3,200	356
Neuchâtel	1797	6		1,604	267
Mulhouse	1806	14	c.	3,290	235
Geneva	1785	11		2,470	225
Geneva	1806	4	c.	880	220
Alsace–Lorraine	1790–1800	37		7,000	189
Hamburg	1790–1800	21		3,200	152
Barcelona	1754	11	c.	1,364	124
Barcelona	1784	80		8,638	108
Franconia	1790–1800	7		700	100
Neuchâtel	1766	17		1,605	94
France	1806	186	c.	14,694	79
Prague	1787	12		936	78
Seine-Inférieure	1806	46	c.	3,542	77
Switzerland	1790–1800	59		4,300	73
Ghent	1793	12		881	73
Austria	1790–1800	18		1,300	72
Saxony	1790–1800	56		3,800	68
Bohemia-Moravia	1790–1800	31		2,100	68
Belgium	1806	55	c.	3,355	61
Prussia	1790–1800	14		700	50
Neuchâtel	1760	16		758	47
London	1719	23		635	28
Silesia	1790–1800	8		100	13

Sources: Chapman and Chassagne, Textile Printers, 11, 175, 213; Caspard,
La Fabrique, 109, 114, 115, 127, 185; F. W. Carter, 'The cotton-
printing industry in Prague, 1766–1873', Textile History, 6, 1975,
133; S. Chassagne, 'L'Enquête, dite de Champagny, sur la
situation de l'industrie cotonnière française au début de l'Empire (1805–1806)', Revue d'Histoire Economique et Sociale, 54, 1976,
366; Wadsworth and Mann, Cotton Trade, 136–7. For Barcelona
the 1754 figure is from Duran Sanpere, Barcelona, ii, 299, and
the labour force has been calculated on the basis of three
workers for the loom figures which are recorded and that for
1784 from BC, JC, Leg. 53, no. 29, ff. 2–21, 15 December 1784.
Note: c. = approximate figure.

Barcelona's position on this table – just above its centre – would
suggest at a first glance that it possessed an average industrial
structure. Closer scrutiny, however, reveals that its industry was
in fact unusual from two points of view: first in so far that calico-

printing concerns achieved large labour forces at an early a stage in its growth, shortly after their foundations and long before any mechanization, which increased economies of scale, took place and second in so far that it came to be composed of so large a concentration of substantial concerns: in 1784 80 calico-printers employed some 8,638 workers or an average of 108 each.[58] The substantial size of manufacture was not in itself unusual in the context of the European industry but Barcelona's grouping of so many large concerns, of relatively uniform dimensions (the average sizes were not, as elsewhere, distorted by the existence of a few giants) was.[59]

There was nothing unusual in the technological characteristics of the Catalan industry which would serve to account for these peculiarities and so the explanation has to be looked for elsewhere. An important part of it resides in the character of the 1728 legislation which provided the basis for the industry's growth. As has been noted, it banned the import of all calicoes, only permitting the import of spun cotton. In view of the lack of an existing cotton industry in Spain, this forced calico-printers to incorporate cotton weaving into their plants, and this necessity provides part of the explanation for the earliness and universality of large scale production in the Catalan industry. A second influence was the *franquicia* system. This, as was noted in the previous section, favoured large scale production for not only were substantial concerns more likely to be privileged but the privileges themselves imposed minimum numbers of looms and were more readily renewed if expansion in scale had been achieved.

There are signs too that the contact between printers and crown occasioned by the *franquicia* system influenced organization, as well as scale, of production. This came to be characterized by vertical integration of the production process in predominantly concentrated manufactures and although there was a clear and well-known technological rationale for this – the need to control quality of production and the character of the printing and bleaching processes which enforced considerable centralization – the contact with the state would seem to have been a further influence to the same end.

It is significant that, initially, such concentration and vertical integration were not practised. Jacinto Esteva's concern consisted of three processes, weaving, printing and bleaching, the first of which was handled on a putting-out basis and the second and third in and around some old huts which had been rented outside

Barcelona's walls. The scale was small, the investment low.[60] Serra's concern originally followed a similar pattern, with some variations: a 1738 agreement reveals that printing was initially subcontracted to an independent artisan and that weaving had been concentrated – a reference is made to a 'house of weavers'; bleaching, of necessity, was concentrated too. By the time Serra was applying for his royal privilege during 1739, however, a concentrated manufacture was being created in which printing was no longer to be subcontracted but carried out, together with weaving and all the other manufacturing processes apart from bleaching, under one roof. The builder's contract listed 'an office to place looms to make indianas, another office to press them, a kitchen for making colours'. The bleaching fields, too, were improved and a house built to hold equipment. The costs involved in these improvements were large (too large for Serra, whose widow was obliged to withdraw from the company in 1741 'for lack of possessions and capital').[61] Why had such a rapid jump been made from the capital-economizing type structure which had characterized the concern in 1738? It seems possible that in addition to the desire to improve quality there was an awareness that a movement towards such an organization of production would favour the request for privilege which was made during 1738. The timing of the investment would support such a hypothesis, in so far as work on expanding the manufacture was started in March 1739 and the privilege request was discussed before the Junta General de Comercio y Moneda in December of that year.[62]

The argument finds some support from the contents of the *franquicias* granted to a succession of calico-printers. The form which these took was as follows: the identity of the person to be privileged is given, a description of the manufacture provided – situation, types of building, equipment, organization of production, technological level, identity of key skilled workers and numbers employed – and the details of the privileges are then listed. The description of the manufacture, though, is not a neutral one: emphasized in it are those factors which had induced the crown to grant the privilege. Some of these factors have been mentioned earlier – scale of production, the provision of employment, the introduction of new technology – but also prominent is an emphasis on size of investment, on centralization of production and the achievement of division of labour. Extracts from *franquicias* will illustrate the point: mentioned in Serra's are the 'great expenses' undertaken by the associates to respond to the royal decree to establish 'new manufactures'; Campins's mention the employment given to 'many people with necessary rooms for them', Guàrdia's the building of a 'house . . . capable of holding more than a hundred looms' and the existence of 'corresponding rooms for the director of the manufacture, the colourist and head of weavers, and the other offices and terraces necessary for the running of the manufacture'; Pongem's include the following favourable response of subdelegate de Montero to his request:

> the same *franquicias* as those of the other manufactures should be conceded to him with respect to maintaining forty looms in action in a large house composed of different offices for all sorts of operations, furnaces, calender, warehouses, ingredients for dyeing, and spun cotton and house outside the walls of the city . . . to boil and bleach the indianas, with corresponding dwellings for workers.

Renewal of Canals's privilege in 1747 is similarly supported by de Montero, both in view of expansion (100 looms were now in use) and the style of the enterprise: 'Under a single roof all the processes of the manufacture were to be noted with the exception of the bleaching meadow and boiling vat, which made it appear very splendid for the beauty and disposition of the materiality of the house.'[63]

The crown, it would appear, favoured concentrated production and extensive division of labour. Possible reasons for this might have included a concern about the quality of production, perceived as best secured by such conditions, a desire to ensure that royal status was only entrusted to distinguished and substantial concerns and the fact that it was such production forms which characterized those enterprises operated directly by the state both in Spain and in other parts of Europe. Calico-printing required scale, division of labour and vertical integration for the purposes of quality control but it seems possible that those of Barcelona's calico-printers who sought privileges accentuated these characteristics of their concerns in order to favour their requests. Serra must have been aware of what was required. Once his *franquicias* were granted other calico-printers in Barcelona had a model to follow. Glòria in 1746 justified his request in terms of his concern being 'of the same type (*calidad*)' as that of Canals,[64] and a representative of the latter's manufacture in addition to claiming its maternity of

11 New Fetter Lane
London EC4P 4EE
Telephone: 071-583 9855
Fax: 071-583 4519

We have much pleasure in sending you
the accompanying book for review

Title: Markets & Manu. in Early Industrial
Europe

Author: Berg

ISBN: Hb 0 415 03720 4

    Pb

Publication Date: 13.12.90

Published Price: £ — 40.00   Hb — — — — —

        £   Pb

A copy of the review would be greatly appreciated.
Reviews should not appear in the press prior to the
date of publication.
For further information please contact:

Vickie Kemp

the others declared that it had given 'motives and patterns (*reglas*) to form those [manufactures] which today ensure the good discipline of the others'.[65] This 'pattern' had partly been imposed by the technical requirements of the trade and, as has been noted, by the details of the 1728 legislation which enforced the incorporation of weaving, but there are signs, too, that it bore the influence of the process of negotiation for *franquicias* between the calico-printers and the state.

PRIVILEGES AND ENTRY INTO THE INDUSTRY

The manner in which contact between calico-printers and government was organized was as follows. The initial privilege request was made directly to the Junta General de Comercio y Moneda. In order to ensure that the request was attended to, the general practice was to appoint what was termed a 'commercial agent' as a representative at the court. Glòria, for example, commissioned Dn Andrés de Pradas in 1739 to act on his behalf 'before His Majesty and royal ministers and officials'.[66] In some cases calico-printers, or associates in calico-printing companies, themselves made the overtures to the Junta. Jaume Campins, for example, was present in Madrid for a full six months in 1746 and 1747 on behalf of the calico-printing concern which he had established in Mataró, a neighbouring town to Barcelona,[67] and in 1756 Canals and Canet commissioned the former's son, Joan Pau Canals, to represent them before the 'Honourable Minister, or Subdelegate of the Royal Junta of Commerce'.[68] The most frequent course of action, however, was the appointment of a commercial agent. In order to assess the request for privilege the Junta commissioned its *juez subdelegado*, Francisco de Montero, to report on the manufacture in question. It was to him as well, as noted above, that jurisdiction over the manufacture was conferred by the *franquicias*.

In 1760 a Junta Particular de Comercio was established in Barcelona which established a regular channel for negotiations with the Junta General de Comercio.[69] This was the culmination of that process of restoring the city's autonomous commercial institutions to which reference was made in the second section of this chapter. The existence of this body relieved the calico-printers of a considerable part of the burden involved in direct negotiation with the crown. Correspondence of this new body gives an insight into the complexity of the process. In 1766 a privilege was granted to Josep Canaleta and Francesc Magarola in connection with cotton spinning and importing cotton. In a letter to its agent in Madrid, Bernardo Marín, who had seen the measure through the Junta General, the Junta mentions that they would finance the 'harsh dues which these offices have claimed for the dispatch of the royal decree . . . and corresponding tips for the secretary of the Junta General, fiscal agent, and others which occur . . . not being by any means just that they should be the responsibility of Canaleta'.[70] Campins, it was noted above, spent six months in Madrid negotiating his *franquicias*. His costs for what he described as the 'laborious measures' were 11,126 *reales*.[71] Uncertainty could be as preoccupying as expense: as the secretary of the Junta Particular noted in 1761, a year after its foundation, 'One realizes that in the affairs of the court nothing is sure or certain until the king decides.'[72]

The calico-printing industry was thus introduced into Spain in a period in which, on the one hand, the impact of state policy and activities on the economy was growing, and, on the other, the administration of the economy was far from fully organized. This placed a considerable onus on the calico-printer himself in the securing of the *franquicias* which were so important to the prosperity of his concern. The fact of these difficulties, difficulties which were both financial – the cost involved – and technical – the complexity of seeing business through the court – had the consequence, it would seem likely, that the *franquicia* system effectively favoured those with large resources and accustomed to involvement in affairs of the crown. Certainly, prominent among those who obtained early grants of *franquicias* were merchants who conform to both these criteria. Glòria's contacts with the state, as already noted, dated back to his ministership in the 1735 Junta Particular de Comercio Marítimo y Terrestre; in addition, during the 1740s, he was a contractor for the supply of uniforms to the army and was granted *franquicias* for two types of woollen cloth production as well as for calico-printing.[73] One of Jaume Campins's commercial roles prior to calico-printing was acting as general contractor to the Real Hospital de Marina in Cadiz[74] and Francesc de Clota's included serving as 'general contractor of the bread manufacture for the provision of the markets and barracks' of Catalonia as well as involvement in the 'general contraction of gunpowder'.[75] Pongem had farmed the 'royal mills' in Catalonia before applying for *franquicias* in 1751, employment which had taken him to Madrid for a court case in 1746.[76] Francesc Bosca's experience as a government contractor is actually cited as an argument in favour of his linen manufacturing request: he is described in the *franquicias* as 'extremely able, on account of his having acquired his experience (*inteligencia*) and capital in France in the contracting company that those people (*naturales*) formed for the army'.[77]

This point should not be overstated and there are clearly arguments which could be introduced against it. Thus it should be pointed out that the majority of the early investors in calico-printing were wholesale merchants, accustomed to investing in a wide range of trades, by no means confined to the affairs of the state. It could be argued that the extent of their involvement in governmental affairs was no more than a natural consequence of the considerable state investment in Catalonia during these years and that it was their possession of good distribution networks, rather than experience of negotiating with the state, which caused them to play so prominent a role in the early development of calico-printing.[78] In addition, the idea that negotiation of terms with royal counsels involved rare and exceptional skills only likely to be possessed by a commercial elite could also be challenged. In a corporative society, as we have noted Spain's was, any type of industrial activity involved reference to some form of legal or governmental framework. Legal or official negotiation, of a type related to that involved in the requests for *franquicias*, would effectively have formed part of any commercial and industrial training, and, indeed, the names of a large number of Catalan artisans is revealed in the lists of petitions contained in the inventory of the papers of the Junta General de Comercio y Moneda for these years and neither of the first two Catalans who made contact with the Junta General in connection with the new industry (Esteva and Serra) came from the contracting elite to which reference has just been made.[79] Finally, as has been noted, *franquicias* for calico-printing were granted more readily from the 1750s; the negotiation problem must thereby have been eased and any advantage enjoyed by the rich and connected decreased.

This last point would confine the relevance of the argument, if it were indeed a correct one, to a relatively short though a most crucial period of some five years or so. To return to its defence, though, two points could be re-emphasized – first, the argument put forward in the second section of this chapter that the years of the extension of the calico-printing industry were a turning-point in the attitude of the crown to industrial initiatives in the principality; and second, the fact that most of the early receivers of calico-printing *franquicias* were involved directly or indirectly in the negotiations connected with this change – Glòria's links have been noted; he, Guàrdia, Pongem and Clota were all members of the new Barcelona company, which finally received royal approval in 1755, the last named being one of those who negotiated its charter.[80] It seems more than possible, indeed it seems probable, that awareness of how opinion was shifting in the court was one factor facilitating their early involvement in the industry. There were, of course, close links, between the Barcelona company and the expanding private trade with the Americas, which preceded its foundation, and the new calico-printing concerns – their product was intended to be, and was to become, a principal export commodity.[81] In a Barcelona short in the necessary colouring, engraving, printing, bleaching and cotton weaving skills necessary for establishing manufactures, the extent of the advantage conferred by the early start which closeness to royal counsels appears to have permitted is certainly not to be underestimated.

CONCLUSION

It should have become clear that the underlying argument of all the five sections of this chapter is that state policies were of great importance to the early development of the calico-printing and cotton industries. That these industries were to play so large a role in the first phases of industrialization adds to the significance which should be attached to the point. As was revealed in the second section, although this issue has not received the emphasis which it merits, some historians have registered its significance, notably Wadsworth and Mann, Rostow and, most recently, François Crouzet.

Clearly the importance to be attached to the possible effects of state intervention in the Spanish case would depend on the extent to which they endured into the post–1760 period when, as has been noted, there was some relaxation in the extent of interventionism. It would seem justifiable to register two points in this connection. First, it is clear that government policy, even if less consistently favourable, continued to provide a high degree of, and for most of the time total, protection – and a relief from the need to compete internationally can hardly be judged a small influence and was indeed having a much commented-on impact on competitiveness by the turn of the century.[82] And second, even if policy became less interventionist, the interventionism of the early years left an enduring legacy.

The character of this legacy can be sub-divided into economic and attitudinal categories. In the case of the former there are signs that the early advantages enjoyed by large-scale manufactures gave them a lead which enabled them to accumulate profit and acquire a commanding position in the industry, permitting them to dominate its later expansion into the basic cotton manufacturing processes. The predominance of the 'manufacture' in this process has been noted by historians and explained in terms of this early accumulation of capital, an accumulation which created a very considerable advantage in so far as circumstances for accumulating capital became progressively less favourable.[83] In the case of the latter it can be shown that the predominance of large manufactures in the early years of the industry gave rise to theirs being regarded as the normal type of unit for calico-printing and cotton manufacturing activity. This attitude came to inform regulations of a corporative kind which were drawn up for the industry in 1767. Defined in these was what a manufacture was to consist in: 'only those manufactures which have twelve looms running, their own or a rented meadow for bleaching, moulds, tables for painting, boiling vats, calenders, burnishers and other necessary tools *will be reputed as fábricas* and will be able to benefit from the *franquicias* which have been conceded or which might be conceded' it was ruled.[84] The style of concern originally developed by Canals (the number of looms is identical) in part, it was the argument of the fourth section of this chapter, to gain royal privilege, had become the legal definition of *fábrica* in the industry. Clearly, more than a question of attitude was involved here. The printers who drew up these regulations had a vested interest in restricting entry into the trade but concealing this motive was facilitated by the years of predominance of large manufactures. The regulation was to be of some assistance in delaying the appearance of smaller concerns.[85]

The viewpoint being expressed in this chapter is related to a point made by Jan de Vries in his *The Economy of Europe in an Age of Crisis*. He notes there that economic development functions like a ratchet, in one direction only: 'The varied impulses that affect an economy', he writes, 'more often move it, however slightly, to new positions from which it is impossible to recapture precisely the former position.'[86] It would be the argument of this chapter that state policies towards the Catalan calico-printing and cotton industry represented impulses of this kind which had lasting influences on the industrialization of the area.

NOTES

*Research for this chapter was financed by a research fellowship granted by the Nuffield Foundation. Translation from French, Spanish and Catalan is by the author.

1 See S. D. Chapman and S. Chassagne, *European Textile Printers in the Eighteenth Century: A Study of Peel and Oberkampf*, London, 1981, 1–4, 49–50; K. H. Wolff, 'Textile bleaching and the birth of the chemical industry', *Business History Review*, 47, 1974, 142–63; L. Gittins, 'Innovations in textile bleaching in Britain in the eighteenth century', *Business History Review*, 52, 1979, 194–204; for the argument concerning conditioning of industrialization M. Lévy Leboyer, *Les Banques européennes et l'industrialisation internationale dans la première moitié du XIXe siècle*, Paris, 1964, 23–62 and 'Le processus d'industrialisation: le cas de l'Angleterre et de la France', *Revue Historique*, 239, 1968, 281–98.

2 See P. J. Thomas, 'The beginnings of calico-printing in England', *English Historical Review*, 39, 1924, 206–16 and *Mercantilism and the East India Trade*, London, 1926, 44–5; A. W. Douglas, 'Cotton textiles in England: the East India Company's attempt to exploit developments in fashion, 1660–1721', *Journal of British Studies*, 8, 1969, 28–43; C. Mukerji, *From Graven Images: Patterns of Modern Materialism*, New York, 1983. On the failure to enforce the French bans on the use of printed calicoes see E. Depître, *La Toile peinte en France aux XVIIe et XVIIIe siècles*, Paris, 1912, 66, 99-103.

3 J. de Vries, *The Economy of Europe in An Age of Crisis*, Cambridge, 1976, 146.

4 See chaps 2, 4 and 11 and P. Hudson, 'Proto-industrialization: the case of the West Riding wool textiles industry, 1700–1830', *History Workshop Journal*, 12, 1981, 34–61.

5 Calculations concerning this are contained in my 'The Catalan calicoprinting industry compared internationally', *Societat Catalana d'Economia: Anuari*, 7, 1989, 72–95.

6 Thus the references in Chapman and Chassagne, op. cit., 7–8 only relate to the period up to 1775, before the industry experienced a rapid expansion. Other references in English texts to the industry include the following: J. C. Laforce, *The Development of the Spanish Textile Industry*, California, 1965, 14–19, 133–44; R. Herr, *The Eighteenth Century Revolution in Spain*, Princeton, 1973, 137–42. The principal Spanish works on the industry are as follows: J. Carrera Pujal, *História politica y económica de Cataluña*, Barcelona, 1946–7, IV, 133–65; F. Torrella Niubó, *El moderno resurgir textil de Barcelona (siglos XVIII y XIX)*, Barcelona, 1961; V. Vázquez de Prada, 'Las fábricas de indianas y

estampados de Barcelona en el siglo XVIII', *Third International Conference of Economic History*, Paris, 1965, v, 277–91; P. Molas Ribalta, *Los gremios barceloneses del siglo XVIII*, Madrid, 1970, 519–38; A. Duran Sanpere, *Barcelona i la seva historia*, Barcelona, 1973, ii, 291–309; R. Grau and M. López, 'Empresari i capitalista a la manufactura catalana del segle XVIII. Introducció a l'estudi de les fabriques d'indianes', *Recerques: História, Economía, Cultura*, 4, 1974, 19–57; C. Martínez Shaw, 'Los orígenes de la industria algodonera catalana y el comercio colonial' in J. Nadal and G. Tortella (eds), *Agricultura, comercio colonial y crecimiento económico en la España contemporánea*, Barcelona, 1974, 243–94; R. Alier, 'La fabrica d'indianes de la familia Canals', *Recerques*, 4, 1974, 59–91; R. Fernández, 'La burguesía barcelonesa en el siglo XVIII: la familia Glòria' in P. Tedde (ed.), *La economía española al final del Antiguo Régimen*, ii, *Manufacturas*, Barcelona, 1982, 3–131; A. Sánchez Suárez, 'Los origenes sociales de los fabricantes de indianas. La familia Rull', *Primer Congrés d'Història Moderna de Catalunya*, i, 779–88; J. M. Delgado Ribas, 'La industria algodonera catalana (1776–96) y el mercado americano. Una reconsideración', *Manuscrits*, 7, 1988, 103–16.

7 P. Mantoux, *The Industrial Revolution in the Eighteenth Century*, 3rd edn, London, 1970, 203. On the legislative reaction to the English industry, see A. P. Wadsworth and J. L. Mann, *The Cotton Trade and Industrial Lancashire, 1600–1780*, Manchester, 1931, 131–44; and Thomas, *Mercantilism*, op. cit. Recent discussions include W. W. Rostow, *How It All Began. Origins of the Modern Economy*, London, 1975, 61–6, 130–1 and F. Crouzet, 'Critiques et autocritique d'une comparaison' in his *De la Supériorité de l'Angleterre sur la France*, Paris, 1985, 82–3. Note, though, the emphasis in J. H. Munro's review of C. Mukerji's *Graven Images*, op. cit. (*Journal of Economic History*, 46, 1986, 1044–5) on the importance of *interruption in Indian supply* as a stimulus for import substitution.

8 L. A. Driessen, 'Calico printing and the cotton industry in Holland', *CIBA Review*, 48, 1944, 1748–51.

9 Chapman and Chassagne, op. cit., 6–8; P. Caspard, *La Fabrique-Neuve de Cortaillod, 1752–1854: Entreprise et profit pendant la Révolution Industrielle*, Paris, 1979, 8.

10 H. Lüthy, *La Banque protestante en France de la Révocation de l'Edit de Nantes à la Révolution*, Paris, 1961, ii, 663.

11 Caspard, op. cit., 46.

12 See L. Bergeron, ' "Pourtalès et Cie" (1753–1801): apogée et déclin d'un capitalisme', *Annales: Economies, Societiés, Civilisations*, 25, 1970, 498–517.

13 Wadsworth and Mann, op. cit., 141.

14 Chapman and Chassagne, op. cit., 6.

15 E. F. Heckscher, *Mercantilism*, 2nd edn, London, 1955, ii, 172; on the bans and restrictions see Depître, op. cit. and S. Chassagne, *La manufacture de toiles imprimées de Tournemine-les-Angers*, Paris, 1971, 38–66. Also C. W. Cole, *French Mercantilism, 1683–1700*, New York, 1945, 36–40, 164–77.

16 References successively are Depître, op. cit., 20, 247; Wadsworth and Mann, op. cit., 207; Lévy Leboyer, op. cit., 50; Chassagne, op. cit., 353–5. See also Rostow, op. cit., 66.

17 Chapman and Chassagne, op. cit., 7.

18 On other types of contemporaneous import-substitution in these areas see, for example, H. Freudenberger, *The Industrialization of a Central European City: Brno and the Fine Woollen Industry in the Eighteenth Century*, Edington, Wiltshire, 1977, and *The Waldstein Woollen Mill: Noble Entrepreneurship in Eighteenth-Century Bohemia*, Boston, 1963. For the theory of such forced draft industrialization damaging market-based growth prospects see A. Gerschenkron, *Europe in the Russian Mirror*, Cambridge, 1970 and Rostow, op. cit., 55–60.

19 J. Fontana, 'Sobre el comercio exterior de Barcelona en la segunda mitad del siglo XVIII: notas para una interpretación de la coyuntura catalana', *Estudios de Historia Moderna*, 5, 1955, 210.

20 R. Davis, *The Rise of the English Shipping Industry*, Newton Abbot, 1962, 244–52.

21 J. Vicens Vives, *Manual de historia económica de España*, Barcelona, 1972, 468–9.

22 ibid., 394–7.

23 ibid., 487.

24 P. Vilar, *La Catalogne dans l'Espagne moderne*, Paris, 1962, i, 706–7.

25 Carrera Pujal, op. cit., iv, 134–5 and for the 1732 visit: Archivo General de Simancas (henceforth AGS), Dirección General de Rentas (henceforth DGR), Segunda Remesa, Legajo (bundle, henceforth Leg.) 4907.

26 K. Glamann, *Dutch Asiatic Trade, 1620–1740*, The Hague, 1958; K. N. Chaudhuri, *The Trading World of Asia and the English East India Company, 1660–1760*, Cambridge, 1978, 547; D. Ormrod, 'English re-exports and the Dutch staple market in the eighteenth century' in D. C. Coleman and P. Mathias (eds), *Enterprise and History: Essays in Honour of Charles Wilson*, Cambridge, 1984, 104, 107.

27 See Wadsworth and Mann, op. cit., 114–15.

28 Cited by Carrera Pujal, op. cit., iv, 135.

29 On this legislation see ibid., 135–65 and A. González Encisco, *Estado e industria en el siglo XVIII: La fábrica de Guadalajara*, Madrid, 1980, 241–7.

30 Carrera Pujal, op. cit., iv, 142.

31 Vázquez de Prada, op. cit., 278–83.

32 E. Herrera Oria, *La real fabrica de tejidos de algodón estampados de Avila y la reorganización nacional de esta industria en el siglo XVIII*, Valladolid, 1922.

33 J. M. Delgado Ribas, 'Política ilustrada, industria española y mercado americano, 1720–1820', *Pedralbes*, 3, 1983, 260–73.

34 Fernández, op. cit., 63.

35 AGS, Consejo Supremo de Hacienda (henceforth CSH), Libro Registro (henceforth Reg.) 213, ff. 54–5, response to request of Dn Migl de Olana y Roca to establish a manufacture of indianas at Alicante.

36 On the Junta of 1735, its members and the Barcelona company see

P. Molas Ribalta, 'La Junta de Comerç de Barcelona. Els seus precedents i la seva base social' in his *Comerç i estructura social a Catalunya i Valencia als segles XVII i XVIII*, Barcelona, 1977, 250–62; for the Duran, Canals, Glòria, Campins, Guàrdia privilege requests: AGS, CSH, Reg. 213, ff. 54, 79, 80, 87.

37 AGS, Secretaría de Hacienda (henceforth SH), Leg. 1103, letter of Glòria to Juan Bautista Iturralde, 22 October 1739.
38 Provided by Carrera Pujal, op. cit., iii, 15, but with no source. On the beginnings of calico-printing in Barcelona, see my *La manufactura a Barcelona al segle XVIII: Origens i comparança a nivell internacional de la indústria d'indienes*, Barcelona, 1990.
39 Archivo Histórico de Protocolos de Barcelona (henceforth AHPB), Notary Severo Pujol, Manual 6, ff. 446–7, 4 September 1736.
40 On 11 August 1737 Serra's request to establish a bleaching meadow for his manufacture was accepted. A similar request was made by Glòria on 26 November 1738 (Archivo de la Corona de Aragón – henceforth ACA – Batllia General, Aa 51, ff. 285–93, Aa 52, ff. 441–52). For the fullest details on these early concerns see Duran Sanpere, op. cit., ii, 292–300.
41 Permission, though, had been obtained by Serra 'from a legitimate superior to form the new manufacture of indianas' it was stated in his bleaching meadow request.
42 As in note 39.
43 Jullian de Canaveras informed intendant Sartine that he had received 'individual notice that in the environs of the "Portal Nuevo" of the city' a calico-printing concern had been established, samples of whose production had been submitted. This was where the Esteva concern was situated (AGS, DGR, Segunda Remesa, Leg. 438, 17 August 1737).
44 AGS, CSH, Reg. 248, ff. 176–7.
45 AGS, CSH, Reg. 213, ff. 92–3, 95, 111, 126; Clota: 12 December 1748, Salomó: 20 February 1749, French: 13 August 1750, Pongem: 6 August 1751; AGS, CSH, Reg. 248, f. 184, certification of Canaleta's *franquicias* of 24 June 1752. On these privileges and calico-printers see Martínez Shaw, op. cit., 248–50.
46 Carrera Pujal, op. cit., iv, 142.
47 As note 40.
48 As note 43.
49 ACA, Registro de la Intendencia, 1/26, f. 151, *franquicias* of 16 December 1747.
50 ACA, Real Audiencia, Diversorum, 495, ff. 18–31, *franquicias* of 19 November 1751.
51 AHPB, Josep Cols, Registro de la fábrica de indianas, *franquicias* of 28 May 1741.
52 ACA, Registro de la Intendencia, 1/26, ff. 214–21.
53 As for note 51.
54 As for note 49.
55 Biblioteca de Catalunya, Junta de Comercio (henceforth BC and JC), Leg. 56, no. 26, ff. 7–12.

56 AGS, CSH, Reg. 248, f. 180, records the Real Audiencia's objection to Campins's privilege to carry arms.

57 See references for *franquicias* listed in notes 36 and 45.

58 BC, JC, leg. 53, no. 29, ff. 2–21, 15 December 1784. This survey has been chosen as it is the only one which enumerates the labour force.

59 For example the Geneva figures are distorted by the giant Fazy manufacture employing 2,000 in 1785 (A.-M. Piuz, 'Note sur l'industrie des indiennes à Genève au XVIIIe siècle' in P. Léon, F. Crouzet and R. Gascon (eds), *L'industrialisation en Europe au XIXe siècle*, Colloques internationaux du C.N.R.S., Paris, 1972, 534).

60 As note 39.

61 AHPB, Josep Cols, manual 12, ff, 122–3, 16 May 1738, contract between Serra and Juan Iber, manual 13, ff. 92–3, 102–9, 5 May and 7 August 1740.

62 AGS, CSH, reg. 248, ff. 176–7 and reg. 213, f. 59.

63 See notes 36 and 45.

64 AGS, CSH, Reg. 213, f. 80, 16 June 1746.

65 As for note 55.

66 AHPB, Miguel Cabrer, Manual 6, f. 77. 6 February 1739.

67 This emerges from the accounts of the manufacture of Mataró. AHPB, Josep Fontana, libro de concordias 5, leg. 91.

68 AHPB, Jaume Creus, Manual 21, f. 77. 6 February 1739.

69 Molas Ribalta, op. cit., 240–305.

70 BC, JC, Reg. 83, Copiador de cartas, letter to Marín, 6 December 1766.

71 AHPB, Josep Fontana, libro de concordias 5, leg. 91. The exchange was approximately 100 *reales* to the pound sterling.

72 BC, JC, Reg. 82, Copiador de cartas, letter to Marín, 12 December 1761.

73 Fernández, op. cit., 100; M. Arranz, 'Demanda estatal i activitat econòmica a Catalunya sota els primers borbons (1714–1808)' in *Actas del Primer Congrés d'Història Moderna de Catalunya*, Barcelona, 1984, II, 261–2; ACA, Intendencia, 1/27, ff. 250–69, *franquicias* of 28 January 1749.

74 Martínez Shaw, op. cit., 256.

75 AHPB, Miguel Cabrer, manual 15, ff. 8–10, 28 December 1742 and Francesc Albia, manual 3, f. 34, 17 June 1747.

76 AHPB, Josep Fontana, manual 15, 27 July 1746.

77 ACA, Real Audiencia, Diversorum, 495, ff. 18–31, 19 November 1751.

78 The importance of this advantage was pointed out to me by Jaume Torras.

79 These types of consequences of a guild system are pointed out in my unpublished paper, 'The state and technological progress in eighteenth-century Barcelona: The experience of Isidro Cathalá y Vives, silk painter in the Chinese style' which was delivered at the European University Institute, Florence, in December 1987.

80 C. Martínez Shaw, *Cataluña en la carrera de Indias*, Barcelona, 1981, 71.

81 J. M. Oliva Melgar, 'La real companyia de comerç de Barcelona a las Indies', *L'Avenç*, 15, 1979, 29–33. It would seem that certainty

about royal commitment to the new industry was one factor determining the pace of its expansion, and particularly the long gap between
the first foundations (1737–8) and the second (concentrated in the
period 1746–9). This is not to discount Martínez Shaw's analysis of
the impact of warfare and trading opportunities on progress (op. cit.,
248–52), but purely to raise one other consideration which was of clear
relevance to investment decisions. For example Canals and Canet,
renegotiating their privilege in 1746, committed themselves to maintaining 100 looms in action 'under the supposition that the prohibition
to import foreign indianas in the dominions of His Majesty will be
maintained' (AHPB, Josep Cols, Registro de la Fábrica de Indianas,
escritura publica giving negotiating powers to the commercial agent
Joseph Antonio de Telleria, 15 July 1746).

82 See, for example, J. M. Delgado Ribas, 'Las transformaciones de la
manufactura al segle XVIII' in J. Nadal Farreras (ed.), *Historia de
Catalunya*, Barcelona, 1978, IV, 254–4 and Torella Niubó, op. cit.,
184–94.

83 Grau and López, op. cit., 35: 'The major transformations, in general,
will be produced within the indiana manufactures, and among these
transformations one has also to situate the incorporation of spinning'
and (p. 39), 'the difficulties in founding new manufactures will be all
the time more considerable. As a general rule, the nucleus of the large
capitals of the cotton sector at the end of the eighteenth century
and beginning of the nineteenth will proceed from manufacturing
accumulation'.

84 BC. JC, Leg. 53, no. 3, ff. 2–7 (my emphasis).

85 On this see Grau and López, op. cit., 29–36.

86 De Vries, op. cit., 2.

Part III

MARKETS, MERCHANTS AND MIDDLEMEN

4

THE OLD AND THE NEW. MARKETING NETWORKS AND TEXTILE GROWTH IN EIGHTEENTH-CENTURY SPAIN*

Jaume Torras

'It is a truth as sad as it is unquestionable', wrote Count Cabarrús in 1783 to Floridablanca, Spain's minister of state, that in Europe 'only Turkey, Portugal and Spain do tolerate in their States these colonies of foreigners that have at their head spies decorated by other Princes ... with special jurisdiction, with privileges, with interests in opposition to those of the State.'[1] Grievances about the excessive importance of foreigners in the economic life of Spain are common in many contemporary or earlier writings. In its most conspicuous form, this foreign presence was closely related to the imperial dimension of the Spanish economy. In spite of efforts to 'nationalize' it, during the eighteenth century colonial trade remained largely in foreign hands, indirectly (through Spanish middlemen) but also directly. A big share of the Spanish trade with Europe was conducted by foreign merchants too.[2]

It was not only the big, long-distance traffic which had attracted the attention of alien interests. Even more striking was the ubiquitous presence of foreign retailers and pedlars throughout the country. In his memorandum, Cabarrús also explained that, besides the foreign commercial houses active in colonial and European trade, there were many

> Companies of Frenchmen in Aragon, Valencia, La Mancha, Andalusia, and the Province of Madrid: their members are mostly Limousins and Auvergnats ... and such companies consist of one hundred, or more, individuals ... thanks to the variety of their skills, every company embraces all kinds

93

of trade, from the repairing of cauldrons to the biggest commercial ventures . . . every year, half the members of the
company go to France . . . there they buy land, there they
have their wives and their children, there they pay taxes and
at the end of the agreed term they come back to relieve their
partners.[3]

In short, commercial life in eighteenth-century Spain was still
largely dominated by the activity of different 'trading diasporas'
or associated networks of foreign merchants and tradesmen.[4] The
counterpart to all this foreign activity was almost inevitably the
flooding of Spanish and colonial markets with foreign goods too.
Surely this was not a sign of economic 'openness', but rather of
the opposite. It is in the context of a backward economy with a
low degree of market integration that commercial intercourse is
likely to be organized in such forms. Social prejudice, the lack of
reliable economic information, the shortage of commercial credit,
the uncertainties of trade – all call for special forms of organization,
the 'trading diaspora' being one of them.

This foreign presence was a legacy of the past, a trait of relative
backwardness that still remained a characteristic feature of
eighteenth-century Spain. In the same period, however, new
elements emerged against this unpromising background. A remarkable new development, one that lastingly altered the economic
landscape of Spain, was the rise of a small but fast-growing industrial area in the north-eastern part of the country. As Sidney
Pollard, in his contribution to this volume, discusses in a broader
context, early industrial developments in Spain must be analysed
in the framework of divergent regional patterns. Eighteenth-
century Catalonia experienced a manifold process of economic
change, in sharp contrast to the prevailing sluggishness of the
contemporary Spanish economy. The Catalan population increased
from around 0.51 to 0.90 million between 1718 and 1787,[5] more
significantly, by the end of the century a highly commercialized
agriculture and the blossoming of industrial initiatives stood wit-
ness to the extent of the transformation under way.[6]

Historians have mainly (and understandably) paid attention to
the emergence first of a calico-printing and then of a fully fledged
cotton textile industry that was to become the leading sector of
Catalan industrialization in the nineteenth century.[7] Effective protection against foreign competition in domestic and colonial mar-

kets and a substantial degree of state intervention were characteristic features of the rise of the calico-printing industry, as argued
in James Thomson's contribution to this volume.

This essay focuses instead on a more traditional sector of the
Catalan economy – cloth manufacturing – in which tariff protection remained low and largely ineffective and state intervention
was only of secondary importance.[8] By its output, as well as by
the amount of labour employed, the Catalan wool textile industry
compared favourably with the cotton industry and its contribution
to the overall growth of this period must not have been negligible.
It expanded strongly during the century and several cloth manufacturing towns featured by 1800 among the major industrial centres of the region. This essay: (1) traces in detail the rise of a
cloth manufacturing family firm in one such town and puts forward
several reasons for its success. In the analysis stress is laid upon
(2) the mercantile side of this business which grew by expanding
its sales outside the region in markets where foreign merchant
colonies were firmly established, and (3) the organization of production and the nature of the changes it experienced.

Instead of colonial trade, new industries and 'enlightened'
reformist policies, the main actors in the story that follows are
domestic markets, old industries and artisan enterprise. This essay
stresses the need to pay attention to the potentiality for growth
and self-transformation inherent in what has been termed 'the
"artisanal" entrepreneurial qualities'[9] so important in the industrial history of neighbouring Languedoc. More specifically, it
points out the ability to build its own 'trading diaspora' in other
regions of the country as a main factor in explaining the remarkable success of the Catalan industry increasingly to sell its goods
in ill-protected Spanish markets where foreign goods (and merchants) had been overwhelmingly present for a very long time.

I

Cloth manufacturing had been an important sector of the Catalan economy since the fourteenth and fifteenth centuries, when
largely export-oriented urban draperies flourished in Barcelona,
Perpignan and other towns. These centres declined with the loss
of the Mediterranean outlets for their cloth in the sixteenth and
seventeenth centuries, while foreign competition also increased in
the Iberian markets. When recovery took place, after 1680, the

wool textile industry had moved to small towns with looser guild structures and easy access to vast rural neighbourhoods.[10] This redeployment was simultaneous with viticultural specialization which, following a well-known pattern,[11] drove out of those rural areas most of the pre-existing local crafts. The growing regional demand for cheap textiles concentrated on smaller supplying areas, which became in turn increasingly specialized. The resulting economies of agglomeration enhanced the competitiveness of Catalan goods in extra-regional markets which became more accessible after 1717, when customs duties were abolished between Castile and the provinces of the old crown of Aragon.[12]

In the eighteenth century, the Catalan wool industry was quite modest in size, even by Spanish standards. In 1765 a tax survey counted 2,200 looms in the region producing for commercial purposes, which meant a fourfold increase since 1723 if credit is given to another similar source.[13] Most of them were operating in manufacturing districts of two broadly different types. The first (and largest) specialized in the production of inexpensive stuffs for low income consumers. Foreign competition was weaker in such goods, while their demand increased in the first half of the century – as long as population growth was not outweighed by diminishing real incomes under pressure from rising rents and grain prices. Small independent producers in these areas marketed their stuffs indirectly through the old-established circuits of regional fairs and local markets. These districts were the traditional heartlands of rural textile manufacturing and many of them experienced deindustrialization in the subsequent period of mechanization of the industry.

A different case was that of the second type of wool manufacturing district, mentioned above, which in 1765 accounted for roughly one-quarter of all Catalan production – but eventually was to prove the more successful.[14] Manufacturing specialized there in the production of so-called 'fine' cloths (to be distinguished from the 'super'-fine ones) of 2,200 to 3,200 threads to the warp; mostly they were mixed fabrics of carded and combed wool. These were the Catalan *paños* that, together with cotton fabrics of the same origin, became common items for sale in urban stores all over Spain after the middle of the century. This was the quality range more open to Catalan producers, who alone were able to cut commercial costs significantly. In the higher quality range foreign competition was too strong and tariff protection ineffective,[15] while in the lower it was difficult to displace locally produced rough stuffs. Only a few manufacturing towns in Catalonia followed this path to growth, based on their ability to compete in urban and mainly extra-regional markets. Such towns (Terrassa, Sabadell, Igualada) later became leading industrial centres in the nineteenth century. There, however, the factory system was not the outcome of the previous development of extensive putting-out networks dominated by big urban merchants. Previous development was of another kind and had involved a differentiation process among independent commodity producers in which old organizational patterns played a not minor role.

Igualada was the largest cloth manufacturing town in Catalonia in the 1760s, though it had only been a minor producing centre until the seventeenth century. In the eighteenth century its population increased at a rapid pace, from around 1,600 inhabitants in 1718 to 6,500 in 1797. The catalyst for this growth was the expanding wool industry, by far the main source of employment in the town.[16] In the 1760s, Igualada manufactured around 1,750 pieces of cloth every year (each one c. 31 metres long, on average), and the twenty local master clothiers (*paraires*) employed at least 2,400 people. In the last twenty years of the seventeenth century, production had never exceeded 300 pieces a year; and the growth was all the more remarkable for the fact that the average quality was higher in the 1760s.[17] An outstanding feature of the industry was the concentration of production in the hands of very few *paraires*: only three of them (Josep Torelló, Segimon Borrull and Josep Anton Lladó) accounted for more than *two-thirds* of the cloth manufactured in 1765. Moreover, Torelló and Borrull were brothers-in-law and in some respects operated as a single undertaking.

An earlier Josep Torelló had become a master in the local clothiers' guild in 1691.[18] In Igualada, as everywhere in rural Catalonia, the *paraires* were the co-ordinators of a cloth manufacturing process that lacked the extreme division of labour (and the corresponding segmentation of craft guilds) so characteristic of urban draperies, and still existing then in Barcelona. These *paraires* purchased wool (usually outside the region, directly or through local merchants), performed the first stages of the production process in their own shops (cleaning, sorting, carding and preparing wool for spinning), then delivered the fibre to spinners and later handed over the yarn to the master weavers who, in Igualada, were organized in a different confraternity and guild.[19] The finishing

97

processes were again carried out or supervised by the clothiers in their shops and in the guild's own (or rented for common use) facilities (tentering grounds, fulling mills). Commercialization was carried out either through the ordering (and, often, financing) merchant or through guilds' stores in urban markets. At the beginning of the eighteenth century, Igualada cloths were disposed of in Barcelona through one such store.[20]

Two years after receiving his mastership Josep Torelló married the daughter of a local gunsmith. His wife died after giving him two sons, who both worked with him and married two sisters, the daughters of another Igualada clothier, Segimon Borrull. In 1711 Torelló married again, this time a peasant girl, and four children were born of this second marriage and survived their father. There was one son, who became a priest, and three daughters, two of whom married two sons of the same Segimon Borrull.[21] Between 1719 and 1740, four marriages took place between the offspring of Josep Torelló and Segimon Borrull: only one daughter in each family married outside the other family – and in both cases outside the clothiers' circle too. Only one of these four marriages ended prematurely (by the death of Torelló's heir, Joaquim).[22] Through such repeated intermarriage a stable co-operation between the two artisan families was ensured, a pooling of information, of relationships and influences and of technical resources too. It also favoured mutual trust when it came to sharing expenses in fixed investments and the risks of commercialization in distant markets.

After the death of his heir, Josep Torelló worked in association with his second son, Josep Torelló *menor*. The need was felt to write down the terms of this father-and-son enterprise in three successive company contracts (in 1726, 1733 and 1735). The 1733 contract established that any resulting profits had to be shared between father and son in proportion to their respective contribution to the running fund (7,000 Catalan *lliures* the father, and 3,500 the son). Except that

> all foodstuffs necessary to eat and drink, all shoes and clothes, expenses on physicians and remedies needed by the said two parts [*father and son*] and their families will be deducted from the profits and earnings of the said company, even if the said Josep Torelló *menor* does not contribute the same capital as the said Josep Torelló *major* to the said company.

The reason for this was that the son's duties involved 'buying wool, selling cloth and spending a great deal of time travelling afar'.[23]

By then, the Torellós were already operating on a much larger scale than most of their fellow-craftsmen in Igualada, though all belonged to the same guild. Several stages can be documented in the then-ongoing process of differentiation. In 1721 Torelló had bought a dyehouse on the outskirts of the town for his exclusive use.[24] In 1735 a more decisive step in the same direction was taken by Torelló and Borrull together. In a neighbouring village they built a fulling mill of considerable capacity, and other premises devoted to the finishing processes (such as tentering grounds and a second dyehouse).[25] Substantial as it was, investment in fixed capital remained modest in comparison with circulating capital. The total outlay required by the dyehouses, fulling mill and related facilities amounted to no more than 5,000 *lliures*, while 10,700 *lliures* made up the running fund needed in 1735 by the Torelló's business alone. Since most of the fixed capital was shared by the two clothiers (Torelló and Borrull), and if we suppose that Borrull had a similar running fund, the ratio of circulating to fixed capital can be roughly estimated at four to one.[26]

By 1735 Borrull and Torelló had become estranged from the more modest clothiers: in that year, the regulations for the use of the guild's own tentering grounds explicitly classed them as strangers (*forasters*).[27] Such 'strangeness' became somehow official in 1745, when a royal decree granted jointly to Borrull and Torelló several tax exemptions and other advantages and distinctions, including the use of the trademark *Fábrica Real de Paños de la villa de Igualada*.[28] The tax exemptions were in fact of slight consequence: their apprentices were not to pay the 'personal' tax; their raw materials and cloth were free from duties in royal inland tolls; they were also free of transport services for the army. Significantly, they were put under a special jurisdiction, that of the *Junta General de Comercio*, [29] in any civil or criminal suit relating to their manufacturing and trading activities.

To be awarded the title of *Fábrica Real* was rather exceptional. In the wool textile sector, this sign of official favour was granted to barely more than fifteen *fabricants* in the whole of Catalonia.[30] They were all clothiers who had broken away from the traditional patterns of activity and scales of operation of the rural *paraires* in Catalonia. Yet, when everything is considered, the royal decree appears as a public sanction of entrepreneurial accomplishment rather than as the starting-point for industrial success – at least in the case of Borrull and Torelló. In 1745 they were already successful manufacturers, and very different from the common *paraires*. They were putting out carded wool to 340 spinners, and had 19 broad looms working for them; together they employed around 500 people.[31] Of course, to be a *Fábrica Real* was no hindrance to continuing prosperity: in 1765, the number of looms working for Torelló and Borrull had increased to 27.[32]

Twelve of these twenty-seven looms were then running for Josep Torelló (the younger), who sold on average 300 pieces of cloth a year. The size and distribution of such sales can be reliably estimated thanks to an accurate register book kept by Torelló since 1759.[33] Map 4.1 shows where the pieces were sold in the years 1762, 1763 and 1764. Fine cloths of 2,600 threads to warp were the main product of the firm, comprising almost two-thirds of the total. It is quite remarkable that regional (Catalan) markets were of only marginal importance for Torelló, who was selling most of his cloth in central Spain – in markets where foreign trading communities played a prominent role, as outlined before. We shall now turn our attention to this aspect.

II

Official favour does not appear to have been the propelling force in the rise of the private *fábricas reales* in this branch of the industry and certainly not in the case of Torelló's. We should, then, look for something else, perhaps the ability of some manufacturers to build their own marketing networks and sharpen the competitiveness of their products by cutting commercial costs. Availability of short-term credit to finance circulating capital was a critical variable, but the sources are extremely unhelpful in this respect.[34] On the other hand, there are relatively abundant data on the mercantile side of the cloth manufacturing business in Igualada.

Since 1726, at least, the Torelló company was selling cloth in distant markets and purchasing raw materials in the producing areas. They marketed their cloth by themselves, outside any guild commercialization scheme, and also independently of merchant capital. They sold directly to dealers and shopkeepers, and even invested in commercial undertakings.[35] In important markets, and especially in Madrid, they had a *correspondent*, a commercial agent selling for them on a commission basis or as an associate in a

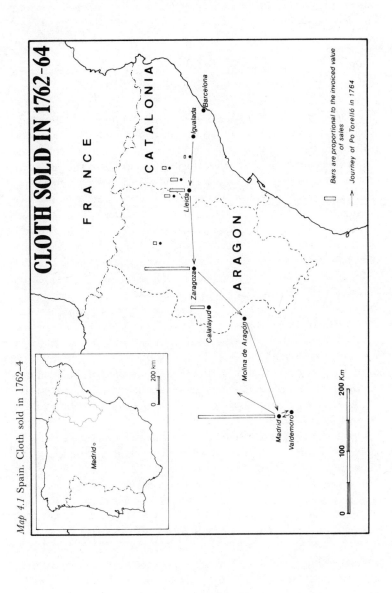

Map 4.1 Spain. Cloth sold in 1762–4

commercial partnership.[36] The Torellós always kept close personal contacts with their agents, as well as with their main wool suppliers. Such contacts implied a regular correspondence and long journeys by some member of the family, usually the heir: at least one every year, covering more than 1,000 km and taking several weeks.

The pattern of such journeys can be sketched through letters which, in the autumn of 1764, Josep Torelló (the second) received from his elder son, Josep Torelló (the third), known as Po.[37] The latter left Igualada (see Map 4.1) at the beginning of October for Lleida (where he sold some pieces of cloth and ordered oil) and Zaragoza, the capital city of Aragón and a major wool market. There he spent several days, during an important religious festival – and fair. After settling accounts with local merchants, selling cloth and purchasing two cartloads of middling quality wool, Po went on to Molina de Aragón (in New Castile). By 27 October he was still in this small town, outside the main road to Madrid, but in the centre of a sheep-raising area. Torelló (and Borrull, too) had been buying wool there for twenty years at least.

One should not imagine Po Torelló as a pedlar or a carter carrying with him the cloth he was selling and the wool he bought. He travelled alone, on a mule, looking for road companions at every stage of the journey. The goods were sent to or from Igualada through the steadily growing transportation network serviced by Catalan carters and muleteers. On his part, Po concentrated on dealing with customers and suppliers and collecting information about trends in fashion as well as about economic prospects. Dependence on commercial intermediaries could thus be avoided in some crucial respects.

On 31 October Po arrived in Madrid and proceeded immediately to Valdemoro, a small town in the province of Toledo. The main regional fair in New Castile was held there every year, which was a decisive event for the success or failure of Torelló's commercial season. On 17 November Po wrote to his father that business looked good: sales amounted to 45,000 *reales* (or *c.* 4,219 Catalan *lliures*), though only 28,000 in cash. The remainder were sales on credit, to be paid in six and twelve months. In a letter sent later from Madrid, probably answering his father's anxieties, Po wrote that 'as for the credits, Mr Cayetano [*Franques, a Catalan merchant active in Castilian markets*] has also been selling to the same people on credit for many years and he tells me that they have never defaulted.' In the same letter (of 1 December), Po announced that he had sold the hinny and would return home 'in the company of some reliable carter' as he now carried a substantial sum in cash. He had spent nine or ten weeks away from Igualada.

A remarkable fact about this correspondence is the very closed nature of the circles in which Po was moving during his journey. The *correspondent* and commercial partner in Madrid, Ramon Nadal, was a Catalan – as all his predecessors in that function had been;[38] Po's informer in Valdemoro was another Catalan merchant; the carters who carried goods and sometimes money to and from Igualada were always Catalan. The only non-Catalan individuals mentioned in the letters are a Castilian wool supplier and an Aragonese merchant. Everything suggests that our merchant-manufacturers evolved within a thick network of trusted fellow-countrymen, a Catalan 'trading diaspora' that made business easier.

Several authors have already pointed out the increasing activity of Catalan merchants during the eighteenth century in Spanish coastal regions[39] and also in the Castilian highland[40]. In what is perhaps the most detailed contemporary account of the state of the Spanish economy, Eugenio Larruga (a long-standing secretary of the *Real Junta General de Comercio y Moneda*) observed in 1792 that in the province of Soria 'in almost every village of some importance there is a Catalan who has settled down there as a shopkeeper to sell different wares . . . The same thing can be said today of the entire Peninsula.'[41] What we know about the behaviour of these Catalan merchants, retailers and carters shows a strong resemblance to that of foreign 'trading diasporas': marriage within the families of the same trading community or with partners from the region of origin; preferential employment of, and commercial association only with other fellow-countrymen; specialization in selling Catalan manufactures and in buying goods for sale in Catalonia, etc.[42] All these signs of a lack of integration in local society are also evidence of continuing mercantile specialization, in which the awareness of being different can be instrumental in creating links of mutual trust and providing exclusive channels of information – both strong commercial weapons in difficult economic environments.

In the eighteenth century, Catalan carters, dealers and shopkeepers could still feel like – and be considered as – foreigners in most of Spain, as they had their own language, a peculiar family law, and a distinct set of mercantile institutions and practices. Perhaps their awareness of being different had been sharpened by their defeat in the War of Succession, which brought full political annexation of the region by Spain.[43] But precisely because of this annexation they were no longer foreigners in the provinces of Castile, which surely could be an advantage. They could feel and behave like foreigners, but legally they were not foreigners. In short, they could form a special 'trading diaspora', and perhaps a very efficient one.

The existing literature and the evidence so far available do not yet allow us to sketch the chronology, the size and the actual workings of this marketing network. But they increasingly suggest that because it lowered risks and cut commercial costs, this old form of commercial organization should be given due consideration when explaining the increasing presence of Catalan goods in Spanish markets after the middle of the eighteenth century.[44] In effect, the competitiveness required to enter these ill-protected markets cannot be explained by technical improvements and cuts in production costs. The next section will consider more closely the developments in the production sphere.

III

Manufacturers such as Torelló and Borrull were still directly involved in the production process. In their workshops (carding shops, dyehouses) or other industrial premises (fulling mills, tentering grounds) several tasks were carried out under their close supervision, namely the preparations prior to spinning and the finishing processes. Dyeing, especially, seems to have been carefully performed or supervised by Josep Torelló himself, and the family kept their own book of recipes.[45] But the two central processes in cloth manufacturing, which required the largest inputs of labour, namely spinning and weaving, were carried out entirely outside Torelló's workshops – in a sense, outside the 'firm' too.

The sources do not throw much light on the relationship between the clothiers and the spinners to whom they delivered wool to be spun – 340 worked for Borrull and Torelló together in 1745, and many more in 1765. Worsted yarn was bought in specialized districts (about 80 km from Igualada) where the spinning of combed wool had become a major source of income for many households in what was a poor mountain area.[46]. Most of the yarn, however, was spun at home by peasant women and children living within a range of 15–20 km from Igualada. We may guess that Torelló subcontracted the time-consuming tasks of delivering fibre and collecting yarn to less fortunate local *paraires*.[47]

As for weaving, it was not carried out in Torelló's own premises: the *post mortem* inventory of the first Josep Torelló in 1745 does not mention even a single loom in his shop, or in the dyehouse.[48] The traditional regulation of cloth-making in Igualada set up a separation between the clothiers' trade and that of the weavers, who were accordingly organized in two different guilds and confraternities (under the advocation of St John the Baptist for the clothiers, and of the Holy Trinity for the weavers). Clothiers must, then, have put out a crucial part of the production process to those master weavers who had an exclusive right to perform all local weaving and who had the legal capacity to regulate, through their guild (subject to the municipal council and, after 1717, to the *Junta de Comercio*), the technical and economic conditions of this operation. Such control enabled the master weavers to negotiate, from a strong position, their share of the value created in the cloth manufacturing process. Clothiers could (and did) bargain by putting out yarn to weavers' guilds outside their own town, which brought about an intricate pattern of spatial segmentation of the production process – since the same or similar regulations existed elsewhere in the middle quality cloth branch of the industry. It seems that at the beginning of the eighteenth century Igualada cloth was mostly woven in smaller surrounding towns, within a radius of 20–25 km, and only two master weavers were active in the town itself.[49]

This pattern did not survive the changing conditions of the early eighteenth century, when some clothiers undertook to improve the quality of their goods in order to compete in new urban markets. Production of higher quality cloths required more skilled weavers, and also a closer supervision of their work; fully specialized artisans had to be attracted to Igualada,[50] which put the local weavers' guild at the hub of this restructuring of the production process. Remarkably, the clothiers succeeded in 1723 in forcing upon the weavers' guild an 'agreement' whereby 'any master clothier (*paraire*) who wishes to be admitted in the mentioned confraternity of the Holy Trinity (*the weavers'*) may and shall be admitted therein as master weaver of wool fabrics without admission examinations nd he will be able to have as many looms and as many journeymen weavers as he wishes.'[51] It is worth mentioning that the agreement was negotiated by a municipal council which at the time counted among its seven members Josep Torelló and his relative, the rich businessman Josep Riera.

Twenty years after the agreement, the confraternity of the Holy Trinity had twenty-two master weavers, four of whom were clothiers admitted without examination. Needless to say, Josep Torelló and Segimon Borrull were among them. But they had not integrated weaving within their 'firm' (thus assuming managerial functions, and risks, in this process), even less concentrated looms and weavers in their shops. This was not the purpose of the 'agreement'. As the master weavers angrily declared in 1753, the journeymen employed by the three big clothiers were weaving 'in their homes [*the journeymen's*] at their behalf and being paid by the piece, and in every respect like master weavers'.[52] In other words, the clothiers delivered yarn to these journeymen weavers in exactly the same way as they had always done to master weavers in Igualada or elsewhere. With one fundamental difference, however: not being masters, such weavers could not organize themselves in a craft guild empowered to regulate the technical and economic conditions of weaving. Their bargaining power must, then, have been significantly lower than that of organized masters.

Thus the ability to bypass the master weavers and directly to put out work to journeymen allowed some *paraires* to appropriate managerial earnings and control which otherwise had to be shared or negotiated with the former. More than the resulting income increases, what really mattered to clothiers was their ensuing greater control over such a decisive phase of the production process. This was achieved without having to incur the additional costs and risks attendant upon concentration and the vertical integration of tasks – and without breaking a guild framework which was versatile enough to adapt to new organizational requirements.

IV

Recent research rather deflates the critical role formerly attributed to the pull of colonial demand in explaining the growth of the Catalan economy in the eighteenth century.[53] The time may be right, then, to look at it from a viewpoint other than its export-oriented and urban-centred side. Small towns, traditional manufactures and domestic trade seem appropriate topics for this new approach. Perhaps case-studies such as the one presented in this essay can help in identifying fields of research which deserve more attention from historians.

The growth of the Torelló enterprise during the first part of the eighteenth century appears to be closely related to expanding sales outside the regional markets, mainly in Madrid, which was achieved without any special protection against foreign or other Spanish goods.[54] Torelló's success was also that of a small number of clothiers in Catalonia whose activity deeply transformed a few manufacturing towns which later became pioneering industrial centres in the age of mechanization. Most of these clothiers were distinguished as 'royal manufacturers', which entailed some (minor) fiscal exemptions and other advantages. But this distinction was a mark of success rather than a starting-point for it. The royal *franquicias* were neither a prerequisite for the rise of these manufacturing concerns out of the craftsmen ranks, nor did they favour concentration and vertical integration of a complex production process – at least in Igualada. In this old industrial branch, state intervention seems to play a much less significant role than in the emerging calico-printing industry studied by James Thomson in this volume.

Good entrepreneurship was no doubt a powerful factor in the success, and the background for this lay in attributes which are characteristic of small-scale producers generally. Easier access to Spanish markets after the War of Succession opened the way to a full exploitation of this potentiality.[55] In Igualada, the accumulation of artisan skills and resources (through repeated inter-marriage between two families) laid the foundation for the emergence of a thriving family concern. The crucial feature which distinguished the Torelló and Borrull families from common clothiers was the broad commercial side of their business, which made them independent from merchant interests and allowed them fully to take advantage of the enlarged opportunities to compete in Spanish markets for textiles. The old pattern of the 'trading diasporas' could be an efficient means of lowering risks and cutting costs in this widening of markets.

Catalonia's rich industrial tradition can explain the readiness to seize those opportunities, which prevented regional economic change from being confined to the agricultural and the outward-looking commercial sectors. But not all the elements of this old industrial tradition were equally fit to sustain this expansion, and the different malleability of guild or other local structures is a relevant point to be considered. In effect, the technical basis of cloth manufacturing remained unaltered but some changes can be traced at the management level.

The ability to bypass the master weavers' guild and directly to employ journeymen allowed some *paraires* in Igualada to absorb managerial earnings and powers, which helped them in their economic rise. Again, this was not the effect of any innovative or reforming measures by the royal government. It resulted from dull political and legal fights at the local level which had different outcomes in different places.[56] Only after the royal decrees of 1769 and especially 1789 did the legal framework generally sanction the situation that the clothiers of Igualada had worked out for themselves since 1723.[57]

Entirely new features emerged in the Spanish economy of the eighteenth century and some of them proved to be decisive for the later experience of small-scale, regionally concentrated industrialization. The case-study presented in this essay suggests that in the explanation of these changes attention should be paid not only to colonial trade, merchant capital or 'enlightened' policies. More research effort should be devoted to flexible guild structures and to small-scale co-operation between artisan and merchant resources at a local level. This is likely to improve our understanding of the social and regional differentiation processes which opened the way to, and were furthered by nascent capitalism.

NOTES

*Research for this essay is a part of a wider study of textile industries in eighteenth century Spain funded by the CAICYT (3553/83). I would like to thank Mrs M. Rita Torelló and Mr Antonió Sánchez for their kindness in granting me access to the Torelló archives, to P. Pascual who smoothed the way for my research in Igualada, and to M. Duran and J. M. Delgado in Barcelona. I am also indebted to Maxine Berg for her suggestions on the first draft of this essay.

The following abbreviations have been used in the notes:

AFT Archives of the family Torelló, Igualada (Barcelona).
ANI Arxiu Notarial, Arxiu Històric d'Igualada.
ACA Arxiu de la Corona d'Aragó (Barcelona).

1 an influential adviser for the Spanish government, Cabarrús, who was himself a Frenchman, advocated a policy of naturalization of the commercial skills embodied in the foreign mercantile colonies. See the

memorandum in *Archivo Histórico Nacional*, Madrid, Sección Estado, leg. 2.944 nr. 434.

2 For a general outline of Spain's colonial and foreign trade during the eighteenth century, see E. *Fernández de Pinedo*, 'Coyuntura y política económicas', 9–173 in E. Fernández de Pinedo, A. Gil Novales and A. Derozier, *Centralismo, Ilustración y agonia del Antiguo Régimen (1715–1833)*, Barcelona, 1980, esp. 124–35. On the legal status, organization, and numbers of foreign merchants in Spain's colonial trade, see W. von den Driesch, *Die ausländischen Kaufleute während des 18. Jahrhunderts in Spanien und ihre Beteiligung am Kolonialhandel*, Cologne/Vienna, 1972.

3 Source quoted in 1 above. For another aspect of the French mercantile community in Spain see D. Ozanam; 'La colonie française de Cadix au XVIIIᵉ siècle d'après un document inédit (1777)', *Mélanges de la Casa de Velázquez*, 4, 1968, 259–347.

4 See P. D. Curtin, *Cross-cultural Trade in World History*, Cambridge, 1984, esp. 2–3.

5 J. Nadal, 'La vraie richesse: les hommes' in J. Nadal Farreras and P. Wolff (eds), *Histoire de la Catalogne*, Toulouse, 1982, 61–90, esp. p. 74. The Spanish population as a whole grew from 8.8 to 11 million in the same period: see Fernández de Pinedo, op. cit., 19.

6 The best short account of this process is in P. Vilar; 'La Catalogne industrielle. Réflexions sur un démarrage et sur un destin' in P. Léon et al., *L'industrialisation en Europe au XIXᵉ siècle*. Cartographie et typologie, Paris, 1973, 421–33. A recent survey of the relevant bibliography in C. Martínez Shaw, 'La Cataluña del siglo XVIII bajo el signo de la expansión' in R. Fernández (ed.), *España en el siglo XVIII. Homenaje a Pierre Vilar*, Barcelona, 1985, 55–131.

7 The initial spurt of the cotton industry was simultaneous with the reform of the legal framework of Spanish colonial trade which entailed the opening of a number of metropolitan ports – including Barcelona – to direct intercourse with America. This has suggested a close connection between both processes. See C. Martínez Shaw, 'Los orígenes de la industria algodonera catalana y el comercio colonial' in J. Nadal and G. Tortella (eds), *Agricultura, comercio colonial y crecimiento económico en la España contemporánea*, Barcelona, 1974. A different view, questioning the relevance of colonial markets for Catalan industrial development, is in J. M. Delgado, 'Política ilustrada, industria española y mercado americano, 1720–1820', *Pedralbes. Revista d'Història Moderna*, Barcelona, 3, 1983 253–63.

8 As far as the Catalan industry is concerned. The State invested large sums of money in royal manufactures for luxury goods (including high-quality cloth) and granted fiscal and other advantages to private producers; the former were located in Castile, and the latter will be discussed below. For general information and references see A. González Enciso and J. Patricio Merino, 'The public sector and economic growth in eighteenth-century Spain', *Journal of European Economic History*, 8, 3, 1979, 553–92. See also Fernández de Pinedo, op. cit., 89–98.

9 J. K. J. Thomson, *Clermont-de-Lodève 1633–1789. Fluctuations in the Prosperity of a Languedocian Cloth-making Town*, Cambridge, 1982, 11.

JAUME TORRAS

10 See C. Carrère, *Barcelone, centre économique à l'époque des difficultés 1380–1462*, 2 vols, Paris / The Hague, 1967 (esp. i, 421–522); M. Riu, 'The woollen industry in Catalonia in the later middle ages' in N. B. Harte and K. Ponting (eds), *Cloth and Clothing in Medieval Europe*, London, 1983, V. Vázquez de Prada and P. Molas Ribalta, 'La industria lanera en Barcelona (s. XVI-XVIII)' in M. Spallanzani (ed.) *Produzione, commercio e consumo dei panni di lana (nei secoli XII-XVIII)*, Florence, 1976, 553–65.

11 F. Mendels, 'Seasons and regions in agriculture and industry during the process of industrialization' in S. Pollard (ed.), *Regions und Industrialisierung*, Göttingen, 1980, 177–95. For Catalonia, see J. Torras, 'Especialización agrícola e industria rural en Cataluña en el siglo XVIII, *Revista de Historia Económica*, II, 3, 1984, 113–27.

12 J. Rodríguez Labandeira, 'La política económica de los Borbones' in M. Artola (ed.) *La economía española al final del Antiguo Régimen. IV. Instituciones*, Madrid 1982, 107–84, esp. 155–60.

13 The 1765 survey, in *Institut Municipal d'Història*, Barcelona, section *Junta de Comercio*, vol. 81; the data for 1725 were published by Geronimo de Uztariz; *Theorica y practica de Comercio y de Marina*, repr. Madrid 1968, 349–50.

14 For more information about the different types of woollen industrial districts in eighteenth century Catalonia see Torras op. cit., 119–24.

15 An outline of eighteenth century Spanish tariff policy appears in Fernández de Pinedo; op. cit., 125–30 British exports to Spain greatly increased during the eighteenth century, and by 1772–4 wool textiles amounted to two-thirds of their total value (and to more than one-third of British wool manufactures exported to Mediterranean Europe). See J. Nadal Farreras; *Comercio exterior y subdesarrollo. España y Gran Bretaña de 1772 a 1914; política económica y relaciones comerciales*, Madrid, 1978, 210–11 and 222.

16 On the economic life of eighteenth-and nineteenth-century Igualada, see J. M. Torras Ribé; 'Trajectòria d'un procés d'industrialització frustrat' in *Miscellanea Aqualatensia* 2, Igualada, 1974, 151–97.

17 Output and labour employed in 1765, in the source quoted in note 13 above (data on Igulada on pp. 74–5). A municipal report estimated in 1770 that 4,000 people were employed, including spinners in the surrounding countryside: Torras Ribé, op. cit., 159. Output in the last decades of the seventeenth century can be estimated from the guild's books, in Museu Comarcal (Igualada), Servei de Documentaoió, *Llibre de la Confraria y Offici de Perayres de la vila de Igualada en lo qual estan continuadas las Ordinacions y determinacions de dit offici.*

18 His father, Joaquim, is the first of the family to appear in the rolls of the guild, and was received as master in 1663: *Llibre de la Confraria*, quoted in note 17.

19 On guilds and confraternities in eighteenth-century Igualada, see P. Molas Ribalta; 'Els gremis d'Igualada a la fí de l'Antic Règim' in *Miscellanea Aqualatensia/2*, Igualada, 1974, 139–49.

20 Castellà Raich, *El Gremio de 'Paraires' de Igualada y sus relaciones con la casa 'Molí Nou'*, Sabadell, 1945, 28. For a general outline of the trade

110

in textiles, see P. Molas; *La burguesía mercantil en la España del Antiguo Régimen*, Madrid, esp. 67–80.

21 The marriage contracts, in *AFT*.

22 But an heiress was already born to him, Josepa, whom later her grandfather married to the heir of a local businessman, J. Riera, a *parvenu* who grew rich during the War of Succession and whose off-spring eventually reached the status of noblemen by the last decades of the century. See on this family J. Mercader and J. M. Torras Ribé *Assaig sobre les oligarquies socials de'Igualada en el segle XVIII*, Igualada, 1970.

23 *ANI*, not. O. Melcion, *Manual*, 1733, fols 25–6. The reason for such contracts between father and son was that the latter was not the universal heir (Catalonia being a land of impartible inheritance), and a difference had to be drawn between the family heritage and the earnings resulting from a given industrial or commercial activity. The family heritage was trasmitted through the (dead) elder son to the Riera-Torelló couple mentioned in note 22.

24 Reference in *ANI*, not. J. Mateu, *Manual*, 1752, fol. 204 Such ownership was not that common, for in 1765 only eight *paraires* (Borrull and Torello among them) had their own dyeing facilities, according to Mn. J. Segura; *Història d'Igualada*, II, facsimile edn., Igualada, 1968, 315.

25 *ANI*, not. O. Melcion, *Manual*, 1736, fols 13–21.

26 *ANI*, not. F. Melcion, *Manual*, 1750, fols 135–46 (for estimations of the value of fixed capital) and not. O. Melcion, *Manual*, 1735, fols 105–6 (for the company contract of 1735). To set this rough estimate in a broader context, see P. Hudson, *The Genesis of Industrial Capital*, Cambridge, 1986, 8–9 and 52.

27 *ANI*, not. O. Melcion, *Manual*, 1735, fols 109–10.

28 The complete text, in *ACA*, sect. 'Reial Audiència. Diversorum', vol. 220, fols 366–71.

29 On this institution see W. Callahan; 'A note on the Real y General Junta de Comercio, 1679–1814', *Economic History Review*, 2nd series, 21,3, 1968 519–28.

30 On *fábricas reales* in a broader Spanish context, see A. González Enciso, *Estado e industria en el siglo XVIII: la Fábrica de Guadalajara*, Madrid 1980, esp. 155–60. Catalan cloth manufacturers who were distinguished as *fabricantes reales* in *Archivo General de Simanoas* (Valladolid), 'Consejo Supremo de Hacienda', libro registro 248, fols 135–74.

31 The data are included in the document quoted in note 28.

32 Data from the 1765 survey quoted in note 13.

33 *AFT*, ms. *Llibre de Comptes ahont se asentaran diferens deutas de diferens particulars, comensan â 9 de 8bre. 1759. Joseph Torello Paraÿre.*

34 The marriage of his grand-daughter (and universal heiress) to the heir to the richest local merchant (see note 22) could have helped Josep Torelló in this respect.

35 They had a partnership of 1,000 *lliures* in a cloth store in the town of Balaguer, in western Catalonia: *ANI*, not. O. Melcion, *Manual*, 1733, fol. 25. Later on, J. Torelló *menor* invested 4,000 *lliures* in a similar

shop in Tamarit de Llitera (in Aragón) managed by his brother-in-law Bartomeu Borrull: *ANI*, not. F. Melcion, *Manual*, 1744, fols 136–7.

36 In Madrid they had had a commercial agent (Solernou) at least since 1731: *ANI*, not O. Melcion, *Manual*, 1731, fols 119–20. In 1763, Torello hired a store there and entrusted its manangement to Ramón Nadal (a Catalan businessman): see *AFT*, ms. *Llibre de comptes*, 43.

37 The following information and quotations come from the collection of letters in *AFT*.

38 Solernou in the 1730s, Prades in the 1740s, Boter in the 1750s (correspondence in Catalan with Boter, in *AFT*).

39 See L. Alonso Alvárez, *Industrialización y conflictos sociales en la Galicia del Antiguo Régimen (1750–1830)*, Madrid 1976; C. Martínez Shaw; 'Las relaciones económicas entre Cataluña y la Baja Andalucía en el siglo XVIII' in *Actas del I Congreso de Historia de Andalucía, Andalucía Moderna (Siglo XVIII)*, Córdoba, 1978, 347–56; M. T. Pérez Picazo and G. Lemeunier; 'Comercio y comerciantes catalanes en la crisis del Antiguo Régimen murciano (1770–1845) in *Primer Congrés d'Història Moderna de Catalunya*, I, Barcelona, 1984, 747–55.

40 A. González Enciso; 'Especialización y competencia regionales: la expansión del comercio catalán en Castilla a fines del siglo XVIII', *Pedralbes. Revista d'Història Moderna*, Barcelona, V,5, 1985, 31–57.

41 E. Larruga, *Memorias políticas y económicas sobre los frutos, comercio, fábricas y minas de España* XXI, Madrid, 1792 (quotation on 168–9).

42 See especially Pérez Picazo and Lemeunier, op. cit., 749–55, and González Enciso, op. cit., 46–55.

43 H. Kamen, *The War of Succession in Spain 1700–15*, Bloomington and London, 1969.

44 See a general view in J. Maluquer de Motes, 'La revolución industrial en Cataluña' in N. Sánchez Albornoz (ed.) *La modernización económica de España 1830–1930*, Madrid 1985, 199–225. (In connection with the role of domestic markets, see esp. 208–9).

45 *AFT*, ms. *Llibre de tints*.

46 See Torras, op. cit., 119.

47 Data about spinning in 1770, in Torras Ribé, op. cit., 159–61. Indications of subcontracting in a statement by the guild's headmen: *ANI*, not. A. Viladés, *Manual*, 1744–6, fol. 22.

48 *ANI*, not. J. Mateu, *Inventaris, 1739–1754*, fols 90–4.

49 A wealth of information on the organization of cloth manufacturing in Igualada around 1720 appears in the proceeding of the lawsuit instigated by the weavers against the clothiers in the 1740s: *ACA*, sect. 'Reial Audiència, Plets civils', expt. nr. 8297.

50 Data on immigration of weavers into Igulada in Torras Ribé, op. cit. 163 and 194.

51 *ACA*, 'Notarials, Igualada', vol. 796 (not. B. Costa, *Manual*, 1723), fols 57–60.

52 *AFT*, doc. B–659. More information appears in the source quoted in note 49.

53 J. M. Delgado, 'Comercio colonial y crecimiento económico en la España del siglo XVIII. La crisis de un modelo interpretativo', *Manu-*

scrits, nr. 3, 1986 23–40. For a general interpretative framework see J. Fontana 'Comercio colonial y crecimiento económico: revisiones e hipótesis in J. Fontana (ed.), *La economía española al final del Antiguo Régimen, -III. Comercio y Colonias*, Madrid, 1982, XI-XXXIV.

54 Catalan (as well as Aragonese and Valencian) clothiers were not exempted from the sales tax in Castile as the other Spanish cloth manufacturers had been since 1752: see Rodríguez Labandeira op. cit., 155–6. The corresponding tax reduction (suppression of the *dret de bolla*) in Catalonia did not take place until 1769.

55 This is suggested by the pattern of development proposed for Languedocian cloth-making towns by Thomson, op. cit, esp. chap. 8. The analaysis is illuminating for our case, in spite of the great differences in scale and national economic context between the Languedocian and Catalan wool industries.

56 The clothiers of Barcelona claimed similar rights in 1721, but the attempt failed mainly because municipal authorities sided with the weavers. See P. Molas Ribalta, *Los gremios barceloneses del siglo XVIII*, Madrid, 1970, 383.

57 Only when the *Reales Ordenanzas para fabricantes de paños de todas clases y bayetas finas del Principado* were issued in 1769 were master clothiers allowed directly to organize the whole cloth manufacturing process. See the full text in F. Torrella Niubó, *El moderno resurgir textil de Barcelona (Siglos XVIII y XIX)*, Barcelona, 1961, 67–75.

5

'NOVELTY, GIVE US NOVELTY': LONDON AGENTS AND NORTHERN MANUFACTURERS[1]

Toshio Kusamitsu

INTRODUCTION

For the historians of the Industrial Revolution the main preoccupation of their research has always been with 'production': either productivity, the human relationship in production, the development of technology and the production process, or the formation of capital and labour.[2] Their tendency to neglect other aspects of economic activity such as circulation and consumption has created a significant gap in our understanding of the totality of economic and social activities. The commodity flows from production to consumption by means of the market, so the important role of the market and consumption in the whole economy is obvious. It must be pointed out, however, that there have been attempts by some socio-economic historians to make 'consumption' an important issue in their investigations. Neil McKendrick, for instance, studied Josiah Wedgwood's marketing techniques, which were a breakthrough and a novel feature among eighteenth-century manufacturers.[3] Eric Jones's study of fashion manipulators is perhaps one of a few pioneering works to show the significance of 'demand side' history. As he puts it, 'Economic history is a supply side subject. This is nowhere more apparent than in the many works written on the industrialization of eighteenth-century Britain. Among them all there are few that consider demand explicitly or extensively.'[4] The recent interest of economic and social historians in proto-industrialization also shows the extent to which commercial activities and the marketing of products – in both national and international markets – became crucial for the development

114

of industry. In periods when there was not much technological advancement, commercial organization was the key factor for an industry's expansion. Also a substantial number of new industries were set up where the potential markets for them could be found. The stimuli for these new industries were 'fashion' and the novelty of the product. People's craze for fashion was immensely important in this context: it opened up new markets, and new industries were created.

The subject of this paper is the importance of design in the marketing activities of manufacturers and merchants. It is still within the confines of supply side history, but it is hoped that it will bridge 'supply' and 'demand' by showing a strong awareness of manufacturers and merchants, and of consumers in their daily activities.

FASHION AND ECONOMIC HISTORY

There still seem to be problems when economic historians discuss 'fashion', mostly about their approach, and about chronology. 'Fashion is accorded a lowly place by economic historians when they account for the rise of the cloth industries and the changing direction of their trade.'[5] Thus Joan Thirsk begins her article on the English stocking knitting industry between 1500 and 1700. She is, moreover, absolutely correct in pointing out the significant role of 'the tyranny of fashion'.[6] Almost all historians of the textile industries have been aware of this, but they mention it only in passing, as something economic history cannot deal with.[7] Instead, they turn their attention to more concrete and 'sterner economic explanations',[8] and abstain from serious discussion of 'fashion' or, for that matter, 'design'.

Although Thirsk's attempt to draw the attention of economic historians to fashion is welcome, she does not fully explain the mechanism by which fashion was interwoven with economic history. What she does suggest is that fashion played an important role in the creation of new industries such as stocking knitting and the New Draperies. Fashion has a significance for the economic historian because of the way in which it acted as an incentive for the transformation of peasant industry into an industry on a national and even an international scale. She seems to use the word 'fashion' in a more *a priori* way, and her research does not reveal much about the day-to-day business of the producers and

115

merchants who had to handle 'the tyranny of fashion' – although, admittedly, in the period she discusses, there is a problem of limited documentation.

D. C. Coleman offers a slightly different approach to fashion.[9] He distinguishes two causes of textile growth in the period between 1450 and 1750: first, a labour-intensive putting-out system in rural areas, which made it possible to lower the cost of production and consequently to reduce prices in real terms; and, second, the ability of the industry continually to develop 'new products'. It is with the latter that we are concerned here. Coleman argues that these new products

> were simply new fabrics, new designs, different colours, dif-
> ferent finishes; changes in yarn, in weaves, in patterns. They
> were, in essence, mutations; and most of them were continu-
> ally disseminated by imitation. . . . More and more the
> market – influenced increasingly by shifts in fashion as more
> substitutes became available – dominated production. Textile
> manufacture provides the supreme example of the pre-indus-
> trial revolution multi-product industry; and, moreover, of a
> consumer-orientated industry, effecting little or no change for
> centuries in the basic techniques of its main production pro-
> cess but frequently changing, in an almost infinitive variety
> of small ways, the combination of inputs which determined
> the look, feel, finish, colour, pattern or weight of the final
> product – and by this route sometimes, though not necess-
> arily, also affecting its cost and profitability.[10]

While Thirsk treats fashion as a 'tyranny' and argues that the survival of frame knitters 'depended always on their ability to retaliate with a new design, or to tap a new market patronized by a different class of purchasers,'[11] in Coleman's view it was precisely this characteristic of the textile trades that enabled them to grow so remarkably, and without much fundamental technological change. In fact, the two explanations are complementary. More-over, these characteristics of textile manufacturing remained unchanged in the nineteenth century. By then they were reinforced by new technologies and methods of work organization which had increased output dramatically. The expansion of markets forced the manufacturer to produce goods with more diversified and speci-alized finishes while, at the same time, the invention of different types of products called for new markets. As we shall see later, the producers and sellers of textiles frequently expressed their concern with this dilemma in business correspondence.

The problem of chronology has also emerged when economic historians try to identify the origins of a consumer society. Joan Thirsk has argued that when new projects were created, in the late sixteenth and seventeenth centuries, domestic industries were activated and stimulated the production of a wide range of consumer goods. This discussion is combined with the proto-industry debate and contributed to the understanding of rural industries in early modern Britain.[12] McKendrick and others, however, have challenged Thirsk's periodization of the birth of a consumer society; they claim that there was a consumer revolution/boom in the eighteenth century, when people's purchasing power rose dramatically and fashion cycles shortened. The scale of consumption became much larger, compared with the seventeenth century, and there was a qualitative change in the habits of consumption, with marketing, advertising and sales promotion now widely employed. The eighteenth century was the first time the desire for consumption was accompanied by consumers' ability to spend.[13] This paper does not attempt to get to the root of the chronological problem. It suggests, rather, that it was in the first half of the nineteenth century that society was more structurally organized to maintain the development of consumerism and the establishment of a close link between merchant and manufacturer.

To the pressure of growing markets, upon manufacturers, which required a continuous expansion of production, was added the forceful demand of fashion. Indeed, the increased output of new patterns *of itself* fostered the growth not only of a more numerous but also of a more discerning consumer market. Mass production made middle-class purchasers aware of new choices in consumption, and prompted the development of 'fashion-consciousness'. Manufacturers responded in turn by the creation of marketing techniques, especially with regard to medium-range goods. Although it continued to be thought very difficult to predict demand, manufacturers and merchants tried to manipulate the taste of consumers by the production of appealing 'novelties'. As will be seen, fashion was to be the creation of producers rather than of consumers.

NOVELTY

Manufacturers who were aware of the significance of fashion were
concerned not simply to imitate, for example, French patterns, but
also to give them a novel flavour. 'Novelty' became a very important feature in the development of the textile industry. J. E. Tennent summarized this tendency:

> In the production of patterns for printed calicoes, novelty
> of conception, and constant variety of effect, are of equal
> importance with elegance and beauty of execution; and . . .
> a perpetual succession of designs is indispensable in order to
> meet the passion for novelty which prevails, not only in
> the home market, but in every country to which we export
> calicoes.[14]

The pursuit of 'novelty' was such that the conscientious manufacturer found it alarming. James Thomson wrote to the Vice-
President of the Board of Trade that 'NOVELTY, the handmaid of
FASHION, and sometimes the enemy of TASTE, enjoys but a short
and fleeting existence – it is of its very essence, quickly to fade
and pass away.'[15] Yet as long as consumers sought new patterns,
as increasingly they did, the majority of manufacturers would
shape their business to the production of continually changing
'novelties'. Daniel Lee, a large calico-printer and dealer, described
the extent to which the trade was under this pressure of novelty:
it was so great that a printer was 'seldom able to sell the same
design a second time to the same individual'.[16] Of course, the
production of a succession of fine patterns was not denied to
anyone working in the trade. It was novelty for the sake of novelty
which Thomson and others condemned.[17] The *Journal of Design*,
for example, was firmly with Thomson when it stated:

> There is a morbid craving in the public mind for novelty as
> *mere novelty*, without regard to intrinsic goodness; and all
> manufacturers, in the present mischievous race for compe-
> tition, are driven to pander to it. It is not sufficient that each
> manufacturer produces a few patterns of the best sort every
> season, they must be generated by the score and by the
> hundreds. We know that one of our first potters brought to
> town last year upwards of a thousand patterns! There are
> upwards of six thousand patterns for calico-printing regis-
> tered annually, and this we estimate to be only a third of

the number produced. . . . One of the best cotton-printers told us that the creation of new patterns was an endless stream. The very instant his hundred new patterns were out he began to engrave others. His designers were working like mill-horses.[18]

This novelty fever, or to use Joan Thirsk's words 'the tyranny of fashion' prevailed, according to many witnesses, mainly in foreign markets. J. E. Tennent pointed out that novelty was the constant pursuit chiefly of those manufacturers engaged in the production of 'medium goods, and those for export'.[19] We shall discuss this point later when the growth of overseas trade is discussed in connection with manufacturers' financial arrangements and their sales strategy. It is appropriate here, however, to stress that the intrinsic value of 'novelty' was promoted rather by manufacturers and merchants than by customers. Or it might be more precise to argue that it was the merchants who were responsible for maintaining this 'tyranny of fashion.'

F. D. Klingender is helpful to the enquiry:

> Already in the second half of the eighteenth century the real arbiter of taste was no longer the designer or even the manufacturer, but the salesman, whose business it was to both sense every fluctuation in the public mood and, if possible, to anticipate change and to motivate fashion by a ceaseless flow of 'novelties'.[20]

Unfortunately Klingender did not pursue his thesis further than this general statement, so it is necessary to develop and modify his assertion. As shall be seen, his point is, generally speaking, remarkably accurate. The implication of Tennent's observation is that the preoccupation of manufacturers with the production of novel medium goods for export was the result of the creation by merchants of new fashions in the market rather than of the demands of consumers. The merchants' attitude was closely connected to an aggressive policy of marketing. If merchants felt pressurized by the need to produce new goods, this pressure was largely created and accelerated by their own marketing strategy. With luxury goods, fashions tended to last longer, and therefore less pressure was felt to manufacture novelties. But it was by the production of medium range goods for export that Britain rose to become a leading commercial nation.

119

The bigger the market became, the more varied the taste. Producers had to possess a clear idea of the distinctive tastes which characterized different markets. Goods had to be dispatched in time for the season as well as in accordance with the specifications sent by foreign and home agents. In such activities, the merchant was required to exercise judgement not only upon economic matters, but also concerning matters of taste. This was especially true in the textile trade, which was so sensitive to changing fashions. The successful expansion of the market for the produce of textile industries has hitherto been explained by such factors as specialization in the production of medium and lower range goods. The role of entrepreneurial skill in marketing these goods, especially in overseas markets, has also been examined by some economic historians. In the section which follows, the latter aspect is considered in connection with the marketing of design.

THE MERCHANT AND THE GROWTH OF THE MARKET

If textile growth was, as Coleman argues, largely caused by the tailoring of products to specific markets, it was merchants who made this interrelationship possible. Merchants played a crucial role in marketing. Yet they have only recently received the attention of historians. Economic historians were previously more concerned with production than with the market. Now, however, interest is being shown in the merchant, and especially in his role in capital formation. The seminal work in this new field is R. G. Wilson's study of Leeds merchants, while S. D. Chapman has published some important articles on cotton printing.[21] The recent studies point out that the cloth trade came to be dominated in the nineteenth century by a class of merchants distinct from those who had held sway in the eighteenth century. Although the main purpose of this essay is to analyse the day-to-day business of merchants in terms of their response to fashion, it is useful as well as important to understand their activities in general.

The change in marketing, in combination with the technological changes which took place around the end of the eighteenth century, resulted in a revolutionary expansion of foreign markets.[22] In the eighteenth century, the output of the Yorkshire wool textile industry was retailed predominantly by Yorkshire merchants, notably by those of Leeds, who exported cloths and stuffs to southern

Europe and to the Americas, especially the United States. The Yorkshire industry relied heavily on foreign markets for the bulk of its sales. This foreign trade continued to be important until the third quarter of the nineteenth century, at which date about two-thirds of the Yorkshire output went abroad. However, the structure of the industry and of merchandising in the district underwent a significant change between the late eighteenth and the mid-nineteenth centuries. The most obvious feature of this change was the transition from domestic to factory production which led successful clothiers to merchandise their own products. The eighteenth-century merchants of the West Riding were mostly descended from Tudor yeomen or small landed families, and their business was conducted in the traditional style, through the cloth halls. The development of the factory system, however, increased output and the necessity of marketing the new products forced the manufacturer to use his own initiative against severe competition, and to dispense with the halls and the middlemen.

A number of developments reflected the advent of the new marketing principles. The speculative system of consignment was characteristic of the new approach. So, too, was the attempt to realize quick returns by mass sales at low unit profit, and the consequent development of the auction system, whereby goods produced in quantity were sold at whatever price they would fetch. Known as the 'Bradford Principles', these methods were employed especially in such distant markets as those of America. Indeed, by the early nineteenth century the domestic and overseas markets were developing along distinct lines. The home market, which took around 40 per cent of West Riding cloth, did not have auction sales and cut-throat price competition, for the products made for this market were less homogeneous, and the trade continued to be conducted on the traditional personal basis.[23]

Between the 1830s and 1850 another significant change took place in Yorkshire. The advantage of specialization in particular products for particular markets was beginning to be felt among manufacturers. The domestic and European markets were still the major destinations for high quality and fancy cloths, whereas cheaper worsted stuffs were being sent to American markets. This period also witnessed the emergence of a new class of merchants, among them numerous foreign merchants who became resident in Britain. As the consignment system declined in importance, trade

121

was conducted increasingly by agents in direct contact with their parent houses.[24]

The structural changes which took place in the wool textile industry in the West Riding were complex. There were, too, considerable differences between the woollen and worsted trades. The worsted industry completed the transition from a domestic to a factory system much earlier than the woollen industry. Woollen manufacturing, meanwhile, was slow to make a similar transition, especially in weaving. The difference was also a geographical one: the rapid growth of worsted was exemplified by Bradford, which became the 'worstedopolis' of England and stole the merchandising of worsted clothes and stuffs from Leeds, which itself had a reputation for specializing in woollens.

The success of worsteds in Yorkshire was promoted by the following: (1) the relatively early transition from a domestic to a factory system, in conjunction with rapid mechanization; (2) aggressive merchandising by Bradford merchants; and (3) the variety of goods which could be adapted to changing fashions. Edward Collinson listed about thirty different goods produced in the West Riding in 1854. They were:

> Lastings, Crapes, Serge, Orleans, Cassinetts, Twills, Dobbies, French Figures, Figured and Embroidered Alpacas, Parisians, Damasks, Camlets, Merinos, Challis, Mousseline-de-laines, Cobourgs, Paremattas, Shalloons, Duroys, Taminets, Khybereen, Poplins, Calimancoes, Bombaseens, Figured Satteens, Cunicas, Mohairs, Fancy Waistcoatings, etc.[25]

Many of these were mixed fabrics, containing wool and cotton or silk. Such mixtures added to the wide variety of fabrics that could be produced.

The cotton industry experienced a development similar to the wool textile industry with respect to finance and marketing.[26] Towards the end of the eighteenth century, manufacturers began to appropriate for themselves the function of merchants, intending to find new markets abroad. According to William Radcliffe, by 1800 'all the great merchants were manufacturers with scarcely an exception'.[27] The old markets such as Europe could only absorb a limited proportion of the vastly increased output. Manufacturers were therefore forced to explore new markets, for they could not stop production. Once the basic machinery of production had been set up, manufacturers were less concerned to add to their fixed asets than to increase their working capital. It is estimated that working capital requirements were about three times as much as those of fixed capital, and the clearance of goods and stocks within a reasonable period was necessary to keep business healthy. Another factor which made manufacturers extend their normal functions of business to include merchandising was the limited terms of credit available to them. The manufacturer felt the necessity of lightening this burden of short credit terms and thus ventured into the merchandising business for himself.[28]

The consignment system was as extensive in the early nineteenth century in the cotton industry as in the wool textile industry, as S. J. Chapman explained:

> The number of small manufacturers, without capital or a merchant patron, was on the increase; and the system of marketing by consigning their goods, which meant the accumulation of risks upon the producer instead of on the dealer, naturally spread when competition among producers was keen, until it was brought to an end by its ravages among those manufacturers who resorted to it.[29]

Small manufacturers were liable to exploitation by the so-called 'slaughter-houses' of dealers. Manufacturers commonly sent their goods to dealers in Liverpool and London to be sold at the best price obtainable. Dealers made advances to the manufacturers, offering one-third to two-thirds of the value of the goods consigned, and frequently nothing more was paid. Dealers would even demand the return of a proportion of the advance if goods did not realize the expected price. A manufacturer wishing to escape this system, and to retail his own products, would be assisted both by a large scale of production and by a distinctive range of products. Even a small-scale manufacturer could operate independently, if his goods were sufficiently out of the ordinary. But, in any case, such a merchant needed to be familiar with the market at which he aimed.[30]

The era of the merchant manufacturers, however, was brief. By the end of the Napoleonic Wars it had already become obvious that recurrent financial and commercial crises produced problems of liquidity. The older generation of merchants, after about 1815, were weakened by the financial strain of selling goods in a dispersed market. At this period, a new marketing system emerged.

Financing and marketing, which had been the combined function of some merchants of the preceding generation, were now separated. Acceptance houses, or merchant banks, emerged as specialists in financing for export, while commission agents now provided market expertise. The former, a small group of London overseas merchants, became increasingly powerful, and the latter, who were permanently resident abroad, supplied detailed information regarding markets.[31] By the 1850s, about 1,500 British commission agents were operating throughout the world, and many continental agents were engaged upon similar business. The manufacturer was now reliant upon men such as these for the foreign distribution of his products. This relationship brought pressure upon the manufacturer to produce the widest possible range of goods – shapes, sizes and designs – to satisfy the middlemen, who were concerned to offer a comprehensive choice of goods. The manufacturer was now constantly in receipt of directions from wholesale merchants and their agents abroad, directing him to produce particular patterns, of stipulated qualities, for specified markets.[32]

Now that we have looked briefly at the development of merchandising in both the woollen textile and cotton industries it is clear that, by the second quarter of the nineteenth century, the merchant class became powerful enough to direct marketing by themselves. Manufacturers were now under the control of merchants who would dictate to them the sort of goods that were required in the market.

MARKETING AND THE SELECTION OF PATTERNS

One of the significant changes brought about by the Industrial Revolution in the woollen textile trade was the decline of the cloth halls and the rise of a new system of marketing. Cloth halls had for long been an essential meeting place for clothiers and merchants wishing to transact business. In Yorkshire, especially, the cloth hall was a crucial institution: there woollen goods were mostly produced by small-scale clothiers and journeymen with limited capital (comprising their tools and materials), who took their cloth weekly to the nearest cloth hall. Whereas the large-scale clothiers in the woollen trades of the West Country and East Anglia practised the putting-out system, while retaining control of the sale of their products to London merchants and factors at

Blackwell Hall, the small-scale clothiers of Yorkshire, who at best produced two pieces a week, relied entirely on the cloth hall to which merchants came from Leeds and Wakefield. In Halifax, a cloth hall was recorded as early as 1572 (although the present building, the magnificent Piece Hall, was erected in 1779). It was in the eighteenth century, however, that the cloth hall began to play a central role in the cloth trade of the West Riding, as Herbert Heaton's study of the Leeds White Cloth Hall shows.[33] R. G. Wilson argues that the supremacy of the Yorkshire cloth industry in the eighteenth century was based largely on the activities of local merchants (primarily those of Leeds and Wakefield), for whom 'cloth was their life, their sole interest'.[34] The advantage of their location was the facility of the closest contact with those who produced the cloth. The weekly visits to neighbouring cloth halls were their chief business. Among contemporary descriptions of proceedings in the cloth halls, Defoe's account of the Leeds Coloured Cloth Market is perhaps one of the most famous:

> Some of them [the merchants] have their foreign Letters of Orders, with Patterns seal'd on them, in Rows, in their Hands; and with those they match Colours, holding them to the Cloths as they think they agree.[35]

As we shall see, this mode of business remained essentially unaltered after the decline of the cloth halls. Merchants continued to use orders with patterns attached to guide them in their purchases. But the significant change was that they no longer attended the halls, and orders were instead directed to the clothiers by post.

Before the early nineteenth century, Blackwell Hall in London played a central role in retailing the woollen manufacturers of the West Country, which relied entirely on London factors and merchants. Factors acted primarily as commission agents, handling money and cloth, with the support of bankers and financiers.[36] Towards the end of the eighteenth century, London factors extended their activities to deal with woollen and worsted manufactures in Yorkshire. A firm of London factors, Hanson and Mills, which has been examined by Conrad Gill, was one of those which tried to extend its business to include north country cloth. Hanson and Mills's method of dealing in northern cloth differed from that of its main business. Instead of receiving goods from clothiers, the firm secured orders in London through half a dozen firms of middlemen in Yorkshire.[37] Pat Hudson argues that merchants and factors in London were, in many cases, more than just commission agents for the cloth manufacturing districts. They also financed the purchasing, storage and sale of the cloth.[38]

The decline of the cloth halls was caused by several factors. First, some merchants began to manufacture cloth themselves. Second, large clothiers who had accumulated sufficient capital and expanded their businesses started to trade on their own behalf. Third, there developed a system of working to the order of merchants and factors.[39] At the same time new ranges of widely diversified goods, especially fancy cloths, became increasingly prominent staples of the West Riding. These undermined the traditional production of broad cloth in the region. The history of the White Cloth Hall in Leeds shows this very clearly. By the beginning of the nineteenth century, the manufacture of undyed fabrics by white clothiers was breaking down, and many clothiers began to make fancy goods, mixed cloths and other new varieties of fabrics. The White Cloth Hall traditionally forbade clothiers to sell these products in the Mixed Hall or anywhere else, but was compelled, under increasing pressure from its users, to make provision for those pieces manufactured by the white clothiers. In 1806 the sale of fancy cloths was permitted, and by 1828 the trustees of the White Cloth Hall further extended the accommodation provided for coloured cloths.[40]

The Huddersfield Cloth Hall experienced a similar development. Among West Riding towns, Huddersfield had the highest reputation for fancy cloths. J. Aiken noted in 1795 that the high quality cloth of Huddersfield was 'as high as the super fines of the West of England'. He also pointed out that the Huddersfield trade 'comprises a large share of the clothing trade of Yorkshire'.[41] Manufacturers in Huddersfield were quick to adapt to the change in fashion in the 1820s, producing lighter and more colourful materials, and they were no less prompt about employing Jacquard looms when they were introduced into the West Riding in the 1830s. Fancy cloths were woven with Spanish wool and the new mill-spun cotton warp, sent from Manchester. Crump and Ghorbal considered the growth of this fancy trade to be one of main reasons for the decline of the Cloth Hall in Huddersfield:

The merchant, and particularly the merchant-manufacturer, began to find it [the Cloth Hall] less indispensable. He preferred to give orders for what he wanted instead of buying

126

what he saw; or he found it an advantage to show his cloth to his customers in a private warehouse. This was especially true in the fancy trade where novelty and design counted for much and privacy was essential.[42]

Crump and Ghorbal found that, in 1822, 102 manufacturers of fancy goods attended the Huddersfield market, but that none used the Cloth Hall. As they remarked, 'The fancy trade was breaking with the old tradition in this as in other respects.'[43]

As far as design was concerned, the market and the cloth hall had functioned as galleries where small clothiers could learn of recent patterns produced by the more fashion-conscious large clothiers. An example is John Rishworth of Keighley, who was said to have started his business with a small capital. 'It was his custom to carry four or half a dozen pieces on his back to Halifax market,' where 'frequently . . . if he saw anything new, he would take drawing of it on the spot, and when he got home introduce it into his own goods'.[44] This method of spreading new designs became less prominent along with the decline of the cloth hall. According to Heaton, the new system of working to order for merchants and factors was increasingly adopted:

> Buyers were giving out samples or specifications direct to the manufacturers, instead of resorting to the Cloth Market, and so small clothiers were becoming more and more dependent upon the commercial class.[45]

Clothiers felt this new dependence not only in financial matters but also in designing. The selection of patterns for production was usually made in two ways: by the manufacturer's own judgement, and by the merchant's or agent's order. Even when a manufacturer chose a pattern from his designer or pattern collector, he normally submitted his choice to the merchant, who then stated his own preference, making suggestions as to further alterations in colour and style. W. H. Maund and Co. of London, for instance, wrote to J. T. Clay in 1841:

> We received the range of the enclosed Patterns this morning & forward you an order for 12 Pieces, so as to engage it to our selves. The Pattern Marke'd with X is the Pattern we approve & which we will thank you to make to the Colours annexed we think the other too Crowded.[46]

The merchant naturally expected the manufacturer to produce new patterns for the new season. For instance, S. and T. Kesteven of London were anxious to have new patterns, but were disappointed by the samples sent by J. T. Clay in June 1839. They asked the latter to send newer cloths: 'The other patterns you sent were not novel enough to enduce us to select from them. We think you have something newer.'[47] Merchants eagerly looked for fresh patterns and urged manufacturers to waste no time in the production of novelties. East, East and Landon wrote in 1842: 'We trust your earnest attention is engaged in producing Novelties for the winter, they must be entirely new & different altogether from what have been out, for we are convinced that the old style of shawl will not do.'[48] Sometimes a request came for patterns of a certain style: S. and T. Kesteven demanded, 'We want something more 'à la Française.'[49]

When a merchant approved a pattern sent from a manufacturer and thought that it was likely to sell, he would try to secure a monopoly of it. This was called 'engaging the pattern', and once a design was engaged to a particular merchant, it would have been a breach of contract on the part of the manufacturer to sell it to others. W. H. Maund and Co. wrote to J. T. Clay in 1842 that

> We herewith send you an order for such colours as we approve which we shall feel obliged if you will give your best attention & make us 1ps [piece] to ea[each] Patterns, we should like to engage the Pattern but would prefer waiting a little to see what colours are most approved amongst our connexion.[50]

A manufacturer who sold patterns already engaged to other merchants would lose the confidence of his customers. In 1847 East, Landon and Holland ordered from J. T. Clay goods of his design. They warned him incidentally that 'of *course any patterns* we send you in this way, both these & those sent yesterday, we consider strictly our own, & *that no other house* should have them'.[51] Clay added to this letter his own note: 'Style to be engaged to them.'[52] The merchant who engaged patterns in this way could therefore offer exclusive goods to his customers. The unauthorized sale of engaged patterns to other shops did, however, occur from time to time. Thus S. and T. Kesteven wrote to Clay in 1837: 'We observe our engaged Jackaurd [sic] patterns in other houses.'[53] Clarkson

and Turner of London, retailers of a superior class of chintz furnishings, engaged patterns from Swaison and Co., printers. The
number of patterns thus engaged was 'not less than 30, and frequently 80 to 100'.[54] In this instance the retailers were most anxious to obtain original designs, exclusive to themselves, for their
customers included the nobility and gentry who were most particular about their purchases.[55]

The manufacturer would visit his merchants and factors in
London with new patterns before the season commenced. It was
more convenient for buyers to see newly produced cloth in their
shops than to travel to the north. Barber, House and Davis, a
firm of London factors, wrote in 1846 to J.T. Clay:

> Please to inform us when we may expect to see you in
> London, with your new spring patterns, or should you be in
> London shortly upon other Business [we] should like to see
> you having a pattern, [which] we think you can make for
> us, for next spring.[56]

J. T. Clay, when he visited his customers in London, jotted down
memoranda which included not only suggestions for patterns but
also technical advice on how to put them into effect. His notebook,
entitled 'Customers' Ideas', contains the suggestions and requirements of his customers. The pages relating to a 'London Journey'
made in November 1844, in preparation for the spring season,
included a number of suggestions from customers who

> want all Goods made so that they wont shrink. Complained
> that we were too late up for the season. Want some new
> pattern in rich *white silk figured* Cashmere – they also want
> some new patterns in Cashmere – white – Buff – Drab and
> other light grounds for spring trade. . . . Would take 50 ps
> [pieces] of the Cotton wp [warp] Woollen on condition they
> were engaged to them.[57]

The manufacturer could learn a great deal from his journeys to
London, gaining first-hand knowledge of current fashions, the
latest news from Paris, Lyons and other continental cities, and the
kinds of business in which his customers specialized. He could
also, if he was an ambitious entrepreneur, broaden his range of
products by studying shop windows in the fashionable quarters of
London. This was especially true of the manufacturer who did not

129

employ his own designers in London; he had to be his own designer, and in a sense was the arbiter of the taste of his products.

The influence of French patterns on the woollen textile manufacturer and merchant was formidable. Fashion-conscious and enterprising manufacturers and merchants not only kept agents in France, they also crossed the Channel themselves to see the latest fashions in Paris and Lyons. E. M. Sigsworth has described Messrs Foster of Black Dyke Mills, who occasionally visited Paris in the 1860s in order to discover new patterns produced by French designers. A friend of the Fosters, J. C. Hart, of a French merchant house in Paris and Lyons, regularly sent them news of fashion and samples of new patterns, and the Fosters relied heavily on him when preparing for a new season. Sigsworth quotes from their correspondence:

> Enclosed you will find samples . . . also patterns of all our new piece goods in your class, besides a new assortment of new styles in Silk Goods from which you may get ideas. You ought to make your *fortune* at Railway speed now that printed goods are entirely out of fashion here, flounced robes are very much fashionable and will continue to be so.[58]

When Hart left for the United States, the Fosters decided to go to Paris to study the fashions for themselves. They visited the shop of a designer who worked for such manufacturers as Salts, Tootal, Broadhurst and Ackroyds, all of them renowned for their high quality patterns.[59]

But it was merchants, even more than manufacturers, who kept foreign correspondents as a source of information. There is abundant evidence of merchants receiving French samples. Once a merchant liked a particular pattern, he would send a sample to the manufacturer for it to be copied. Bidgood and Jones, for example, wrote to Clay: 'Please copy the enclosed *immediately* they are French just recd and let us see a range of d[ar]k *rich* colorings [as] soon as possible.'[60] They were naturally afraid of their patterns being pre-empted and asked Clay to be 'sure to preserve the pat*n* and *sent it back again*'.[61] Another merchant who wrote to Clay was 'glad you like the French Patterns we sent you', and requested that the pattern should be engaged to him.[62] A merchant would not only send to a manufacturer patterns that the merchant liked but also others which he cared for less. Kennerley and Sons of London, for instance, wrote in 1840: 'We enclose 2 patterns of

Shawls French . . . but we do not think much of them, we thought you would like to see what was going.'[63] And a month later they wrote again to Clay: 'We are in no hurry for the French Shawls but we think both patterns worth your notice for the advanced Autumn trade.'[64]

Agents were sensitive about the quality of the goods they ordered, especially when the patterns were of the French style, as these normally attracted a good sale. An agent would insist that a manufacturer imitated as closely as possible the quality of original French designs. Bidgood and Jones advised Clay, when the expected quality of French imitations was unobtainable, that 'they are not quite equal in richness to the French ones (and it it very desirable they should be)'[65] The merchants seem to have been well acquainted with the processes of weaving, and they would write to the manufacturer with suggestions for possible improvements:

This pat*n* in appearance comes pretty near the French, their cord is rounder than yours, which *I think* may be on account of the yarn forming the cord being harder twisted.[66]

Agents continually expressed confidence in their own taste in their correspondence with manufacturers, sometimes giving very detailed directions to manufacturers to produce as nearly as possible their own requirements. W. Barber, for example, wrote to Clay:

I have enclosed you 2 of the French Patt again, which I think looks better, they appear rather looser on the face, and the figure is triffle larger if you look into it, and a very little press on it, no doubt you will be able to make the piece, near to the French patt*n*, if you observe the 2 small patt*n* you will find the contrast in the colours much better there's more *Blk[black] and darker Green*, which shows the figure much better and throws up the white.[67]

The popular style called 'French pattern' was not necessarily produced in that country. It was, rather, *à la française* in spirit and in taste. John W. Gabriel, showing the shrewd eye of his kind for new design characteristics, wrote in a letter of enquiry to Clay:

The enclosed French pattern is being manufactured by an English house & if it should be yourself & you could send me a price of it by the very first conveyance with patterns of your other colourings I shall be obliged.[68]

SEASONALITY

'The tyranny of fashion' was intensified twice a year, at the commencement of the spring and autumn seasons. Preparation for the season, however, began several months ahead. Agents and factors would write to manufacturers, when one season was at hand, with regard to that which was to follow. The design process, therefore, although affected by the seasonal cycle, especially in the putting-on and engraving departments, continued throughout the year. Designers produced patterns almost every week, although not all the designs went into production. One calico-printer gave evidence that

> There is no month in the year in which we do not produce a considerable number of new patterns, of course more in the spring and autumn; but having a great variety of markets to prepare for, we produce them week by week and month by month, so as constantly to have something new to offer to our customers.[69]

In some branches of calico-printing seasonality did not prevail to the same extent as in the production of garments. The demand for printed handkerchiefs, furnishings and certain luxury goods was constant. One Kent printer, whose chief business was silk-printing but who had also been in the business of printing calico for some years, declared in 1840:

> We have no particular rule in our fancy trade; we endeavour to keep the men employed all the year around; we are not like the great Manchester houses, who have particular days and particular seasons, our pattern is cut and printed at once.[70]

This printer, Augustus Applegath, was renowned for his high quality, elaborate block prints. His testimony suggests that he had regular customers for whom he printed exclusively. The importance of fashion in such a case was not related to heavy seasonal demands, but to the specific requirements of private customers. But, for the large-scale manufacturers, fashion was less predictable and systematic organization of marketing was necessary.

132

The stocking of goods for the spring season began with the new year. W. H. Maund and Co. wrote to Clay that they wanted to receive goods by January, 'as our Travellers leave at that time on their first Spring Journey.'[71] Bidgood and Jones, writing on 4 January, urged their manufacturers to

> Please send up any spring goods of ours that you have ready and large patterns . . . of the others *as soon as you possibly can. You must* give us a better variety of colouring of the pattern *recd this morning.*[72]

In the preceding months business could be quiet, as William Lupton wrote to his agent in Italy, in a letter of 19 December:

> We are sorry to hear that business is dull with you, it has been the case here for two or three weeks past, but it is always so with us at this season of the year & we hope shortly to have a revival, when our Spring demand commences.[73]

The merchants, however, would typically have placed their spring orders even before this date. Kesteven and Sons made it clear, when writing to Clay on 5 October 1836, that they did not want a repeat of the previous year's loss which had been caused by the late delivery of goods:

> We have enclosed two styles we wish you to try a pattern range for next Spring. The design must be considerably reduced, in fact reduced as much as possible to retain the effects. The last pattern produced to our design was most admirably worked . . . if it had been finished sooner [it] would have sold much better.[74]

The firm also complained that Clay had supplied only a scant variety of goods in comparison with other houses.

Business continued to be active during the season itself. One merchant house wrote on 16 May, in forwarding patterns for the autumn season, that they wanted more goods immediately for the current spring season. They exhorted their manufacturer to 'send us the ranges as soon as possible as the Season is advancing'.[75]

June and December were generally regarded as slack periods, being sandwiched between the main seasons. There were, however, exceptions. On 25 June 1831, William Lupton wrote to his agent in Scotland:

> We may here remark that we never felt less inclined to send

out goods that are ordered than we do at this present time – the Country dealers appear to have got the impression that goods are falling, we presume from the idea that this is *generally* a dull season of the year; they are however much mistaken. Goods are continually becoming scarcer & there has scarcely at any time been known a brisker demand than there is now.[76]

One month prior to this letter, Lupton wrote to his Naples agents that 'the advance of Wools in this country since July last year has been so very great – the demand for cloths has been more extensive for some months past than it was ever known to be before,'[77] and he was also very optimistic about the autumn trade. But this prolongation of the season was unusual. As the same merchant's letter of December in the same year shows,[78] the autumn trade was commonly followed by a lull.

The autumn season started in July and lasted until October, but its peak was in August and September. It was necessary that goods for early sale should be delivered by the middle of July. One merchant wrote impatiently to his manufacturer, in a letter of 1 August: 'It is getting very late, we ought to have the goods of this substance in Stock by this time.'[79] When the autumn season was drawing to a close, agents, as in spring, were anxious to receive fresh supplies of cloth which would sell easily. The same merchant urged on 26 September: 'Pray do all you can to supply us with a few *short lengths*, send the next two or three parcels by the *Railway Company*, the carriers keep them about too long.'[80]

In the calico-printing trade, too, seasonality was one of the most significant factors for manufacturers and merchants. Salis Schwabe, a calico-printer who specialized in light goods, stated that he generally began work 'in the Month of June' and then proceeded throughout July and August 'in preparing my designs and drawing them, and then giving them out to engravers'.[81] Since most manufacturers were producing goods not only for home but also for foreign markets, the exhibition of goods for the spring season necessarily started as early as September. It was typical for a firm which exported goods principally to Mexico and the West Indies to start delivery in September, 'to meet the Christmas market'.[82] Schwabe, who exported some of his products to South America, had his first exhibition in October. The spring season for the home market commenced in February,[83] and the taking of orders became brisk in January.[84] This season lasted for six months, until July, when business slackened. During the season, when certain patterns proved successful, the manufacturer would press hard on printers to meet the demand.

CONCLUSION

Fashion was therefore a 'tyranny' for manufacturers and merchants as well as, once successfully employed, the best opportunity to capitalize in increasing profit. They tried to catch the signs of changing taste in the market and to create new demands by responding to it. Those with sound judgement and the ability to adjust themselves to changing fashions produced new designs and products every year, even every season. Their reaction to fashion changes were closely connected with their marketing strategy – and their response to fashion changed along with the development of financial and trading structures. In the early nineteenth-century English textile industry the basic technological changes were completed and, in response to productivity increases, significant changes took place in circulation. The competition became more severe and new types of marketing were required. Against this background merchants began to take the lead in the new field of marketing. They were a different class of merchants from their pre-nineteenth-century counterparts, who had been gentleman-merchants; they traded much more aggressively. Manufacturers were now more subordinate to merchants, as far as the marketing of products was concerned; the manufacturers were innovative and positive about fashion changes but it was always the merchants who dictated the line of designs and fashion for every season. They were the arbiters of taste, and their taste mattered. Manufacturers were there to satisfy the demands of the merchant, and unless they went along with them, they could not sell their goods. The English textile industry thus established a merchant-orientated structure and would maintain it until well into the twentieth century.

NOTES

1 This article was originally given to the Pasold Fund Conference on the 'Social and Economic History of Dress' held in London in 1985, and to ERC-sponsored conference on 'Custom and Commerce' at

Warwick University in 1987. Its Japanese version was also given to the Socio-economic History Society of Japan in 1986. I am extremely grateful to those gave me useful comments and criticism of my paper. I thank particularly Dr Maxine Berg, who gave me a helpful guide for the revision of this paper.

2 D. Cannadine, 'The past and the present in the English Industrial Revolution 1880–1980', *Past and Present*, 103, 1984, discusses the history of the studies of the Industrial Revolution, and clearly shows how past historians were preoccupied with 'production'.

3 N. McKendrick, 'Josiah Wedgwood: an eighteenth-century entrepreneur in salesmanship and marketing techniques', *Economic History Review*, 2nd series, 12, 1960. See also E. Robinson, 'Eighteenth-century commerce and fashion: Matthew Boulton's marketing techniques', *Economic History Review*, 2nd series, 16, 1963–4; N. McKendrick, J. Brewer and J. H. Plumb, *The Birth of a Consumer Society: Commercialization of Eighteenth-Century England*, London, 1982.

4 E. L. Jones, 'The fashion manipulators: consumer tastes and British industries, 1660–1800' in L. P. Cain and P. J. Uselding (eds), *Business Enterprise and Economic Change: Essays in Honour of Harold F. Williamson*, Kent State, 1973, 198.

5 J. Thirsk, 'The fantastical folly of fashion: the English stocking knitting industry, 1500–1700' in N. B. Harte and K. G. Ponting (eds), *Textile History and Economic History*, Manchester, 1973, 50.

6 ibid.

7 H. Perkin, in *The Origins of Modern English Society*, London, 1969, points out the importance of 'consumer demand' and 'social emulation' (91–7) but remains an observer of the phenomenon of 'fashion'.

8 Thirsk, op. cit.

9 D. C. Coleman, 'Textile growth' in Harte and Ponting, op. cit. See also the same author's article, 'An innovation and its diffusion: the "New Draperies" ', *Economic History Review*, 2nd series, 22, 1969.

10 Coleman, 'Textile growth', 9.

11 Thirsk, op. cit., 73.

12 J. Thirsk, *Economic Policy and Projects: The Development of a Consumer Society in Early Modern England*, Oxford, 1978.

13 McKendrick *et al.*, op. cit.

14 J. E. Tennent, *A Treatise on the Copyright of Designs for Printed Fabrics* London, 1841, 24.

15 J. Thomson, *A Letter to the Vice-President of the Board of Trade, on Protection to Original Designs and Patterns, Printed upon Woven Fabrics*, Clitheroe, 1840, 21.

16 Tennent, op. cit., 24.

17 Thomson, op. cit., 21.

18 *Journal of Design and Manufacture*, I, 1849, 4.

19 Tennent, op. cit. 24.

20 F. D. Klingender, *Art and the Industrial Revolution*, London, 1947, (repr. 1972, edited and revised by A. Elton), 40.

21 See, for instance, R. G. Wilson, *Gentlemen Merchants: The Merchant Community in Leeds 1700–1830*, Manchester, 1971; S. D. Chapman,

'Financial restraints on the growth of firms in the cotton industry, 1790–1850', *Economic History Review*, 2nd series, 32, 1979.

22 The following description of the development and the structure of the West Riding wool textile industry is, unless otherwise mentioned, based on J. James, *History of the Worsted Manufacture in England, from the Earliest Times*, London, 1857; R. G. Wilson, op. cit.; P. Hudson, *The Genesis of Industrial Capital: A Study of the West Riding Wool Textile Industry c. 1750–1850*, Cambridge, 1986; E. M. Sigsworth, *Black Dyke Mills: A History*, Liverpool, 1958; D. T. Jenkins, *The West Riding Wool Textile Industry 1770–1835*, Edington, 1975.

23 Hudson, op. cit., 167–74.

24 ibid., 174–81.

25 E. Collinson, *The History of the Worsted Trade, and Historical Sketch of Bradford*, Bradford, 1854, 80–1.

26 The following paragraphs on the calico-printing industry are based on the accounts of S. D. Chapman, op. cit.; S. J. Chapman, *The Lancashire Cotton Industry*, Manchester, 1904; E. Baines, *History of the Cotton Manufacture in Great Britain*, London 1835; M. M. Edwards, *The Growth of the British Cotton Trade, 1780–1815*, Manchester, 1967; J. H. Clapham, *An Economic History of Modern Britain*, Cambridge, 1926.

27 W. Radcliffe, *Origins of Power Loom Weaving*, Stockport, 1828, 131.

28 S. D. Chapman, op. cit., 52.

29 S. J. Chapman, op. cit., 136.

30 ibid., 138–9.

31 S. D. Chapman, op. cit., 54.

32 P. L. Payne, *British Entrepreneurship in the Nineteenth Century*, London, 1974, 43.

33 H. Heaton, 'The Leeds White Cloth Hall', *Thoresby Society*, xxii, Leeds, 1915.

34 R. G. Wilson, 'The supremacy of the Yorkshire cloth industry in the eighteenth century' in Harte and Ponting, op. cit., 241.

35 Daniel Defoe, *A Tour Thro' the Whole Island of Great Britain*, ed. by G. D. H. Cole, 1927, 612.

36 C. Gill, 'The Blackwell Hall factors, 1795–1799', *Economic History Review*, 2nd Series, 6, 1954, 274.

37. ibid., 276.

38 Hudson, op. cit., 156–7.

39 Heaton, op. cit., 168.

40 ibid., 160–1.

41 J. Aiken, *A Description of the Country from 30 to 40 miles around Manchester*, London 1795, 554.

42 W. P. Crump and G. Ghorbal, *History of the Huddersfield Woollen Industry*, Huddersfield, 1935, repr. 1967, 102.

43 ibid., 108.

44 J. Hodgson, *Textile Manufactures and Other Industries in Keighley*, Keighley, 1879, 145.

45 Heaton, op. cit., 168.

46 W. H. Maund to J. T. Clay, 1 November 1841, J. T. Clay and

Co., Business Letters (Central Public Library, Archive Department, Halifax), CLA: 19.

47 S. and T. Kesteven to Clay, 29 June 1839, CLA: 24.
48 East, East and Landon to Clay, 9 April 1842, CLA: 47.
49 Kesteven to Clay, 13 June 1841, CLA: 25.
50 Maund to Clay, 12 December 1842, CLA: 19.
51 East, Landon and Holland, 15 June 1847, CLA: 49.
52 ibid.
53 Kesteven to Clay, 8 May 1837, CLA: 23.
54 *Minutes of Evidence taken before the Select Committee on the Copyright of Designs, Parliamentary Papers*, 1840, vi (hereafter PP 1840), Q. 2160.
55 ibid., Q. 2081.
56 Barber, House and Davis to Clay, 29 July 1846, CLA: 65.
57 'Customers' Ideas' 1844–7, 8 November 1844, CLA: 70.
58 Sigsworth, op. cit., 326.
59 ibid., 327.
60 Bidgood and Jones to Clay, 5 July 1842, CLA: 32.
61 ibid.
62 Maund to Clay, 12 December 1842, CLA: 19.
63 Kennerley and Sons to Clay, 18 March 1840, CLA: 38.
64 ibid., 25 April 1840, CLA: 38.
65 Bidgood and Jones to Clay, 12 June 1841, CLA: 31.
66 ibid., 14 December 1842, CLA: 32.
67 W. Barber to Clay, 6 July [n.d.], CLA: 63.
68 J. W. Gabriel to Clay, 18 October 1844, CLA: 61.
69 PP 1840, Q. 3652.
70 ibid., Q. 2996.
71 Maund to Clay, undated, CLA: 19.
72 Bidgood and Jones to Clay, January 1841, CLA: 30–1.
73 Lupton to *Cde* Binard of Leghorn, 19 December 1831, William Lupton Correspondence (Brotherton Library, University of Leeds), vol. 19.
74 Kesteven to Clay, 5 October 1836, CLA: 23.
75 Maund to Clay, 16 May 1843, CLA: 19.
76 Lupton to John Stewart of Glasgow, 25 June 1831, Lupton, vol. 19.
77 Lupton to Fr. Trabuchi and Muck, 12 May 1831, Lupton, vol. 19.
78 See note 73.
79 Bidgood and Jones to Clay, 1 August 1840, CLA: 30–1.
80 ibid., 26 September 1840, CLA: 30–1.
81 PP 1840, Q. 92.
82 ibid., Q. 3241.
83 ibid., Q. 97.
84 ibid., Qs. 99, 101.

6

THE ORGANIZATION OF SEWING OUTWORK IN LATE NINETEENTH-CENTURY ULSTER

Brenda Collins

Traditional accounts of the success of the linen industry in the north of Ireland have usually delineated its expansion in terms of spinning mill and weaving factory production. This emphasis on yarn and cloth output has tended to underestimate the contribution of the making-up trades which were an integral part of the linen industry. Even within the academic debates on proto-industrialization, the distinction is commonly blurred between the contribution of the component stages of production. Thus, in textile production, outwork has been considered in terms of what it contributed to a central workshop or proto-factory rather than as a system of manufacture in its own right and subject to the operations of the market place. Yet it was precisely the outwork products which encountered the volatility of consumer choice to a degree not experienced in either yarn or cloth production. The widespread continuance of sewing outwork in the making up and embellishment of clothing and household drapery during the nineteenth and early twentieth centuries in Ulster is therefore of interest in any analysis of the connections between industrial change and market structures.

The outwork organization was not based on some unilinear progress towards a factory system but was embedded in social institutions and non-economic values which defined frameworks of perception. These took differing forms in the two aspects of sewing outwork discussed here. First, in the hand embroidery industry of north-west Donegal, the organization and distribution of the work took place within a paradigm of close-knit community relationships which reinforced local power structures and which was eventually institutionalized by state involvement. In the second case, the expansion of the shirt industry in the same geographical region affords a contrast in its technical duality of hand and machine production which permitted internal flexibility in product development. The persistence of both industries, almost as anachronisms, into the twentieth century, may suggest that regional success does not altogether imply transformation to full-scale industrialization.[1]

I

Linen manufacture in the north of Ireland expanded initially with the rural household as a complete production unit, from the growth of flax to the sale of woven brown (unbleached) cloth at linen markets. The application of the process of machine spinning to flax in the 1820s extended, through the putting-out system, the viability of the rural hand loom weaving households in those areas near to spinning mills. In the two decades before 1845 the continued livelihood from hand loom weaving and the dependence on the potato as a main food item encouraged population increase; only after the Irish Famine, when the rate of population growth slackened substantially, were power looms introduced to the industry and the weaving sector began to be centralized, as spinning already had been, in factories and mills in Belfast and other towns of east Ulster.[2]

Sewing and making up became an integral part of linen manufacture. The outwork sewing or needle trades can be categorized into two types of activity, embroidery (fancy stitches, flowering, sprigging) and sewing (plain stitches and seams), both processes which used hand and machine technology. This categorization admittedly owes more to the late nineteenth-century confusion in the Census classification of occupations based on industrial type than it may ever have done to reality; its application to Ireland defined seaming and shirt-making as part of *dress-making*, and embroidery as part of the residual *mixed materials* class. Throughout the earlier part of the century, too, the problems of ambiguity of definition between plain and fancy stitches as well as the inevitable under-recording of self-defined outworkers combine to make any strict assessment of the chronology and spatial location of the industry too sweeping. Several aspects, however, stand out with consistency: first, sewing as wage labour became a widespread activity occupying between one in four and one in nine working women and girls between 1850 and 1914; second, although the sewing industry was originally situated in Co. Down, its rapid expansion in the 1840s involved a once and for all shift to the north-west counties of Donegal, Londonderry and Tyrone; third, those latter three counties (together with Co. Down) retained their pre-eminence even as absolute numbers fell at the end of the period and, in particular, the shirt industry dominated Derry city and its immediate hinterland.

Table 6.1 Spatial distribution of women sewers in Ulster 1841–1911

%	1841	1851	1861	1871	1881	1901	1911
			(Shirt ind.)*				
Down	63	29	29	2	24	27	22	21
Donegal	2	13	17	40	21	19	27	15
Londonderry	3	8	12	27	13	14	16	17
Tyrone	4	12	13	22	13	11	12	10
Belfast	N/A	N/A	N/A	–	N/A	7	13	29
Other counties	28	38	29	9	29	22	15	8
Total in 000s	29	125	92	7	67	52	49	31

Sources: 1841 Census, PP 1843, xxiv; 1851 Census, PP 1856, xxxi; 1861 Census, PP 1863, lxi; 1871 Census, PP 1874, lxxiv, pt 1; 1881 Census PP 1882, lxxviii; 1901 Census, PP 1902, cxxvi and cxxvii; 1911 Census, PP 1912–13, cxvi.

Note: Sewers include sewed muslin workers, embroiderers, seamstresses, shirt-makers and fancy goods (textile) workers.

*It is only possible to show figures for the shirt industry for the year 1861 because these figures were not published separately before or since.

The origins of sewing for the market lay with the development of the late eighteenth- and early nineteenth-century mechanized cotton industry in Belfast and the west of Scotland.[3] The widespread use in Ireland of the term 'Ayrshire needlework' to describe embroidery on fine cotton muslin for dresses confirms that the connection extended beyond the merchant level down to the rural workforce through the putting-out networks by which hand loom cotton weavers and embroiderers obtained work. These networks were especially strong over an area up to thirty miles from Belfast in Co. Down. With the changeover from cotton to linen production in Belfast in the late 1820s, several of the largest sewed muslin warehouse owners moved their headquarters to Glasgow and continued to put out work in Ulster. Several other Scottish merchants established agencies in Ulster, through patronage, industrial schools and urban warehouses. The latter were viable only in Belfast and other towns where there was a steady supply of labour within walking distance. Their hold, however, was crucial in the dissemination of basic skills and providing knowledge of a loose structure of economic opportunity for agent, girl worker and ultimately the merchant. One sewed muslin firm in Armagh city employed four hundred girls over the period 1837–43 and those who had left their premises continued to take work from the warehouse to sew at home. The school at Dungannon, Co. Tyrone, had between fifty and sixty children on its books and one hundred more 'outside' who 'having been trained in it [the school] are furnished with muslin to flower at home for which they are paid as when at school'.[4] Agencies were also established which were based on a commercial relationship, such as those of the weekly urban linen markets, and the numbers employed in the linen industry increased dramatically between 1841 and 1851. It was estimated in the 1850s that there were about fifty Scots and Irish warehouse owners employing four to five hundred agents, many of whom acted on behalf of more than a single warehouse.[5] Most of the Irish work for the Scottish warehouse was said to be exported from Glasgow to London and abroad as 'Scotch work',[6] and hence the significance of the Irish contribution to the industry was lost.

Several exogenous factors combined in the late 1850s to remove the Scottish base of the industry and thereby to change the end result from a cotton to a linen product. The immediate cause was a financial crisis in 1857 in the USA, which was the destination of most of the embroidery exports. Wholesale warehouses became overstocked with goods, whose prices fell rapidly. In these changing market circumstances, competition from the Swiss machine embroidery industry was effective in drawing away the higher end of the trade. Finally, the American Civil War interrupted the availability of cotton supplies, leaving open the possibilities of substitution. Just as Irish linen yarn and cloth production expanded in the late 1860s, taking up sales opportunities in the markets left open by the diminution in cotton production, so also did the embroidery and making up of fine linen goods expand in Ulster using the existing trading networks and establishing others.[7]

II

During the 1860s and 1870s in Ulster, embroidery and sewing on fine cambrics for clothing and heavier linen cloths for household drapery both intensified and became more extensive under an outwork system of production. It intensified in terms of increasing output to meet the clear indication of increasing demand from the middle classes in Europe and America. Household furnishing and individual adornment had always been badges of status; what was new about the late nineteenth century was the extent to which mass sales dictated mass, in the sense of extensive, production. The industrial dualism which this implied arose because of the need to supply an extended variety of choice for consumers. The development of American and European consumer demand for fashion in the sense of changes in style required the customizing of the product which was, in the nineteenth century, the antithesis of intensive mechanization. The degree to which the sewing industries were consumer dominated is illustrated by the report of the Irish consul in Portland, Oregon to the Department of Agricultural and Technical Instruction in Ireland in 1907. 'The superiority of British [subsumes Irish] goods in the higher grades is unquestioned but their sale is necessarily limited. It is the great middle class consumption which tells . . . all other things being equal, the patterns at once decide the choice.'[8]

The Irish industry competed in the international markets with German, Austrian and Swiss production which had been widely mechanized with foot-(treadle-) operated embroidery machines as early as the 1840s. It was only in the immediate pre–1914 period that such machines began to be adopted on an indoor warehouse basis in Belfast, copying the continental examples.[9] The lateness and slowness of mechanization can be explained by the degree to which hand-made goods retained a novelty value for the purchaser so that the advantages of longer production runs and lower retail prices to some extent cancelled each other out. But where novelty implied variety, its production under an outwork system also implied uncontrollability, both of workers and of the dissemination of design. Herein lay a dilemma recognized by the warehouse owners whose marketing decisions took into account their lack of authority over their outdoor workers and the difficulties of propagating good (that is, profitable) standards of design.[10]

The numbers ever employed as embroidery outworkers and

agents in north-west Ulster are impossible to obtain with total accuracy. This was due to the ambiguous position of outworkers and home workers in relation to the various Factory (Extension) and Workshops Acts of the later nineteenth century. District councils and employers were required by law, in 1901 and 1906 respectively, to keep lists of their outworkers. Councillors, who were often employers as well, tended, with a few notable exceptions, to the view that this was impossible because of the undefined relationship between the outworker and her ultimate payer of wages. A reasonable estimate would be 25,000–30,000 workers in good times throughout the period, falling to half that number on occasion. One government committee in 1912 listed 117 agents in north-west Ulster; however, the problem of estimation was compounded by the tendency of agents to 'give employment to hundreds of people, many of whom, probably, work for other agents also'.[11] Moreover, the numbers of workers also varied in relation to the annual rural work cycle. Most of the embroidery workers were the wives and daughters of agricultural labourers and farmers of small pastoral farms so their labour was required, first, for planting and harvesting food crops for household consumption and also, in the summer months, for running the farms while the men were seasonal migrants in great Britain. They were thus 'freer' to turn to sewing in the winter months of the year. The October–November period of every year provided the steadiest availability and highest piecework rates, while the March–May period generally saw output reduced by at least one-third. Thus outwork and Ulster farming practice dovetailed exceedingly well on the supply side. Market demand, however, was intensely seasonal, and varied according to export destinations. While the home trade was recognized as being more regular, the American trade peaked for a month in spring and again in autumn. The southern hemisphere trade made opposing demands on the calendar.[12]

The matching supply to demand was borne by the merchant warehouse owners, mainly in Belfast, who stored the goods and employed indoor staff to launder, finish and pack them for transportation. In order to play this role, the merchant warehouse owners retained flexibility in their indoor workforce also, by generally working under hours (i.e. below the maximum permitted under the Factory and Workshops Acts), so that when orders were required they could increase output by temporary overtime, rather than by taking on extra workers. As one managing director of a

Belfast firm which combined all the stages of cloth production expressed it, 'We to some extent protect ourselves by employing more than we actually want at other times, in order to meet this pressure.'[13] The firms which combined the spinning, weaving and ornamentation processes in one ownership were those which were best able to handle flexibility in the narrow sense of shifting production from one product to another within a range of linen goods.

With this type of production process, therefore, it would be farcical to attempt to estimate weekly, average or even typical earnings. 'Exceptional' earnings were 2s 6d per day in 1857, 10s per week in 1914 – and there seems to be a general reiteration over the period that 1s per day or 5s per week was a common, if not typical wage. At the same time, 9d per day was described as 'usual' and many 'older women' earned 3d–6d.[14] Over the sixty years after 1850, piecework prices seem to have varied little, except between the seasons. Earnings were thus determined solely by availability of work and by the availability of time to do it. Girls who 'sit constant' at their work managed perhaps an eight-hour day, but constancy over more than a few weeks was unlikely in view of the competing land and domestic obligations. Nor were the piecework rates such that more detailed work paid a higher return to the embroiderer. This seems to have been because of the power with which the large USA retail firms dictated their wholesale purchasing strategies:

> An American buyer gives a large order for a particular class of goods and because of the size of the order he expects the price charged to be small. The manufacturer accepts the order in order that he may not lose smaller and better paid orders, but the transaction entails that an immense amount of work is sent out for which a low price is paid.[15]

In addition, in the First World War period, the USA imposed tariffs of 60 per cent on all imported finished embroidered goods, whether produced by hand or machine. This acted adversely on the sales of the higher quality imported Irish articles and depressed wages, 'a cheap coarse roughly embroidered cushion cover bringing in a higher wage to the worker than the expensive finely embroidered handkerchief or tray cloth'. Girl embroiderers demonstrated their distance from a craft tradition in assessing the relationship between their earnings and their labour by describing the former work as 'good' and the latter as 'bad'.[16]

The agency system was a vital part of the structure of this section of Ulster society. Agents received the cut-out but unfinished goods with the patterns stamped on them, and the thread for distribution to the outworkers. They commonly worked on a 10 per cent commission on the value of the wages they paid out. The agents received an invoice with the work and were expected by the suppliers to pay the stated wages, but this could only be verified in the rare cases where the price was stamped on the cloth. Because the agents had to pay the one-way carriage of the goods some may have been inclined to exact fines arbitrarily for poorer quality work. In addition some agents, presumably in order to avoid their own travelling costs in distributing the work, used subagents who did not receive a commission and looked for a return for their involvement in regular work for themselves.

In this type of economic relationship much depended on trust and goodwill. One of the first lady factory inspectors, Miss Hilda Martindale, who took a special interest in the condition of Irish outworkers, summarized their weak position: 'The workers receive work many times a day and the prices they receive vary considerably, and as they are often paid only once a fortnight they complain that . . . they are unable to compute the amount of their earnings.'[17] However, one of the most important aspects of the agency system was the brake it put on the development of conventional commercial relationships. Miss Martindale was told that 'to give out sprigging is a very profitable employment, and that the development of a shop has been rapid once an agency has been obtained . . . the district [west of Donegal town] is almost studded with little shops in which sprigging for distribution to outworkers is to be seen on the shelves, and in the windows, together with the ordinary groceries and draperies'.[18] The sewing agency brought custom to the shop while the customers who dealt regularly with a shopkeeper expected him to provide them with sewing work. Often the payment in coin by the agent to the worker was immediately returned, in whole or in part, as payment for goods in the shop. A dispensary nurse described the position in 1908:

> All the agents round here have shops and they will only give their best work to customers . . . only yesterday a girl came to me and said 'You're doing sprigging for Mr A and you'll have to leave all your money with him, for he has said he's going to give out no more work to a sewer unless she gives

the money back to him.' I said, 'I'll spend my money where
I like', but you see I'm not dependent on the sprigging, but
the poor folk who are have to spend it all at the agent's
shop.[19]

Thus the relationship of employed to employer was integral to the
relationship of customer to shopkeeper. 'Indeed and it's ashamed
I'd be not to leave my wages at the shop.'[20]

Such commercial relationships underlined the centrality of the
rural trader in determining the status of individuals through the
provision of goods. They were reinforced by the general lack of
ready cash in a household economy which depended on subsistence
production, with the major inputs of money, apart from sewing
earnings, being the cyclical earnings from emigration and farm
service. This brought about a general reliance on credit which
took the form of supplying dry goods such as tea, sugar, flour and
draperies and requiring the outworker to pay off her debts by
means of her work.[21] This undoubtedly evaded the spirit, if not
the letter, of the Truck Acts but the agency structure continued,
even after a notoriously successful legal prosecution against a
Donegal outwork employer in 1899. As agents of industrial discipline, the Irish justices were by no means unambivalent about the
lady inspectors; an Irish QC declared in 1900 that they were 'an
army squatted round Dungloe, watching every little industry and
striving to throttle them'.[22] Indeed, the long-term outcome of the
prosecution was precisely the opposite of the intentions of the lady
inspectors, in strengthening these aspects of the agency system by
placing outworkers in Ireland outside the protection of the Truck
Acts, except where there was a direct contract of service between
them and the central supplier. This perpetuated economic practices which ordered the labour market in a way far beyond that
of economic rationality. The close-knit nature of community
relationships reinforced the multiple levels of social bargaining
between agent/shopkeeper and embroiderer/customer. Equally
these bargains reinforced patterns of trust and networks of aid.[23]

III

Contemporaneous with the intensification of outwork embroidery
was the extension of the other major needle trade, the making up
of men's shirts and ladies' underclothing. The technological

advance of mechanized sewing created production possibilities where they had not existed before and also extended them beyond their original boundaries. This was true of the better documented case of the London 'sweated' clothing trades and also of the development of the Derry shirt industry, both of which are examples of 'industrial districts' whose viability rested on the existence of dual technology.[24]

The industry began in the hands of two or three firms in Derry city in the 1840s and 1850s. In 1861 the area around Derry city contained nearly 90 per cent of all the shirt workers in Ulster and this pattern continued until after the Second World War. Built into its structure from the outset was a combination of indoor and outdoor workers and, in contrast to the embroiderers, hand and machine technology. The combination was not transitional or subordinate to mechanization as the organization of production in this way made maximum use of all inputs – capital, technology and labour. Men's shirts and ladies' underclothing were the first garments to be mass manufactured using the concept of proportional body measurements. This was an important advance, raising the quality and thus extending the demand for such items of clothing. Men's shirts were the paramount example of this application, because their construction could be varied within an essentially limited number of standard-sized pieces of cloth. This conceptual advance was allied with the invention and application of a steam-powered cutting machine in the 1860s. Cutting out was an inside process, being dependent on power; it was therefore highly controllable in terms of volume of output and design.[25] Production grew dramatically, though precise statistics are difficult to obtain with any consistency. In 1867 it was reckoned that 2,000 were employed within the Derry factories and 10,000 sewers in the counties of Londonderry, Donegal and Tyrone. In 1875 there were 4,000 to 5,000 indoor employees and 12,000 to 15,000 outdoor workers. By 1902 Coyne estimated 18,000 indoor workers and over 60,000 in rural districts.[26]

The introduction of sewing machines was crucial to implementing the semi-customization required to market a mass-produced garment to a growing number of urban white collar workers. The first batch of foot-operated treadle machines was installed in a Derry factory in 1856, when there were estimated to be only about three thousand machines available throughout the world. This anticipated by at least a decade the diffusion of the sewing machine in the London clothing trades. Not only did foot-treadle and hand-operated machines speed up production by at least five times the rate of hand sewers but, because the precise capabilities of the machine were initially confined to straight seaming, they redefined the subdivision of tasks in the overall production process. Final making-up required the detail of hand finishing of buttons and front bands and 'of course, from the technical nature of the trade, a large amount of the best work is done by hand'.[27] The use of the sewing machine also perpetuated the structural advantages of the outdoor shirt worker by moving the potential bottleneck in the supply chain just one stage further along, in only partly making up the goods. Thus the ratio of outworkers to factory workers in the shirt industry was five to one in the 1860s, declining only to three to one in the 1870s, a ratio which was maintained until after 1914. Ladies' underclothing was even more of an outwork industry, with about 85 per cent of its workforce outside the factory.

Nor was the distinction complete between factory=machine and outwork=hand. Hand sewing work continued within the factory while, by the 1890s, sewing machines were used outside the factory setting. The application of steam power to sewing machines in the Derry shirt industry had only a limited impact on this structure because of the tightness of integration between factory and outwork which was achieved by the use of the lower technology machine. Even in the 1860s the largest Derry city factory owners recognized that inanimate power provided 'uniformity of pace and regularity of stitching . . . where no two persons work exactly the same'.[28] This gave them an advantage in productivity over smaller workshops without power, because the women 'have nothing to do but plant their feet upon the spring and the machine goes . . . whereas it is very fatiguing and very injurious to the health of delicate women driving some of the sewing machines eight or nine hours a day by the foot'.[29] However, there was continuing competition from the smaller workshops and factories which were not subject to the same regulations regarding hours as those larger ones under the Factory and Workshops Acts. In addition coal had to be imported at a comparatively high cost. These factors served to stave off the tremendous degree of reorganization required fully to adopt powered machine technology.[30]

Although the deliberate development of the shirt and ladies' underclothing industries based on a combination of factory and outwork labour seems an anachronism in the late nineteenth century, the business decisions were also based on the labour supply. 'Considerably over 80 per cent of the persons engaged are females, and it is always difficult to get a large supply of female labour unless there is work in the neighbourhood for their male relatives.'[31] In this respect, Derry was compared unfavourably with Belfast, where the linen, shipbuilding and engineering industries provided complementary job opportunities. An immobile rural workforce, accustomed to the networks of distribution of sewing, therefore fulfilled a crucial role.

There were several methods of supplying the outwork. First, indoor workers in the shirt factories were encouraged to take work home for others in their family to complete. This was seen by both factory owners and workers as a means of reinforcing the household as a production unit. 'That is one thing which enables the business to succeed so well, as it enables parents to employ children under their own roof, and give them a profitable and clean employment'.[32] Many of the workers walked four or five miles daily from their parents' homes,[33] and, to allow for this, the working hours of the shirt factories were kept deliberately low (in comparison with spinning mills, even after they were brought under the same regulations), at 51 hours per week, with a late starting time, after breakfast, of 8 a.m. The short hours meant that those who were able to take work home in this way were, in effect, often able to double their potential earnings contribution to the household budget.

Second, the larger city firms established agencies in a forty-mile radius in the countryside. Agents were representatives of the various firms but were paid a salary rather than relying on commission. Few overlapped with the embroidery agencies, for there seem to have been distinctive locations for each. As with embroidery, the numbers of workers on the books was probably, at the most, two-thirds of all those who actually did the work. The supply of work from the shirt factories was much less seasonally erratic because the factory owners chose to keep up a stock of shirts. This was possible because shirts and associated clothing were not so subject to the tyranny of fashion. Nevertheless, this had the effect of making the possibility of earnings more continuous for the outworker. Typical earnings throughout a year seem to have been 4s or 5s per week and work patterns seem to have been more regularized than with the embroidery, with the sewers in a household doing little else, 'other members of the family doing the housework'. [34] Thus there was a transfer of work patterns of discipline from the factory to the household, which actually strengthened the viability of the small farming household.

A third way in which sewing was distributed, particularly in the underclothing industry, was through outstations in Limavady, Strabane, Letterkenny and other small towns and villages of northwest Ulster. These were staffed by salaried employees of the Derry city firms. Chas Bayer & Co., who were leading underclothing manufacturers in the pre–1914 period, employed three or four thousand outworkers through their stations. Some girls worked in the stations, which were really warerooms or sheds, while others took work from them to do at home. The major characteristic of the outstation structure as opposed to the agency network was that the former extended the sewing machine technology to the outworkers. Some firms supplied machines free to outworkers on condition of a guaranteed return of finished goods. By the end of the period a hire purchase system was common, where machines were supplied by the factory owner and eventually became the workers' own property. Once a woman owned a machine in her own home she was free to take work from anyone and also to clothe herself and her family. The household's function in production and consumption was thus totally interconnected and reinforced.

However, in contrast to the embroidery industry, the structure of organization of outwork in the shirt and underclothing industries did not depend on transactions built on multiple relationships. Work was given out with a price affixed, and this was paid providing the goods were completed and returned within the required time period, which was usually one week. Whether the outwork was distributed in the factory or by agents or salaried employees, the transaction was confined to the defined monetary value of the labour rather than existing as part of a set of customary role relationships. A contemporary guide to Irish commercial development gave approval to the underclothing industry that it was conducted on 'business lines'.[35] Why there should have been this contrast is not clear. It may have been related to the relative spatial closeness of the rural shirt and underclothing workers to their employers in Derry city, compared with the 80–100 miles distance in the networks sending embroidery work from Belfast. If workers were distant from the control of their employer, the multiple levels of social bargaining would act as an alternative method of work discipline. In contrast, the shirt workers' patterns of labour and distribution were more tightly organized and bureaucratic. As important in permitting bureaucracy, which was seen in the standardization of work and wage patterns within the industry, was the nature of the product. Whether using hand or machine sewing, the shirt and underclothing production gave a much more standardized end product compared with the ornamentation of embroidered goods. This permitted objective standards of quality control and appropriate uniform piecework rates which could not be applied to home embroiderers. The product thus determined the organization of production.

IV

Sewing outwork in north-west Ulster intensified during the second half of the nineteenth century, not only despite, but also because of, the industrialization of the Belfast area. Certainly, the census statistics of the turn of the century would suggest that there was a gradual shift from a rural-based sewing industry to a city base, where outworkers were only a residual part of the whole textile workforce. However, the framework of the organization of the sewing trades was much more enduring because, as was argued above, it was crucial to the continuance of rural society. Indeed, outwork in the country districts expanded numerically between 1881 and 1901.[36] Moreover, the extension of a rail network reduced distribution costs and so made flexible production more accessible to the manufacturers and exporters of the Belfast area.

The extent and type of outwork in any community seems to have depended on a combination of geography, local actors and networks. The one consistent feature of the rural communities was the level and regularity of men's earnings. Where the majority of family men were labourers and small farmers, with limited opportunities for wage labour or cash from the sale of farm produce, then outwork became the cash crop. Together with male seasonal migration it provided a substantial proportion of the cash input in a household budget. Commentators universally agreed that though families were not dependent on sewing outwork yet it made an important contribution by 'enabling the family to live when it could not live from its other sources of income'.[37] For this reason, the Congested Districts Board, which was set up by the government in 1891 to examine means of raising the living standards of communities in the north-west and west of Ireland, took as one of its model budgets a family where 18 per cent of the annual cash receipts were derived from home industries.[38] In particular, the outwork sewing stations were emphasized as leading to 'a marked improvement all round – physical, social, mental'. Cash earnings were spent on improving home comforts and on better dress, accepting, at a distance, the standards of late nineteenth-century urbanization:

> Young women, too, find it pays to consider themselves . . . overcoming their natural reluctance. They no longer, where [sewing] work can be obtained . . . assist in field labour save perhaps just at harvest time. It roughens their hands for fine work; so does baking the domestic oatcakes and they encourage the carts of the Derry bakers. They become smarter in appearance and more civilized altogether.[39]

On a wider level, the earnings from outwork are widely supposed to have been used to finance emigration passages to America and Australia. Certainly, in the period 1890–1911, female emigration from Co. Donegal was at a much higher level than male emigration. Paradoxically, outwork also enabled those who stayed behind to better themselves. After the land legislation of the 1880s there were opportunities for small tenant farmers to buy their land and many did so with the aid of their womenfolk's earnings from sewing outwork.[40] The organization of sewing outwork thus helped to create the adult generation of 'peasant proprietors' in rural Ulster immediately before the First World War – a generation which displayed more stability than had perhaps been evident since the daisy days of hand loom weaving almost a century earlier.

NOTES

1 The linen industry in Ulster could well be classified as an 'industrial district' (A. Marshall, *Industry and Trade*, London, 1919). The article by C. Sabel and J. Zeitlin 'Historical alternatives to mass production', *Past and Present*, 108, 1985, 133–76, reinforces many of the interpretations given above, while useful comparisons are provided by J. Schlumbohm, 'Seasonal fluctuations and social division of labour: rural linen production in the Osnabrück and Bielefeld regions and the urban woollen industry in the Niederlausitz (*c*.1770–*c*.1850), in M. Berg, P. Hudson and M. Sonenscher (eds), *Manufacture in Town and Country before the Factory*, Cambridge, 1983.
2 B. Collins, 'Proto-industrialization and pre-Famine emigration', *Social*

153

BRENDA COLLINS

History, 7, 2, 1982, 127–46. L. Kennedy and P. Ollerenshaw (eds), *An Economic History of Ulster 1820–1939*, Manchester, 1985.

3 See B. Collins, 'Sewing and social structure: the flowerers of Scotland and Ireland' in P. Roebuck and R. Mitchison (eds), *Economy and Society in Scotland and Ireland 1500–1939*, Edinburgh, 1988. Also H. McCall, *Our Staple Manufactures*, Belfast, 1855 and E. R. R. Green, *The Lagan Valley*, Manchester, 1949. This paper does not pretend to be exhaustive. In particular the handkerchief industry awaits analysis and interpretation.

4 *Children's Employment Commission*, Appendix to Second Report, pp. 1843, xv, n54, n68.

5 J. Strang, 'On the rise, progress and value of the embroidered muslin manufacture of Scotland and Ireland', *Transactions of the British Association*, 27, 1857, 167.

6 Mr and Mrs S. C. Hall, *Ireland, Its Scenery, Character etc.*, iii, London, 1843, 85.

7 E. Boyle, 'Linenopolis: the rise of the textile industry' in J. C. Beckett *et al.*, *Belfast: The making of the City 1800–1914*, Belfast, 1983, 41–55.

8 *Department of Agricultural and Technical Instruction, Ireland, Journal*, iii, 1902–3.

9 In 1909 the DATI sent a representative to Switzerland and the Austrian Tyrol to examine the possibility of establishing machine embroidery in Ulster organized along the Swiss lines in order to recapture the embroidery orders which Belfast manufacturers were placing abroad. (DATI *The Machine Embroidery Trade in Switzerland and Austrian Tyrol*, Dublin, 1909, Introduction.) There is a photograph of one of the embroidery 'factories' established in rural Ulster as a result of this investigation in W. A. Maguire, *Caught in Time*, Belfast, 1986. The exterior and its interior machinery bear a striking resemblance to the photographs in the DATI pamphlet.

10 See R. Price, 'Structures of subordination in nineteenth-century British industry' in P. Thane, G. Crossick and R. Floud (eds), *The Power of the Past*, Cambridge, 1984.

11 *Royal Commission on Labour*, Reports on the Employment of Women, PP 1893–4, xxxvii pt 1, X, Donegal, 327.

12 ibid. See also *Children's Employment Commission*, PP 1866, xxiv, Fifth Report. Mr Lord's report and evidence on warehouses in Bradford and Belfast; *Committee on the Insurance of Outworkers (Ireland)*, PP 1914–16, xxxi, Report i, 10, 15, 17.

13 *Children's Employment Commission*, PP 1866, xxiv, Fifth Report, 191. York Street Spinning Company Ltd.

14 *Insurance of Outworkers*, PP 1914–16, xxxi, evidence of Dr Mowbray and Appendix iv.

15 *Factories and Workshops Annual Report for 1907*, PP 1908, xii, Principal Lady Inspectors' Report. *Appendix IV. Truck and Gombeening in Donegal* (by Miss Martindale), 216.

16 *Machine Embroidery in Switzerland*, op. cit., 5–6; *Truck and Gombeening*, op. cit., 216; M. H. Irwin, *Homework in Ireland*, Glasgow, 1913, 21.

17 *Factories Report, 1907*, op. cit., 193.

18 *Truck and Gombeening*, op. cit., 214.

19 ibid., 217.

20 ibid.

21 L. Kennedy, 'Retail markets in rural Ireland at the end of the nineteenth century', *Irish Economic and Social History*, V, 1978, 46–63.

22 A. Anderson, *Women in the Factory*, London, 1922, 81.

23 See the reference to the work of C. Geertz in P. Joyce, 'Introduction' in P. Joyce (ed.), *The Historical Meanings of Work*, Cambridge, 1987. The importance of the shopkeeper in Irish rural society is excellently described in H. Brody, *Inishkillane*, Harmondsworth, 1973, while M. D. McFeely, *Lady Inspectors*, Oxford, 1988 uses the lady inspectors' diaries to reach similar conclusions to my own.

24 See S. Lilley, 'Technological progress and the Industrial Revolution 1700–1914', *Fontana Economic History of Europe*, III, London, 1970, chap. 3. J. Smiechen, *Sweated Industries and Sweated Labour*, London, 1984. Sabel and Zeitlin, op. cit.

25 A. Baron and S. E. Klepp, 'If I didn't have my sewing machine' in J. M. Jenson and S. Davidson (eds) *A Needle, a Bobbin, a Strike*, Temple, Pa, 1984, 20–59.

26 E.H. Slade, 'A History of the Londonderry Shirt Industry', M. A. thesis, Belfast, 1937, 31. *Report of the Commission on Factories and Workshops Acts*, PP 1876, xxx, vol. II, qn. 17297. W. Coyne, *Ireland Agricultural And Industrial*, Dublin, 1902, 417–9. In the 1907 Census of Production, the Derry area contributed 22 per cent by value of the total UK shirt, collar and cuff production.

27 *Industries of the North*, Belfast, 1886, repr. 1986, 91.

28 *Children's Employment Commission*, PP 1864, xxII, Second Report, 192. Messrs. Tillie and Henderson.

29 *Commission on Factories and Workshops Acts*, PP 1876, xxx, vol II, qn 17328. Mr. Tillie.

30 See also a very relevant discussion in relation to the bicycle industry in C. K. Harley, 'Skilled labour and the choice of technique in Edwardian industry', in *Explorations in Economic History*, II, no. 4, 1974, 391–414.

31 Coyne, op. cit., 418.

32 *Factories Commission*, PP 1876, xxx, qn 17335.

33 Many of the shirt industry workers in Derry city lived in Co. Donegal. Their daily journey to work assumed a political significance after the partition of Ireland in 1922 when the county and city of Londonderry remained in the United Kingdom and Co. Donegal became part of the Irish Free State.

34 *Committee on the Insurance of Outworkers (Ireland)*, PP 1914–16, xxxI, Report, 19. Evid. of Dr Mowbray, Castlederg.

35 W. T. McCartney-Filgate, 'The fine underclothing industry in the counties Londonderry and Tyrone' in W. T. McCartney-Filgate (ed.), *Irish Rural Life and Industry*, Dublin, 1907, 182–5.

36 See Table 6.1. *County Borough of Belfast*, Health Reports, 1913–15, 89. 'Outwork in the city has been reduced as employers prefer it to be done on their premises because of punctuality, combined with sending

it to the country districts where it can be embroidered at a cheaper rate.'

37 *Outworkers*, PP 1914–16, xxxi, 21. Evidence of Revd Maguire, Inishowen.
38 *First Annual Report (1893) of the Congested Districts Board for Ireland*, quoted in Coyne, op. cit., 260–1.
39 *Factory Inspectors' Reports for 1888*, PP 1889, xviii, 146–7.
40 See E. Boyle, *The Irish Flowerers*, Belfast, 1971. 'Many a farm round here was bought with the money' (70). Also 125–7, on emigration. On 'peasant proprietorship' W. E. Vaughan, *Landlords and Tenants in Ireland 1848–1904, Studies in Irish Economics and Social History*, 2, Dundalk, 1984.

Part IV

MARKETS AND URBAN MANUFACTURE

7

URBAN MANUFACTURES IN THE PROTO-INDUSTRIAL ECONOMY: CULTURE VERSUS COMMERCE?

*Paul M. Hohenberg**

In the thirteenth century, most would agree, urban producers working in a system of guilds enjoyed a near-monopoly in manufacturing throughout Europe. With the exception of such trades as mining, any rural production served only immediate local needs. By 1800, on the other hand, rural domestic industry flourished on a mass scale in many regions, notably in lines such as textile spinning that were already proving highly amenable to mechanization and factory concentration. In many ways it is this explosion in the scope and location of domestic industry that was revolutionary; while the subsequent transformation involved great technological advances, it probably broke fewer institutional and organizational barriers.

In recent years the interest aroused by the concept of proto-industrialization has drawn wide attention to the scale of rural domestic production and thus to the magnitude of a change that occurred somewhere over a five-century span.[1] Proto-industrialization (p-i) is commonly defined as the growth of rural domestic manufactures for non-local consumption. By itself this definition says nothing about the concomitant evolution of urban production. But clearly towns must have lost at least their relative share of the secondary sector and perhaps even suffered absolute losses as well. Theorists of p-i have firmly fixed their sights on factors conditioning rural growth – the links with commercial agriculture on the one hand and the family economy and its demography on the other – and hence have largely neglected questions relating to the timing, extent and causes of the urban-rural shift. To what extent are we dealing with a zero-sum game, with rural gains

159

stemming from urban losses? How did the costs of production differ in town and country? Did relative costs alone determine industrial viability or were there also systematic differences in demand for urban and rural goods?

In what follows I explore these issues principally from the urban point of view. It is not difficult to soften the somewhat cartoon-like contrast that one can derive from too quick a reading of the p-i literature and too narrow a focus on manufacturing activities destined for early mechanization. I focus on economic consider-ations both to balance the picture – restoring some sense of the continuing industrial importance and vitality of European towns – and to put into perspective the very real urban rigidities that remain. The analysis points towards the hypothesis that urban manufacturing was carried on in a cyclically unstable world within an inherently inflexible structure. Moving work into the country-side not only offered a way of reducing costs, but also constituted one of a number of strategies whereby towns attempted to manage and minimize change. The energies unleashed proved far too strong for towns to control, however, and short-term defensive measures sometimes undermined their long-term positions.

Economists look for economic explanations; that is, they fashion arguments to make observed behaviour consistent with economic or market rationality. In the present case, however, unless we account for the vulnerability of towns to fluctuations in activity in economic terms, we must not only appeal to 'non-economic' factors but also face a real paradox. How is it that towns, 'with their relatively open, fluid, competitive, and acquisitive societies', could allow so much of the economic future to escape them?[2] By looking at industry – Braudel's 'capitalism away from home' by contrast with trade – we can see that, if mercantile urban cultures seemed so unwilling to bend to the laws of commerce, perhaps it is because the spirit of capitalism was blunted by the search for stability.[3]

MANUFACTURING COSTS IN COUNTRY AND TOWN

A simple account of what drove change focuses on labour costs. The traditional economy of rural Europe harboured considerable reserves of labour. At a minimum they derived from the seasonal rhythm of agricultural tasks and from the structure of households; in addition, patterns of inheritance and land tenure, incipient overpopulation or man-land imbalances, and even leisure preference – given exploitative social relations and a lack of goods to buy – could swell the potential labour surplus. Thus rural labour was available at low opportunity cost. Agricultural work ensured much of its subsistence and held the population in place.

Over time the rural labour supply could change systematically. One important mechanism focuses on shifts from arable to pastoral husbandry, which would reduce the demand for agricultural labour. Such shifts have been associated with enclosure and with other progressive or capitalistic developments; yet much of the new agriculture was arable or 'convertible' and more rather than less intensive than the old, demand for labour increasing and also spreading more evenly over the year. For the most part p-i did not develop in the best agricultural areas but in marginal zones accessible to commercial food supplies. The second mechanism, even more powerful and hotly debated, ensured an elastic labour supply by having the p-i system 'grow its own' labour, as manufacturing employment made it feasible for rural people to marry earlier and increased the economic value of young children.

Of course, wage rates are only one aspect of unit labour costs. Skill, control and productivity matter as well. Rural work was largely restricted to materials of limited value and to techniques that could be broken down into manageable component tasks. In a very real sense rural domestic industry was a rehearsal for mechanized mass production in the factory; it lacked only direct supervision and greater recourse to machinery and inanimate sources of power.

Typically, labour cost conditions in urban industry are seen as little more than the dark obverse of the rural side. Operating under the guild system, urban producers maintained a high-cost, tradition-bound mode of production that resisted change and fought to ward off market forces and the adaptation they demanded. Costs inherent in urban locations included the need to import food and maintain the built environment and to make up for the absence of part-time agricultural employment; there is also the element of monopoly rent resulting from guild control. Marxist analysis uses the term 'costs of reproduction' of labour to capture the first category and portrays the second as resistance to capitalist exploitation.

But the urban cost picture is not so simple, even for labour. To begin with, one cannot easily compare rural workers to urban craftsmen who acquired skills through a long apprenticeship. Also,

161

urban subsistence wages might be less volatile than rural ones: towns were far better equipped to deal with dearth because of their organized access to distant food supplies. Finally, it is even said that urban residents were taxed more lightly in *ancien régime* France; certainly, seignorial and other claims against the income of most European peasants drove a wedge between their earnings and the gross cost of their labour.[4]

Even more important than the static level of wages, however, is the elasticity of supply of labour. Here getting rid of unwanted workers may be quite as significant as being able to hire more without sharply driving up wages. The argument about costs of reproduction of labour amounts to saying that rural labour was elastically supplied (all the more so if p-i stimulated population growth) and could be disposed of as readily. We shall see that supply did pose problems for towns, but they also enjoyed some advantages as regards both skilled and unskilled labour. The supply of skilled labour often depended on migrants, whether drawn by economic opportunities or driven by political per-secutions.[5] Such migrants preferred to move to towns, notably the larger ones (at least until empty lands in the New World beckoned). While autonomous cities could and did control access to citizenship, they could not withdraw it once granted. On the other hand, many urban labourers were temporary immigrants vested with no rights, whom the town could in principle exclude as readily as the merchant manufacturer could dispense with cot-tagers when work was short.

Labour may be the principal input to manufacturing, but it is not the only determinant of costs. Because working capital played a greater role for the merchant manufacturer than fixed capital, the longer period of production implied by a scattered workforce constituted something of a handicap. Transport costs could deter-mine a rural location near raw materials or an urban one with better market access. Although the p-i literature plays down tech-nological change, growing reliance on wind and water power drew industry to suitable – chiefly rural – sites, while heat-using process industries found 'sea coal' in ports. New gadgets abounded. Some helped break complex operations down into simple tasks, anticipat-ing mechanization but in the meantime favouring decentralization; others gave greater scope to skilled labour.[6]

Relative costs of rural and urban location differed greatly from product to product. If the producer had to ensure the highest quality or respond quickly to a changing market, close control over a largely skilled labour force was necessary. New goods and processes as well as luxury goods in general are cases in point. For common goods produced in large quantities, on the other hand, economies of production were a greater concern. Decomposing the work into simple steps gave spatial flexibility as well as scope for using unskilled labour, at least for part of the process. In its simplest form, the p-i model postulates a division of labour between urban merchant and rural workers. But other arrangements were equally eligible: urban as well as rural production steps (fulling and dyeing versus spinning and weaving, for example) for a single product; urban – more likely suburban – workshops or domestic workers; or proto-factories in town or outside it.

Even large-scale production, still atypical but growing, did not necessarily imply an urban location. Putters-out could employ hundreds of workers.[7] Estate or monastery workshops, manufactures, mines, forges or arsenals could employ large numbers in self-contained units apart from any established town. Indeed, urban authorities resisted large concentrations of workers, certainly for fear of disruptive protest but also, perhaps, because failure of the single enterprise could so drastically affect the town.

Adapting an idea from the modern theory of international trade, one can think of a product cycle in which location shifts from urban to rural as a new good or technique develops, matures and becomes routine. At first, labour skill, access to finance and markets, and entrepreneurial control are dominant considerations. Gradually they are replaced by access to abundant labour and raw materials (including energy). A secular flow of work should ensue from town to country and from more central cities – in touch with world-wide currents of trade, travel and ideas – to lesser towns and villages. Of course, such a picture of ongoing renewal places a particular burden on the adaptability and readiness to nurture innovation of urban societies, precisely the areas in which they are said to have been deficient.

THE PATTERN OF DEMAND

Before turning to the issue of urban inflexibility, however, it is necessary to look at the composition of demand for manufactures, since some goods offered less scope for highly developed spatial divisions of labour than did others. For ease of argument, I draw an excessively neat distinction between urban-made luxuries, consumed by recipients of property income or rent, and rural-made wage goods, whose market depended on the discretionary income of workers. This conveniently ties the composition of demand to the functional distribution of income. And, in fact, long-run changes in income distribution do correspond to shifts in relative strength between urban and rural manufactures over the period.

Over the very long term, the most striking change in the composition of output by type of product resulted from a broadening of the market for manufactures, as the mass of the population gradually became at least occasional consumers of bought articles. Cloth and metalwares – nails and knives, for example – loom large alongside processed products of the food, drink and tobacco sector. Paper, pottery and glass, leather, and even wooden articles slowly spread to customers of modest means, either because of rising living standards or as a result of sharper divisions of labour. Even servile labourers on estates in relatively backward areas would buy something. With the additional benefit of cheap backhaul rates, overseas sales of wage goods also grew in the long term, in exchange for slaves and for the products of the Americas. Mercantilist governments worked hard to ensure markets for the metropolis in colonies where European settlers threatened to develop import substitutes. In general, wage goods were simple to make and price-elastic in demand, and therefore natural candidates for rural p-i or a regional division of labour.

However, trade in relatively complex, higher quality goods destined for a more affluent clientele, goods embodying much more skilled labour as well as higher valued raw materials, also expanded enormously in the early modern period. Colonial elites, for example, were faithful clients of imported consumer goods. The palaces and pageants of Europe's kings and their courtiers – as well as their wars – depended on a multitude of skilled hands; so did the more discreet but also more comfortable lives of the famously rising bourgeoisie. A host of articles gained an association with place names – Meissen, Faenza, Delft and Limoges from one industry alone – a sure sign of greater specialization and commerce. The list of new or increasingly 'industrial' luxury products is endless: weapons and art goods, clocks, books, tapestries and rugs, velvets and calicoes, furniture and glassware. Import substitution played a part here; the case of printed cottons (calicoes) attests to Europe's gradual advance on Asia. Wherever they might

164

be consumed, town house or manor house, nearby or halfway around the world, these luxuries had their origin in urban workshops or centralized manufactures.

Wage goods and luxuries followed different rhythms over the nearly five centuries that concern us. After the general crisis of the fourteenth century, a first expansion of rural crafts in the fifteenth century paved the way for renewed urban growth in the sixteenth.[8] A climacteric is observed by the early to mid-seventeenth century, after which the major p-i push gathers momentum in the last decades and continues on through the following century and beyond. One point to note is the lag between 'urban crisis' and (rural) proto-industrial expansion. For example, northern Italy's towns declined in the early seventeenth century, whereas the p-i zone on the fringes of the Po plain apparently emerges only a century later.[9] Moreover, Europe as a whole presents no close spatial correlation between urban losses and rural gains in manufacturing over the longer term. Some regions, such as the southern Low Countries, exhibit both. Here, as in northern Italy, the urban share of the regional population may have had to decline from its precociously high levels before rural industry could develop. But in southern Germany and Spain rural p-i does not compensate urban losses, while England sees more rural gain than urban decline.

I have argued elsewhere that the distribution of income between wages and rents was driven by movements in population, specifically by the competition of workers for land or of landlords for tenants.[10] A sparse population – relative to available resources – could obtain holdings on terms that left workers sufficient discretionary income to offer a market for wage goods. Population growth, however, would gradually tip the balance in favour of those with claims to surplus, that is, to the excess of per capita output over the social subsistence wage. The claimants included landlords as well as feudal, church and secular powers. Their prosperity translated into demand for luxuries (and construction). However, when and where population density rose enough to trigger subsistence crises, the property incomes on which luxury industries depended would in turn decline. Following a drop in population, wage incomes would recover well before prosperity returned to the *rentier* class, the more so as recovery from major population declines tended to be delayed in Europe.

The focus on demand suggests, paradoxically, that rural

165

industries would tend to flourish during periods of high real wages, such as the early eighteenth century, whereas urban industry should do best while wages were falling in real terms, as in the sixteenth century.[11] Without question the simple argument that low rural wages drew industry out of the towns needs qualification. My analysis also sheds light on what might have happened in towns. Money wages would presumably respond to early stages of a long-run inflationary period because the prices of these goods would be associated with strong demand for luxury goods and urban labour. As food prices peaked and crop failures became frequent, however, demand for urban products was likely to weaken and employment to fall, a situation inviting protest and strenuous efforts to assert traditional privileges and suppress competition. Since the market for many urban goods would remain weak, even after rural activity recovered, historians understandably interpret the urban troubles as triggering a long-lasting flight of capital to smaller, non-corporate places and to rural cottages.

URBAN INFLEXIBILITY: AN ECONOMIC INTERPRETATION

I have so far used three sets of arguments to account for the ruralization of manufactures: *longue durée* trends towards both market provision of wage goods and deskilling divisions of labour, and long-run fluctuations in demand patterns resulting from movements in income distribution. Innovation, on the other hand, whether autonomous or in response to market stimuli, enhanced the urban role. It remains true, however, that towns often failed to adapt flexibly to changed conditions. Though home to markets and merchants, and often politically dominated by commercial elites, they tried to counter market threats by clinging to old monopolies rather than with innovative products or cost-cutting. Twentieth-century experience with the highly contagious British disease makes us sensitive to these issues. A variety of explanations compete, some focusing on economic forces and others on what economists tend to dismiss as 'culture'. Early modern towns are said to have suffered from sclerosis – medical metaphors abound – but the question is, to what extent did this represent a loss of earlier vigour and to what extent a dysfunction in relation to a changed environment? That the environment did become more variable and demand more adaptability seems clear from everything I have said. There remains the need to examine why the pre-industrial town was poorly equipped to cope with a more widely integrated and changeable economic environment.

The accepted interpretation of urban resistance to competitive forces focuses on craft guilds. These associations of producers are portrayed as steadfast against change and strong enough to frustrate and drive off powerful merchants. Though mainstays of the communal spirit, guilds are seen as prepared to court collective economic ruin rather than sacrifice short-run self-interest. Surely this picture cannot be even remotely accurate. By the fifteenth century, and ever after, guilds were far weaker and less autonomous than it implies.[12] Moreover, any suggestion that guilds prefigure modern trade unions is quite off the mark. As Goubert notes, 'It is superfluous to mention that workers played no role in them.'[13] Working within the guild structure, masters had largely closed off access to membership to all save their own sons, and so created a permanent class of journeymen-workers. These guilds had then, typically, come under the control of the merchant elite that also governed the town. Finally, in centralized states such as absolutist France, guilds served largely as vehicles for implementing mercantilist fiscal and regulatory policies.

All these arguments suggest that the problem of guilds could be more than symptomatic of a commitment to stability that must have involved the whole urban community, including its oligarchy. I believe that this focus on stability can be explained in the framework of conventional microeconomics, although translating the realities of the early modern town into the conceptual apparatus of production and cost theory requires attention to cultural factors. In the simplest terms, urban costs were not systematically higher than rural costs, but they were more sensitive to the scale and scope of production, and the choice and level of output. Figure 7.1 shows the distinction schematically in terms of the unit or average cost curves. The narrow parabola for urban manufacturing is characteristic of a capital-intensive mode of production, with high fixed costs and little flexibility of the capital. By contrast, average cost in a rural p-i setting varies little from one scale of output to another.

The capital involved in early urban industry was tangible and intangible, and private as well as collective. Private intangible capital is exemplified by the knowledge, skill and experience of craft workers and masters. However, this human capital was

Figure 7.1 Urban and rural average costs

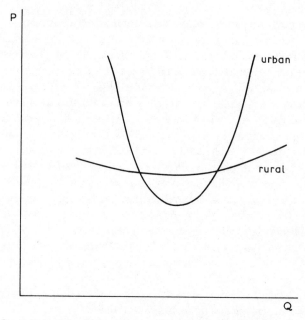

specific to a particular technique or product and did not imply a capacity to innovate. The more valuable a technology and a reputation for quality, the more peril there was in allowing experimentation. By contrast, private tangible capital – structures or equipment – was generally modest. The principal tangible capital was collective, namely the physical town itself, its walls, market and guild halls, houses and religious buildings. The municipal institutions and private networks that protected and administered the town and sustained the citizens' solidarity, loyalty and pride also represented capital, collective and intangible. Most important, the social and political structure of the community, the distinctions and ties of blood, status, clientele and affinity underpinning the urban culture, were interwoven with economic functions and sources of wealth. A shift in the dominant type of production activity could call into question the whole urban fabric and the infrastructure of services, support and power that made the town productive.

Without question, at its best the urban mode of production was efficient in contemporary terms. All over Europe it generated the profit that built, sustained and protected a splendid built environment and a privileged community. Changes in scale as well as type of production were chancy, however, because the costs of the urban environment were so nearly fixed. Expansion resulted in congestion, with the danger that the town would undertake irreversibly costly expansion to accommodate unsustainable growth. Most daunting, in all likelihood, was the need to feed distressed inhabitants, the more so as we have noted that periods of frequent dearth were also likely to coincide with falling demand and rising unemployment. Shrinkage in demand would saddle production with higher unit fixed costs, and this process could cumulate disastrously as the higher costs aggravated the competitive disadvantage that had induced skrinkage in the first place.

Not many economic historians have looked at the early modern town as an economic system, so most attention has focused on rent-seeking activities – attempts to establish or maintain monopolies and other privileges – rather than on deliberate efforts to stabilize the type and volume of industrial production. The work of R. DuPlessis and M. Howell on Lille and Leiden constitutes a noteworthy exception.[14] They show rich and powerful merchants helping small local rival producers survive, placing community interests ahead of their own. In fact, one can readily interpret much urban economic behaviour as intended to offset or soften the effects of external market shocks and trends.

Towns often attempted, and sometimes succeeded in, changing over to a more promising line, though few apparently matched Geneva's switch from cloth to watches and cotton prints in the eighteenth century.[15] Other cities gave up their industrial vocation and concentrated on finance, transport or administration, or they attracted *rentiers* and sought to consolidate their control over regional surpluses. Towns controlled migration and limited what non-citizens could do and where. Citizenship was rationed by quotas as well as by price. And towns transferred work outside the walls in good times, and recaptured it, or attempted to, when volume contracted. Yet, in the long run, neither urban *Gastarbeiter* nor the moving of work proved successful strategies for stability. Moreover, as their political autonomy declined, towns lost the ability to exclude outsiders and to control their surroundings.

While urban merchants continued to dominate the entrepreneurial and distributional functions in rural p-i, towns could not maintain a regional commercial monopoly any more than they could an industrial one. Long-distance networks of trade extended

PAUL M. HOHENBERG

tentacles by which local merchants could circumvent local centres
and gain direct access to wider markets. This was particularly true
in regions criss-crossed by commercial currents and may help to
explain the density of proto-industrial development in a swath
across north-western Europe from Lower Normandy to the Duchy
of Berg through (or around) such traditional manufacturing centres as Rouen, Beauvais, Amiens, Lille, Ghent, Liège, Aachen and
Cologne.[16]

CONCLUSION

The towns just mentioned are good examples of what happened
to strong urban manufactures during proto-industrialization. None
ceased to be active, yet all faded in comparison with the industrial
development – not always rural – around them. By 1800 their
population was for the most part growing moderately and the
industrial share of employment may not have been much greater
than in cities we rarely associate with manufacturing, such as
London and Paris. The great capitals offered a superb market for
the most quintessentially urban goods, from modish clothes to
scientific instruments. Besides drawing on their own large populations and on the court, the capital cities found a thriving market
in the rich and thinly urbanized agricultural regions around them,
with their gentry and substantial farmers who relied more and
more on the shops 'in town'. And streams of travellers came from
the more distant provinces and abroad.

We think of nineteenth-century urban industrialization in terms
of factory towns and factories in and around cities. Yet small-
scale, weakly mechanized manufactures proved hardy survivors in
the urban economy, continuing or renewing a long tradition.
Plenty of towns had long-standing or more recent industry that
survived and flourished. A quickening pace of innovation and the
elimination of remaining municipal obstacles to free commerce
provided carrot and stick. Some new labour-intensive mass industries – furniture, shoes and ready-made clothing, for example –
would gravitate to towns with no obvious lure for modern industry.
Even the new urbanization built around mines and mills was
prefigured as early as the sixteenth century in the meteoric – if
short-lived – rise of Hondschoote as a textile centre.

Over the long early modern period, the manufactures of urban
Europe experienced many fluctuations and vicissitudes. Exports,

170

a widening consumer base and some innovations in techniques, products and forms of organization and finance offered opportunities, but also added new competitive threats to the still-potent danger from subsistence crises. These islands of precocious modernity were committed to a search for stability that went beyond an unwillingness to compress wages or change work rules. Sometimes urban societies had to settle for stagnation or for an auxiliary role; on other occasions they adapted successfully. This rich and varied urban experience should not be reduced to a caricature against which the important story of rural cottage industry is played out. Europe's proto-industrialization was urban as well.

NOTES

* I thank Lynn Hollen Lees for valuable comments.
1 This essay draws on two collections of papers prepared for sessions of successive International Economic History Congresses: 'Proto-industrialization: Theory and Reality', Budapest, 1982, and 'The Dynamics of Urban Decline in the Late Middle Ages and Early Modern Times: Economic Response and Social Effects', Berne, 1986. Specific references to these unpublished papers are omitted.
2 P. Corfield, *The Impact of English Towns, 1700–1800*, Oxford, 1982, 97.
3 F. Braudel, *Civilisation matérielle, économie et capitalisme, XVᵉ-XVIIIᵉ siècle*, II, Paris, 1979–81. Work in progress by Robert DuPlessis develops the theme of urban stability for cities in the Low Countries.
4 P. Goubert, *L'ancien régime*, II, *Les pouvoirs*, Paris, 1973, 81.
5 B. Supple, 'The nature of enterprise' in E. E. Rich and C. H. Wilson (eds), *The Cambridge Economic History of Europe*, V, Cambridge, 1977, 397.
6 M. Berg, P. Hudson and M. Sonenscher (eds), *Manufacture in Town and Country before the Factory*, Cambridge University Press, 1983, 10–12.
7 G. Gayot, 'Dispersion et concentration de la draperie sedanaise au XVIIIᵉ siècle: l'entreprise des Poupart de Neuflize', *Revue du Nord*, 61, 1979, 127–48.
8 F. Braudel, op. cit., II, 270–1; B. Chevalier, *Les bonnes villes de France*, Paris, 1982, 167.
9 D. Sella, *Crisis and Continuity: The Economy of Spanish Lombardy in the Seventeenth Century*, Harvard, 1979; A. Dewerpe, 'Le triangle industriel italien', *Annales (ESC)*, 39, 1984, 897.
10 The original statement is in a paper from the Budapest congress (see note 1); see also P. M. Hohenberg and L. H. Lees, *The Making of Urban Europe*, Harvard, 1985, chap. 4.
11 Nominal wages tended to remain sufficiently stable for the course of real wages to be dominated by price movements, notably for food grains.
12 F. Braudel, op. cit., 274–5.

13 P. Goubert, *L'ancien régime*, I, *La société*, Paris, 1969, 203.
14 R. DuPlessis and M . Howell, 'Reconsidering the early modern urban economy: the cases of Leiden and Lille', *Past and Present*, 94, 1982, 49–84.
15 A. Perrenoud, *La population de Genève, XVIe-XIXe siècle*, Geneva, 1979.
16 For the German regions, see H. Kisch, 'From monopoly to *laissez-faire:* the early growth of the Wupper valley textile trades', *Journal of European Economic History*, 1, 1982, 298–407 and 'The textile industries in Silesia and the Rhineland' in *Industrialization before Industrialization*, Cambridge, 1981, 179.

8

COMMERCE AND CREATIVITY IN EIGHTEENTH-CENTURY BIRMINGHAM

Maxine Berg

The Industrial Revolution is no longer what it was. Recent quantitative evidence has turned it from an age of 'widespread ingenuity' to one of steady but unspectacular growth. Though it is clear that the industrial sector in the eighteenth century was much larger than previously thought, the gain in aggregate productivity was modest. Such gain as there was, moreover, has been attributed to agriculture and to a very small part of the manufacturing sector.[1] We have passed, in effect, from an 'Industrial Revolution' to 'slow aggregate growth', and economic history has passed into a phase of disillusioned revisionism that parallels the recent revisionism in seventeenth- and eighteenth-century political history.

At the same time, the focus of research on the sources of industrialization has shifted to the countryside. The theory of 'proto-industrialization' has seen the main locus of early industrial expansion in rural manufacture organized on the putting-out system. The cities have been treated as peripheral – as backwaters of guild-dominated luxury industries or, at best, as centres for mercantile and financial services.[2] Together, the 'proto-industrial' and 'aggregate growth' research regimes have pushed the once-celebrated phenomena of urban growth and technological innovation well forward into the nineteenth century, where their appearance has little of the heroic originality of the century past. Except for the obvious, isolated examples of large-scale manufacturing, factories and industrial cities in and around Manchester, the technologies of the eighteenth century are now widely regarded as primitive.[3] Until the factory and the industrial city were generalized across the country it seemed obvious to ask how there could have

173

been significant aggregate growth. How could proto-industrialization pass into industrialization proper? The interesting thing
about this question is not its obviousness, and certainly not its
putative quantitative and conceptual radicalism: it is its dependence on the very orthodoxy it seeks to dethrone. The theses of
'slow aggregate growth' and 'proto-industrialization' both presup-
pose that industrialization really does consist, in the end, of factories and large-scale technical change. Prometheus may not have
burst out of his bonds in a sudden surge of energy; but he did
eventually wriggle out of them. We must simply accept on the
basis of these new conventions that industrialization, the factory,
the industrial city, were, in Britain at least, gradual, rather unspectacular and perhaps never really completed developments, of a
piece with our gradual, unspectacular, unexciting political evolution.[4]

The historiographic fortunes of the particular city of Birmingham have changed in parallel with those of the 'Industrial Revolution'. Once Birmingham was the admitted exception. It appeared
to encapsulate an alternative social structure, in undeniable contrast with that of Manchester. In a pioneering essay, Asa Briggs
postulated the existence of a 'Birmingham tradition' based on a
distinctive social and economic structure. Birmingham's differences
from the great textile centres were manifold: diversity of occupation, a relatively skilled labour force, small workshops, close
relations between master and men and opportunities for social
mobility. Manchester's big capitals, large-scale organization and
unskilled workforce were Birmingham's worker-entrepreneurs and
organic specialization.[5] Continuous with this interpretation, the
city has been described as a pre-industrial survival in an industrial
world or, more recently, as the historical focus of an alternative
style of industrialization. A centre for skill, flexibility and market
specialization rather than mass production, it generated a consensus between skilled workers and employers rather than the class
conflict of the factory towns.[6] The classic contrast was that perceived in the nineteenth century between Birmingham, where
'association, negotiation, argument and compromise were the stuff
of politics and business' and Sheffield, which, though also based
in the small-scale metal trades, was an altogether simpler society
of starkly demarcated divisions. Extensive trade unionism and
popular opposition to machinery were Sheffield's trademark while
Birmingham's were consensus and innovation.[7]

Another recent examination of the Birmingham tradition, however, has sharply qualified this picture of the 'exceptional' city. The nineteenth-century city, it is argued, was dominated by large capitals, its workers were less skilled and less highly paid than was formerly thought, and ultimately its differences from Manchester were not so significant.[8] The city's industrial structure was transformed in the first half of the nineteenth century from the mercantile circulating capital of the workshop system to the fixed capital of the factory. Small firms were subordinated to large ones, succumbing to the garret or sweating system. The class outlook of Manchester was not missing from Birmingham's trade societies by the second quarter of the nineteenth century. The Birmingham image of social cohesion reflected local discourse in the nineteenth century, not the realities of the workplace.[9] On this interpretation, Birmingham did not long remain an exception; indeed, in the perspective of 'aggregate growth' it was not an exception at all. Its small-scale workshop manufacturing simply passed into industrialization in step with the overall indices of growth in the nineteenth century. Prior to that, in the eighteenth century, it was, at best, a bastion of traditional, small-scale technology. Again, however, it is the conservatism of the revisionist position which is noticeable: Manchester remains the point of reference.

In the older picture, Birmingham represented the exceptional continuity of an urban and industrial structure separate from the Manchester model. Now it simply exemplifies the break with the eighteenth-century artisan past into the capitalist industrial city in the first half of the nineteenth century, with a social structure much less unlike Manchester's than the earlier understanding supposed. Both views assume that Birmingham must be compared with Manchester as the prototype of the modern capitalist industrial city. It is the object of this paper, however, to argue that analysis of Birmingham as a manufacturing city in the eighteenth century must take us outside that standard concept of the industrial city. I shall contend that Birmingham's economy and industrial structure in the eighteenth century were much more complex than the simple model of artisan-workshop manufacturing suggests. An historical explanation for the growth of the city should be sought, not in the description of internal structures, but in the analysis of relationships between the city and its region and, beyond this, in its national and international connections.

There is a special eighteenth-century dimension to the growth of this city which is not captured by comparing it with England's other rising industrial towns and cities. This context is first that of indigenous regional growth; second, that of commerce and empire. Birmingham was the centre of a great coal and iron region whose rapid transformation from the seventeenth century was part of a broader coal-based expansion long pre-dating the classic textile-based Industrial Revolution. Its greater rival and more important point of comparison in this pattern of regional development was the North-East and Newcastle. Birmingham also bears comparison with the great commercial cities of eighteenth-century empire – Glasgow, Liverpool and Bristol, all ports to be sure, but with a trading wealth that depended, like Birmingham's manufacturing wealth, on colonial empire and European commerce. Their financial and commercial sophistication further provided the kind of connections and counterpoints to London that Birmingham's commercial classes aspired to. As a manufacturing city, Birmingham also had European models. It had, as Briggs noted, features in common with Lyons, long a node of European commerce, as Birmingham was of English trade and transport. Like Lyons, too, Birmingham's manufacturing was not a new product of the Industrial Revolution – its industrial importance was established in the seventeenth and eighteenth centuries; that of Lyons in the sixteenth and seventeenth centuries. Both, in addition, were small workshop economies supporting major export industries.[10] Birmingham's regional, European and international framework in the eighteenth century thus call for analysis in terms of broader models of urban development in early modern Europe.

MODELS OF THE CITY

Two models of city development have recently been propounded in order to illuminate the development of manufacturing cities in the eighteenth century: one by Jan de Vries in *European Urbanization 1500–1800* and the other by Paul Hohenberg and Lynn Lees in *The Making of Urban Europe 1000–1950*. Both of these works are large macroeconomic surveys analysing the relationship between urban and industrial growth within the framework of proto-industrialization and industrialization. De Vries's pan-European pattern of cyclical growth and decline of cities gives special significance to the role of the city in developing its hinterland. Proto-industrial development, he believes, had two essential hallmarks – it was co-ordinated by urban merchants and it was dependent on distant markets. The rise of proto-industrialization was, to a large extent, a consequence of city-centred investment. Proto-industrialization frequently undermined urban industrial employment, but urban commercial and service functions grew stronger. In consequence, the urban stagnation which characterized Europe between 1600 and 1750 was succeeded by the rapid growth of smaller cities and the addition of new cities during the classic Industrial Revolution period. An urban 'growth from below' of resource-based industries like metallurgy and a clustering of proto-industrial textile manufacture set the scene for the industrial towns and cities of the nineteenth century.[11]

England, however, appears to have been a major exception to the European pattern discerned by de Vries. Between 1600 and 1750, just when the smaller towns of Europe were stagnating while industrial production shifted to the countryside, in England the metropolis, rural industry and small towns all surged ahead. England's big industrial cities of the nineteenth century – Manchester, Leeds, Birmingham, Liverpool, Nottingham and Sheffield – gathered their burgeoning populations in a long sweep from the late seventeenth century right through the industrial period. Birmingham, in particular, seems to have grown rapidly, its manufacturing base changing in relationship to its hinterland, but growing along with its regional investment and commercial services. In terms of population growth, Birmingham and the other major industrial cities can, however, be set apart from the whole range of smaller industrial towns that only crested the wave of urban expansion at the end of the eighteenth century: Stoke, Wolverhampton, Stockport, Leicester, Paisley. These towns definitely joined the upward trend of de Vries's urban cycle in the late eighteenth century. (See Table 8.1)[12]

The reciprocal growth of town and country manufacture was, however, predicated in de Vries's model of the city's priority as a regional centre. This suggests a need for further analysis of the relationship between the city and its hinterland. The Hohenberg and Lees model of the proto-industrial city is such a model of regional interaction, reassessing the neglected 'role of the citizen as a large-scale producer of industrial goods'. Their model related incomes and, with this, demand in urban centres to conditions in the countryside. Agricultural productivity is related in the model to property incomes or Ricardian rents. Improvements in

Table 8.1 Selected British commercial/industrial towns and cities. Population estimates in thousands

1600		1670		1700		1750		1800	
Bristol	12	Bristol	20	Bristol	21	Bristol	50	Manchester	89
Newcastle	10	Newcastle	12	Newcastle	16	Newcastle	29	Liverpool	83
Glasgow	2	Glasgow	–	Glasgow	13	Glasgow	24	Glasgow	77
Aberdeen	7	Manchester	6	Birmingham	8–9	Birmingham	24	Birmingham	74
Dundee	7	Leeds	6	Manchester	8–9	Liverpool	22	Bristol	60
		Birmingham	6	Hull		Manchester	18	Leeds	53
				Leeds		Leeds	16	Sheffield	46
				Leicester	} 5–7	Aberdeen	16	Newcastle	42
				Liverpool		Nottingham	12	Hull	30
				Nottingham		Sheffield	12	Nottingham	29
				Aberdeen		Dundee	12	Aberdeen	27
				Dundee				Dundee	27
								Sunderland	26
								Stoke	23
								Wolverhampton	21
								Bolton	
								Leicester	
								Stockport	} 17
								Greenock	
								Paisley	

Sources: Wrigley, 'Urban Growth,' p. 686. Jan de Vries, European Urbanization 1500–1800, pp. 269–87

productivity raise the share of income going to profits, reducing the shares going to wage payments and rents. A rising population would lead ultimately to diminishing returns in agriculture and, with this, higher rents. Diminishing returns in the countryside, reducing productivity and bringing high grain prices and lower discretionary incomes, would rapidly affect rural manufacturers. The rising population which brought higher rents would, in this model, also entail higher urban incomes, since the holders of power and property lived in the towns. Taxes and government revenue would also flow into the towns. Those in the central city might thus for a time retain their prosperity, buoyed up by high rents and property incomes, but demographic crisis would eventually cut rental incomes and break the urban boom.[13] The model effectively displays the close distributional connections between central cities and hinterland towns and villages, and in the countryside, between industrial producers and food producers. It can thus provide a way of specifying Birmingham's relationship with the rest of the Black Country. But its limitations are those of all closed economy models. The neglect of international markets raises major reservations about its applicability to Birmingham, and indeed to all proto-industrial centres. The rural wage in such areas was linked not only to the harvest and diminishing returns in agriculture, but also, and perhaps primarily, to international markets for manufactured goods. Urban prosperity depended less on neighbouring property incomes than on the vagaries of war, and financial and international markets. The models of urban development offered by de Vries and Hohenberg and Lees do illuminate regional interaction and the cycles of urban and rural expansion. But in not accounting for the international framework of eighteenth-century cities, they are subject to potentially critical limitations.

These limitations have been recognized recently, and a much more complex model of urban linkages devised. Two urban systems coexisted and interpenetrated. One system was a hierarchy of central places, culminating in a regional capital and ultimately in the capital of a multi-region state. The other system related those cities involved in long-distance trading networks together with their secondary outposts or satellites. The cyclical fluctuations of a town or city would depend, therefore, on its place in the network system or central place connections, and the one system might offset the other.[14] Birmingham was indeed the centre of the

Black Country region; but its horizons and rhythms had their own distinctive European and colonial setting.

THE CHARACTER OF BIRMINGHAM

Was Birmingham the quintessential proto-industrial city? Let us look at its demographic and regional history. Birmingham first appeared among the towns with populations of over 10,000 between 1700 and 1750. Its close contemporary rivals were Manchester and Leeds. But these newly growing towns were, at the time, only joining several large cities of much older vintage. Bristol, Exeter, Newcastle and Norwich, along with the metropolises of Edinburgh and London, had 10,000 inhabitants by 1500; York had 10,000 by 1600 and Sheffield and Glasgow by 1700. It should not, therefore, simply be assumed, retrospectively, that early eighteenth-century Birmingham was a new type of town, distinct from the older centres which it drew alongside. In fact, Birmingham was distinct from Manchester in that its really striking growth occurred in the first half of the eighteenth century, when population rose from 8,000 in 1700 to 24,000 in 1750. Between 1700 and 1750 Birmingham moved from the fifth-largest to the third-largest town in England and Wales, its population rising to 40,000; only London and Bristol were larger. Growth continued, up to 74,000 in 1800. But while Birmingham had led Manchester and Liverpool in 1750, by 1800 it had fallen behind their 89,000 and 83,000 inhabitants respectively.[15] Birmingham stayed in their shadow throughout the nineteenth century, with a population of only 294,000 in 1850 compared with Manchester's 412,000 and Liverpool's 422,000. It only regained a place close to Manchester in the late nineteenth century, when Manchester's population was 1,255,000 to Birmingham's 1,248,000. Birmingham's demographic history was thus not of a piece with the Manchester model of the industrial city; rather, it was outstanding in the early industrial, not the classic industrial period.

The city's regional setting was also different from that predicted by the models. The coal and iron of the West Midlands were the basis not only for the country's largest mining and iron output after that of the North-East, but also for the extensive metal manufactures of the Black Country and Birmingham. Further, product differentiation within the region set in rapidly. Primary producers collected on the water-power sites around the Birmingham plateau, particularly on the western edge, close to the Severn waterway. Nailers, cutlers and edge tool-makers congregated in the Digbeth district of Birmingham in the seventeenth century, but left for the countryside at the beginning of the eighteenth. The Black Country nailers collected around the margins of the coalfield and grew to 35–40,000 by 1799, in communities like Sedgley, West Bromwich, Oldbury and Darlaston. Foundry products, hollow ware, edge tools and other hardwares, and glassware were produced in the subregions of Walsall, Wolverhampton, Stourbridge and Wednesbury.[16] Birmingham itself turned to the gun trade and to a whole new class of products directed to luxury markets – buttons, 'toys', brass articles, jewellery and plated goods. The gun trade involved the Black Country region and the city of Birmingham: semi-finished gun locks and other parts were made in Bilston, Wednesbury and Darlaston, and the guns were then assembled and finished in Birmingham itself.[17] In terms of manufacturing, there was in this instance a clear regional division of labour between processing and intermediate manufacture in the hinterland, and finishing and assembly in the centre. This bold demarcation does not hold for all the regions and industries. Bilston was a case in point. From early in the eighteenth century it was dominated by toy-makers and buckle-makers, and it later became an important centre for japanning.[18]

Fashion, not lower-class wages, dictated trends in production. Boulton conceived of many of his products as part of dress fashion and designer houseware. As Eric Robinson has put it:

> For the London season the Spitalfields silk weavers produced each year their new designs, and the Birmingham toy-makers their buttons, buckles, patchboxes, snuff boxes, chatelaines, watches, watch seals . . . and other jewellery.[19]

Birmingham's new trades were quite different from their Black Country counterparts – not merely higher quality or more finished versions of the same thing, but new commodities directed to the aspirations for luxury consumption of European and colonial buyers and not to the humble home market.

Not only were Birmingham's markets international; so too was its outlook. Its interdependence with the rest of the West Midlands, while important, was subordinated to its position as a nodal point of national communications and transport. The Birmingham trades were largely export industries, with sophisticated networks of merchants and agents in Birmingham, London and overseas. Approximately £600,000 worth of toys were produced in 1759, of which £500,000 were exported. Extensive trade networks with the American colonies, Italy, France and Germany were supplemented by the opening of new markets in Russia, and by the close connections between the British and Neapolitan nobilities in the latter half of the eighteenth century.[20]

World-wide markets were well established by 1760. The significance of overseas trade, though not quantified, was clear; there were major upswings in overseas trade in the periods 1700–15 and 1745–60, both times of substantial industrial growth in the West Midlands. Interruptions of overseas trade were quickly reflected in overstocked warehouses.[21] But most of the overseas wars before 1793 do not appear to have had any long-term effect on Birmingham's export trade. It was not until the French Wars that there was a substantial and sudden setback to trade. By the end of the eighteenth century foreign trade was of at least equal significance to the home trade. The proportion of Birmingham's industrial output exported in 1801 was higher than the national proportion of industrial output exported.[22]

Transport and finance transcended the regional framework to link the city to the nation, taking the hinterland with it. The promotion of the Trent and Mersey canal in the 1780s unleashed revealing conflicts between local Black Country and metropolitan Birmingham interests. Proposals for branch lines between Wednesbury and Coventry canal at Fazeley, between the Severn and the Dudley collieries at Tipton were based on local concern over the costs of carrying coal within the West Midlands; other proposed links between Birmingham and Worcester, Warwick and Stratford, Dudley and Netherton would likewise help to integrate the region. But Birmingham, its interests expressed by Samuel Garbett, wanted more – it wanted the wider world. As Garbett argued, instead of 'allowing speculators to make partial patches as private jobs; inland navigation should be considered a national political object.' The real priority was a direct connection with London. The final settlement was the Coventry canal's connection with the Trent and Mersey canal in 1785. And, within the next five years, canals linked Lancashire to the Midlands and the Thames.[23] The actual effect of the canal network across the West Midlands eventually established by the end of the century was, however, to facilitate cheaper transport of heavy goods and raw materials, rather than to carry the output of Birmingham's workshops. Industrial growth in the town was accelerated by, rather than created by, its canals.[24]

If the regions could not contain the town, neither could the metropolis confine to itself financial growth. Birmingham became a financial centre in the eighteenth century, and was so well endowed with banks that by 1800 the West Midlands had a lower ratio of population to bank offices than any other region in England, including London. A certain amount of this banking financed the regional trades. Lloyd's Bank, started in 1765 from family wealth in the iron trades, soon served a range of Birmingham and Black Country trades – file-cutting, hinge-making, the toy manufacture and the traditional food and drink trades. Samuel Galton moved from gun manufacture to banking in the first years of the nineteenth century, and soon handled much of the financial servicing for the gun trade. But finance was also a diversion from industry. Most Birmingham manufacturers relied more on trade credit and partnerships than on the large banking sector, which had an independent existence within the wider commercial world.[25]

Birmingham, then, took a different route to the stark contrast between regional development and the national metropolitan trajectory stressed recently by Pat Hudson.[26] Birmingham's integration with its region was thus only one dimension of its character. Pulling against this were its distinctive manufactures and its cosmopolitan mercantile networks. The fluctuating fortunes of its hinterland beat a contrapuntal rhythm to its own European and imperial cycle. The town's character made it not just an adjunct to rural proto-industrialization; it stood in no simple continuity with industrialization from below. Rather, it stood apart from other Black Country towns. The eighteenth-century context of this town was national as much as it was indigenous and regional. The volatile 'frontier markets' both abroad and at home of these classic 'sunrise industries' affected the nature of innovation and its reception.[27] How, then, did this framework affect the nature of invention in this highly creative town?

MENTALITIES OF INVENTION – THE MANUFACTURER'S PRACTICE

Jane Jacobs in her *Cities and the Wealth of Nations* (1984) argues that city regions, especially those which have expanded on the basis of import replacement, have a special vitality founded on their diversified yet concentrated markets and the symbiotic relations among producers. 'The strengths of tight-packed branches of symbiotic enterprises . . . have always been the strengths of creative cities.'[28] The creative city, on this account, has a special industrial structure. Such cities have been credited with economies of agglomeration, making a fertile environment for small firms. And so, as it is now argued, these small firms are carriers of innovation in their adaptability and symbiotic efficiency.

But Birmingham's economy was distinctive. Large-scale firms – Boulton, Taylor, Clay, Welch and others – held a dominant position in the economy. They led the way in 'organizing' the industrial sector by setting the political and legal framework. And because of their size, they had direct access to national and European markets through their own agents. The marketing of Birmingham ware for a whole range of smaller scale firms was dependent on these larger manufacturers.

Their dominance was, however, mediated by a substantial group of manufacturers of middling wealth. These cannot be described as small artisans for, up to a threshold at least, they ran numerous workshops and employed significant numbers. This was an economy of surprisingly substantial workshops – many aspiring, indeed, to a kind of mass production of luxury products. The small artisan could coexist with the giant – but the crucial feature of this economy was its middling manufacturers. Defusing the great polarity between the large millowners and small outworkers apparent in the textile districts, they entailed a more equitable distribution of income if not political power in the manufacturing sector. New techniques, materials and products were the life-blood of this sector. Distribution of income in the manufacturing sector in this place at least may well have made new technology an opportunity rather than the issue of conflict it proved to be in other major industrial centres.

Birmingham's inventive activity was proverbial. Richard Prosser argued that it was a famous centre for invention until the 1850s, with more patents to its credit than anywhere outside London. These inventions were small in scale – tools, metal compositions and scientific instruments; the major eighteenth-century innovations were stamp, press, drawbench and lathe. But all of these actually dated back to earlier centuries, and were simply adapted to new uses with the rise of the toy trade in the eighteenth cen-

tury.[29] This 'hardware' of technology was combined with a significant 'software' of product development, materials adaptation and
division of labour. Indeed, the proverbial small-scale technical
change or intermediate technology of hand tools was only one side
to the Birmingham achievement. The other was rapid responsive-
ness to and leadership of the markets and a new luxury consumer
culture which set its framework. Innovation in products and
materials are rarely captured by the economists' productivity indices, built as they are on capital-labour ratios. Experimentation
with alloys spearheaded new commodities. Manufacturers sought
market and design leadership in competition with London and
Paris.

Birmingham's own historians have hitherto explained its outstanding creativity by reference to several factors: its absence of
guild restrictions, its skilled workforce and its close-knit workshop
culture. Most recently its success has been linked to community
mentalities. The city's manufactures, it is argued, combined the
flexible use of a widely adaptable technology with an institutional
context balancing co-operation and competition among firms.
Sabel and Zeitlin have credited the city with co-operative ventures,
the collective learning of technologies and a 'community ethos'
that gave scope to competitive ambition, 'rewarding talent, but
keeping the struggle for advancement within safe limits'.[30]

On closer examination, however, it appears that the contemporary perception and practice of innovation were much more complex than this admirable picture of positive market opportunity,
egalitarian social structures and community spirit suggests. Birmingham had a highly divided manufacturing social structure,
even in the eighteenth century, and invention was pursued not
through isolated individualism or mutual agreement, but within a
strict institutional context of patenting and quality controls, and
a non-institutional code of secrecy.

Though patents were taken out for small improvements and
tools, they were pursued relentlessly only by a section of the
Birmingham trades. In a highly localized setting, where news of
novelty travelled fast, there seems to have been no attempt at
sharing improvements, as happened later in the nineteenth-century
iron trades.[31] Larger manufacturers pursued patenting, while the
small frequently resorted to secrecy. Boulton saw strict patent laws
as an incentive to innovation, arguing that they 'tended to encourage industrious and ingenious men to labour for the common

185

good'. Against the current legislative unpopularity of patents, Boulton argued:

> It tends to destroy the greatest of all stimulants to invention, viz. the idea of enjoying the fruits of one's own labour. Some late decisions against the validity of Patents have raised the spirits of illiberal, sordid, unjust, ungenerous and invention-less misers, who prey upon the vitals of the ingenious and make haste to seize upon what their laborious and often costly application has produced.[32]

With this reasoning he threw his political weight behind Watt's difficult campaign to have his steam engine patent renewed in 1775 – the success of which ensured a patent monopoly to the Boulton and Watt partnership until 1800. But large-scale manufacturers like Boulton pursued their patent rights in the same spirit as seventeenth-century projectors. They fought just as readily to break the patents that infringed on them. Boulton led the way in founding the Birmingham Brass company, a large-scale joint stock venture set up to bypass the external patent and monopoly of the Anglesea company which supplied Birmingham with 2,000 tons of copper a year mined in Cornwall and smelted in Swansea.[33] Birmingham patents were perceived as monopoly rights. Whether they were merely stockjobbing monopolies to the heirs of seventeenth-century projectors or real incentives to ingenuity, patents were only as good as their defence, and few but the wealthy Birmingham merchants could afford the legal costs.

Secrecy was the more effective protective device of the poorer manufacturer – and Birmingham was a very secretive place. Cautions were issued to manufacturers in 1783 and again in 1786 against 'showing workshops to strangers', and of the dangers of 'foreign emissaries with views to entice your workmen and to rob you of your newest and most important inventions'. Business was conducted in an atmosphere of secrecy, with patterns, prices and terms of credit all cleverly concealed.[34]

Monopoly rights established the institutional framework for invention; quality controls then reinforced it. Larger manufacturers campaigned relentlessly for controls on production practices and output standards. They aspired, furthermore, to the institutions of traditional corporate towns. The Birmingham trades had founded their success on freedom from product constraints, and their ability to copy high quality craft products of precious metals in cheaper metal imitations. But some tried as soon as possible to restrict these activities within a legally defined framework. First there was the campaign for Assay Offices in Birmingham and Sheffield, achieved in 1773. Then there was the proof house, establishing standards for gun manufacture, standards still not high enough to meet the stricter regulations of the Board of Ordnance. Though 50,000 guns were made per year to barter in the slave trade, many did not reach the standards required for the army and navy. Birmingham manufacturers protested that their guns, though not perfect, were safe, and should be used by troops – if not the English than at least the Irish.[35]

In Birmingham we see attempts to create standards and impose controls on an industry which had never had such traditions, and indeed on an industry which had flourished on producing articles in imitation of and substitution of guild craft work. Not only were controls created, but the language of old guild customs in traditional industries was invoked. The controls were, furthermore, a subject of conflict between the manufacturers and artisans who set the controls and those who bypassed them.[36]

The campaign for the Button Act of 1796 which laid down rules and definitions of the quality of gold in the gilting of buttons was one example. Again organized by Boulton, the project was conceived entirely within the framework of guild traditions, corporate towns and the protection of traditional commodities. Success would make Birmingham ware like wrought plate, linen, woollens, Sheffield cutlery and gold lace, all protected and regulated commodities. Prosecutions were to establish the moral priority of the 'the trade' over rights to individual property. There were to be:

> a caution to others, whose Principles may have been seduced by the Influence of bad Example, or by the Temptation of Excessive Profit, to endanger the Public Credit and the permanent Prosperity of Birmingham. No traffic, however great, can be valuable if it bears not the stamp of Honesty. . . . Let our Townsmen carry all their Gold to the Assay of Conscience.[37]

Boulton was the apostle *par excellence* of mass production, mechanizing, extending the division of labour and introducing cheaper metal alloys to cut costs. His views on mass marketing were renowned. 'It would not be worth my while to make for three countries only; but I find it well worth my while to make for all the world.'[38] His views on this did not change over his long years in business. In 1778 he declared, 'I rather choose to make great quantities with small profits, than small quantities with large profits.' And in 1794 he reiterated, 'We think it of far more consequence to supply the People than the Nobility.'[39]

But while he based his profit margins firmly in the mass market, Boulton sought to have his goods identified with quality, fashion and aristocratic taste. He placed great emphasis on new designs, taking up the Greek revival and using his connections in Naples with Sir William Hamilton not just for markets, but for obtaining and copying originals of Greek and Etruscan art. He ran a drawing school, used leading engravers and displayed and sold his ware in galleries, showrooms and auctions at Christies. He used royalty and nobility, making commemorative issues on royal birthdays, and sending new patterns to members of the aristocracy.[40]

It was clearly very important to Boulton and to other major manufacturers such as John Taylor that at least some of their products carried all the paraphernalia of exclusive luxury craft items. This was vital to a pricing policy, which involved making goods desirable in a socially emulative market, then making them accessible in price and place of sale to a broader middle-class market.[41]

The object of Birmingham's industrialists was thus not to create viable institutions for invention in a rising industrial city, but to legitimize and shape trading and manufacturing practices within a traditional corporate structure. These controls were achieved, furthermore, through lobbies of Parliament, something the Birmingham men were very good at. It is this lobbying, as much as anything, which has earned Birmingham its reputation among historians as the leader of the new industrial towns. 'Before there was an Anti-Corn Law League there was a Birmingham Political Union. Before there was a Manchester School there was a Birmingham school of political economists.'[42] There was the Birmingham Commercial Committee and Samuel Garbett's national General Chamber of Manufacturers in the 1780s. But in fact these were precarious groupings, rent by internal division, and ultimately lobbying was intermittent and piecemeal, carried out by particular trades and industries.[43] The principal lobbyists, moreover, perceived their efforts as an extension of landed society and the traditional political order. John Money has argued that Garbett and Wedgwood thought of the General Chamber of Manufactures in eighteenth-century terms as a permanent interest group which would take its rightful place alongside the older landed and commercial interests in the fabric of national politics. Thomas Walker of Manchester, on the other hand, thought of it as an open body much like the later pressure groups of the nineteenth century.[44] Boulton cultivated his connections with the local gentry as well as the metropolitan aristocracy.[45] He rallied support for the government's coercive acts against the American colonies in 1774, in opposition to the rest of the mercantile community, arguing quite incongruously that the Birmingham trades would be little affected by the American dispute.[46]

This attempt to establish an institutional framework for manufacture in the town through monopoly rights in invention, quality controls and the lobbying of interest groups reveals a dimension of Birmingham industry rarely mentioned by historians: its internal divisions. The initiatives taken in favour of controls were made by large-scale manufacturers supported by those smaller manufacturers closely dependent on them for subcontracting and marketing outlets. Their metropolitan, landed and commercial-imperial outlooks were not those of all manufacturers in the town; indeed a regional focus and different consumer market assumptions may well have developed among the smaller manufacturers.

The priorities of the large manufacturers were certainly not universally accepted in the town. An articulate opposition pointed to the growth of the larger firm, and explicitly raised the spectre of monopoly.[47] Product controls were also disputed:

By this inducement any dishonest fellow's oath is promised to be kept secret and the industrious mechanic prevented from the natural exercise of his talent, being also in fear of the constable's search warrant – is not this made more likely to destroy trade than to increase it?[48]

Others noted that the houses of the rich lay increasingly outside the town boundaries, and that there was growing physical segregation of working manufacturers to certain parts of the town.[49]

The economic divisions between the large-scale firms and the others were very large. By 1783 94 manufacturers had a capital greater than £5,000, 80 more than £10,000 and 17 more than £20,000.[50] But even in 1812 most Birmingham manufacturers were men of small capital, deploying from £300 or £400 up to £2,000 or £3,000, and employing between 5 and 30 hands.[51] The perception of the town by the very large manufacturers must have been very different from that of the common run of small and medium sized firms. The evidence of an industrial sector marked by large internal divisions is accumulating. There is also some limited evidence, as we have seen, for a divide in perceptions and priorities among those in the trades. It is important, at this point, however, to indicate the diversities in the scale of manufacture, and the existence of a substantial core of medium-sized businesses with different investment and market horizons rather than the few large manufacturers and their small-scale dependents whose outlook has dominated literary and political images of the town.

MENTALITIES OF PROPERTY – THE ARTISANS' PRACTICE

It is difficult to establish any clear picture of the distribution of wealth or the degree of concentration in the trades. Findings presented here are those based on the early stages of research, and thus represent only the broad outlines of an account of industrial structure. But the case built up by those who claim a social structure based on small-scale capitals, close relations between master and man, and organic growth from artisan to merchant capital is now open to serious challenge. First there was the great divide between small-scale and large-scale capitals[52] – but even the small tradesmen appear much more substantial than we have been led to believe. Apart from the very large firms we know of, newspaper references reveal another level of medium sized businesses. Those in the button, buckle and japanning trades in the 1780s who advertised for partners all sought those with a capital advance of £400-£600. Bankrupt or deceased firms advertising tools in the 1780s left much more than could be used by the typical family firm. William Orchard, a button-maker, advertised tools in January 1789 which included 21 lathes. In June of the same year, a buckle-maker had 20 buckle vices, lathes and vices to sell.[53] The better known medium sized firms who reported to the Committee of 1812 included George Room and Joseph Webster, manufacturers of japanned goods. They employed 40 and 100 hands respectively, out of 600–1,000 in the trade. Benjamin Cook had 40–50 employees in his toy and jewellery business; Thomas Osler had 30–100 in his glass, toy and button works. William Bannister, a plater,

190

employed 120, and Thomas Clarke who produced webbing, brass and toys employed 150.[54]

But even the broad range of small firms had more resources than we have been led to expect. Probate and fire insurance records allow an insight into a much greater range of resources in the metal trades than we have previously had access to. My research on these is not yet complete, but my work thus far has revealed extensive artisan property holding. The Royal Exchange Fire office records cover about 70 metal workers for the period 1777–87. Of these a little less than one-quarter insured five or more houses, and just under half had assets insured at £500 or more. The Sun Fire records, which cover 136 firms, reveal approximately 18 per cent with five or more houses and 42 per cent with policies valued at £500 or more. (See tables 8.2 and 8.3.) Probate records show that just under half of a sample of 250 metal workers examined for 1730–75 left two or more houses. These numbers must be treated with reservation. There are many among those who do not mention property who simply did not specify their wealth. Among those who did, there is still no indication of the value of this property. These houses are not valued at probate, but values are obtainable from title deeds used by C. W. Chalklin. Between 1746 and 1780 over 5,000 houses were added to Birmingham's housing stock. Major building booms took place in 1746–50 and the 1780s, and most of these houses sold for just under £100. Those in Boulton and Watt's Foundry Row and Low Row, built in 1796 and 1801 respectively, sold for £120. A number of smaller buildings frequently built at the backs of these houses, sold for £35–£60 and were rented for £3–£5. Many from the metal trades were heavily involved in this eighteenth-century property development, and were frequently multiple owners.[55]

The Birmingham manufacturers were much more prominently involved in the property market than were those in the Nottingham and Manchester textile industries. Why did they invest in housing? First, a number of these metal workers did have means beyond that of the small outworker. The outlays on building projects were often larger than those for units in outwork or small workshop manufacture. Expenditure on housing also rivalled the outlays on storage and materials of the smaller capitalist employer of outworkers in nail-making, or the outlay on tools, premises and materials of the small Birmingham button-maker. Other investment outlets included landed property and local business, but these often

Table 8.2 Royal Exchange Fire Assurance, 1777–87: metal working trades in Birmingham

Date	Policies	Houses		W/H*, shops		Trade goods, tools	Total £ value
		No.	£ value	No.	£ value	£ value	
1776	6	10	950	1	100	430	1,650
1777	7	25	2,950	4	80	760	3,790
1778	4	4	480	2	120	1,700	2,400
1779	5	16	1,329	3	340	500	6,200
1780	3	3	510	1	90	750	1,500
1781	10	79	3,190	14	1,210	2,770	8,530
1782	6	4	510	3	900	330	2,000
1783	3	12	430	1	50	50	550
1784	2	23	1,702	5	220	410	3,600
1785	4	5	340	5	160	1,000	1,650
1786	11	34	1,900	6	250	230	4,650
1787	9	21	2,285	13	1,685	2,700	7,400
Total	70	236	16,576	58	5,205	11,630	43,770

Notes:
No. of policyholders with 5 houses or more   16
No. of policyholders with 10 houses or more   8
No. of policyholders with assets insured at £500 or more   32
No. of policyholders with assets insured at £1,000 or more   10

*W/H = warehouses

Table 6.5 Sun Fire Assurance, 1776–86: metal working trades in Birmingham

Date	Policies	Houses No.	Houses £ value	W/H, shops No.	W/H, shops £ value	Trade goods, tools £ value	Total £ value
1776	4	9	2,510	14	5,420	150	8,100
1777	21	44	2,530	44	2,580*	4,755	10,560
1778	11	52	2,885	51	1,775*	1,015	6,500
1779	31	77	9,240	58	2,975	8,925	22,750
1780	13	28	2,798	29	1,052	2,240	6,400
1781	14	23	2,210	19	1,150	2,230	5,560
1782	8	28	1,535	22	1,185	1,020	4,320
1783	7	20	1,850	26	6,020	200	8,110
1784	11	24	1,985	15	295	890	3,700
1785	10	33	2,620	13	370	1,020	4,730
1786	6	13	675	9	325	1,050	1,300
Total	136	351	28,333	300	23,147	23,515	82,030

Note: *includes some trade goods and tools.

Date	Policies	5+ Houses	10+ Houses	Insured for £500+	Insured for £1,000+
1776	4	–	–	2	1
1777	21	4	1	6	3
1778	11	3	1	7	3
1779	31	7	–	18	6
1780	13	1	1	6	1
1781	14	2	–	6	–
1782	8	1	1	4	1
1783	7	1	1	3	2
1784	11	2	–	3	–
1785	10	2	1	3	2
1786	6	1	–	–	–
Totals	136	24	6	58	19
%		17.6	4	42	13

required much greater capital, sometimes over £1,000, for low yields in the first case and high risk in the second. Urban property ownership, on the other hand, offered a safe investment for a reasonable yield of 7–12 per cent, compared to 4–5 per cent in land, 4 per cent on Funds and 4–5 per cent on mortgages, and 10–15 per cent in manufacturing.[56] The Birmingham tradesmen appear to have invested where possible in property, and possibly not on extending their manufacturing enterprises. Several went so far as to require the dissolution of their enterprise at death, for reinvestment in a safe and steady asset, that is, property. Family strategy also appears to have been an important factor, with many attempting to accumulate enough property to pass one rental asset to each surviving child.[57]

Birmingham was also the home of an extensive development of early building clubs, and building societies were established as early as 1781. Hutton commented:

> The itch for building is predominant: we dip our fingers into mortar almost as soon as into business. This is attended with a public benefit of the first magnitude, for every house to be let holds forth a kind of invitation to the stranger to settle in it, who being of the laborious class promote the manufactures.[58]

Artisans and small tradesmen expressed their independence by thus helping each other to buy houses. Shares in these building clubs were usually £60–£120, with monthly subscriptions set at 5s–10s. Subscriptions were frequently met by building smaller tenements in backyards which were then rented out to employees or others.[59]

The property-owning trades of eighteenth-century Birmingham bore a close similarity to those of its rural hinterland, and to those of non-industrial parts of the country in the late seventeenth and very early eighteenth centuries. The rural metal workers of late seventeenth-century South Staffordshire invested, when they prospered, mainly in cottage property and workshops which they leased to their neighbours.[60]

At this point I can only speculate on the extent to which this investment was directed to housing rather than to plough back into industrial enterprise, i.e. whether this investment was complementary or alternative to manufacturing investment has yet to become clear. It may be, as Morris has argued for the nineteenth-century middle class of Yorkshire, that these artisans had a property cycle whereby assets were shifted from business and manufacturing to rental income and dividends when individuals reached their forties and fifties. Fire insurance records indicate generally greater assets in housing than in fixed capital. Those who insured with the Royal Exchange had equal amounts in housing and total capital. Those with the Sun had just over 60 per cent of the value of assets in capital goods insured in housing. Relatively low priority or valuation was attached to household goods and wearing apparel. The evidence of inventories thus far examined also indicates a relatively low level of stock and goods in process, along with a relatively basic range of consumer goods.

The generally small to medium scale of enterprises, along with this pattern of artisan property investment, indicates that priority may not have been placed on the increasing size of production units. This in turn may relate back to the organization of production and the techniques of these trades. Larger scale or even multiple workshops would require a shift in the levels of required supervision. A small family-run workshop would not just grow organically into something larger. It would require complete changes in organization and management which may have taken production outside the horizons or desires of an artisan producer. A range of small-scale, highly adaptable and flexible technologies also allowed the options of product and materials innovation without the requirements of large-scale production using extended divisions of labour. In other words, the scale economies of the Birmingham products and techniques were not all that great.

At the same time, it can be said that investment in housing was also investment in the town, and in its new housing estates. The Birmingham artisans' investments may have been safe and traditional, but they were also a stake in, and a commitment to the town. For the wills I have covered, most of the housing mentioned was to be found in the town; by the middle of the eighteenth century, at least, most of the Birmingham metal workers who left wills had left behind their agrarian roots.[61]

Many of Birmingham's big manufacturers built their homes outside the town and sought out social connections with landed society. At the same time, as we have seen, they aspired to a traditional corporate order for Birmingham's manufactures. The town's small and medium sized metal workers also staked their not insubstantial means in property, but this was urban housing, a reflection of their urban self-perception.

CONCLUSION

Jan de Vries argues that the striking feature about early modern Europe's rank-size distribution of cities as compared to that of China was the existence of many more smaller cities. The foundations of European industrialization were to be found in the growth of these cities in Europe from 1750; in England, exceptionally, for the seventeenth century. These cities were succeeded by what Hohenberg and Lees refer to as 'the modern urban economy', where economies of scale complemented economies of agglomeration, a process of 'consolidation, concentration, hierarchy'. De Vries predicts the possibility of a new cycle of urban renewal, one based not on the megalopolis mentality which has succeeded the large nineteenth-century industrial city, but on the formation yet again of smaller cities. He concludes: 'If future urbanization should take the form of city creation rather than urban concentration, it will not be for the first time, nor will it necessarily imply the wholesale abandonment of historic urban forms.'[62]

This bold recasting of the whole relationship between urbanization and industrialization, placing the origins of growth in new, indeed proto-industrial towns may present an appealing historical framework and indeed political message. It integrates urban and rural expansion, displacing preoccupations with factory concentrations and big cities. But just as we must disaggregate the process of urbanization into the types of city formation, especially as between large cities and newer small cities, so we must disaggregate once again this concept of 'urban growth from below', of the 'grass roots' of Europe's urban system. Here lies the significance of eighteenth-century Birmingham. This was one of Europe's new towns, though its growth dates from the seventeenth century, not from the last half of the eighteenth century. It was a regional centre and, in its manufacturing, a hub of technical ingenuity. So far, therefore, it seems to exemplify a grass roots industrial city. But it was not. After 1700 it was beyond classification as a smaller town in relation to England's other towns and cities. By 1750 it was among the top five. Its international and commercial focus cast it in a mercantile and imperial framework. Its place was not perceived by its industrial leaders as separate from, but as an extension of landed society and corporate towns, and its artisans were property holders. And yet this town grew phenomenally in the eighteenth century, its manufacturing output and diversity prodigious, its technical virtuosity unsurpassed. It was a city of the eighteenth century, neither traditional nor an early version of the Manchester model.

To return in the end to historiography, what are the implications of Birmingham's history for our understanding of the relationships between urbanization and innovation? What does Birmingham tell us about technical change and the Industrial Revolution? First, it is clear that unlike the predictions of the simple proto-industrial model, this town was not a technical backwater, a refuge of guild restrictions. It was instead a technological leader. The prominence of the town and its industries tell us that the early phases of British industrialization were urban at least as much as they were rural. Although reasons for Birmingham's technological leadership have still to be elucidated fully, many contributory factors have been identified: lack of institutional regulation, religious toleration, long historical concentrations of skilled workers, traditions of artisan mutuality, and urban economies of agglomeration. But even if all of these explanations have validity, which as I have shown is doubtful, they are not sufficient. The diversities of scale in Birmingham manufactures mean that the town cannot be squared with the model of the 'creative city', as a versatile centre of symbiosis for networks of small innovative firms.[63] Nor can Birmingham's achievements be explained by psychologistic appeals to a consensual ethos which balanced 'co-operation and competition among firms'. The 'collective learning of technologies, markets and codes of behaviour across and within generations' combined with the 'scope for competitive ambition'[64] were not general characteristics of the Birmingham achievement: relatively few such values were shared by the whole manufacturing class.

Instead, it was in the conflict and competition between the larger manufacturers and the lesser, in conjunction with its hinterland, but also separate from it, that the town forged its own record of technical innovation. This was notably a record of participation in, and not resistance to new techniques, something which set Birmingham apart from the Industrial Revolution of the textile regions. Many of Birmingham's inventions were reputedly those of small artisans and working men and women, protected by secrecy and individuality. They were of the type which Hawkes

Smith described as 'that alone which require more force than the arms and tools of the workman could wield, still leaving his skill and experience of head, hand and eye in full exercise'.[65] Birmingham's machinery was in the main hand operated, only supplemented in some cases by horse and water power. Large firms like Taylor's toy works and Boulton's Soho factory did indeed develop extended divisions of labour, and made use of machinery powered by water mills. But there appear to have been no overriding economies of scale which made the larger firm the norm. And in an industry of highly differentiated markets and extensive product innovation, the diseconomies of scale associated with rigidity, management and hierarchical supervision made the small adaptable firm a viable alternative. Larger firms with their innovations in organization and division of labour, their commercial empires and corporate mercantile aspirations, still developed and used similar technologies to the small ones. This process of city-centred innovation, confined neither to factories and powered machinery nor to artisan tinkering, but achieving a competitive development of both, made for a distinctive eighteenth-century record of technological development. This is a record which the historian of aggregate growth passes by: aggregate productivity estimates do not encompass or account for innovations in products and materials. But it was these innovations as much as any factory or steam-powered machine which constituted Britain's Industrial Revolution.

NOTES

1 N. F. R. Crafts, *British Economic Growth during the Industrial Revolution*, Oxford, 1985.
2 F. Mendels and P. Deyon, 'Proto-industrialization: theory and reality, *Eighth International Congress of Economic History*, Budapest, 1982. Also see F. Mendels, 'Des industries rurales et la protoindustrialisation: historique d'un changement de perspective', *Annales ESC*, 39, 5, 1984–5.
3 Crafts, *British Economic Growth*, op. cit, 17 and 'British economic growth 1700–1850: some difficulties of interpretation', Paper to the Workshop on Quantitative Economic History, University of Gröningen, September 1985, 3–4. Also see J. Mokyr, 'Has the Industrial Revolution been crowded out: some reflections on Crafts and Williamson', *Explorations in Economic History*, 24, 1987, 315.
4 See, for example, J. V. Beckett, *The Aristocracy in England 1660–1914*,

Oxford, 1986; and J. Cannon, *The Aristocratic Century: The Peerage of Eighteenth Century England*, Cambridge, 1984.

5 A. Briggs, 'Birmingham' in his *Victorian Cities*, London, 1963, 185–245.

6 C. Sabel and J. Zeitlin, 'Historical alternatives to mass production', *Past and Present*, 108, 1985, 133–76.

7 D. Smith, *Conflict and Compromise: Class Formation in English Society 1830–1914. A Comparative Study of Birmingham and Sheffield*, London, 1982, 34.

8 E. Duggan, 'The Impact of Industrialization on an Urban Labour Market – Birmingham, England 1770–1860', Ph.D. thesis, Wisconsin, published in New York, 1985, 117–33.

9 C. Behagg, 'Myths of cohesion: capital and compromise in the historiography of nineteenth-century Birmingham', *Social History*, 11, 1986, 381.

10 A. Briggs, 'Social structure and politics in Birmingham and Lyons, 1825–1848' (1950) in A. Briggs (ed.), *The Collected Essays of Asa Briggs*, I, Brighton, 1985, 214–40; P. Hohenberg and L. Lees, *The Making of Urban Europe 1000–1950*, Cambridge, Mass. and London, 1985, 190–1.

11 J. de Vries, *European Urbanization 1500–1800*, Cambridge, Mass., 1984, 238–46.

12 E. A. Wrigley, 'Urban growth and agricultural change: England and the Continent in the early modern period', *Journal of Interdisciplinary History*, 15, 4, Spring 1985, 708.

13 Hohenberg and Lees, *Making of Urban Europe*, op. cit., 113–20. For further development of this model see Hohenberg and Lees, 'Urban decline and regional economies: Brabant, Castile and Lombardy, 1550–1750', *Journal for Comparative Study of Society and History*, 1989, 439–61.

14 Hohenberg and Lees, 'Urban decline', op. cit., 457.

15 See Table 8.1; Hohenberg and Lees, op. cit., Wrigley, op. cit., 686.

16 See M. W. Flinn, *The History of the British Coal Industry, II, 1700–1830, The Industrial Revolution*, Oxford, 1984, 27; M. J. Wise and B. L. Johnson, 'The changing regional pattern during the eighteenth century' in M. J. Wise (ed.), *Birmingham and its Regional Setting. A Scientific Survey*, Birmingham, 1950, 161–74; and G. C. Allen, *The Industrial History of Birmingham and the Black Country 1860–1927*, London, 1929, 51.

17 Duggan, op. cit., 18.

18 See M. B. Rowlands, 'Continuity and change in an industrializing society: the case of the West Midlands industries' in P. Hudson, *Regions and Industries*, Cambridge, 1989, 193. This article also provides a detailed chronology of the development of industry in the West Midlands.

19 See E. H. Robinson, 'Matthew Boulton and Josiah Wedgwood, apostles of fashion' in R. P. T. Davenport-Hines and J. Liebenau, *Business in the Age of Reason*, London, 1987. For a recent treatment of the development of middle-class consumption see L. Weatherill, *Consumer Behaviour and Material Culture in Britain 1660–1760*, London, 1988.

20 See *Journals of the House of Commons*, 32 Geo. III, Martis 20, 1759, XXVIII, 496–7 and E. Robinson, 'Boulton and Fothergill, 1762–1782

and 'The Birmingham export of hardware', *University of Birmingham Historical Journal*, VII, 1959–60.

21 Rowlands, 'Continuity and change', op. cit., 184.

22 E. Hopkins, *Birmingham. The First Manufacturing Town in the World 1760–1840*, London, 1989, 63, 74.

23 J. Money, *Experience and Identity, Birmingham and the West Midlands 1760–1800*, Montreal, 1977, 25–9.

24 Hopkins, *Birmingham*, op. cit., 30.

25 Duggan, op. cit., 47, 53.

26 See P. Hudson, 'The regional perspective', in Hudson (ed.), *Regions and Industries. A Perspective on the Industrial Revolution in Britain*, Cambridge, 1989, 5–38.

27 On the modern sunrise industries of the Third World see R. Pahl, *On Work*, (essays by Pearson, Alic and Harris), Oxford, 1988.

28 J. Jacobs, *Cities and the Wealth of Nations*, New York and Toronto, 1984, 40.

29 See Hopkins, *Birmingham*, op. cit., 7–8 and Rowlands, 'Continuity and change', op. cit., 186.

30 Sabel and Zeitlin, op. cit., 155.

31 R. A. C. Allen, 'Collective invention', *Journal of Economic Behaviour and Organization*, IV, 1983.

32 Cited in Samuel Smiles, *Lives of Boulton and Watt* (2nd edn), London, 1866, 341.

33 H. Hamilton, *The English Brass and Copper Industries to 1800*, London, 1926.

34 See J. A. Langford, *A Century of Birmingham Life: A Chronicle of Local Events 1741–1841*, Birmingham, 1841, 318 and 326; E. H. Robinson, 'Boulton and Fothergill, 1752–1782,' op. cit., 72.

35 Assay Office Papers, Birmingham Reference Library: Samuel Garbett Papers.

36 See D. Hay, 'Manufacturers and the criminal law in the late eighteenth century: crime and police in south Staffordshire', paper for *Past and Present* Coloquium, Oxford, 1983. Also see Hay, 'Crime, authority and the criminal law', Ph.D. thesis, Warwick, 1975.

37 Assay Office Papers, Birmingham Reference Library.

38 N. McKendrick, J. Brewer and J. Plumb, *The Consumer Revolution*, London, 1983, 77.

39 E. L. Jones, 'The fashion manipulators: consumer tastes and British industries 1660–1800' in L. P. Cain and P. J. Uselding (eds), *Business Enterprise and Economic Change*, Ohio, 1973, 218.

40 ibid., 271; Robinson, 'Matthew Boulton and Josiah Wedgwood', op. cit., 109–10.

41 McKendrick, Brewer and Plumb, op. cit., 74.

42 Briggs, *Victorian Cities*, op. cit., 187.

43 J. Styles, 'Interest groups, lobbying and Parliament in eighteenth-century England', unpublished paper, 1986.

44 Money, *Experience*, op cit., 44.

45 J. Money, 'Birmingham and the West Midlands, 1760–1793: politics

and regional identity in the English provinces in the later eighteenth century', *Midland History*, I, 1, 1971, 10–11.

46 B. D. Bargar, 'Matthew Boulton and the Birmingham petition of 1775', *William and Mary Quarterly*, series 3, 13, 1956, 31. Boulton argued, 'I do but little business myself to America. Not so much as one-twentieth of our manufactures is sent thither. The nailers might be seriously affected . . . but this was a negligible factor, for the quantity of nails sent . . . does not exceed one-fourth of the whole made in this city.' Quite the reverse was claimed by several merchants and manufacturers in 1812. See *House of Commons Minutes of Evidence taken before the Committee of the Whole House to Consider Several Petitions against the Orders in Council, Reports from Committees*, PP 1812, III, 2–51.

47 See *Address to Manufacturers in General* (1763); cited in Money, *Experience*, op. cit., 260.

48 Assay Office Papers.

49 This point was made in opposition to the Police Bill of the late 1780s and again in the *Appeal to Manufacturers on the Present State of Trade* (1795). See Money, *Experience*, op. cit., 15 and 267. On the origins of the separation of home from work in the Birmingham middle classes see L. Davidoff and C. Hall, *Family Fortunes. Men and Women of the English Middle Class, 1780–1850*, London, 1987, chap. 8.

50 Hamilton, *Brass and Copper*, op. cit., 273.

51 Hopkins, *Birmingham*, op. cit., 91.

52 See Duggan, op. cit., and Behagg, op. cit.

53 *Aris's Gazette*, 26 June 1778; 7 May 1781; 22 April 1782; 26 April 1784; 13 June 1785.

54 House of Commons Committee, PP 1812.

55 C. W. Chalklin, *The Provincial Towns of Georgian England. A Study of the Building Process 1740–1820*, London, 1974.

56 ibid., 160–3.

57 Probate Records, Birmingham parish.

58 Cited in Chalklin, op. cit., 237–8.

59 S. D. Chapman and J. N. Bartlett, 'The contribution of building clubs and freehold land societies to working-class housing in Birmingham' in S. D. Chapman, (ed.), *The History of Working Class Housing: A Symposium*, Newton Abbot, 1971.

60 M. B. Rowlands, 'Industry and social change in Staffordshire, 1660–1760. A study of probate and other records of tradesmen', 39. *Lichfield and South Staffordshire Archaeological Society Transactions*, 9, 1967–8.

61 Probate records, Birmingham parish.

62 De Vries, *European Urbanization*, op. cit., 261, 266.

63 Jacobs, op. cit.

64 Sabel and Zeitlin, op. cit., 155.

65 W. Hawkes Smith, *Birmingham and its Vicinity as a Manufacturing and Commercial District*, London, 1836, 18.

Part V

MARKET PRODUCTION AND WOMEN'S WORK

9

LOVE AND POWER IN THE PROTO-INDUSTRIAL FAMILY

Gay L. Gullickson

In 1983 Martine Segalen's *Mari et femme dans la société paysanne* was published in English under the title *Love and Power in the Peasant Family*.[1] While the English title bears little resemblance to the French, it does convey the central issue of the book and indeed of much of social history – what was life like in the peasant family? Were wives subservient to their husbands? Were men oblivious to the feelings of their wives and daughters? Or did husbands and wives love each other and their children much as husbands and wives and parents do today? Were marriages hierarchically organized economic units forged solely to facilitate survival? Or were they economic partnerships based on mutual respect and shared work and responsibility?

The answers to such questions are difficult to discern in the material available to social historians, and opinions vary widely.[2] Charivari rituals, marriage rituals and peasant proverbs indicate that there were strongly prescribed gender roles in peasant communities and that these roles were hierarchically arranged.[3] The husband was to exercise authority and his wife was to obey him. When wives became too powerful or husbands too subservient, each could be publicly humiliated (charivaried) as the community attempted to restore the 'proper' male – female relationship in the marriage. While the charivari, marriage rituals and peasant proverbs tell us a great deal about prescribed gender roles and gender stereotypes, they do not tell us to what degree men and women conformed to or rebelled against these roles. Some rebellion is clear, simply from the existence of charivari, but its extent is not, nor is the extent to which couples may have publicly conformed and privately rebelled against rigid roles.

Although he couched them in different terms, the questions of love and power that Segalen and others have raised about peasant families were raised about proto-industrial families by Hans Medick in a widely cited 1976 article.[4] Medick spoke of status rather than power, but his concern was much the same as Segalen's – the relationship between husbands and wives in families that worked for the putting-out merchants. Medick argued that the return of men's work to the house and the creation of jobs for women in proto-industrial regions had a profound effect upon roles and relationships. The picture he painted was one of increasingly important female earnings followed by greater co-operation between the sexes, a breakdown in the sexual division of paid labour and, in regions where the demand for female labour was high, the assumption of household tasks by men. In Medick's view, these increasingly egalitarian gender relationships were symbolized, but not limited to, husbands' and wives' joint participation in status consumption, i.e. the consumption of alcohol and tobacco both within the household and in public.[5] In short, in Medick's view, earning ability and status (respect, decision-making power within the family, access to public leisure and consumption) went hand in hand for women. As one improved, so did the other.

Medick raised an intriguing possibility – that proto-industrialization, by providing jobs for women, increased their power within the family and the larger community. In the absence of diaries and letters from the men and women who were employed by the putting-out industries, Medick's hypothesis is difficult to pursue. In fact, the evidence he cited was sparse and it is not clear that all of it came from regions that we today would define as proto-industrial.[6] His conclusions have continued to interest scholars, however, since they pose for the proto-industrial period the question that studies of women's work have raised and debated since 1919, when Alice Clark[7] first tackled it in her study of the *Working Life of Women in the Seventeenth Century*: have economic changes improved or impaired women's lives and raised or lowered their status or power within the family, the workplace and the community?

A decade after Medick's article, I think it is time to examine the issue of women's status or, to use the language of Segalen's translator, of love and power, in the proto-industrial family again. None of the proto-industrial jobs performed by women and men in rural areas in and of themselves conferred high labour status.[8] They did not give individuals autonomy or control over economic resources. Workers were at the mercy of the putting-out merchants

206

and travelling porters for the supply of raw materials and the payment of wages. They had no independent access to supplies or markets. When raw materials were in short supply, or prices were low, they suffered loss of work and income without recourse. Status is relative, however, and the question I wish to address here is the extent to which women's status – i.e. access to higher wages, power within the family or community, access to public leisure and consumption, independence, respect, etc. – improved in relationship to that of men.

Most of the evidence I will present in reference to this question is drawn from my own study of the manuscript censuses, notarial and judicial records, *cahiers de doléances* and local *mémoires* from the pays de Caux in Upper Normandy in the late eighteenth and early nineteenth centuries. Although there is much variety among proto-industrial regions, I think the situation in the pays de Caux and those presented in other published case-studies supports a different conclusion from the one reached by Medick in 1976. In general, there appears to have been little or no improvement in women's status within the community during this period and shifts in the love and power relationships within the family are almost impossible to detect, despite a widespread expansion of demand for female labour and the entry of women into previously all-male occupations in many proto-industrial regions.

FEMALE EMPLOYMENT AND EARNINGS

The eighteenth century

The Seine river, winding slowly towards the English Channel from Paris, passes through the old province of Normandy, dividing it into two distinct sections. Rouen, the capital of the province, lies midway to the English Channel, on the northern bank of a large loop in the river. Connected to both the domestic markets of Paris and the export markets of England, Spain and Portugal by short water routes, Rouen was an important commercial centre well before the beginning of the eighteenth century.[9]

North of the city lies the pays de Caux, a large triangular-shaped plateau covered with grain fields and woods and traversed by a major road leading from Rouen to Dieppe. By virtue of its location near a large international market town and its relatively easy traversability, the Caux was a major source of labour for the

Rouen merchants well before the proto-industrial era. Work was put out into the countryside by travelling porters and then returned to the city for finishing and sale. From at least the beginning of the seventeenth century, the small size of Rouen's population, its merchants' desire to increase production, and the Caux's location meant that *cauchois* peasants often alternated work in agriculture with work in cottage industry. As long as farming was highly seasonal in its labour demand, and the Rouen merchants were content with a decline in yarn and cloth production during the planting and harvest seasons, agriculture and the textile industry could and did share the same workforce.

At the turn of the eighteenth century, a development that would lead to the proto-industrialization of the Caux occurred – the Rouen merchants began to experiment with the spinning and weaving of cotton. Female spinners readily abandoned wool and flax for the cleaner, better smelling and more easily worked cotton, and rural weavers began to ply their linen warps with cotton wefts. By the 1760s the cotton industry was expanding rapidly and the wool industry was in full-scale decline.[10]

The half-cotton half-linen fabric produced in the Caux reminded people of Oriental fabric and was called *siamoise*. Most *siamoises* were not of high quality, and their major purchasers were peasants, urban workers and colonial planters who bought the material to clothe their slaves. They came in several varieties and three colours: red, white and blue solids, and red and white, and blue and white stripes and checks.[11]

Before the introduction of spinning machines at the end of the eighteenth century, fabric production could only be expanded by increasing the number of workers. It is impossible to determine the exact number of *cauchois* women, men and children who were employed in the cotton industry, but it was a substantial and ever-growing number. Arthur Young was so impressed by the size of the industry that in 1788 he recorded in his diary as he passed through the region that he saw 'farmhouses and cottages everywhere, and the cotton manufacture in all'.[12] This may have been hyperbole on Young's part, but inventories of possessions made after death, as well as contemporary estimates of the number of spinners and weavers in the Caux support the basic thrust of his statement. Based on the number of looms operating in the region, M. Goy, an Inspecteur des Manufactures at Rouen, estimated in 1782 that 188,207 persons were employed by the Rouen textile merchants, most of whom were in the Caux.[13] (The total population of Upper Normandy in the 1780s was approximately 590,000.)[14]

For the Caux, as for other places, estimates of the number of spinners (and carders) necessary to keep one weaver working full time vary from observer to observer and historian to historian, but eight to ten is the likely number. Goy assumed that there were 9.5 workers per loom, or approximately eight spinners to every weaver, to arrive at his 1782 figure of 188,207 cotton workers.[15]

The importance of spinning as a source of employment for women and of income for the Caux can be seen in a cluster of villages known administratively in the eighteenth century as the canton of Auffay. Located along the eastern edge of the region, approximately halfway between Dieppe and Rouen, the twenty-one villages ranged in size from tiny Bazomesnil with an adult population of only 96 to the village of Auffay with an adult population of 668 in 1796.[16] This part of the Caux lay well within the range of the Rouen putting-out merchants, and three-quarters of the women in the villages worked for the Rouen merchants as spinners. In the small village of Sevis, an astounding 98 per cent of the women (120 out of 123) were spinners. In the village of Auffay, 223 of the 365 women were spinners (61.1 per cent).

In comparison with spinning the other employers of female labour – harvest work in the fields, sewing, and merchant and artisan businesses – were insignificant in the Caux. Weaving, however, was only one of the major employers of male labour. Large numbers of men also worked in artisan crafts, ran merchant businesses, and worked in agriculture as farmers, domestics and day labourers.[17] In the canton of Auffay as a whole only 15 per cent of the men were weavers, quite low in comparison with the 75 per cent of women who spun for the merchants. Only in the small village of St Denis sur Scye did the percentage of weavers reach 40 per cent of the male population in this part of the Caux.[18]

In the eighteenth century, the adult sexual division of labour between spinning (and other preparatory steps in the production of yarn) and weaving was maintained quite rigidly in the Caux. No women appear in eighteenth-century records as weavers and very few adult men are listed as spinners. Most of the men who were spinners were generally too young or too old to work at more strenuous tasks (only forty men over the age of sixteen are listed as spinners in the 1796 Census for the canton of Auffay and twenty-six of those were aged sixty or older),[19] and the others may have been disabled in some way that would have excluded them from other occupations, as Michel Léonard Girot of Auffay was. Girot suffered from muscular spasms and worked as a spinner and warper, attaching the warp threads to the loom. Even this work was difficult for Girot since sudden, unexpected sounds would cause him to jump and break his threads.[20]

Table 9.1 Spinners and weavers in the canton of Auffay, an IV (1796)

Commune	Spinners	Women	%	Weavers	Men	%
Auffay	223	365	61.1	32	303	10.6
Bazomesnil	41	50	82.0	10	46	21.7
Bracquetuit	117	179	65.4	15	155	9.7
Cressy	114	149	76.5	2	123	1.6
Cropus	98	107	91.6	27	97	27.8
Etaimpuis	59	66	89.4	19	67	28.4
Fresnay le Long	87	122	71.3	14	110	12.7
Heugleville sur Scie	228	292	78.1	54	269	20.1
Montreuil	148	215	68.8	12	191	6.3
St Denis sur Scie	78	85	91.8	33	82	40.2
St Hellier	77	108	71.3	13	94	13.8
St Maclou de Folleville	112	185	60.5	29	167	17.4
St Sulpice	74	89	83.1	7	67	10.4
St Victor l'Abbaye	173	206	84.0	12	184	6.5
Sevis	120	123	97.6	19	99	19.2
Totes	61	71	85.9	19	112	17.0
Varneville	102	133	76.7	16	129	12.4
Vassonville	99	177	84.6	42	110	38.2
Total	2,011	2,662*	75.5	375	2,405*	15.6
Biennais**	–	74	–	4	57	7.0
Loeuilly**	29	97	29.9	8	67	11.9
Notre Dame du Parc**	8	58	13.8	11	59	18.6
Total	?	2,891	?	398	2,588	15.4

Source: ADSM L367.
Notes
* The imbalance in the male and female populations is probably accounted for by the absence of men who were serving in the French army. In 1800, 348 men from these villages were listed as absent soldiers.
**Biennais, Loeuilly, and Notre Dame du Parc left most female occupations unrecorded, and Notre Dame du Parc, unlike the other communes, left many male occupations unrecorded.

While it seems likely that the wives and daughters of weavers took turns at the small looms used in the Caux when the men were ill, or tired, or working in the fields, there is no direct evidence to this effect.[21] Similarly, there is no evidence that men helped their wives by spinning or carding during winter months when there was no farm work to be done in the fields, although such a practice again seems likely since many men had learned to card and spin as children.[22]

Estimates of how much spinners and weavers earned in the Caux vary from observer to observer, but it is clear that female spinners earned far less than male weavers. Spinners were paid according to the quantity and quality of the yarn they produced. Lighter, more finely spun yarn received a higher piecerate than heavy yarn. Inspector Goy estimated that spinners earned between ten and fifteen *sous* per day, depending on how many hours they worked.[23] Arthur Young, the travelling agronomist, reported that spinners earned nine *sous* a day.[24] If we average these figures, we are left with the estimate that *cauchois* women earned about twelve *sous* per day. This may be a high estimate, however, because there is no way of telling whether the time a woman spent cleaning, carding and washing raw cotton is included in the estimates of how much yarn she could spin a day. If this work was not included in time estimates for spinning, then Arthur Young's figure of nine *sous*, the lowest of the eighteenth-century estimates of average daily earnings for spinners, may be the most accurate. (For the estimates of several historians see Table 9.2.)

Like spinners, weavers were paid by the piece. Rates varied according to the size of the piece, the difficulty of the work and the fineness of the weave.[25] Average wages are again difficult to determine because we know nothing about the weavers' hours and days of work on either a weekly or an annual basis. It is clear, however, that experienced weavers earned more than beginners because they worked more quickly and with greater skill. It is possible that highly skilled weavers earned as much as thirty or forty *sous* in a day,[26] although Goy estimated that the average *cauchois* weaver earned only twenty *sous* per day.[27]

While it is impossible to be precise about the earnings of men and women in cottage industry, it is important to note that whenever a range of wages is cited, the lowest wages paid to men are higher than the highest wages paid to women. Nevertheless, women's wages were crucial to their families. Without them, many *cauchois* families would have been forced to choose between sending sons and daughters away from home to work, making the husband/father a seasonal migrant, and moving out of the region, since the population of the region exceeded the needs of agriculture. None of these survival strategies was necessary in the Caux. There is no evidence of seasonal migration by adult men, and most children, both daughters and sons, remained at home until they married. Women's earnings thus helped keep the family together.[28]

Table 9.2 Estimated daily earnings (in *sous*)

Estimated by	spinners	weavers
Goy	10–15	20
Bouloiseau	8–15	30–40
Sion	8–12	20
Evrard	12–14	15–18

Sources: AN F12 560 (Goy's Report); M. M. Bouloiseau, 'Aspects sociaux de la crise cotonnière dans les campagnes rouennaises en 1788–1789', *Actes de 81ᵉ Congrès National des Sociétés Savantes*, Rouen-Caen, 1956, Paris, 1956, 405–6; Jules Sion, *Les paysans de la Normandie Orientale*, Paris, 1909, 184–5; Fernand Evrard, 'Les ouvriers du textile dans la région rouennaise (1789–1802)', *Annales historiques de la Révolution française*, 108, 1947, 349–50.

Table 9.3 Premarital geographical mobility, Auffay, 1751–1817

Marriage date	Men			Women		
	Non-orphans*	Co-resident**	%	Non-orphans*	Co-resident**	%
1751–86	111	101	91.0	124	116	93.5
1787–1817	157	130	82.8	165	162	98.2
1818–50	215	149	69.3	214	185	86.4
Total	483	380	78.7	503	463	92.0

Source: Family Reconstitution Study, Auffay.
Notes: *Individuals with at least one living parent at the time of marriage.
  **Living in the same village as parent(s) and presumably with them.

While their earnings remained low, women did exercise some control over them since they worked directly for the putting-out merchants rather than for weaver-husbands. The procedure in the Caux was for the women to sell their completed yarn in the local textile markets or back to the merchant from whom they had 'purchased' the raw cotton. The yarn merchants then sold the completed yarn to other merchants who had the thread washed and dyed, and put it back out into the countryside to be woven.[29]

In Auffay, the spinners rose in the middle of the night to carry their skeins of yarn several miles in leather backpacks to the textile market in Bacqueville, where trading began at dawn. The trip to the market was an exclusively female pilgrimage. Neither men nor children were allowed to accompany the women on their weekly treks.[30] Fabric, on the other hand, was too heavy to be carried to markets and was retrieved by the same travelling porters who distributed spun yarn and prepared warps to the weavers.[31]

In addition to selling their yarn alone at the textile markets, spinners in Auffay gathered in each others' homes during long winter evenings to work and talk. Such occasions for female community may have strengthened individual *cauchois* women when it came to dealing with their husbands or children, and may have been duplicated in other communities.[32] They did not, however, improve women's status within the community. While women gathered to work, men often gathered in the local cafés to drink and bet small sums on dominoes. The cafés were where high-status consumption was taking place and, judging from the complaints about their deleterious effects on the behaviour and morality of young men in the 1789 *cahiers de doléances* for the Caux, the cafés were male enclaves.[33] It was women's earnings from spinning that gave the men pocket-money and that made the existence of the cafés possible. Women had no comparable gathering place. They gathered to work, not to relax – not a sign of improving status.

While most studies of proto-industrialization have not included detailed information about the female labour force, high female employment, low female wages and a sexual division of labour between spinning and weaving appear to have been widespread but not universal in these regions. In the Flemish linen industry, studied by Franklin Mendels, four female spinners plus one-and-a-half workers in ancillary tasks (children of both sexes as well as adult women) were needed for every male weaver.[34] Despite the demand for their labour, spinners were paid such low piecerates that they could barely survive, let alone acquire a dowry for marriage.[35] Similarly, in the English framework knitting industry in Shepshed, Leicestershire, David Levine's research reveals that women and children spun, while men knitted, and that individual earnings were so low that all members of the nuclear family as well as co-resident kin had to work in the industry for a household to make ends meet.[36] In the north-western and western counties of Ireland, studied by Brenda Collins, spinning also remained women's work and families with few daughters or other female kin hired live-in female spinners to help spin the family's flax, since the income generated by spinning was crucial to their ability to pay the cash rent on their farms.[37]

Of the major case-studies that focus on the social and demographic consequences of proto-industrialization, only Rudolf Braun's work on the highlands of Zurich reveals a situation in which spinning and weaving were not sexually segregated tasks in the eighteenth century, although the extent to which women and men crossed the traditional gender divisions in textile production remains unclear from his study.[38]

Despite the low piecerates for which most spinners worked, women's earnings had a positive effect on the standard of living, family formation and family cohesiveness in proto-industrial regions. In the Zurich highlands, Braun has argued, cottage industry gave the sons and daughters of landholding families more freedom in choosing marriage partners since land was no longer the sole source of a family's income. What might be foregone in the acquisition of land could be made up in diligent work at the spinning wheel and loom. For landless peasants, the simple possession of two spinning wheels now made marriage possible and marriage frequency increased while marriage ages fell.[39] Braun regarded these marriages, based on personal attraction rather than economic considerations, as a sign that a major transformation in erotic consciousness was occurring in the highlands. Marriage became 'enveloped in a much more intimate aura. . . . [It was now] a reciprocal commitment of two people, who hope with it to realize their individual happiness.'[40]

While other historians have not gone as far as Braun in analysing the effect of proto-industrialization on the erotic or romantic dimension of peasant life, most have agreed that cottage industry affected family formation and strengthened family ties by allowing people who would otherwise have had to leave in search of work to remain at home. Braun himself argued that it became less necessary for highland daughters to work as servants in Zurich, for sons to join the army and for fathers to look for seasonal work in the lowlands.[41] Similarly, Collins found that in the north-western and western flax- and linen-producing counties of Ireland, adolescents no longer had to leave the family farm to seek work, and adult men no longer had to seek winter work in cities and other regions.[42] And Levine's research reveals that the availability of work in the hosiery industry in Leicestershire villages like Shepshed made it possible for children to remain at home while their counterparts in purely agricultural villages were forced to leave in search of employment as farm labourers or domestic servants.[43]

In some regions, the presence of cottage work also affected marriage patterns. In his pioneering work on Flanders, Mendels found that marriage frequency entered an upward spiral during the proto-industrial period, with the number of marriages increasing in years when the price of linen was high in comparison to that of grain, and not declining in bad years.[44] Even more dramatic, Levine found a five-and-a-half-year decline in the mean age at first marriage for both men and women in the late eighteenth and early nineteenth centuries, when framework knitting was at its peak in Shepshed.[45]

Such changes in marriage ages and frequency did not always accompany proto-industrialization, however. In the pays de Caux, marriage frequency was high in the eighteenth century when cottage spinning provided a job for virtually any woman who was willing to work, and labour demands in weaving, artisan and merchant crafts and farming created full male employment. The the low wages paid to spinners kept marriage ages high, however, and later, when spinning disappeared as an employer of female labour, marriage frequency for women declined as male migration to the urban textile centres increased. (See Table 9.3.)[46] Similarly, Myron Gutmann and René Leboutte found that the mean female marriage age remained high and stable throughout the eighteenth and early nineteenth centuries in three proto-industrial Belgian villages,[47] and James Lehning has shown that proto-industrialization did not always lead to lower marriage ages and higher marriage frequency in the *département* of the Loire in France.[48]

In some regions, the steady employment offered by the spinning merchants allowed women to create their own living arrangements, a development that was usually impossible because female earnings were so low. In the Caux, for instance, some single and widowed women were able to support themselves without the assistance of an adult wage earner. Although eighteenth-century tax rolls do not list the occupations of most of the women who headed households (and never list them for other women), given the predominance of spinning in the occupations of women, it seems likely that most of them were spinners.[49] Their earnings from this, combined, perhaps, with the produce from a garden and a few chickens, and sometimes with the earnings of their children, allowed them to live in their own homes rather than board with relatives or neighbours. Throughout the second half of the eighteenth century, between 10 and 15 per cent of the households in Auffay were headed by women, a fairly high percentage for an eighteenth-century village.[50]

It is not clear from Collins's published work whether all-female households developed in the north of Ireland, but it was certainly the case that the more female spinners a family or household contained, the better. So much so that there was a clear trend away from households in which women spun yarn for male weavers towards households in which women spun yarn for the market.[51] In Shepshed, however, women's earnings were so low that widows who could not find lodgers or a family to share a household were forced to enter the workhouse.[52] And in Flanders spinners earned so little that they were often 'condemned to celibacy', and special lay and religious communities were set up specifically to aid spinsters.[53]

In general, it appears that proto-industrialization brought some improvements to the lives of women in the eighteenth century. Their work raised the economic security of their families, who could now more easily pay the rent on the land or cottage than they could before. Adolescent girls and boys could remain with their families until they married, which reduced the chances that they would be economically or sexually exploited by an employer or his male employees, and their chances of marrying improved as they and young men found steady work from the putting-out merchants. Their wages remained lower than those of men, however, and in most regions a woman alone faced dire poverty. Even in a village like Auffay, where some women were able to maintain their own households, their economic well-being should not be exaggerated. Survival was based on constant work and full employment, and the increased employment offered by the spinning merchants was to be short-lived.

The nineteenth century

At the end of the eighteenth century, machines replaced hand wheels and spinning moved into factories, whose locations were determined not by the presence of a labour force (as the location of proto-industries had been) but by the presence of running water to power the machinery. The first workers to be affected by mechanization were the women who spun wool for the hosiery industry in villages like Shepshed.[54] Cotton spinners in regions like the Caux were also affected early on, although the trade blockades of the Revolutionary and Napoleonic eras somewhat delayed the transition to machine spinning in France. Flax spinners in regions like the north of Ireland and Flanders, where linen yarn had substituted for cotton simply because it was stronger, watched the market for hand-spun flax disappear as more and more cotton was produced by machines. Finally, but not until well into the nineteenth century, women who spun wool for worsted and woollen weavers watched machines take over their work.[55]

The large populations of proto-industrial regions could not be sustained without the employment offered by the putting-out merchants. In regions where women could find no other work the loss of spinning was devastating. As an eighteenth-century Swiss pastor cited by Braun observed, 'These people came with cotton and must die with it.'[56] Once again adolescents had to leave home to find work, standards of living declined, and both men and women began to contemplate migration to urban manufacturing centres. Typical of the declining regions were the counties in northern and north-west Ireland, already on the periphery of the proto-industrial system, where 'the small farm combining flax production and spinning was destroyed'.[57] Young adults sought refuge in emigration, leaving large demographic holes in the rural population. One-quarter to one-third of adolescents aged eleven to twenty in 1821, and 15 to 20 per cent of younger children emigrated out of the economically declining counties in the 1820s and 1830s.[58]

Some proto-industrial regions were reprieved from the effects of mechanization by the expansion of jobs in hand weaving. Since men had not lost any of their traditional employments, the merchants turned to women to meet the increased demand for weavers as the water-powered mills generated ever larger quantities of yarn. Desperate for work, and probably already knowing how to weave or knit despite the fact that they had not been formally employed in such work in the past, women whose mothers and grandmothers had worked as spinners now took up weaving and knitting.

By mid-century, in the Caux, women again dominated the cottage labour force. In Auffay there were three times as many women as men weaving in 1851 (54 women as against 17 men). In other villages the figures were even larger. In St Maclou de Folleville, 51 women and only 6 men were weavers; in Totes, 200 women and only 40 men; and in Biville la Baignard, 160 women and 120 men.[59] A similar situation existed further south in the mountains around Saint-Etienne, where both women and men wove ribbons for urban merchants. James Lehning's research reveals that, as in the Caux, women dominated the rural weaving labour force in the first half of the nineteenth century. In the canton of Saint-Genest-Malifaux, 87.8 per cent of the 1,976 ribbon weavers were women.[60]

While the dominance of weaving by women that occurred in the Caux and the Stephanois may not have been typical of proto-industrial regions in the nineteenth century, the sexual integration of weaving was. In Shepshed, 'vast numbers of women and children', many of whom had previously spun, now worked alongside men at the knitting frames.[61] In northern and north-west Ireland, wives and daughters who had previously spun turned to weaving and 'multiple loom households' became common.[62] And in some families in the Zurich highlands, daughters were especially desired because of the income they could produce by weaving.[63]

In all of these cases, women's employment in weaving followed the mechanization of spinning and the concomitant increase in demand for weavers. Nineteenth-century observers attributed this development not only to changes in labour demand, however, but also to changes in the arduousness of weaving. In Ireland one independent weaver (presumably male) reported that women were able to switch from hand spinning to weaving because ' "even little slips of girls could weave linen . . . with the mill spun yarn" '.[64] And in the Caux, women wove lightweight calicoes rather than the heavier *siamoises* because, one male weaver suggested, 'they are more suited to their [weaker] physical strength and their inferior intelligence'.[65] In Shepshed, where observers apparently saw no decline in the physical labour demanded by framework knitting, men were reported to be able to undergo 'the fatigues of labour for longer hours than the weaker physical energies of women and children enable them to bear'.[66]

Whether women were significantly weaker than men in the early nineteenth century is debatable, however. Studies of women's farm labour demonstrate that rural women were as accustomed to strenuous farm work as men were,[67] and the size and strength differences between the sexes were probably not large. In fact, it

218

seems more likely that the paeans to male strength (and intelligence) which began to appear in the nineteenth century are more a reflection of male psychological distress over the entry of women into weaving and knitting than they are evidence of women's inferiority. In this regard, it becomes difficult to read the sexual integration of weaving and knitting as a sign of improving female status, since the arguments not only laid the basis for ongoing male claims of superiority but also justified paying lower piecerates to women in regions like the Caux.

In fact, even to say that weaving became a sexually integrated occupation in the Caux is somewhat misleading. From the beginning of the nineteenth century, men and women wove different kinds of fabric. This new division of labour between the production of all-cotton calicoes and heavier fabrics made it possible for the merchants to continue to pay women less than men, just as they had during the spinning era. Male weavers earned 0.75 to 1.25 francs a day in villages like Auffay while female weavers earned 0.50 to 0.90 francs.[68]

In Shepshed, male and female knitters were paid the same piecerate and apparently produced the same quality fabric, but women, nevertheless, continued to earn less than men. While male observers attributed this difference to greater male strength, which enabled men to 'turn off more work',[69] it seems just as likely that it was a result of women's continuing responsibilities for child care and food preparation which would have taken them away from the knitting frames for at least short periods of time.[70]

Indeed, in view of the fact that we have no evidence that men helped women more or assumed more responsibility for household tasks under proto-industrialization than they did before, we have to assume that women continued to bear responsibility for and to perform this labour. In fact, given the evidence that men did not take up women's paid work during the spinning era, even when the demand for workers was very high, it seems unlikely that they would have taken up women's unpaid labour when weaving and framework knitting became sexually integrated occupations.

WOMEN'S STATUS

The research on proto-industrialization has clearly supported the first half of Medick's equation. Large numbers of women worked for the putting-out merchants in these regions, and as their work increased so did their cash contributions to their families. Indeed, female labour was the key to the success of the proto-industrial textile industries. In addition, the sexual division of labour in weaving and framework knitting broke down in the early nineteenth century as the merchants hired women to perform what had been exclusively male tasks. Further research has not revealed, however, that divisions of labour within the family broke down, that male – female relationships became more egalitarian, or that women began to participate in high-status consumption.

Only Rudolf Braun has ventured to suggest that proto-industrialization had a significant effect on personal relationships, and his argument is that the emotional or romantic content of peasant life improved, not that male – female relationships became more egalitarian. If Braun is correct, then it might be the case that proto-industrialization created a situation in which the emotional attachment (love) of married couples for each other increased and power hierarchies between spouses decreased. It is, in fact, possible to imagine families in which the men helped their wives and daughters by carding yarn during the winter and by keeping an eye on younger children while the women spun; families in which resources (food, clothing, alcohol, leisure time, etc.) were shared equally between spouses; families in which decisions were made jointly regardless of community norms and the possibility of being charivaried. No such arrangements are mentioned in the archival material that is available to and cited by historians, however, and such role sharing remains a matter of speculation both for the Caux and for the other proto-industrial regions that have been studied.

In fact, what little evidence there is either points in the opposite direction or is ambiguous. The arguments about male strength and intelligence that arose in the Caux and Shepshed in the nineteenth century indicate male resistance to the sharing of paid work and, by extension, to the creation of egalitarian relationships and increased female wages and independence. And the increased consumption of alcohol and leisure activities that followed in the wake of the putting-out merchants in the Caux was limited to men. Both of these developments are signs that peasant society in the Caux, at least, continued to be hierarchically organized.

Judicial records present similarly ambiguous and sparse evidence about the status of women. In the year II (1793–4), for instance, an Auffay peasant sued for forty *livres* in damages after his wife was beaten with a piece of wood by another man, temporarily disabling her, a development which we might interpret as a sign of his regard for his wife's well-being as well as her earning ability.[71] Even if such a conclusion is warranted in this case, however, it is difficult to interpret another complaint lodged in the year VII (1798–9) as a sign of improving female status, unless one regards the simple filing of a complaint as a sign of increasing self-esteem. Even so, one isolated case is hardly the basis on which to pass such judgement. In this instance, Marie Adelaide Beaudouin sought a restraining order against her weaver husband after he 'kicked her with his feet and beat her with his fists . . . and threw her out the door which he closed and locked on her without allowing her to take any clothes or linens other than those on her back'.[72] More than a sign of improving respect for or self-respect among women, these two cases might more logically be seen as evidence of a culture in which men resorted to violence when either their own wives or other women failed to obey their wishes or to satisfy their needs. The cases involving husbands and wives in the Caux are so few in number, however, that it seems unwise to generalize from them. We are left, once again, without a clear picture of gender relations and whether they were changing.

The key to understanding the failure of women to acquire new status and respect when the demand for their labour was high, and especially when they became weavers lies, I think, in a phenomenon identified by Anne Phillips and Barbara Taylor. Status was attached to the worker, not to the work, and women were inferior workers.[73] When women began to perform the same tasks as men, the greater likelihood was not that women's status would rise, but that the status of men in those occupations would decline, now that they could conceivably be seen as performing women's work. As a result, at least some men tried hard to differentiate either their abilities from those of women or their work from that of women by establishing new divisions of labour within what had been a unified craft. It is also noteworthy that the sexual division of labour broke down in only one direction. Even when the demand for spinners was very high, able-bodied men did not do this work (except, apparently, in the Zurich highlands where economic need may have overridden all other considerations), a sign perhaps of just how much men stood to lose psychologically if they did women's work.

It is, of course, possible that peasant men and women had

more egalitarian relationships than their public behaviour and the statements of a few nineteenth-century weavers and other observers indicate. Men might have valued women's work highly, both in cottage manufacturing and in the family sphere, especially since their economic contributions were so important to the family's ability to pay the rent on the farm and to stay together during winter months – and, indeed, throughout the adolescent years of their children. The problem is that we have no evidence to this effect. The records that proto-industrial historians have used so far have not allowed us to see behind the cottage door. Perhaps we will eventually find sources that will reveal to us some aspects of the personal relationships within proto-industrial families. At the moment, however, the preponderance of the available evidence – the very low piecerates paid to female spinners, the appeals to male strength and intelligence when weaving was sexually integrated, and male control of public spaces and hence of status consumption – combined with a total lack of knowledge about the sharing of labour within the family leads inescapably, I think, to the conclusion that whatever may have been happening between husbands and wives in the private sphere, there is no sign of any significant improvement in women's economic and social position in the public sphere.

NOTES

1 M. Segalen, *Mari et femme dans la société paysanne*, Paris, 1980. (English translation by S. Matthews, *Love and Power in the Peasant Family*, Chicago, 1983.)

2 See, for instance, P. Bois, *Paysans de l'Ouest*, Paris, 1971; E. Shorter, *The Making of the Modern Family*, New York, 1975; L. Tilly, J. Scott and M. Cohen, 'Women's work and European fertility patterns', *Journal of Interdisciplinary History*, 6, Winter 1986, 447–76; F. Zonabend, *La Mémoire longue: Temps et histoires au village*, Paris, 1980; and Segalen, *Mari et Femme*, op.cit.

3 Segalen regards peasant proverbs as revealing less hierarchical relationships between husbands and wives than I do. See, Segalen, op. cit. Also see N. Zemon Davis, 'Women on top' in her *Society and Culture*, Stanford, 1965; and E. P. Thompson, ' "Rough Music" le charivari anglais', *Annales, E. S. C.*, 27, 1972, 285–312.

4 H. Medick, 'The proto-industrial family economy: the structural function of household and family during the transition from peasant society to industrial capitalism', *Social History*, 3, October 1976; 291–315; reprinted in P. Kriedte, H. Medick and J. Schlumbohm, *Industrializ-*

ation Before Industrialization, trans. Beate Schempp, New York, 1981. All references are to the 1976 article.

5 ibid., 310–15.

6 Medick, 'Proto-industrial family economy', op. cit., 312, notes 84–9. For his statement about women's improving status, Medick relied on R. Braun's study of the Zurich highlands, E. Sax's 1888 study of Thuringia and J. N. von Schwerz's 1816 study of Westphalia and the Rhineland. Slightly better documented was his claim about the breaking of the gender barrier on various paid occupations as proto-industrial merchants searched for ever larger numbers of workers, although whether the evidence he cited comes from proto-industrial regions or traditional cottage industry regions is not entirely clear.

7 A. Clark, *Working Life of Women in the Seventeenth Century*, 1919; repr. London, 1982. This question has also been pursued by Ivy Pinchbeck *Women Workers and the Industrial Revolution 1750–1850* (1930), London, 1981; Edward Shorter, *The Making of the Modern Family*, London, 1975; Louise A. Tilly and Joan W. Scott, *Women, Work and Family*, 2nd edn, London, 1987.

8 See M. C. Howell, 'Women, the family economy and the structures of market production in cities of northern Europe during the late middle ages', unpublished paper delivered at the Conference on Commerce and Custom at the University of Warwick, March 1987.

9 J. Levainville, *Rouen: Etude d'une agglomération urbaine*, Paris, 1931, 188–93.

10 Archives Nationales (hereafter listed as AN) F12 560M: Latapie, 'Réflexions préliminaires sur un mémoire intitulé Voyage de Rouen ou observations sur l'état actuel des arts et manufactures de Rouen, Elbeuf, Louviers, Evreux et Andely faites dans le mois de mai, juin et juillet 1773'; Archives Départementales de la Seine Maritime (hereafter listed as ADSM) 6MP5110; J. Sion, *Les paysans de la Normandie Orientale: Pays de Caux, Bray, Vexin Normand, Vallée de la Seine. Etude géographique*, Paris, 1909, 12, 168–86; P. Dardel, *Histoire de Bolbec des origines à la Révolution: Le commerce et l'industrie à Bolbec avant 1789*, Rouen, 1939, 52, 77–80.

11 AN F12 560 (1782 report on manufacturing); L. Reybaud, *Rapport sur la condition morale, intellectuelle et matérielle des ouvriers qui vivent de l'industrie du coton*, Paris, 1862, 268–9; Sion, *Paysans*, op cit., 174–5; C. Fohlen, *L'industrie textile au temps du Second Empire*, Paris, 1956, 193. Some pure cotton cloth was produced in the Caux, but the cotton fibres produced by hand spinning were generally too weak to withstand the pressure applied to warp threads in the weaving process.

12 Arthur Young, *Travels in France during the Years 1787, 1788, 1789* (edited by Jeffry Kaplow), New York, 1969, 83.

13 AN F12 560. Historian Pierre Dardel, using the same technique, estimated that only 56,992 persons were similarly employed by the merchants in 1732. Dardel, *Histoire de Bolbec*, op. cit., 84.

14 ADSM L367.

15 There were 19,865 looms in 1782. See AN F12 560.

16 ADSM L367. Enumerated Census, Canton of Auffay, *an* IV (1796). Children under the age of twelve were not listed in the census.

17 In Auffay there were 14 female servants, 25 seamstresses, 48 merchants and 19 artisans in 1796. In comparison there were 223 spinners. ADSM L367. In Auffay there were 28 women employed in agriculture (including 25 who either alone or with their husbands were cultivators), 14 female servants, 25 seamstresses, 48 merchants, 19 artisans and 223 spinners in 1796. In comparison, there were 32 male weavers, 54 merchants, 93 artisans and 90 men employed in agriculture as farmers, day labourers and farm servants. ADSM L367.

18 ADSM L367.

19 ADSM L367.

20 I. Mars, *Derniers souvenirs du bon vieux temps d'Auffay depuis 1793 jusqu'à 1840 environ*, Dieppe, 1876, 110–13.

21 This seems especially likely in light of the sexual integration of weaving in the early nineteenth century. *Cauchois* looms were small and the daughters of weavers probably learned to weave as their brothers did.

22 M. M. Bouloiseau, 'Aspects sociaux de la crise cotonnière dans les campagnes rouennaises en 1788–1789', *Actes de 81ᵉ* Congrès National des Sociétés Savantes, Rouen – Caen, 1956, Paris, 1956, 406; Sion, *Paysans*, op. cit., 184. Children began to work in cottage industry around the age of six. As young children, their work was not segregated by sex, and both boys and girls helped clean and comb cotton and learned to spin.

23 AN F12 560.

24 Young, *Travels in France*, op. cit., 436, 503 (1792 edn). Unfortunately, Young did not indicate his source of information.

25 ADSM 6MP5122.

26 Bouloiseau, 'Aspects sociaux', op. cit., 406, n. 3.

27 AN F12 560.

28 Family Reconstitution Study for the village of Auffay. Between 1751 and 1786, 91.0 per cent of the men and 93.5 per cent of the women who married in the village of Auffay were living in the same village as their living parents at the time of the marriage.

29 Dardel, *Histoire de Bolbec*, op. cit., 96.

30 Mars, *Derniers souvenirs*, op. cit., 38–9.

31 Claude Fohlen, *L'industrie textile au temps du Second Empire*, Paris, 1956, 148–53.

32 Mars, *Derniers souvenirs*, op. cit., 34, 37–8.

33 E. LeParquier, *Cahiers de doléances du bailliage d'Arques (secondaire de Caudebec) pour les états généraux de 1789*, 2 vols, Lille, 1922; and G. Dubosc, 'Le jeu de dominos en Normandie', *Par-ci, par-là: Etudes normandes de moeurs et d'histoire*, Rouen, 1927, 48. The names given to various dominoes, the favourite café game in the Caux, also indicate that the cafés were male domains. The double six was the 'big daddy' ('*le gros papa*' or '*le gros père*'); the double blank, 'the laundress' ('*la blanchisseuse*' or '*la blanchinette*'); and the five, 'the patrol' ('*la patrouille*'), the spots representing four men and a corporal, an apparent reference

to the days men spent in the National Guard in the late eighteenth and early nineteenth centuries.

34 F. Mendels, *Industrialization and Population Pressure in Eighteenth-Century Flanders*, New York, 1981, 200.
35 ibid., 207–8.
36 D. Levine, *Family Formation in an Age of Nascent Capitalism*, New York, 1977, 46–57.
37 B Collins, 'Proto-industrialization and pre-Famine emigration', *Social History*, 7, 2, May 1982, 133, 137.
38 R. Braun, 'The impact of cottage industry on an agricultural population' in D. Landes (ed.), *The Rise of Capitalism*, (New York, 1966, 53–64. Braun's research pre-dates the literature on proto-industrialization, but is widely accepted by proto-industrial historians.
39 ibid., 58–9.
40 ibid., 58.
41 ibid., 64.
42 Collins, 'Proto-industrialization and emigration', op. cit., 134–5.
43 Levine, *Family Formation*, op. cit., 47.
44 F. Mendels, 'Proto-industrialization: the first phase of the industrialization process', *Journal of Economic History*, 32, (March 1972), 250–2.
45 Levine, *Family Formation*, op. cit., 61–4.
46 For a fuller explanation of these trends in the pays de Caux, see *The Spinners and Weavers of Auffay*, chap. 7.
47 M. P. Gutmann and R. Leboutte, 'Rethinking protoindustrialization and the family', *Journal of Interdisciplinary History*, 14, Winter 1984, 595.
48 J. Lehning, 'Nuptiality and rural industry: families and labor in the French countryside', *Journal of Family History*, Winter 1983, 333–45.
49 This conclusion is supported by the 1796 Census. In that year, forty-one of the sixty-one women who headed their own households in Auffay were employed as spinners. See ADSM L367.
50 ADSM 219BP364, C1730.
51 Collins, 'Proto-industrialization and emigration', op. cit., 133–4.
52 Levine, *Family Formation*, op. cit., 56.
53 Mendels, *Industrialization and Population Pressure*, op. cit., 207–8.
54 Levine, *Family Formation*, op. cit., 32.
55 P. Hudson, *The Genesis of Industrial Capital*, Cambridge, 1986, 29–43.
56 Braun, 'Impact of cottage industry', op. cit., 61.
57 Collins, 'Proto-industrialization and emigration', op. cit., 138.
58 ibid., 139.
59 ADSM 6MP83 (1851 Census for the canton of Totes).
60 J. Lehning, *The Peasants of Marlhes*, Chapel Hill, 1980, 28–30, 40.
61 Levine, *Family Formation*, op. cit., 27.
62 Collins, 'Proto-industrialization and emigration', op. cit., 140.
63 Braun, 'The impact of cottage industry', op. cit. 62.
64 B.P.P. 1840 XXIII, 646, cited in Collins, Proto-industrialization and emigration', op. cit., 140.
65 Charles Noiret, *Mémoires d'un ouvrier rouennais*, Rouen, 1836, 18–19.
66 Cited in Levine, *Family Formation*, op. cit. 27.
67 See, Ivy Pinchbeck, op cit., part I; Olwen Hufton, 'Women and the

family economy in eighteenth-century France,' *French Historical Studies*, IX, Spring 1975, 1–22; Clark, op. cit., *Seventeenth Century*, ch. 4.
68 ADSM 6MP5154.
69 Cited in Levine, *Family Formation*, op. cit., 27.
70 For an analysis of the traditional divisions of labour between women and men, see Hufton, 'Women and the Family Economy;' Pinchbeck, op. cit.; Segalen, op cit.; Louise Tilly and Joan Scott, op. cit.
71 ADSM L8247: Justice of the Peace Records.
72 ADSM LP 8255: Justice of the Peace Records.
73 Anne Phillips and Barbara Taylor, 'Sex and Skill: Notes towards a Feminist Economics,' *Feminist Review*, no. 6, 1980, 79, 85.

10

APPRENTICESHIP: TRAINING AND GENDER IN EIGHTEENTH-CENTURY ENGLAND

Deborah Simonton

THE NATURE OF APPRENTICESHIP

The locus and pattern of eighteenth-century upbringing varied from the modern one, which relies on the centrality of school, in that occupational training and experience in other households were far more important. Apprenticeship was one such route to adulthood which supplemented schooling or provided the entirety of a child's formal education. The purpose of this paper is to evaluate the character of apprenticeship and its role in educating, training and preparing girls for the adult world. No attempt has been made, except where relevant, to describe apprenticeship in terms of labour experience and industrial relations.[1] An understanding of female apprenticeship requires an evaluation of two separate but intrinsically related characteristics. First, apprenticeship was intended to provide skill and training for adult work. Second, during apprenticeship the values and behaviour which society considered important were transmitted to the embryonic adult. The operation of apprenticeship and the relative weight assigned to these two aims within male and female apprenticeship illustrate the divergent attitudes toward education and occupational opportunities for each sex.

Throughout the early modern period, English children from all levels of society were sent to homes other than their own for work, service and vocational training, and for the acquisition of manners and patterns of behaviour. Substitute adults took on the responsibility for bringing up and training them. For their part, the children served the family in positions which depended on their social

227

status; likewise their integration into the host family varied. The stage of life between childhood and adulthood coincides with the period of preparation for adult life. Primarily during those years, children learn the values, beliefs and roles which underwrite the social system in which they participate. Gillis calls this pre-adult stage 'youth' and modern Europeans distinguish it as two separate stages: adolescence followed by youth.[2] Ariès suggested that the pre-adult years were regarded ambiguously, so that childhood was confused with adolescence while the relationship between them and youth remained vague.[3] However, the practice of placing out children suggests that eighteenth-century people identified a life-cycle stage between childhood and adulthood. Kett also shows how the language of age implied such a stage of development.[4] From the timing, character and language of schooling, service, apprenticeship and 'placing out', eighteenth-century commentators appeared to associate this stage with learning. It was a transitional period, characterized as semi-dependent in contrast to the complete dependence of childhood and the independence of adulthood. The modern term of adolescence and youth were merged into a single stage during which the essential transmission of culture took place as well as training in the economic skills needed to make a living.

Apprenticeship coincided with this stage of 'youth' for eighteenth-century children. Structurally distinct from domestic and farm service, formal apprenticeship tied master and apprentice by a written contract, an indenture, to a certain term of years and conditions. In contrast, servants engaged in verbal or tacit contracts, typically of one year.[5] Additionally, apprentices, their parents or guardians paid the master for training while servants were paid for working, and could save to set up on their own in a way apprentices could not. Apprenticeship as a formal method of vocational training in crafts and trade originated in the guild system of medieval times. Ideally, a master or mistress agreed to train a child in a trade for a specified term of years and to board and house the child. In return the master was paid the agreed premium and the child contracted to serve faithfully and keep the secrets of the trade.[6]

Before the eighteenth century, the institution was modified by legislation on artificers and the poor law, and by changes in the economic structure of society. The Statute of Artificers (1563) added legal regulation of apprenticeship to the customs and rules of the guilds.[7] At the same time the act extended to urban England the guild practices of the City of London and other corporate towns. Children aged ten to twenty-four could thereby be apprenticed to husbandry or divers other trades. The act required an apprenticeship of seven years before setting up in certain crafts and provided legal remedies for either party in cases of misconduct.

Significant to apprenticeship was Tudor adoption of the institution as a means of removing pauper children from the parish poor rates. Pre-dating the Statute of Artificers, the Poor Law of 1536 authorized parish officials to put 'single' children aged between five and fourteen with masters of husbandry or other crafts or labours. They were to be taught so that they could support themselves as adults.[8] The Elizabethan poor laws supplemented this act, extending parish apprenticeship to the children of beggars and ultimately to children whose parents the overseers of the poor thought unable to maintain them.[9]

Thus a variety of apprenticeship patterns existed by the eighteenth century, based on the guild model and practices but diverging from it in purpose and emphasis. Private apprenticeships most resembled the model in that training was undertaken by a master in exchange for a premium and a specified term of service by the child, usually seven years. Those emanating from private charity adhered to similar conditions and terms but the premium was paid by the charity and the trades and premiums tended toward the more modest end of the scale. Yet charity apprenticeship could resemble either private or parish schemes. Poor law officials arranged the details and paid the premium for parish apprentices, often putting out children with more regard for the rates than for the child's benefit.

Central to the idea of apprenticeship was the expectation that children should receive training in a craft or trade. Indentures carried the stipulation:

> That the said [Master/Mistress] the said Apprentice in the Art of [trade] which s/he now useth shall teach and Instruct or Cause to be taught and Instructed in the best way and Manner that s/he can.

Defoe stressed this element, for a boy's 'apprenticeship is and *ought to be* [his emphasis], a school to him, where he ought to learn everything that should qualify him for his business'.[10] Adam Smith built his case for the abolition of apprenticeship on what he saw as the fallacy that apprenticeship produced a skilled and industrious workforce, underlining the contemporary belief that learning a skill was a prime function of apprenticeship. The thrust of his attack was precisely that few trades required extensive skills to practise them:

> Long apprenticeships are altogether unnecessary. The arts, which are much superior to common trades, such as those making clocks and watches, contain no such mystery as to require a long course of instruction. The first invention of such beautiful machines, indeed, and even that of some of the instruments employed in making them, must, no doubt have been the work of deep thought and long time, and may justly be considered among the happiest efforts of human ingenuity. But when both have been fairly invented, and are well understood, to explain to any young man, in the compleatest [sic] manner, how to apply the instruments, and how to construct the machines, cannot well require more than the lessons of a few weeks. . . . In the common mechanic trades, those of a few days might certainly be sufficient.[11]

If skill were the most important aspect of apprenticeship, most apprentices' terms could have been far shorter.

Apprenticeship indentures refer to the 'mysteries' and 'practices' of trades, not to skills. Thus the language of apprenticeship itself suggests that vocational training embodied passing on the practices and behavioural patterns expected of one who carried out the trade. In other words, the training had less to do with expertise and rather more to do with the status carried by the trade. Within this construction were the seeds of a regulated method of social advancement. In an age which made fine distinctions between artisan and labourer, between master and journeyman, access to apprenticeship, particularly in a 'good' trade, was seen as enhancing a child's opportunities. In practice, of course, these distinctions were blurred, and a glut of journeymen made this more an ideal than a real solution.[12]

Historically, the terms and uses of apprenticeship were applied to other forms of education including universities, as exemplified by the term 'master of arts'.[13] Likewise, Ariès's evidence supports the view that:

> in order to obtain initiation in a trade of any sort whatever

– whether that of courtier, soldier, administrator, merchant
or workman – a boy did not amass the knowledge necessary
to ply that trade before entering it, but threw himself into it;
he then acquired the necessary knowledge through everyday
practice, from living and working with adults who were
already fully trained.[14]

Reminiscent of placing children in other households, this implies
a broader view of their expectations of apprenticeship than simple
training.

The contract itself specified that the master would regulate the
apprentice's conduct. Even where vocational teaching was important, the duty of providing moral training, to act *in loco parentis*,
was manifestly expected by society. Defoe made this explicit,
explaining that in their first years of apprenticeship children could
not understand the trade, but were to be taught submission to
family orders, subjection to their masters and dutiful attendance
in their shops and warehouses. Throughout the remainder of their
terms, in addition to preparation for work, they were to be
instructed 'in such things as may qualify them best to enter upon
the world, and act for themselves when they are so enter'd'.[15] For
many children, the apprenticeship system, the formal mechanism
for transmitting skills in English society, clearly was intended to
answer the wider needs of bringing up children.

Apprenticeship also carried within it an inherent contradiction.
On one level, it served as an initiation to the heavy responsibility
of citizenship and adulthood. Corporation organization suggested
this most strongly since apprenticeship frequently led to becoming
a freeman with civic rights and responsibilities. On another level
it was radically different from adulthood. For example, it imposed
a ban on marriage, and legally described a dependent status so
that apprentices lacked the economic and social rights of adults.
The legal rather than the moral restrictions on behaviour which
were contained within apprenticeship meant that the institution
could not and did not provide preparation for certain aspects of
adult life, including freedom of movement and decision-making.

The apprenticeship of paupers had additional functions which
overlapped, and in certain respects further blurred, the original
purposes of the institution. Because children were put out to relieve
the parish poor rates from the burden of their support, vocational
training was less prominent, while support of the child became

paramount.[16] Frequently, pauper apprenticeship was criticized for providing ratepayers with cheap labour. Undoubtedly this was true in certain respects, though by the end of the eighteenth century the development of 'outdoor' apprenticeship made this criticism more valid for the system as a whole.[17] Parish apprentices were more prevalent in poorer trades, such as cordwaining and weaving, than in prosperous ones, which lends weight to their being cheap supplementary labour instead of receiving meaningful training. Yet in jobs like husbandry and housewifery, the line between training and work was obscured by the nature of the task. In occupations requiring highly sophisticated skills, a formal training was more justified, but where expertise was acquired by association with experienced workers, the training is harder to define. England remained primarily agricultural, so that many children, as adults, would be employed in agriculture. In these cases, apprenticeship provided them with useful knowledge and experience. But, as long as pauper apprentices were concentrated in poor or overstocked trades, the industrial training was of less economic value. Also the value of parish apprenticeship may have varied by its application in urban as opposed to rural trades.

These, then, were the dominant features of apprenticeship as an institution as it moved into the eighteenth century. In many respects they remained valid throughout the century. However, economic and social changes altered and influenced the shape of eighteenth-century apprenticeship and brought it under attack. Also its application to girls often operated in quite different ways from its use in boys' education. These issues are the focus of the next two sections, which rely on a sizeable body of quantitative data derived from eighteenth-century material relating to Essex and Staffordshire.[18]

Records of apprenticeships were kept by a variety of institutions, including central and parish administration, corporations and guilds, and private firms and individuals. In theory, inland revenue records of apprenticeship should be complete for all non-parish indentures. They recorded payment of duties on apprenticeship indentures which came into force from May 1710 to January 1811.[19] Pauper indentures did not need to be, and usually were not, registered, nor were those where no money changed hands. The duty was payable by the master or mistress, but when they refused the parents or apprentice paid the duty in order to avoid prosecution and to ensure a legal apprenticeship for the child.

The records are not comprehensive, but the extent to which children, and especially girls, are under-represented is unknown. Because these records were created for the purpose of collecting duty, circumvention is to be expected. Similarly, given the administrative weakness of the system, a fair amount of successful avoidance was likely. The expense of formally putting out a child because of the premium and tax may have outweighed the advantage to be gained in status and adult position. The importance of registration probably varied with the status of the trade and the social position of the apprentice or the master or mistress. Although average premiums were not very high and many menial, low-status trades were registered, the perceived obligation to register may have been taken more seriously as one moved up the social scale. The likelihood of under-registration was greater for girls, since certain of the advantages were not in fact obtainable. They could not usually gain the freedom of the corporation, nor did apprenticeship necessarily enhance their trading or political position as it did with boys.[20] They were largely restricted from guilds and the advantages of a collective work group, and women were often seen by men not as trading partners but as threats to their own position. Since they had less to gain from the formalities of indenturing, their families may have been less interested in fulfilling all obligations.

As the century progressed, other pressures operated to undercut apprenticeship both in new trades and the less established ones which could not fight for exclusive rights. On the one hand there were those like Adam Smith who argued against apprenticeship on economic grounds, as a restrictive practice. On the other, for many new trades, 'on the job' or limited periods of training sufficed. Also new trades were regarded as legally outside the Statute of Artificers. Together these considerations may have diminished the reliance on apprenticeship for training, or at least vigorous adherence to the formalities of indentured service. Similarly, many new trades fell at the lower end of the status range and, being concentrated outside corporate areas, pressures for following guild traditions were weaker. If status were an important feature of registration, these factors operated to lessen further the sense of obligation to register.

The poor law and charity indentures and the overseers' account books comprise the other major body of records. The accuracy and completeness of this material is coloured by the standard problem of historians: survival of material. Certainly the records of Essex and Staffordshire are not complete, and so represent a sample imposed by the vicissitudes of time.[21] The quantifiable data from the records were processed by a computer programme which allows apprenticeship variables to be compared with each other, e.g. sex to trade, to length of service or to premiums required for apprenticing a child. A detailed classification of trades was devised to evaluate and combine the hundreds of trades into meaningful groups. This permits regrouping in order to discover the relationships which best describe the form and function of female apprenticeship. The quantification and subsequent analysis of the records is a way of building up a picture of the sexual differentiation of work and of the assumptions made by contemporaries about the need for girls to be trained for their economic roles. Comparing premiums and terms of service allows an estimate of the status of trades and possibly their skill requirements. Evaluating the level of female involvement in the apprenticeship system and women's participation in the trade hierarchy helps to locate their economic role in its historical context.

The inherent limitation of the data used here means that they alone cannot resolve the issues of the content of apprenticeship and its value to the participants. Other material, such as settlement examinations, could be brought to bear to help to describe more fully the content and purposes of female apprenticeship. Also, reliance on this data ignores the large numbers of girls who did not want, need or have a trade apprenticeship or who were not pauper children subject to the overseers' dictates. Apprenticeship was only one form of educating girls for adult roles, and a great many children, especially girls, did not experience formal apprenticeship. For them other forms of education and upbringing such as family, schooling, work or informal arrangements were significant.

EIGHTEENTH-CENTURY APPRENTICESHIP

In the last half of the eighteenth century, legal and political opinions about apprenticeship shifted. An acceleration in industrial productivity, coupled with the realization that changes in work organization could facilitate profit-making, led to a challenge to the institution of apprenticeship. At the same time, the increasing numbers of poor and the application of parish apprenticeship to reduce the poor rates, especially from the 1770s, led to legal changes in that system as well. Shifts in attitudes and economic conditions operated together to effect changes throughout the institution with regard to terms, premiums, trades and its sexual configuration.

For the most part, eighteenth-century legislation operated to amend but not significantly alter parish apprenticeship. The terminal age was reduced for London boys in 1767 and for all others in 1777 to twenty-one years.[22] The long period of parish indenture to age twenty-four had become recognized as a period of legalized slavery. It may have controlled vagrancy or prevented marriage when the Elizabethan legislation was passed, but its depiction by Hanway as more damaging than beneficial led to the reduction.[23] At the same time a minimum premium of £4, payable in two instalments, was established. The staged payment was intended to procure better masters and provide an incentive for improved treatment. Eden believed that these two measures saved many lives, though on balance George was less certain.[24]

Several legislative changes aimed to provide more protection for the parish apprentice, in response to the ill-treatment reported in quarter sessions records and chronicled by historians of apprenticeship.[25] Since the Statute of Artificers, apprentices could be discharged on reasonable cause by either their own or their master's application to quarter sessions. However, apprentices whose premiums were less than £5, especially parish apprentices, were not protected. Then, in 1747, the law was extended, allowing their application to the justices on the grounds of 'any Misusage, Refusal of necessary Provision, Cruelty or Ill-treatment'.[26] If the justices thought it reasonable, restitution of a proportion of the premium was also granted. In 1792 and 1793, further protection was extended to parish apprentices.[27] That this legislation did not resolve the problem is testified to by continued cases and criticism of the system by contemporaries such as Catharine Cappe.[28]

Changes in the economic structure during the century, particularly the decline of some industries and the rise of new ones, reshaped apprenticeship and its role in economic and social life. Legal opinion, as well as the economic frame of mind, increasingly tended to reject apprenticeship as inhibiting the basic common law right to exercise a trade. Blackstone explained:

> At common law every man might use what trade he pleased; but this Statute [of Artificers] restrains that liberty to such

as have served as apprentices. . . . However, the resolutions
of the courts have in general rather confined than extended
the restriction.[29]

The statute was enforced by complainants bringing cases before
the courts, thus the onus for compliance rested on injured parties.
Rule points out that remarkably few prosecutions were brought
during the century, with a general absence of litigation from mid-
century. While the trend varied regionally, and certain trades were
more likely to maintain apprenticeship regulations, he argues that
'case law had clearly established the equivalence of seven years'
working to a fully indentured apprenticeship'.[30]

Practice and case law established two fairly clear interpretations
which held throughout the last half of the century. In view of
industrial changes, the statute was held not to extend to trades
which were not in existence when it was passed in 1563. Thus
many of the industries of the period, including cotton manufacture
and many Black Country trades, were regarded as exempt. Similarly, contemporary acceptance of a period of seven years as equivalent to indentured apprenticeship undermined the strength and
supposed universality of the institution. A third and less certain
restriction of the statute was the claim that it only extended to
corporate and market towns.[31] In Essex and Staffordshire, with
the growth of rural industry since the sixteenth century, this view
of the act could have significantly altered the role of apprenticed
labour in those two counties.

Economic opinion which favoured removal of trade restrictions
was aggressively opposed to apprenticeship. Adam Smith's classical statement of this position gave theoretical force to views which
were already widely held. He argued that apprenticeship restricted
entrance to certain employments, by limiting the number of
apprentices allowed to each master. Lengthy training, which
increased the expense of education, restrained it indirectly. Similarly, apprenticeship obstructed the free circulation of labour from
one employment to another, by requiring seven years' training in
any craft or trade before it could be practised. Long apprenticeships, he wrote, were no guarantee of good workmanship nor did
they encourage young persons to industry. Most trades, especially
the 'common mechanic trades' could be learned in a few days or,
occasionally, a week.[32] Smith saw apprenticeship as a deliberate
attempt by craftsmen to restrain competition, and protect their

own position and earnings. In the climate of free ebullient competition, with the abolition of apprenticeship 'the publick [sic] would be a gainer, the work of all artificers coming in this way much cheaper to market'.[33]

In opposition to the forces of free trade stood the skilled workers who wished to protect their position within a trade and the trade's position within the economic and social structure. Smith argued that apprenticeship regulations offended against the property each worker had in his own labour. In contrast to this, skilled workers maintained that apprenticeship conferred a particular property right to the exclusive exercise of their trade. Their seven-year service was thought to have purchased this right for them, enhanced in the better trades by sizeable premiums which guaranteed admission to a trade with status and prospects.[34] In addition to providing a 'closed shop', the right to control numbers of apprentices helped to prevent dilution of the trade, thus maintaining its levels of prices and wages.[35] These depended, however, on economic conditions and, in the growing number of disputes about wages, apprenticeship was usually only a contributory factor. The fundamental issue was that craftsmen believed they had earned an exclusive property right to exercise their trade, while economic pressures backed by ideological debate were pressing for the individual's natural right to employ his labour. The irony is that in appealing increasingly to the terms of the Statute of Artificers in the early nineteenth century, craftsmen focused attention on it, which led to repeal of the apprenticeship sections in 1814.[36]

Nevertheless, apprenticeship remained the premier method of providing formal vocational training in the eighteenth century. But here, too, its position was challenged. With growing interest in schooling, the position of apprenticeship in the typical life-cycle of the child gradually altered, often being removed altogether. School preparation for the professions was increasingly common for middle-class boys while eighteenth-century writers on apprenticeship indicated that certain basic schooling should precede the learning of a trade. In Campbell's 1747 guide to apprenticeship, he saw reading and writing as so useful for all trades 'that we need not, it is presumed, use many Arguments to recommend Children being well founded in these before they are bound'.[37] Additionally, he recommended arithmetic and drawing as useful skills to acquire before entering upon an apprenticeship.

Charity schools and Sunday schools coupled with Evangelical

and Methodist educational activity provided alternative forms of education for many children of the labouring orders. The pattern of bequests also suggests an important change in the value of apprenticeship as a form of education. In Essex and Staffordshire, the proportion of educational charity for apprenticeship fell from 43 per cent to 22 per cent during the eighteenth century, with very few new donations after 1750. This decline was partly the result of and offset by a rise in the number of donations for schooling.[38] Charity school records show that schooling was being interjected into the educative cycle, preceding apprenticeship. Colchester Charity School, from 1714, taught boys to 'write a fair hand to suit them for apprenticeship', while Wolverhampton included the 'Grounds of Arithmetic to fit them for Service or Apprenticeship'.[39]

One of the key questions about apprenticeship during the eighteenth century is: 'Did it decline as a practice?' The implication of the pressures described above are that it did. Yet the available data suggest the number of indentures remained fairly stable from 1750, though linked to an underlying rise. Parish apprenticeships rose consistently from 1760 to 1790, but in the decade which produced the Speenhamland decision, the number of parish apprentices returned to the level of the 1770s. When compared to the population growth in the two counties, the proportion of apprentices again remained fairly stable from 1750, though dropping from 1791. But by comparison to the age group, which grew more rapidly than the overall population, apprentices were clearly a declining proportion from 1771, with a fairly steep drop from 1786. Thus while the data do not suggest a dramatic decrease in the use of formal apprenticeship, the decline in the proportion of the relevant age group placed as apprentices is notable. While more children were apprenticed, clearly the institution did not keep pace with the increasing numbers of children, exhibiting yet another factor putting pressure on the system. This was particularly true for the traditional apprentices, put privately to trades, who were the largest group.

Even allowing for lost indentures, avoidance of tax and poor recording, a remarkably small proportion of children appear to have experienced apprenticeship. An average of 0.4 per cent of the age group (5–14) were placed as apprentices in any one year in the two counties. With an average term of 7.4 years for all apprentices, at any one time about 3 per cent of the children in those

counties were serving as apprentices. This does not invalidate the
further study of apprenticeship for several reasons. It was perceived as important to contemporaries either as training or as a
means of relieving the poor. It was also a model of the social
relations between adults and young. As many as 3,000 children at
a time could have been serving out their indentures in Essex and
Staffordshire. If these figures hold for the whole country, some
56,000 children could have been serving apprenticeships at one
time. For some areas, such as London, the figures were probably
higher. Also, formal apprenticeship is only the tip of the iceberg,
since historians of domestic and farm service, household economics, labour and apprenticeship recognize the importance of
less formal forms of apprenticeship-like service.[40]

Most private apprenticeships coincided with the period of adolescence, lasting from fourteen to twenty-one. The parish apprentice's experience was usually quite different, beginning earlier and
therefore lasting longer. Most pauper children were put out
between ages seven and nine and only 6 per cent were indentured
at fourteen. Certainly the early age of indenturing could imply the
use of cheap labour, although they probably began their apprenticeship as a liability. They were too young to work well and
frequently spoiled materials. However, these apprentices were far
more useful at the end of their lengthy terms than initially, particularly where little skill was involved. Such young apprentices also
reflected the parsimonious desire to remove children from the rates,
which was very much in keeping with the general administration
of the poor laws at that time.

The length of the terms also varied by the type of apprenticeship
to which a child was indentured. The traditional guild term of
seven years was clearly the most popular, although parish apprentices were most frequently placed 'to age 21' or 'to age 24'. Practice
could and did vary, however, since a small proportion of privately
placed children were indentured for these long terms, while some
parish apprentices were bound for terms which were more like the
guild model. Despite the relative stability of the seven-year term,
over the century it was gradually eroded, so that the average
(excluding those put 'to age 21', 'to 24', etc.) dropped from just
over seven years at the beginning to 6.3 years by the end of
the century. Though a slight change, the trend does support the
contention that traditional controls over apprenticeship loosened
throughout the century.

Premiums paid with a child's indenture rose consistently during the last half of the century, as did prices. From just under £14 in 1750, the average premium by 1799 was over £23, a 45 per cent increase, while consumer prices rose by 64 per cent.[41] Premiums ranged from nil to £500, but the great mass of them (85 per cent) were £25 or less. Sixty per cent of all children were apprenticed with £10 or less, and a third with £5 or less. Thus there was less differentiation among the great mass of apprenticed trades than might have been expected. These data undercut somewhat the idea that charity apprentices, with a premium of £5 or £10, were in a less favoured position than privately indentured children. The data also imply that, for the great majority of trades, the premium alone was not particularly likely to purchase them a secure niche in life.

In order to group similar trades and related processes, a trade classification was derived.[42] Clustering the trades in this way produced a surprisingly even distribution across ten major occupational categories, based on the raw material used in the process. The evenness of the pattern is partly because apprenticeship did not reflect the economic structure well. Indeed, the data tell us more about how apprenticeship was used than about the economic organization of society. Agriculture, which probably employed the largest number of people in the economy, was less likely to use apprenticeship for training than the craft-orientated sectors of the economy such as the metal, wood or leather trades. Husbandry was well represented in the data because of numerous parish apprentices. Also other agrarian traders such as millers, butchers and bakers took large numbers of non-parish apprentices. The leather trades were the single most popular craft area, representing over one-fifth of apprentices, and included cordwainers, the largest single craft taking apprentices. These were followed by agriculture, the timber trades and then textiles.

Of course, the trade pattern of apprentices is dependent upon the type of indenture. In private apprenticeship, leather and related crafts rise to nearly a quarter of the whole but, again, the pattern is fairly even. Parish apprenticeship contrasted sharply in that twice as many children were placed in agriculture and three-and-a-half times as many in services: the areas which included husbandry and housewifery. The other two groups which took a significant number of parish apprentices were textiles and metal working, the main economic activities in Essex and Staffordshire.

Indeed, the data illustrate the growth in metal trades and the relative decline in textiles as destinations for parish apprentices over the century.

The difference between these two patterns of apprenticing is not simply that parish apprentices were put to poor overstocked trades, since many children placed out by private indenture also went to unpromising trades. Instead the patterns suggest that, independently of prospects, some trades were considered appropriate for 'real' apprentices and others for paupers. The four most popular pauper trades contained only negligible numbers of private apprentices, while tailoring and cordwainers, which appear at the top of the list for private indentures, drew relatively few paupers. Indeed the correlation in the rank order is not very high at all. Not surprisingly there were no paupers placed to grocers, mercers, surgeons, ironmongers, saddlers, cabinet-makers and attorneys; both the status and the premiums made these an impossible choice for poor children and the overseers.

Forty per cent of children placed out by poor law officials were sent into housewifery or husbandry with farmers, yeomen or husbandmen. This reflects, in part, the rural character of the two counties and of England as a whole. It also demonstrates the willingness to board children out to relieve the rates. However, as explained earlier and underlined by Marshall, in these rural communities the work upon which they were set was preparation for the life they could expect as adults. Their position as adults would probably be little different from others in the rural community.[43]

Interestingly, the rank order and pattern of charity apprentices matches that of private apprentices better than it does the parish pattern. Potentially these children were selected as 'deserving' poor who would benefit from a craft apprenticeship. They may or may not have been paupers. In most cases, the charities were attached to a charity school from which a deserving boy was chosen. The proportion of these children in agriculture was untypically low, implying that charity apprenticeship was used specifically to put poor children to a trade rather than husbandry, the pauper apprenticeship 'catchall'. The proportion put into service also matched the private pattern rather than the pauper one. On the other hand, the high proportion of charity apprentices in textiles suggests it was the alternative to agriculture for a poor but deserving child.

As with trade categories, pauper and private apprenticeships

241

created two distinct patterns when the stage of processing to which children were apprenticed is considered. Three-quarters of trade apprentices engaged in secondary production, while pauper apprentices were strongly situated in primary processing. The strong link between private apprentices, production of goods and the so-called traditional trades implies an emphasis on skill. Most trades related to agriculture, heavy and preparatory trades and cloth-making were classed as primary production, while secondary manufacturing included finishing work, the hardware trades and making artefacts and clothing. Thus apprentices in secondary processing usually worked in trades which created finished products. This in itself could not be characterized as more skilled work than that in the primary stages. More probably many of the trades in this category were associated in social perceptions with the traditional guild model of craftwork. From this ensued the identification of these trades with the appropriate status and role for a boy whose parents could afford to pay a premium. Thus the distinction in placing private and pauper apprentices probably had more to do with perceptions of status and position than with the actual skills involved, or even the potential prospects.

The service sector illustrates the distinctions in standing which can occur throughout the trade classification. Prosperous occupations carrying good prospects and prestige, such as law and medicine, were found side by side with overcrowded poor trades, such as housewifery. Though these disparities are disguised by statistical averages, the apprenticeship system operated in large part to preserve lines of demarcation and a sense of status. Most of these apprentices came from the lower levels of society, but moving up the social echelons the more prestigious trades appear, carrying with them status and prospects.

Their standing was identified by the premiums and terms which they commanded, because of course the levels of premiums and terms were affected by the trade to which a child was apprenticed. The services and chemicals groups drew very large premiums – over £40 – primarily because they contained professions like surgeon, apothecary, attorney, etc. Only the timber and leather products groups, with averages of just above £10, fell well below the average of £18 11s 2d. The large number of apprentices to carpenters, wheelwrights, cordwainers, shoe-makers and glovers, with premiums under £10, held down the average premiums in those sectors of the economy, since together they included a quarter of all apprentices and nearly a third of private apprentices. The discrepancy between premiums illustrates the disparity between the upper and lower ends of some trade groups. Textiles, for example, included mercers and milliners who could regularly demand over £30, and weavers who received an average of £3-£4 for taking an apprentice. Similarly metal work contained jewellers, clock-makers and ironmongers, who could ask high premiums, and blacksmiths, buckle-makers and locksmiths who averaged premiums between £5 and £6. Even within one trade, such as tailoring, there were differences between those at the top, asking something like £77, with an apprentice and those at the sweated end, taking only £1 15s.

The clearest differences in the use of apprenticeship appear between parish and private indentures. Parish children were apprenticed younger for longer and for smaller premiums on average than children whose parents attended to their indentures. The areas of the economy to which each was apprenticed also differed. Parish children were more prominent in agriculture and services and in the primary stages of manufacture. Privately placed children were fairly evenly spread over the first five trade categories, encompassing most of the crafts, and they were engaged primarily in secondary manufacture. On a trade by trade basis there was little correlation, in that trades which were heavy in private apprentices took relatively few parish children and vice versa. These differences are partly a manifestation of the different purposes and perceptions which underpinned parish and private apprenticeship. Private apprenticeship carried with it the sense of skill, training, status and the mystery of the craft. This was true even if many children were put into trades which were already overcrowded and might bring small returns. Parish children were seen by contemporaries as cheap labour, as objects of pity or in need of inculcating in hard labour, and apprenticeship was a useful way to shift the burden of the poor. The issue is less one of skill and expertise than of status and social position.

FEMALE APPRENTICESHIP

Historians usually treat apprenticeship as a male preserve, although girls are more frequently mentioned when parish apprenticeship is studied. Nevertheless, most authors continue to perpetuate the impression that the important historical questions are those which involve boys. It has been left mainly to historians concerned with female work and its economic implications, such as Ivy Pinchbeck, Alice Clark and Eileen Power, to deal with the issues arising from female apprenticeship.[44] The other notable exceptions are Jocelyn Dunlop and R. D. Denman who dedicated a chapter to putting women into context in *English Apprenticeship and Child Labour*.

The impression that apprenticeship was almost exclusively male is given credence by some records, notably those of guilds and corporations, which did not actively encourage female involvement. However, apprenticeship as a system of training applied to girls as well as boys during the eighteenth century. Girls were a significant proportion of the apprentices recorded by the inland revenue and by parishes, though the level of their participation depended upon the form of the apprenticeship undertaken. Similarly, though in fewer numbers, guild and corporation records refer to females as mistresses and apprentices.[45] The gender differentiation of trades indicates that female experience of apprenticeship diverged markedly from male. The nature of the trades open to girls, the terms of service and the levels of premiums suggest a devaluation of female work and female status, and reflect a narrowing of occupational opportunities. Yet occupational training may not have been the most significant feature of female apprenticeship. As a regulated system of upbringing, apprenticeship taught both boys and girls the values and behaviour expected of them.

The terms of the Statute of Artificers applied equally to both sexes, and frequently it was invoked to restrain unapprenticed women from practising a trade. In these disputes, craftsmen regarded the employment of women as a means of introducing untrained cheap labour.[46] However, guilds traditionally allowed the wives and daughters of members to work in a trade and to continue as full guild members after the death of husbands and fathers.[47] Also, many women gained their trading position because contemporaries accepted seven years of experience as equivalent to apprenticeship. Often girls were taught during service with their parents or others in an informal arrangement.[48] Additionally, some work which was seen as traditionally female usually did not take apprentices. Such a case is spinning, a common female occupation which Morant claimed employed the majority of Essex women in the 1740s.[49] Only eight wool spinning apprentices and twenty-six cotton spinning apprentices were recorded from both counties for the whole century. Thus apprenticeship records are not a true indication of the extent and nature of women's work, nor do they necessarily accurately reflect their training opportunities.

Much female work was subsidiary to and supportive of men's work, particularly in domestic industry, and women combined household tasks with their industrial activities. They were less likely than men to be seen working in their own right, and their social and economic position was defined by the men with whom they were linked. As a result, apprenticeship training was less likely to be regarded as a part of a girl's life. Yet the lack of enforcement of the statute affected women in two ways. Through casual untrained labour, large numbers of girls were employed who otherwise could not have been. But where they were not apprenticed, their work remained casual and subordinate; they were not qualified at law and in effect could work only as assistants to male relatives.

This is not to say that they were not apprenticed nor that they did not receive similar training to boys. Some girls who worked for their fathers were no doubt as carefully taught as boys. Others were apprenticed on the same conditions as brothers and served a formal term. When they completed their apprenticeship, they could set up as independent mistresses, legally the equivalent of masters, and take apprentices themselves. In Essex and Staffordshire, 3 per cent of those taking apprentices were women acting alone, another 0.5 per cent were couples. Nevertheless, as a training scheme, apprenticeship affected girls less systematically and less formally than boys.

Girls comprised 9 per cent of apprentices in Essex and Staffordshire during the last half of the eighteenth century. They accounted for just over 4 per cent of private apprentices and about 3 per cent of charity indentures. Parish indentures showed a strikingly different pattern, since nearly a third were girls. Also 60 per cent of all female apprentices were put out by the parish rather than by their parents; this compares to about an eighth of boys. Girls' increasing prominence in parish apprenticeship has particular significance in conjunction with the trade structure of apprenticeship discussed below. Overall, the evidence confirms that apprenticeship was preponderantly male, but that girls constituted an important element.

The records of charity schools in the two counties corroborate female participation in apprenticeship. Unfortunately, the minute books did not distinguish clearly between 'apprenticeship' and 'service' when recording why pupils left.⁵⁰ According to their rules, those who completed the stipulated period of attendance were found a place, and nearly a quarter of children specifically minuted as 'going apprentice' were girls. The proportion of girls rises to a half when the numbers leaving for 'service' and 'apprenticeship' are combined. The distinctions between service and apprenticeship were blurred in the case of girls, because apprenticeship was often another way of entering service. Some donations specified that girls going into service were to be assisted in a manner similar to a charity paying a boy's apprenticeship premium.⁵¹ At many schools, girls were to find a place in service before they were allowed to leave.⁵²

The suspected informality of training arrangements further obscures any clear line between apprenticeship and service. It is worth remembering that only a small proportion of children of either sex underwent formal indentured apprenticeship. Many gained experience and any 'training' through annual hirings as servants. Settlement examinations illustrate how apprenticeship could become a series of hirings or how a hiring could turn into apprenticeship.⁵³ The line between formal and informal modes of training was very thin indeed.

Not only were girls less likely than boys to be apprenticed, but the structure and characteristics of their indentured service varied significantly from the male pattern. There are clear implications that girls' training was perceived differently from that of boys. For girls, the economic educative functions seem to have been devalued and their situation seen as inferior. From another viewpoint, girls' apprenticeship may have satisfied different aims which had value in their own right. Apprenticeship did not mirror accurately the economic roles and divisions in society, and roles were constructed along gender divisions, so that male and female apprenticeship should have reflected differences as well as similarities.

The length of girls' terms demonstrate two contrasting patterns. A significant proportion of girls were indentured for shorter periods than boys. Private female apprentices served on average only 4.8 years, with half serving four years or less. Less than 6 per cent of their male counterparts served four years or less. On the other hand, 60 per cent of female apprentices, including some private ones, were placed out until the age of twenty-one or marriage.

Privately apprenticed girls, then, served appreciably shorter periods than female parish apprentices and than most boys.

The shortness of these terms suggests that the institution played a different part in girls' lives. Perhaps the trades to which they were apprenticed required little training, but the more probable reason was that the acquisition of status through apprenticeship was far less significant for girls than for boys. Short terms held throughout private female apprenticeship, not just in trades with fairly good premiums. Thus girls were not following the 'traditional' guild model which carried with it certain prestige and rights. Also, girls apprenticed for short terms were available for work up to two years earlier than boys. While they were able to earn sooner than boys, perhaps saving for a dowry, their ultimate prospects both financially and socially were potentially diminished. These girls' situations were distinctly different from those whose apprenticeship, though of short duration, could be identified as providing 'finishing' and status.

On the other hand, only one-eighth of boys served the long periods associated with parish apprenticeship while three-fifths of girls did. Thus a parish girl apprenticed at the average age of ten would serve eleven years, far longer than the vast majority of boys. A number of pauper boys obtained apprenticeships for seven years (16 per cent), but several girls apprenticed privately served until they reached twenty-one (5 per cent). This emphasizes the disparity and also demonstrates that two different models were perceived as appropriate to girls' and boys' apprenticeship. Different purposes and results were construed within each model, reinforcing perceptions of adult gender roles. Again girls' apprenticeship carries with it the image of cheap labour as opposed to training, suggesting that girls' prospects were of little consequence.

Similarly premiums diverged by sex, averaging nearly £14 for girls and £18 for boys. Overall, a wider range of premiums existed for boys while, on a trade by trade basis, girls' premiums were regularly lower. Premium values were a function of trades, which were themselves sexually differentiated. Girls were bound to trades throughout the economy and clearly women were regarded as able to do heavy and unpleasant work. Despite the sexual differentiation of trades, women and girls were regularly engaged in work which a later generation would have distinguished as distinctly non-female. From 1750, 46 per cent of girl apprentices were in the services, mainly housewifery, while 40 per cent worked in various

247

textile trades. The small mining and chemical groups were almost exclusively male, but so were the leather and timber trades which accounted for well over a third of all apprentices. The large agricultural and metal groups together included a tenth of apprenticed girls, primarily in farming and smithing. The pattern indicates that certain areas of work were considered to be more appropriate for female participation, and that others were difficult for them to enter. Yet the presence of girls across the spectrum underlines the extent of their activities and the lack of a rigid definition of female work, at least for those social groups from which apprentices primarily were drawn.

Pauper boys had a wider range of opportunities than girls, being spread more evenly throughout the trade areas, while three-quarters of pauper girls were apprenticed to the services, virtually all to housewifery. Girls apprenticed privately fared somewhat better in that three-quarters went into textile trades while the rest were a little better spread between the sectors of the economy. The high proportion in textiles was caused by two 'female' trades, mantua-making and millinery, taking nearly two-thirds of these girls.

Within trade groups, individual trades show an even more marked sexual differentiation, since those commanding higher premiums and offering better returns were usually exclusively male adult trades. For example, within agriculture, millers and grocers demanded premiums averaging £23 and £42 respectively. Yet only one girl, a pauper, was placed with a miller and none with grocers. The same was true of cabinet-makers, plumbers and curriers, to name but a few. The exclusion of females from those trades further suggests that women's work and training was devalued. In those agricultural, textile and metal trades in which women were best represented (husbandry, locksmithing, buckle-making and weaving), their premiums were low, averaging £2-£5. The terms tended to exceed seven years, while the skill required to practise the trade was minimal, suggesting that they were cheap labour.

The textile trades were an exception. Though they figured throughout the group, the numerous apprentices to milliners and mantua-makers paid good premiums and served short average terms of four years. Both female trades, millinery drew higher premiums, of £25-£75, while mantua-making required £12 on average, still a relatively good premium. Millinery as a prestigious female occupation was recommended to girls of 'good family'. It was a skilled trade and offered scope for women, attracting those with capital and some social standing. Good profits could be made by women with the ability and finance to establish themselves once their apprenticeship was complete. Contemporary commentators such as Campbell thought a woman could begin business with capital ranging from £100 to £1,000, but he stressed the need for parents to be able to provide adequately for their daughters since wages for underworkers were very poor. In spite of the 'vast profits' made by the mistresses, they 'yet give but poor, mean Wages to every Person they employ under them'.[54] For the top end of the trade and the well-capitalized employer it could be a good business enterprise, but for the less fortunate, and especially for employees, prospects were much less optimistic. Mantua-makers, usually capitalized with under £100, likewise were known for paying poor wages. According to Campbell, their journeywomen 'may make shift with great Sobriety and Oeconomy to live upon their Allowance; but their Want of Prudence, and general Poverty, has brought the business into small Reputation'.[55] He warned that the pay was frequently so low as to make prostitution their alternative form of employment. Certainly such a life was a problem for women in seasonal urban trades where they were subject to periods of slack employment and low wages. Premiums varied considerably for mantua-makers' apprentices, from £2-£31, illustrating the range within the occupation.

In all likelihood, milliners' and mantua-makers' apprentices obtained a training and a trade through apprenticeship in a way which many girls probably did not. Also, by apprenticeship to a trade with the potential of good status, girls conceivably expected to learn the polish and ways of a social class into which they might hope to marry. The apprenticeship of girls to mercers and drapers suggests this likelihood even more forcefully. It could have been a form of 'finishing' similar to boys who were apprenticed to gentlemen for similar sums and terms. In such cases, the wife probably took responsibility for the girls' education. This characteristic of female apprenticeship is also a clear reminder of the social class distinctions represented within apprenticeship, invalidating any attempt to treat it as a monolithic form of training with a single function.

It might have been expected that more women shopkeepers would have been identified. Clark suggested that women were more likely to be apprenticed to retail than guild trades during the seventeenth century, while for the following century Pinchbeck argued that a decline in apprenticeship and non-enforcement increased considerably the proportion of women traders.[56] However, the retail trades probably involved capital out of the reach of most women. Those with financial resources were the same ones who began to withdraw from the labour force as the ideological pressure embodied in the domestic ideal of women began to have greater impact. Also women may be hidden as shopkeepers working in partnership with husbands. In any case, data based on indentures and trade names do not clearly identify the retail trades.

Since the retail group as a whole is quite small, those apprenticed to mercers and drapers were probably in a favourable position with their large premiums and short terms. In most instances, girls in the retail trades probably served as shop assistants for the vintners, victuallers, pawnbrokers and shopkeepers, and as barmaids to the innholders, particularly as most were parish apprentices. Thus their prospects of setting up on their own must have been slim, given the capital required, while remaining as an assistant was not particularly lucrative or promising.

Within service occupations the sexual differentiation is marked, just as the status differentials are. Professions requiring large premiums, such as law and medicine, were exclusively male. Yet twice as many girls as boys went into the teaching profession, which also drew good premiums. All the girls apprenticed to school teachers were indentured after 1780 but with premiums two-and-a-half times greater than the boys who were placed with schoolmasters throughout the century. At the other end of the group, domestic service was virtually all-female, with small premiums (except one at £40). Most of these girls were parish apprentices. Importantly the services represent the variation between menial and professional service. The difference between the standard deviation for females' premiums (£15.04) and males' (£67.54) illustrates the wide spread of boys' premiums within the services compared with those of girls. The clear sexual differentiation within the sector, which grouped girls at the menial end of the range, suggests in part that apprenticeship remained a respectable form of training for middle-class boys where professions were important, while many middle-class girls were less likely for social reasons to seek apprenticeship.

The relationship of apprentice to master is further evidence of sexual differentiation. Clearly it was usual to apprentice boys to men: 99 per cent were. Girls were also apprenticed regularly to males, since fewer than 4 per cent of indentures involved a mistress. Even in housewifery, girls were often apprenticed formally to men, but wives or other females in the household may have taken charge of them. Part of the reason may have been that men were more likely to be legally responsible for any apprentice, since wives were restricted by law from making contracts as feme coverts.[57]

Mistresses illustrate the gender divisions of trades even more markedly than the apprentices do, because they indicate areas in which women were more likely to take up an occupation. Bonnet-making, pencilling and silkwinding were all-female occupations, corresponding to the strong female presence in textiles, and there was an overwhelming preponderance of mistresses and women apprentices in millinery, mantua-making and even ribbon weaving. Housewifery and husbandry were also conducted by numerous mistresses, reflecting the importance of these areas to parish apprenticeship and to female apprenticeship. Several mistresses took only boys, probably where they carried on a husband's trade. This was especially true where the trade was predominantly male, such as fishing, chandlery and glazing. But in some heavily 'male' trades, women took girls as hatters, mercers, drapers, peruke-makers, glovers and millers. Interesting contradictions appeared, with female grocers taking only boys but women victuallers taking only girls. Grocers could get high premiums, so that these women could have been bringing up boys, perhaps even a relative, to a lucrative trade. The girls, on the other hand, may have been shop assistants, as suggested earlier. In other trades like plumbing, oyster dredging, printing and gardening women appear only with their husbands. Mistresses' trades show marked sexual differentiation in that they were overwhelmingly in 'feminine' trades. Again, this indicates the limited prospects for journeywomen. Large numbers of women were undoubtedly 'hidden' by joining forces with husbands, but the likelihood of the girl becoming mistress in her own right, especially in a trade outside the female trades, was very slim.

As described above, the stage of processing varied significantly by the type of apprenticeship, with two divergent patterns suggesting a skill/status differentiation between private and parish apprenticeship. Private apprentices were strongly associated with the traditional crafts, the production of goods and secondary stages of processing, all aspects which could claim an emphasis on skill, but which were closely associated with the idea of status and the 'mysteries' of a closed group. Parish apprenticeship contrasted sharply with the above pattern in that the majority were split between agriculture and services and it was very strongly biased to the primary stages of processing. The implications for girls are crucial. If parish apprenticeship was seen to provide less training and less prosperous occupations, it was devalued. Thus the relatively strong female involvement in parish apprenticeship implies that girls were subject to an inferior occupational training, proportionally more than boys. Rarely did a female parish apprentice find herself put to a trade with good prospects. While a similar trend is also true for boys, parish apprenticeship could operate as an avenue to a trade with a financial future and good status for a poor boy. Once again, this relationship implies a diminished regard for girls' training, implying that apprenticeship primarily fulfilled other functions for girls.

Apprenticeship was not intended solely as industrial training for either sex. Passing on values and behaviour from one generation to the next was a significant component, as numerous apprentice-master relations suggest. Apprenticeship may also have promoted girls' mobility, because training or 'finishing' in a respectable female trade could enhance social position. Where emulation was an important feature of the initiation to adulthood, apprenticeship could be quite important. Frequently, non-pauper girls were apprenticed to trades which they probably never carried out. Girls apprenticed to farmers, mercers, drapers or even to housewifery with large premiums suggest that 'finishing' or transmitting values and behaviour may have been a significant part of their education. In such cases, the purpose of the apprenticeship may have been provision of general education and discipline, rather than teaching a trade. Aspiring females, whose families could afford the premium, may have seen such apprenticeships as a means of improving their status and prospects, possibly with an eye to marriage within the trade or at least the social group.

A finishing education was also available at a wide range of schools for middle-class girls. Within the social structure, which was layered into overlapping strata, apprenticeship and schooling were utilized by individuals for their own ends. Where the pauper girl had little choice in the nature of her apprenticeship, lower middle-class parents may have seen a suitable apprenticeship as an attainable means of achieving improvement in their daughter's status and position in society. Schools were still too expensive for some, while for others a good apprenticeship seemed preferable to a poor school. Two consecutive millinery firms in Colchester regularly apprenticed young women, keeping two on the premises, and increasing the premiums over time. Their reputation was sufficiently respectable to attract regular applicants. One Chelmsford firm required over £70 as a premium after 1790. While the practice of apprenticeship was concentrated among the girls of the labouring orders, it certainly reached into the middle classes, at certain points overlapping with schools to provide the sort of education and preparation wished for.

Similarly large numbers of female parish apprentices were maintained and probably given general education in addition to any technical instruction they might have received. There were economic and political reasons for apprenticing pauper girls, but the female advice literature of the last half-century made it clear that girls' moral upbringing was of paramount concern to the middle classes. For girls lower down the social scale education in demeanour, propriety and sobriety could be derived through apprenticeship. The system was sometimes seen as a means of raising children in an appropriate environment. Many contemporaries thought that the poor benefited if children were taken away from miserable and depraved parents and placed with a better sort of person, who provided an example to emulate.[58] Avoiding the patronizing tone of those writers, socialization, as education in the values and behaviour expected by society, was probably an important element of female apprenticeship. In an age which was redefining the female character, that motive may partly explain the increasing number and proportion of female apprentices.

CONCLUSION

Training was the primary aim of apprenticeship, and girls shared in gaining industrial skills in this way. However, occupational skills were probably a less important element than the transmission of cultural values. Apprenticeship as an institution was socially constructed so that it reflected the values of eighteenth-century life. Distinctions of class and status were integral to an understanding of the relationships of the time, and individuals' roles and positions were determined less by ability and more by the niches

253

into which they fitted. As such, whereas skill and training for an occupation were explicitly regarded as central to the experience of apprenticeship, the period of learning was implicitly used to perpetuate status distinctions. Thus a crucial element of apprenticeship as a preparation for life was the role of the master in transmitting culture and acting as a status model for the novice to emulate. Similarly, apprenticeship embodied gender distinctions which reflected socially determined evaluations of women's status and worth. Division of labour throughout the economy was sexually constructed so that although women made a vital contribution, their status and position was usually devalued.

The elements of apprenticeship described above suggest that the nature of many trades to which girls were apprenticed and the training component of their terms of service were given less weight than was the case with boys. The shorter terms of girls have been taken to suggest that less training was likely to be provided for them, while boys' apprenticeship more clearly matched the pattern established by guild tradition. The sexual differentiation of trades meant that girls with high premiums found their way into 'female' work, while the wide range of professional and profitable trades were largely restricted to boys. Schoolteaching was one modest exception. Boys also dominated the middle range of 'respectable' trades while girls were involved in those requiring less skill, training and prestige. Girls were more likely to be found in the 'general' categories of production which, because of the way the groups were constructed, meant that less complex tasks were required. They were poorly represented in trades like cutlery or the manufacture of mechanical devices, which imply a greater skill component. Although the range of girls' opportunities was not limited to female trades, girls do not appear throughout the trade groups equally with boys.

In instances like mantua-making and millinery, girls were probably taught the trade, both because these were 'female' trades and because girls were usually apprenticed to a mistress. A similar case could be made for schoolteachers. But with those significant exceptions, girls were in largely overstocked or menial trades with low premiums, such as weaving and the small metal trades. And even millinery and mantua-making were seen as overstocked by contemporaries. Similarly, the relationship between parish apprenticeship, the content of trades and sex likewise suggests that girls were more likely than boys to obtain an inferior training. This is not to suggest that women's work was not skilled or important, but that it was not recognized as such through apprenticeship. Nor does it mean that no occupational training was provided. While numerous girls were educated through apprenticeship, their experiences diverged markedly from those of boys.

Though the concept of status is fraught with dangers, the over-whelming feeling is that girls' opportunities were sharply limited. They were most likely to be found in the low-status occupations carrying with them modest future prospects. They were left in an economically vulnerable position, restricted to menial and over-stocked trades, a situation which reflected and further reinforced their subordinate social position. The construction of apprentice-ship for girls owed less to any feminine ideal and rather more to a status evaluation which described girls and women as subordi-nate and their work, albeit economically valuable, as inferior in status to male work.

NOTES

1 For this reason a number of fascinating but tangential problems have had to be put aside. For the history of apprenticeship, particularly legal and economic relations, the classic work is O. J. Dunlop and R. D. Denman, *English Apprenticeship and Child Labour: A History*, London, 1912. A discussion of the changes in eighteenth-century apprentice-ship, its problems and debates can be found in J. Rule, *Experience of Labour in Eighteenth-century Industry*, London, 1981, 95–123. Dorothy George relates apprenticeship to its London context and trades and includes useful interpretations of the special problems of parish apprenticeship in *London Life in the Eighteenth Century*, London, 1925, repr. Harmondsworth, 1953. Dorothy Marshall in *The English Poor in the Eighteenth Century*, London, 1926, 181–206, places parish apprentice-ship in the changing context of poor relief.

2 The evolution of the idea of youth is discussed in J. Gillis, *Youth and History, Tradition and Change in European Age Relations, 1770-Present, Studies in Social Discontinuity*, London, 1974, 1–9; P. Ariès, *Centuries of Childhood*, Harmondsworth, 1973, 23–30 relates adolescence to both youth and childhood. See also J. F. Kett, 'The stages of life' in M. Gordon, (ed.), *The Family in Social-Historical Perspective*, New York, 1978, 166–91.

3 Ariès, *Centuries of Childhood*, op. cit., 27.

4 Kett, 'The stages of life', op. cit., 166–8.

5 For clarification of the relationship between domestic and farm ser-vants and apprentices, see A. Kussmaul, *Servants in Husbandry in Early Modern England*, Cambridge, 1982, 4; Kussmaul's use of 'formal' coincides with mine in that the contractual nature of indentured apprenticeship is regarded as formal, while the customary relationship

between servants and employer is referred to as informal. For the contractual elements of domestic service, see J. J. Hecht, *The Domestic Servant in Eighteenth-Century England*, London, 1956, repr. 1980, esp. 72–4. Also W. Blackstone, *Commentaries on the Laws of England*, ed. E. Christian, London, 1800, I, 425–7 explains late eighteenth-century legal definitions of servants and apprentices.

6 Rule listed the essential features of guild apprenticeship in *Experience of Labour*, op. cit., 97.

7 5 Eliz. I, c. 4.

8 27 Henry VIII, c. 25.

9 14 Eliz I, c. 5 (1572); 39 Eliz. I, c. 3 (1597); 43 Eliz. I, c. 2 (1601).

10 [Daniel Defoe], *The Complete English Tradesman in Familiar Letters*, London, 1727, repr. New York, 1969, I, 14.

11 Adam Smith, *An Inquiry into the Nature and Causes of the Wealth of Nations*, ed. R. H. Campbell and A. S. Skinner, 1776, repr. Oxford, 1976, 139–40.

12 See Rule, *Experience of Labour*, op. cit., 33. A useful discussion of social distinctions in London trades can be found in George, *London Life*, op. cit. 159–66.

13 Smith, *Wealth of Nations*, op. cit., 136–7.

14 Ariès, *Centuries of Childhood*, op. cit., 186.

15 Defoe, *English Tradesman*, op. cit., I, 6.

16 See Marshall, *English Poor*, op. cit., 181–206.

17 On outdoor apprenticeship: see Rule, *Experience of Labour*, op. cit., 100–1.

18 For more detail on the database and related research problems encountered, see D. Simonton, 'The education and training of eighteenth-century English girls, with special reference to the working classes', Ph.D. thesis, Essex, 1988, 178–82.

19 Enacted by 8 Anne, c. 5 (1709); repealed by 44 Geo. III, c. 98 (1814).

20 See M. Prior, 'Women and the urban economy' in her *Women in English Society*, London, 1985, 102–4.

21 In many cases, such as Romford's, the records simply do not exist. This is particularly unfortunate since other materials including the charity school have proven so valuable and reliable. An interesting case is Gnosall, Staffordshire where the overseers' records turned up by accident in an old chest in the early years of this century. Even among existing collections, damage and loss have taken their toll. Such a case is Enville, Staffordshire where despite plentiful indentures before and after, there are only three for the years 1720–40. By contrast, in several Essex parishes few records survive after the first half of the century such as Tolleshunt D'Arcy after 1727, Chigwell after 1744 and Canewdon after 1750. It is possible that apprenticeship fell off at that time, but the usual historical view is that parish apprenticeship was employed more frequently in order to offset rising poor rates. Loss of records is a more plausible explanation in view of the existence of large groups of records for the later period for parishes all over Essex, such as Walthamstow and Bocking. In some cases, like Burstead Magna, the early years are missing.

APPRENTICESHIP: TRAINING AND GENDER

22 7 Geo. III, c. 39 and 18 Geo. III, c. 47.

23 On Hanway's activities in favour of the infant poor and especially the 1767 act, see J. S. Taylor, 'Philanthropy and empire: Jonas Hanway and the infant poor of London', *Eighteenth-Century Studies*, 12, 3, Spring 1979, 285–305. See also *Report from the Select Committee on the State of Poor Parish Children*, PP 1767, xxxi, 248.

24 F. Morton Eden, *The State of the Poor*, i, London, 1797, 338–9; George, *London Life*, op. cit., 236–8; Marshall, *English Poor*, op. cit., 201–5.

25 8 and 9 Wm. III, c. 30 (1696–7), 20 Geo. III, c. 36 (1780). The motives and impact of this legislation are discussed in I. Pinchbeck and M. Hewitt, *Children in English Society*, i, London, 1969, 248–50. On the treatment of apprentices see Marshall, *English Poor*, op. cit., 198–206, George, *London Life*, op. cit., 224–30 and Rule, *Experience of Labour*, op. cit., 98–104.

26 20 Geo. II, c. 19 (1747).

27 32 Geo. III, c. 57 (1792), 33 Geo. III, c. 55 (1793); see also Blackstone, *Commentaries*, i, 426.

28 C. Cappe, *Observations on Charity Schools, Female Friendly Societies and other subjects connected with the views of the Ladies Committee*, London, 1805, 45.

29 Blackstone, *Commentaries*, i, 427–8. Elizabethan courts had ruled that in unskilled trades such as husbandry, brick-making and milling an apprenticeship was not essential, J. H. Clapham, *An Economic History of Modern Britain*, 2nd edn, Cambridge, 1930, i, 370.

30 Rule, *Experience of Labour*, op. cit., 109, and see also 106–14.

31 Smith, *Wealth of Nations*, op. cit., 137.

32 ibid., 135–40, 150–2.

33 ibid., 140.

34 See the examples cited by Rule, *Experience of Labour*, op. cit., 106–7, and E. P. Thompson, *The Making of the English Working Class*, London, 1963, repr. Harmondsworth, 1968, 279.

35 See the cases cited in C. R. Dobson, *Masters and Journeymen: A Prehistory of Industrial Relations, 1717–1800*, London, 1980, 56, 114, 134 and George, *London Life*, op. cit., 233–4.

36 55 Geo. III, c. 96.

37 R. Campbell, *The London Tradesman*, London, 1747; repr. Newton Abbot, 1969, 20.

38 *Abstract of Returns of Charitable Donations for the Benefit of Poor Persons, 1787–88*, PP 1816, xvi, 351–90, 1117–1160.

39 'Colchester Charity School Cash Book and Ledger, 1710–70', Essex Record Office T/A 613, 9; 'Wolverhampton Charity School Minute Book, 1716–1797', Staffordshire Record Office D1157/1/5/1. A similar stipulation was included in the charitable bequest in the will of Humphrey Perye of Bilston in Wolverhampton, Great Britain, Commission to Inquire Concerning Charities, *Reports, 1819–1837*, v, 597.

40 Peter Laslett's figures for servants are significantly higher. Whether or not he included apprentices is not clear. See his discussion on the life-cycle of servants in *Family Life and Illicit Love in Earlier Generations*, Cambridge, 1977, 34.

257

41 Prices from P. Mathias, *First Industrial Nation*, London, 1968, 69 based on Schumpeter-Gilboy price indices, 1696–1823. These averages do not consider those cases for which no premium was indicated, though most of them were parish apprentices placed out with very small premiums.
42 See Simonton, 'Education and training', op. cit., 285–7.
43 Marshall, *English Poor*, op. cit., 194.
44 I. Pinchbeck, *Women Workers and the Industrial Revolution, 1750–1850*, London, 1930, repr. London, 1981; A. Clark, *Working Life of Women in the Seventeenth Century*, London, 1919, repr. London, 1982; E. Power, *Medieval Women*, Cambridge, 1975.
45 Dunlop and Denman, *English Apprenticeship*, op. cit., 150–1.
46 Dobson, *Masters and Journeymen*, op. cit., 63; Pinchbeck, *Women Workers*, op. cit., 160–1.
47 See Prior, 'Women in the urban economy', op. cit., 104.
48 Dunlop and Denman, *English Apprenticeship*, op. cit., 148–9; Pinchbeck, *Women Workers*, op. cit., 126, 160; *Report on Disputes between Masters and Workmen Engaged in the Cotton Manufacture*, PP 1802–3, viii, 343, 344, 383.
49 Cited in A. F. J. Brown, *Essex at Work, 1700–1815*, Essex Record Office Publications No. 49, Chelmsford, 1969, 2.
50 Simonton, 'Education and training', op. cit., 142–4.
51 Two Staffordshire examples are the Envil Free School for Girls where they were prepared for service and the governors were required to find an appropriate place for them and, in Stafford, Isaac Walton's Charity of 1696 set aside £5 annually for maidservants: Charities Commission, *Reports*, v 617; xi, 602–3. These reports frequently used the terms 'apprenticeship' and 'service' interchangeably.
52 See, for example, 'Wolverhampton Charity School Minute Book', S.R.O., D1157/1/5/1, 1730.
53 Birmingham Diocesan Record Office, 'St Peter, Harborne, Settlement Examinations, 1752–1807', DRO 61/7/12 and 'St Lawrence, Northfield, Examinations re: Settlement, 1699–1802, Overseers of the Poor, Bundle II,' DRO 14.
54 Campbell, *London Tradesman*, op. cit., 336, 208.
55 ibid., 227.
56 Clark, *Working Life of Women*, op. cit., 200–1; Pinchbeck, *Women Workers*, op. cit., 294.
57 Blackstone, *Commentaries*, i, 442–4.
58 Sarah Trimmer, *The Oeconomy of Charity, or an Address to Ladies Concerning Sunday Schools*, London, 1787, 11–15; Cappe, in *Observations on Charity Schools*, op. cit.,19–20, makes this argument but later argues against apprenticeship as a solution.

Part VI

MARKET STRUCTURES AND SOCIAL INSTITUTIONS: COMMERCE AND CUSTOMARY CONTEXT

11

LANDHOLDING AND THE ORGANIZATION OF TEXTILE MANUFACTURE IN YORKSHIRE RURAL TOWNSHIPS *c.* 1660–1810*

Pat Hudson

In the century or so before the advent of widespread factory production in the British textile trades the bulk of cloth was produced in rural and semi-rural areas, largely on domestic premises. In the eighteenth century manufacturing sectors became more and more concentrated geographically, as deindustrialization in some regions accompanied rapid proto-industrialization in others. In this process of change the West Riding of Yorkshire came to dominate the British manufacture of wool textiles. Clearly the region proved an attractive and receptive location for the expansion of a highly commercialized form of domestic production. This was often carried out alongside farming and other agrarian pursuits, dovetailing with them and securing a supply of labour and other factors of production from within established communities. The structures of rural production varied, depending partly on the nature of cloths and their markets, and the technology, finance and type of labour required in their manufacture. In addition, and related to these economic factors, the character of particular localities within the West Riding (their agrarian base, social structure, institutions and customs) also appears to have influenced the organization of pre-factory manufacturing and its evolution into more centralized forms. This impact upon industry of regional and local variations in the social and power structures of rural communities is the central concern of this chapter. The focus here is the West Riding but the issues have wider relevance for the study of other proto-industrial regions both in Britain and elsewhere. How did such aspects as the division of labour, the relation-

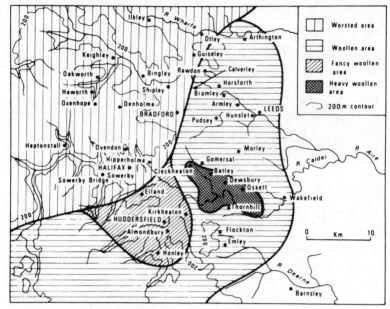

Map 11.1 The location of Sowerby and Calverley within the worsted and woollen areas respectively of West Yorkshire, *c. 1780–1830*

Source: Based on Hudson, *The Genesis of Industrial Capital: A Study of the West Riding Wool Textile Industry, c. 1750–1750*, p. 28.

ship between production and marketing, the sources of capital, credit and enterprise come to differ between different regions (and subregions) even where very similar commodities were the end result? And what long-term influence did regional and local social and agrarian arrangements have upon the later emergence of more centralized and capital-intensive manufacturing?

Yorkshire's rise to dominate the production of coarse and medium quality woollen and worsted products during the eighteenth century was accompanied by increasingly distinctive subregional specialization as illustrated in Maps 11.1 and 11.2. Heaton's classic study stressed this emerging spatial pattern, as did Sigsworth, and later work by Jenkins and Dickenson was set in the context of the marked distinctiveness of manufacturing in the different branches of the industry and in the different localities of the wool textile belt.[1] Many different organizational forms of production coexisted in the region by the mid-eighteenth century, from workshop and artisan structures to specialized forms of putting out, from small-scale sideline activity to large-scale business

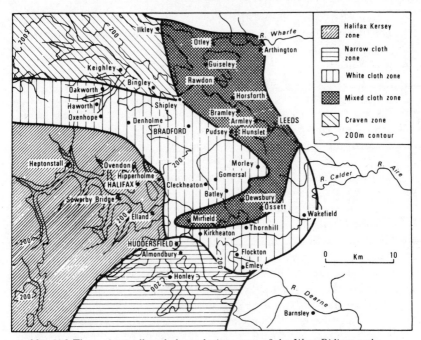

Map 11.2 The main woollen cloth producing zones of the West Riding, early eighteenth century
Source: Based on Dickenson, 'The West Riding Woollen and Worsted Industries', p. 63.

and from largely independent farmer/artisan labour to proletarian pieceworkers. Although a wide spectrum of forms was notable the major feature of variations in the organization of manufacturing, outside the larger towns, was the contrast between the production of woollen fabrics on the one hand and worsted cloths on the other. The increasing variety of woollen fabrics, which had been the traditional manufacture of the area since medieval times, continued, as in the past, to be largely associated with independent artisan families who bought their raw material from the local stapler, and sold a finished or semi-finished product to merchants in the regular market of the local cloth halls. By contrast, worsted production, which expanded rapidly from the mid-eighteenth century, was dominated by medium and large-scale putting-out concerns who often went far afield for both wools and marketing. Thus the spatial pattern of rural manufacture in the late eighteenth century, exhibited in Map 11.2, with woollen production

263

concentrated chiefly in the east and south of the Riding and worsted production in the north and west, represented a broad divide in organizational terms as well as in the nature of commodities produced.[2]

There are some well-rehearsed arguments which help to explain why proto-industry, in its various forms, was widespread in Yorkshire by the eighteenth century: the insufficiency of agriculture, through much of the Riding, to provide the subsistence needs of a growing population and a tradition of peasant skills in woollen cloth production for household and local needs based on the use of local woods. This general environment was given further stimulus by the expansion of Britain's textile trade with southern Europe and across the Atlantic, as well as by generally buoyant domestic demand conditions.

What is much more difficult to explain is the existence and success of different organizational forms.[3] There was, for example, nothing in the nature of the production processes of woollen textiles which dictated that they should be produced on an artisan basis rather than by putting out. Indeed, in the West Country, the manufacture of woollen cloth was dominated by large-scale clothiers who put out wool to journeymen and their families to complete the various stages of production. J. de L. Mann has argued that the organizational contrast between Yorkshire and the West Country was determined by the sorts of cloths produced and that it would have been impossible to produce superfine cloth, with its expensive raw materials, on the Yorkshire system.[4] But although Yorkshire was dominated by the production of fabrics at the lower end of the market, the region also contained areas, for example in Leeds and around Huddersfield, where types of high grade and fancy woollens were produced by small-scale artisan concerns. Indeed, it was the cheapest line of blanket production around Dewsbury which saw some of the earliest movements away from small-scale to larger-scale enterprises.[5] Furthermore, although the worsted branch in Yorkshire was equally famed for its cheap goods it developed, almost from its inception, on a putting-out basis. Clearly a more convincing explanation of organizational patterns in the industry is required and it is here that the spatial aspect of the woollen/worsted contrast assumes a central importance.

In my earlier work I examined the agrarian and manorial histories of the woollen and worsted areas of Yorkshire.[6] At the regional level of analysis this work suggested that the agrarian and institutional environment was the major influence on the ways in which textile manufacture was conducted outside the larger towns during the eighteenth century. Worsted production on a putting-out basis supplanted woollen manufacture in the north and west of the region. This was accompanied by considerable division of labour between households articulated through putting-out concerns of some size which extended their spinning distribution into the North Riding and the Yorkshire Dales through a complex web of intermediaries. The worsted area had previously supported kersey manufacture by domestic households often living on the brink of subsistence and increasingly relying on their textile earnings to provide basic foodstuffs. The independence and viability of these households was threatened by the subdivision of holdings and by the rise of larger freeholders and leaseholders who developed putting-out systems employing spinners and weavers on piecerates. The viability of these small domestic concerns was further undermined by their heavy reliance on the fluctuating fortunes of foreign markets. Thus what was to be the worsted belt was already in the early eighteenth century characterized by a social polarization which included a large group of proletarianized households precariously dependent on their textile activities. Much of the worsted belt lay above 200 metres, which made it climatically and agriculturally less hospitable than the woollen area and for this reason it was never strongly manorialized. Control over the land market was weak and so subinfeudation and enfranchisement had proceeded apace since the sixteenth century, creating the accumulation of land in the hands of a socially diverse but limited class who rented cottages to the larger army of the landless. I argued that this type of social structure and institutional history created a favourable environment for putting out to take root and flourish. Potential commercially minded employers with landed assets existed alongside a proletarianized group whose landlessness made it difficult to function independently as household manufacturers.

By contrast, in the woollen belt the more fertile agricultural holdings and the manorial histories of the white and mixed cloth zones may well have imparted a greater resilience to the independent artisan structure. The balancing of the dual occupation of farmer and manufacturer was an important feature of the stability and success of this structure as was the ability of small firms to raise cash on the basis of their farming assets. The soil and climate, suitable for a mixture of arable and grazing, also made this area more attractive for large estate owners and earlier it had been more strongly manorialized than the worsted belt. The manorial history of the woollen area promoted the continuation of copyhold leases, delayed piecemeal enclosure and made the land market less fluid than it was on the Pennine slopes to the west. This may have retarded proletarianization or at least promoted an environment with tenurial and inheritance practices and a structure of parish authority which bolstered the existence of small family-run businesses.

Thus my earlier work suggested that the organization of manufacture of the different branches of textile production found in eighteenth-century Yorkshire owed much to the pre-existing agrarian structures of landholding and land use. I have also argued that the motivation and finance of those responding to commercial stimuli as the century progressed were shaped largely by the mores and socio-economic relationships embedded in the localities and their histories. The exogenous stimulus of expanding domestic and overseas markets therefore came up against the internal structure and dynamic of the localities, and this did much to determine the extent to which communities were able or felt it necessary to respond to the opportunities which presented themselves.[7]

In order to test these notions and to enquire exactly how the institutional agrarian environment functioned to influence the social structure via landholding, inheritance, poor relief systems and in other ways, two townships (which have good survival of archival material) were chosen for a major reconstructional study: Sowerby and Calverley. Sowerby lies to the west of Halifax in the worsted belt, while Calverley is in the Aire valley to the northwest of Leeds at the edge of the woollen area. Of course these townships have distinctive histories and social features peculiar to themselves, but the idea of this comparative research project is that the two townships will be sufficiently representative of their regions that their development in the eighteenth and early nineteenth centuries will be better understood with reference to the broad hypotheses which emerged from my earlier work.

The research relies heavily upon the use of the IBM mainframe computer at Liverpool, employing an IBM database software called ISQL (Interactive Structured Query Language). This enables nominal data to be united across a large range of files and also facilitates the storage, reordering and retrieval of a mass of tabulated material. Thus, for example, taxation data can readily be linked to occupational information from parish registers, probate material can be linked to demographic events and land transfer and estate papers can be united with information on parish administration. In this way the computer-aided study of manufacturing townships can uniquely illuminate the social and economic relationships which lie at the heart of economic development. It can also provide a window on the lives of ordinary people whose profiles can only be traced by squeezing out and reassembling every small piece of evidence surviving from the townships.[8] The full results of analysis of the mass of data extant for the two townships must await the completion of the project, but here we examine some initial findings from the reconstructional work using record linkage and looking in turn at occupations, social structure, landholding and inheritance.

SOWERBY AND CALVERLEY: OCCUPATIONS

Sowerby was a bigger township than Calverley in terms both of population and of land area. At the 1811 Census Sowerby had a population of 5,177 compared with Calverley's 2,390. Their difference in population size appears even greater in the late seventeenth century when the hearth tax listed 127 households in Calverley-cum-Farsley and 312 in Sowerby. Both of these figures from 1664 include those households, about a third in each township, who were exempt from the tax by reason of poverty.[9]

The dependence of both Sowerby and Calverley on the manufacture of textiles is apparent from the late seventeenth century as indicated in surviving wills and probate inventories.[10] As illustrated in Table 11.1, almost half of Sowerby will-makers had textile occupations while in Calverley the proportion was 38 per cent. But in neither case does this represent the full commitment of the township to its main branch of manufacture because will-making was biased in favour of the upper income groups whereas textile crafts on a part- or full-time basis were ubiquitous among the poorer groups. In Calverley, because of the greater proclivities of the soils, a significant proportion of the non-textile will-makers were yeomen farmers with no obvious textile involvements, although the existence of credits on bond among the assets of many is indicative of considerable lending and borrowing between the farming and textile groups.

Table 11.1 Occupations as described or listed in probate data, Sowerby and Calverley, 1690s–1760s*

Occupations	Sowerby	Median value of probate inventories Sowerby	Calverley	Median value of probate inventories Calverley
Clothiers	17	£27	38	£56
Yeomen/putting–out merchants	16	£184	–	N/A
Weavers	14	£13	2	£8
Other textile employments	6	not calculated	2	not calculated
Non-textile employments	58	not calculated	69	not calculated
Total cases	111		111	

Source: Probate inventories and wills, Borthwick Institute, University of York.
Note: *Sowerby here includes Soyland and Calverley denotes Calverley parish.

The textile occupations of will-makers differed between the townships, reflecting the nature of production in the two places and the organizational structure of the industry. In Calverley the majority of will-makers included in the textile trades are described as clothiers, a term which in that township covered a vast range of types of concern, from those with assets valued as low as £2 to those over £500 but typically lying in the £30-£138 range (the interquartile range). Most of these clothiers, with the exception of the very poor, held land (particularly copyhold land) and carried out arable and livestock farming alongside textile production. Often their assets were fairly equally balanced between the two, although credits and stocks on the textile side of their operations seem to have run up large (textile) assets in one or two cases. In Sowerby the term clothier seems to have been applied both to dependent weavers and to more substantial independent concerns, but assets of clothiers in that township seldom exceeded £100. Putting-out employers with assets of between £50 and £800 were typically termed yeomen. These Sowerby individuals were often involved in agriculture as well as trade and industry but the bulk of their assets were clearly in trade, especially in credits and stocks of wool and cloth. The term yeoman in Calverley was, by contrast, almost exclusively applied to landholding farmers only.[11]

By the early eighteenth century the occupational information provided by the parish registers enables more detailed understanding of the occupational structure across the whole of the social

scale. Again there is indicated a heavy reliance on weaving in
Sowerby. Whether one analyses the occupations of fathers of baptised children, relatives of those buried or the occupations of the
deceased, the results are very similar (see Table 11.2). Around 45
per cent of Sowerby's male population were weavers in the second
quarter of the eighteenth century, a further 20–30 per cent had
textile occupations other than weaving (principally clothiers, dres-
sers, spinners and combers). Thus around 70 per cent of the male
employed population was dependent on textiles for their main
source of livelihood. Female dependence is harder to estimate
because the work experience of so few women is reflected in the
parish register data. Where a glimpse is obtained, a very high
proportion of spinsters is indicated.[12] Sowerby's other occupations
in the first half of the eighteenth century were principally the
service trades (shoe-makers, innkeepers, victuallers), and building/
labouring. Agricultural occupations are simply not found recorded
in the parish registers, with the exception of one or two woodcut-
ters. Clearly the soil and its products was very much a secondary
activity in the township. Many people held land (as we shall
see) and worked it, but few regarded it as their main source of
livelihood.

Table 11.2 Occupations taken from parish registers, Sowerby St Peters,
1729–40

Occupations of fathers of those baptised 1729–40		Occupations of first relatives of those buried 1730–6	Occupations of the deceased 1730–6
	%	%	%
Weavers	48	54	40
Other textiles	22	14	38
Service trades	23	25	12
Building trades, labourers etc.	4	5	3
Yeomen/woodcutters	3	–	7
	100	100	100
Total cases	212	80	42

Source: Parish register, Sowerby St Peters, West Yorkshire Archive Service,
Halifax.

At the end of the eighteenth century the dependence on textiles
remained, although the numbers concentrating on weaving had

269

PAT HUDSON

increased as had the numbers of service occupations directly associated with commercial textile production (see Table 11.3). The
same high proportions dependent on the textile industry are also
found in the early nineteenth century: 45 per cent of the fathers
of baptised children were weavers and a further 23 per cent were
involved in other aspects of textile manufacture. A large proportion
of the rest were in trade and services allied to the textile industry.[13]

Table 11.3 Fathers' occupations from Church of England baptisms,
Sowerby St Peters, 1777–98

Occupations	Number	Percentage of total
Weavers	482	56
Other textiles	162	19
Service trades	77	9
Tradesmen and merchants	30	4
Building trades	84	10
Farmers	1	0
Soldiers	19	2
Total cases	855	100

Source: Parish register, Sowerby St Peters, West Yorkshire Archive Service,
Halifax.

Interestingly, the parish register material provides some insights
into occupational and residential mobility. Of the 855 cases of
fathers of the baptised 1777–98, only 62 were recorded with more
than one occupation and 48 (77 per cent) of these were weavers
(shifting to or from being soldiers, clothiers, combers and/or
labourers mostly). Twelve per cent of the fathers moved one or
more times, within the township, during their child-bearing years
and a further 7 per cent moved into or out of Sowerby (from or
to neighbouring townships in the main). Of the total movers, 88
per cent were weavers, showing them to be the most mobile group
as well as those most likely to shift occupations or to carry on two
occupations at once. Clearly Sowerby's weavers formed a fluid and
mobile group.

The wide use of the term clothier to cover a variety of size and
type of undertaking, together with the dependence of Calverley's
population on artisan cloth-making in the early eighteenth century
is illustrated in Table 11.4 which analyses the occupational data
from the parish register for the years 1721–6. No one was classified
as a 'weaver' or a manufacturer as in Sowerby. Apart from the

270

overwhelming dominance of clothiers, the importance of the husbandry group, which had no direct counterpart in Sowerby, shows up. Although not yet complete, study of the parish register data for Calverley at the end of the century shows the continuing numerical dominance of the clothier group in the population, although this is reduced to nearer 50 per cent of stated occupations.

Table 11.4 Occupations as stated of fathers of children baptised at Calverley parish church, 1721–6.

Occupations	Number	% of total
Clothiers	452	70
Other textiles	5	1
Husbandmen	64	10
Innkeepers	11	2
Tailors	23	4
Masons	12	2
Blacksmiths	13	2
Shoe-makers	10	1
Other services	41	6
Others	15	2
Total cases	646	100

Source: Calverley parish registers, vol. 2, West Yorkshire Archive Service, Leeds.

SOCIAL STRUCTURES

Our earliest indications of the different social structures of the two townships during the period 1660–1820 come from the hearth tax returns and are illustrated in Tables 11.5a and 11.5b which analyse the returns for 1664. The Sowerby figures are inflated by the inclusion of Soyland in the returns for the township. Soyland was to become a separate township but fell within the same constabulary as Sowerby for hearth tax purposes. As Soyland appears to have been very similar in social and occupational structure to Sowerby, the Sowerby/Soyland hearth tax figures can be regarded as representative of the nature of Sowerby (though inflated by about 28 per cent in terms of numbers of taxpayers). The Calverley and Sowerby hearth tax returns highlight remarkable contrasts between the two townships in social structure, as reflected in hearth ownership. These, to a large extent, accord with our initial understanding of the differences in social structure pertaining as a result of very different patterns of prior manorialism, of land-ownership, leasing and inheritance.

Table 11.5 Analysis of the hearth tax returns, Sowerby and Calverley, 1664

(*a*) Sowerby hearth tax, 1664 (includes Soyland)

Hearths	Number of household heads	% of household heads
Exempt	140	30
0	3	1
1	185	39
2	72	15
3	29	6
4	27	6
5	10	2
6	2	<1
7	1	<1
8	1	<1
9	1	<1
Total	471	100

(*b*) Calverley hearth tax, 1664

Hearths	Number of household heads	% of household heads
Exempt	43	34
0	0	0
1	58	45
2	18	14
3	6	5
4	1	1
5		
14	1	1
Total	127	100

Source: Hearth tax returns, E179/210/393, 16 Charles II, Lady Day 1664, PRO, Chancery Lane.

In Sowerby, no taxpayer paid on more than nine hearths through the four tax points 1664–74, but fifteen or so individuals in Sowerby paid tax on five or more hearths.[14] At the other end of the social scale (in hearth terms), 56 per cent of the taxpaying public paid on one hearth with a further substantial group of 30 per cent paying on between two and four hearths. Thus although the social structure was by no means polarized at this date, there certainly appears to have been a stratum of the sort of substantial individuals who might be capable of finding the credit and capital to finance trade and putting out on a considerable scale. These persons existed alongside a significantly large exempt class of potential employees, but the middling strata were also highly visible.

Turning to Calverley, a very different picture emerges in the distribution of hearths in the returns. Sixty-nine per cent of tax-payers (or 45 per cent of total household heads) paid on only one hearth, in 1664, with a further 21 per cent paying on two. Only one person paid tax on more than four hearths – Sir Walter Calverley, by far the largest landowner in the township. Thus Calverley township, as reflected in the hearth tax returns, had a very large group of one-hearth payers, a smaller middling stratum than Sowerby and one family, the Calverleys (succeeded by the Thornhill's during the eighteenth century) who controlled much of the land of the township. Calverley's 'one-hearth payers', as we shall see, were mainly small landholding clothiers and, as in Sowerby, about one-third of householders (the landless and small cottager group in the main) were recorded as exempt from taxation by reason of poverty.

We have thus established that Sowerby and Calverley conform to the typologies regarding occupation and social structure boldly stated in my earlier work, although Sowerby, and possibly also the other townships of the worsted area, possessed a much more significant and varied middle stratum than was originally thought. Also Calverley, and possibly most of the rest of the woollen area, had a class of poor and landless cottagers from the late seventeenth century which was as significant as the proletarianized element of the worsted belt. To understand fully the place of this stratum in the society of the woollen textile area it will be necessary to discover the occupational structure of the proletarianized group. To do this we must first enquire a little more into the relationship between landownership, landholding (and working) and the organization and finance of the textile industry.

LAND AND INDUSTRY

Although the subject of much debate relating to their precise accuracy and the question of calculating acreage equivalents, land tax returns can provide valuable information on the structure of landholding and (from the 1780s) on landownership and occupation.[15] Land tax analysis of owners and, where possible,

occupiers has been calculated for Sowerby at five benchmark years –
1750, 1761, 1782, 1788 and 1794. For Calverley land tax analysis
has been undertaken only for the latter three dates because of
poorer survival of the earlier records. Additionally, for the Blackwood quarter of Sowerby only (covering more than one-third of
the land area and the population of the township), a detailed rate
assessment of 1804 has been analysed against the occupational
data from the parish registers to form a case-study of the relationship between landholding and manufacture.

Sowerby is remarkable for the survival of early land tax returns
dating (sporadically) from 1750. The tax paid (mainly by owners
rather than occupiers of land) in 1750–1 and 1761 is detailed in
Table 11.6. Between these two dates a revision of Sowerby's assessment occurred so that individuals were made to pay an increase
of some 25 per cent. This accounts for the overall upward shift in
assessments, but Table 11.6 is most remarkable for the stability
which is shown in the distribution of taxes. In 1750–1 and 1761
85 per cent and 78 per cent respectively of taxpayers paid sums
between 4s and £2 10s. Relatively few (7 per cent and 6 per cent)
paid less than 4s but this was matched and, in 1761, exceeded in
size by a group of substantial taxpayers paying more than £2 10s.

Table 11.6 Sowerby land tax payers 1750–1 and 1761

Categories	1750–1*	1761
Less than 4s	11	8
4s–<£1	79	51
£1–<£2 10s	44	46
£2 10s–<£5	7	12
£5–<£10	2	6
£10–<£20	1	1
£20 and more	–	1
Total paying tax on land	144	125

Source: Land tax returns, SPL 145, 146, 150, West Yorkshire Archive Service,
Halifax.
Notes: *Includes Sowerby and Westfield quarters for 1750, Blackwood and Pallas,
1751

This sort of wealth distribution is similarly reflected in poor rate
and window tax assessments of the mid-century.[16] These are clear
in showing the class of substantial wealth-holders which Sowerby
possessed in contrast to Calverley and other places like it. The

window tax, like the poor rate but unlike the land tax, was assessed on the occupation of houses and is thus, perhaps, a more accurate representation of wealth-holding and social status, especially for a manufacturing township, than the land tax, which simply reflected the ownership of landed assets. The spread of wealth-holding in the upper-middle social range is conspicuously absent in the Calverley indicators throughout the period, although a lay subsidy and a war tax of the 1690s both show a substantial social group in the lower, yet 'solid', taxpaying ranges. The 1692 war tax schedule shows clearly that Sir Walter Calverley paid three times as much as his nearest 'rival' down the social scale.[17]

The more directly comparable figures for both ownership and occupation of land in the townships (from the later eighteenth-century land tax) highlight the same contrasts, but here we can now also see the different distributions of owners, occupiers, owner-occupiers and owner-part-occupiers. If we take landownership first, Table 11.7 illustrates the percentage distribution of land tax payers in the two townships which nicely reflects their differences in social structure. In Calverley, Thomas Thornhill paid more than £70 in 1782, rising to £95 in 1794. By the latter year he was paying more than nineteen times that of the next person on the tax scale. In Sowerby, on the other hand, George Stansfield and Sir Watts Horton shared the top tax bracket, but both paid only £25-£35 throughout the period and several others paid more than £2 10s. Many of those in the Under 4s tax bracket in Calverley paid less than 1s, but the lowest Sowerby payment was 3s, indicating either the existence of a stratum of poor taxpayers in Calverley or the fact that many smallholders owned and were liable for only part of the land which they held. Supplementary copyhold land was probably also held or small plots rented from Thornhill.

A difference is also indicated in the proportions of owner-occu-piers and owner-part-occupiers. Sowerby had a significantly greater proportion of people directly involved in working their own land which, along with the greater dispersal of ownership, implied a much greater freedom in the land market. Most of the owner-occupiers of Sowerby were in the 4s–£1 tax category. In Calverley, owner-occupiers were predominantly found in the under 4s group, those with bigger farms consisted of tenants, many of whom rented land from Thornhill who obviously exerted considerable control over the land market.

Table 11.7 Percentage distribution of land tax payers, Sowerby and Calverley, 1782, 1788 and 1794

Land tax assessment category		Percentage paying				
	1782		1788		1794	
	S	C	S	C	S	C
1 <4s	14	33	15	41	14	41
2 4s–<£1	36	48	35	39	35	36
3 £1–<£2 10s	29	15	30	16	31	19
4 £2 10s–<£5	12	2	13	2	11	2
5 £5–<£10	7	–	4	–	6	–
6 £10–<£20	–	–	1	–	1	–
7 £20 and over	2	2	2	2	2	2
Total %	100	100	100	100	100	100
Total cases	122	46	111	44 (55)*	107	42
Total cases of owner-occupation	32	11	30	18	32	15
Total cases of owner with part occupation	18	5	20	3	21	4
% of owners with direct involvement with their own land	41	35	45	38	50	45

Source: Land tax returns for Sowerby and Calverley, West Yorkshire Archive
Service, Wakefield.

Turning to the sizes of tenanted farm plots most common in
the two townships, as detailed in Table 11.8, it becomes obvious
that the typical farm in Calverley was one on which 4s–£1 was
paid in land tax. There also existed a sizeable number of cottages
with small patches of taxable land attached. It is highly likely that
these farms were the province of the dual-occupation clothier.
Large units were occupied mainly by specialist yeomen farmers
and graziers, working to supply the Leeds market in particular.
In Sowerby, the most common farm-size group was also taxed
4s–£1, but the next category of £1–£2 10s was also very substantial
and several persons occupied farms taxed at £2 10s–£5. But almost
no one classed themselves as farmers in the parish register entries
of the period[18] and many Sowerby yeomen, as evidenced by probate inventories, were involved in textile putting out and trade.
The sizeable farms of Sowerby were thus intimately related to

textile manufacture and trade, acting as a source of collateral and spreading risks just as the small farms and holdings of Calverley enabled balancing of occupations among the clothier group.

Table 11.8 Percentage distribution of occupiers of land in Sowerby and Calverley, 1782, 1788 and 1794

Land tax assessment category	1782		1788		1794	
	S	C	S	C	S	C
1 <4s	10	15	9.5	28	10	25
2 4s–<£1	48	65	46	57	47.5	59
3 £1–<£2 10s	36	16	38	11	34	9
4 £2 10s–<£5	6	3	6	2	8	4
5 £5–<£10	–	–	0.5	–	0.5	–
6 £10–<£20	–	1	–	2	–	3
Total %	100	100	100	100	100	100
Total cases	221	106	211	119	208	118

Source: Land tax returns for Sowerby and Calverley, West Yorkshire Archives Service, Wakefield.

When research has progressed further it should be possible to match the parish register occupational data with the land tax results to get some idea of exactly which occupational groups owned and occupied the very different distributions of land in the two townships. This sort of information is currently available only for 1804 for about one-third of the township of Sowerby. Tables 11.9 and 11.10 give the results of matching the parish register occupational data against the rate valuation for that year for owners and occupiers respectively.

More than half of the landowners' occupations were identified, indicating the importance of sizeable holdings on the part of textile merchants and tradesmen and of merchant-manufacturers. Few of these individuals occupied their land, however, preferring to rent it out in small farms for additional income where it could still also form a valuable collateral on mortgage for credit and loans. Those weavers who owned land typically did the same. Only two, John Whitely and Jonathan Speak, worked their 9-acre plots; the rest appear to have concentrated on manufacturing, supplementing their income with rent. A similar split between weaver-farmers and those, mostly landless, who concentrated just on manufacturing becomes evident in the analysis of tenants' occupations given in Table 11.10. These findings considerably sophisticate our understanding of the weavers of Sowerby, previously thought to be almost entirely a proletarianized group by the end of the eighteenth century.

Table 11.9 Occupations of landowners in the Blackwood quarter of Sowerby, 1804

Occupation	Name	Land owned to nearest acre	
Weavers	Wm Clay	3	
16	Henry Cockroft	40	
	David Greenwood	11	
	Wm Greenwood	0	
	John Haigh	9	
	John Hellowell	0	
	John Meller	19	
	Geo Normanton	18	
	Jno Radcliffe	8	average holding
	Jas Ratcliffe	1	=11
	Matthew Scott	0	
	Jonathan Speak	9	
	John Sutcliffe	0	
	Richard Sutcliffe	21	
	Wm Walker	20	
	John Whiteley	9	
Widows and spinsters			average holding
11			=20
Textile merchants and tradesmen			
5	William Barker	10	
	Richard Ingham	12	
	Peter Pickles	15	average holding
	Wm Rawson	27	=20
	Wm Sutcliffe	38	
Putting-out merchants/ manufacturers			
6	Richard Hincliffe	35	
	James Holroyd	33	
	Jos Priestley	148	
	Jas Riley Junr	13	average holding
	Jas Riley Senr	33	=31
	Geo Stansfield	43	
Reverend	Nathaniel Phillips	14	
Shopkeeper	Ogden Sawood	0	

Source: SPL 310, West Yorkshire Archive Service, Halifax.
Notes: Total of owners with 'occupations' identified = 40, acreage = 799. Total number of owners = 74, acreage = 1,638.

Table 11.10 Occupations of tenants identified in the Blackwood quarter of Sowerby, 1804

Occupations	No.	No. of owner-occupiers	Average land held to nearest acre
Weavers (landless cottagers)	30		0
Weavers with land	33	2	19
Combers (landless cottages)	8		0
Combers with land	1		3
Tradesmen	5	1	17
Surgeon	1		12
Spinner	3		1
Labourer	1		0
Manufacturers	2	1	26
Clogger/shoe-maker	2		0
Innkeeper	1		0
Wiredrawer	2		0
Farmer	1	1	27
Total tenants with identified occupations	89		
All tenants	198		
Proportion identified	45%		

Source: SPL310, West Yorkshire Archive Service, Halifax.

Clearly, Sowerby's population was less proletarianized than was previously thought and Calverley's was more so, although the basic division of clothier/farmer structure in Calverley and landholding employer/landless employee in Sowerby does remain the most salient observation. The landless in Calverley typically found farm or service trade work or worked for clothiers as journeymen and termed themselves clothiers.

A breakdown of the 1804 Sowerby rate assessment by size of tenancy shows just how small average landholdings were in the township and how few, especially of the small plots, were owner-occupied (see Table 11.11). This is the clearest statement we have about the extent of land-subdivision and proletarianization which had occurred in Sowerby by the end of the eighteenth century.

Table 11.11 Blackwood tenancies by size, 1804

Size categories	No. of tenancies	No. owner-occupied
Landless cottages and land under 1 acre	111	2
1–4 acres	124	3
5–9 acres	17	5
10.14 acres	16	2
15–19 acres	17	2
20–4 acres	10	2
25–9 acres	6	1
30–4 acres	0	
35–9 acres	2	1
40–4 acres	4	2
More than 45 acres	4	–
Total tenancies	311	20

Source: SPL310, Rate Assessment 1804, West Yorkshire Archive Service, Halifax.

INHERITANCE

The final part of this enquiry concerns inheritance practices. So far we have considered findings from various cross-sectional observations reflecting social structure and landownership. A study of inheritance practices, and the changing grid of custom and practice within which these operated, indicates how landholding patterns (ownership and occupation) were perpetuated or destroyed. This then had important implications for changing social structure, wealth and status distribution over time and, hence, important implications for the structure and development of trade and industry in the two townships.

Over 100 wills from each township area have been examined for this study.[19] Preliminary findings suggest that in both townships considerable care was taken in will-making to see that landholdings passed intact to a single beneficiary. In Sowerby, the wife, if she survived, usually inherited for life first and then land was passed to a male heir, usually the eldest son. Land was only subdivided in Sowerby in two circumstances. First, where it lay some distance away, outside the township, and formed a separate estate for a second beneficiary. Second, where there were no male heirs but more than one female to provide for.

In Calverley land was more often subdivided among two or more male heirs, particularly where large holdings were involved which could provide more than one farm of a size suitable to run alongside manufacturing. In Calverley, also, fewer wives inherited land – brothers or even male cousins were preferred, particularly where they were clothiers. There also seems to have been tighter control, by testators, over future marriage of widows in Calverley than in Sowerby.

In both townships primogeniture was accompanied by the recognized need to provide portions for younger and secondary heirs, especially females. In Calverley, female (and some male) beneficiaries extended well beyond the nuclear family throughout the period, nieces, aunts, sisters and cousins commonly receiving sums of money or goods to a much greater extent than occurred in Sowerby where the bulk of lands and goods appear to have been left to immediate relatives of the nuclear group or, through them, to grandchildren.

One or two examples of Calverley and Sowerby will-makers might serve to highlight the aspects mentioned. William Dawson, a Calverley clothier, died in 1693 leaving an estate worth £346 12s 6d. Interestingly, about £200 of this was in credits owing and Walter Calverley owed him £100. He left lands in the neighbouring township of Yeaden to his eldest son; his two other sons and a daughter received substantial cash portions of £60 each (largely to be used for their education); and the two elder sons were also bequeathed a loom when they reached the age of twenty-one. Sarah, his wife, was given all chattels and the right of tuition of her children but only if any remarriage was approved by 'my beloved friends', Joseph Marshall of Horsforth and William Hollings of Yeaden, clothiers. These friends were themselves left 20 shillings each.[20] In 1700 Benjamin Sandall, a clothier of Calverley, died leaving an estate of £216 11s. Of this £53 was owed to him by his creditors. He obviously died without issue but expressed considerable concern for relatives and dependents in his will. His lands and personal estate were divided equally between his two clothier brothers but first £40 was to go to his sister, 40s annually to his father for life, 20s each to two uncles, 20s to the poor of Idle, 20s plus the use of lead and tenters to a clothier cousin, 5s each to three servants and a new suit of clothes to Robert Brewer, his apprentice.[21]

Sowerby wills abound with interesting illustrations of inheritance practices; considerable variation occurred. Jeremiah Riley died in 1715 leaving a movable estate of £776 14s 6d. He termed himself a yeoman but, from his inventory, it is obvious that he was a putting-out merchant. His considerable landed estates, which he occupied in Sowerby, were left to his eldest son, his second son receiving £150 and a smaller estate leased out to tenants. His daughter, Abigail, was left £300 at twenty-one, 'the interest on which to be used to maintain her with meat, drink, apparell, washing, lodging with all convenient education, learning and accomplishments fit and needful for such a one'. Riley's wife received only £50, and the remainder of the estate went to the eldest son.[22]

A part, and in Calverley a considerable part, of land bequeathed was copyhold and had first to be surrendered to the lord of the manor before it could be left by a testator. Tenures unsecured by a will or by a clear lineage of hereditable descent could, in theory at least, fall back into the hands of the lord of the manor. In a place like Calverley one may assume that the lord was likely to enforce this, so blocking the inheritance process as there was much profit to be made in reorganizing land for leasing into the size of plots suitable for the farmer-clothier. Evidence suggests that this was a very important aspect of estate improvement on the part of Sir Walter Calverley, and in the Aire valley generally, during the eighteenth century.[23] Lords of manors and large estate owners with reversionary leases could call back lands into their purview, thus controlling and rigidifying the land market and perpetuating a structure of small farms at lease.

The weight of portions ensured the need for Sowerby landowners to maintain an efficient and commercial attitude to their undertakings, hence the prime importance of expanding commercial manufacture and trade and the ubiquity of leasing out land rather than working it direct. The relatively freer land market in Sowerby, compared with Calverley, did mean that male heirs being left portions could lease a plot or two with relative ease.

Another feature of the inheritance systems of the two townships arising out of their very varied agrarian and manorial legacies was the different 'grids of inheritance': the complex web of custom and practice concerning use-rights which accompanied the passing of land from one generation to the next.[24] E. P. Thompson has argued that these grids were being extinguished in the eighteenth century, long before parliamentary enclosure. With the disappearance of gleaning and grazing and other communal use-rights, younger sons and daughters had less and less chance to make do with legacies

282

of cash or moveables. Thus, Thompson argues, impartible inherit-ance with portions resulted in the decline of the yeomanry as a class. However, in the case of manufacturing townships such as Sowerby and Calverley this process was considerably modified by the possibilities of incomes earned in manufacture and the leasing of land. Furthermore, much land was held on bond or mortgage or as security for debts, especially in Calverley where most cloth-iers' assets included a high proportion of credit extended. This holding of land as security brought with it temporary use-rights of value to clothiers.[25]

The structure and practice of inheritance tended, in both town-ships, to perpetuate the traditional structure of landholding and the continued importance of leasing and short-term transfers. The proliferation of copyholders in Calverley ensured some continu-ation of traditional use-rights, particularly until the (partial) Enclosure Act of 1758. At this point the continuation of the same inheritance practices in new circumstances appears to have acceler-ated the process of proletarianization of a portion of the population while maintaining the more substantial ex-copyholder clothier dyn-asties on a stable footing.

In Sowerby enclosure by act came late – in the 1840s – but use-rights had been considerably reduced long before. Primogeni-ture with portions did not here result in the decline of the 'yeo-manry' but meant that those who survived, flourished and bought up the land which others were forced to sell were those involved in the lucrative spheres of trade and putting out. This was the new yeomanry class of Sowerby. They never called themselves clothiers (though that is what, in many respects, they were) but instead termed themselves yeomen and rose during the eighteenth century to positions of power and authority in the township elite. Here they administered the poor law, relief, pauper apprenticeship and settlement in a manner which appears rather different from that found in Calverley where older landholding families continued in power. In Calverley older yeoman families functioned in town-ship administration alongside a group of stable landholding cloth-iers who eventually financed co-operative company mills on a joint stock basis. They exhibited aspects of communal organization, affiliations and loyalties in the sphere of familial affairs and local government. Sowerby, by contrast, seems to have manifested a more 'individualistic' culture. But this aspect of the story of Calverley and Sowerby opens a different chapter, which requires considerable additional research.[26]

THE DYNAMICS OF PROTO-INDUSTRY

This paper set out to test some preliminary hypotheses established at subregional level concerning the relationship between landholding (ownership and leasing) patterns and the organizational structure of commercial textile manufacture. To a large extent the basic hypotheses hold good for the two townships examined, although the strength of the middle-income social stratum in Sowerby, its relative absence from Calverley, plus the importance of the poor and proletarianized group in Calverley from the late seventeenth century are a surprise and necessitate some restructuring of thought on the subject of social structure and textile manufacture. Of course it may well be the case that social structure was as much a product as a precondition of the organizational forms which the industry manifested. Thus, once established, from the mid-seventeenth century, if not earlier, the multitude of artisan clothiers in Calverley both reproduced themselves (through natural increase and inheritance practices carried out within a framework of substantial proportions of copyhold and leasehold land), and increasingly produced a proletarianized group of portioned offspring who failed to get a foothold on the manufacturing/landholding ladder. This group was swelled by immigration – largely from neighbouring townships, migrants being attracted by the possibilities of textile employments. We know that migration in (and out of) Sowerby was also a feature of the eighteenth century, although net migration may well have been outward here, helping to control the numbers of landless poor naturally created by the structure of landholding. Inheritance practices, together with the initial structure of landownership and landholding from the sixteenth century and earlier, served in Sowerby to aid the rise of a 'new yeomanry' of commercial manufacturing employers. In Calverley it seems to have ensured the relative stability of a huge group of small landholding clothiers in the population throughout the eighteenth century.

This, of course, had important implications for the gradual transition, experienced throughout the West Riding, from domestic to factory-based methods of textile manufacture. Both the speed and the nature of this transition varied, as did worker resistance to change. Much of the story of the development of woollen and worsted mills during the period *c.* 1780–1860 can only be understood with reference to the structure and evolution of proto-industrial production in the different branches of the industry.

A major development in the woollen sector of the late eighteenth century was the fairly rapid mechanization of scribbling and carding and their location alongside fulling in water-powered mills.[27] Traditionally, fulling mills had been owned and financed by landowners, a legacy of manorial monopolies. In some cases landowners provided the larger premises and machinery necessary for scribbling and carding, but in many localities, such as Calverley, scribbling and fulling mills were established by groups of artisan clothiers on a joint stock basis. They thus avoided the delays and monopolistic charges of the traditional establishments and evolved arrangements regarding pricing and credit terms which were of considerable advantage to subscribers. Such 'company mills', established under the precarious legal arrangement of a trust deed, required the existence of considerable communal loyalty among the clothier subscribers. They also required stable groups of clothiers whose assets were sufficient to afford shares in the mills. These conditions appear to have been fulfilled in clearly defined areas of the woollen zone where they arose directly out of the legacy of manorialism, landholding and local norms and practices. Interestingly these mills did not arouse opposition and were never termed factories. Contemporaries who used them saw them fitting in with the needs and the structure of the domestic artisan system, strengthening it and serving its needs.[28]

Unlike the development of scribbling mills, the expansion in number and scale of operations of merchant-manufacturers in the woollen areas in the period *c.* 1780–1820 did arouse great hostility among the artisan concerns as they threatened to undermine the whole structure of the industry and the livelihood and independence of its workers.[29] Resentment and opposition, together with the considerable economic efficiency of the structure of small units (deriving from credit channels, the incorporation of centralized preparatory and fulling processes, and corporate solidarities) were major reasons why the number of integrated woollen factories grew so slowly before the 1820s and why the most notable feature of the woollen sector well after this remained the domestic clothier.[30] The household unit of production was still the most viable in most branches of woollen production before 1850, particularly where use was made of the public and company scribbling mills. In 1844, John Nussey, woollen manufacturer of Birstal, commented:

> The woollen manufacture of this district may still be termed domestic. Many of the small clothiers have shares in the mills and those who have no interest in the mills enjoy the advantages of them. Wool is generally bought sorted of the stapler and sent to the mill for scribbling and slubbing for which a small sum is paid per 1b weight. It is then returned to the clothier who spins and weaves and looks after the processes of manufacture in his own home. It is again sent to the mill to be fulled. The clothier then prepares it for market and it is sold in bulk in the cloth halls to the merchant who dyes and finishes it.[31]

This artisan structure remained viable and competitive partly because the volatility of the trade cycle was felt relatively more by factory producers with their high overheads than it was by the dual occupational structure of the artisans. The agricultural holding could form a valuable cushion against hard times, and the self-exploitation mechanism of the proto-industrial family economy compared with the greater rigidities of wage labour was recognized by businessmen in the region.[32]

When one considers the transition to factory production in the worsted sector a different pattern of development and a different relationship with the proto-industrial structure emerges. It is clear that the putting-out system was creating considerable inefficiencies and diseconomies in the increasingly competitive environment of the late eighteenth century. In particular, frauds committed by workers became increasingly problematic. This was a difficulty not generally experienced in the woollen branch, where there were fewer waged workers and those there were tended to be closely supervised in small workshops. In the worsted branch, however, woolcombers commonly embezzled their employers' wool and spinners reeled 'false' or short yarn. Combinations of operatives were often successful in ensuring that these appropriations continued with impunity, despite attempts by the Worsted Committee to stamp them out.[33] The growth rate of the Yorkshire worsted industry in the late eighteenth century, impelled particularly by the expansion of overseas markets, was faster than that of the woollen trade. This put sudden intense strains on the putting-out system. Worsted yarn proved suitable for the Arkwright technique of mechanical spinning and thus benefited greatly from the developed technology of the cotton sector. But the changeover to power spinning on the Arkwright system required the construction of a four- or five-storey mill to make use of the power of a water wheel or steam engine and this imposed a high threshold of entry into centralized worsted manufacture. It appears that the key figures in early worsted mill building and finance were merchant manufacturers, including putting-out capitalists, wool staplers, merchants and entrepreneurs previously involved in cotton, flax and even silk spinning. The high threshold of entry meant that there was very little upward mobility into factory production on the part of small clothiers or small-scale putting-out employers.[34]

Given the potential for accumulation of capital in the hands of merchants of the putting-out system, and the diseconomies of such systems as business expanded, it is perhaps surprising that the pace of centralization of worsted spinning was in fact rather slow before the 1820s.[35] Most employers continued to employ large numbers of men, and especially of women, in the absence of and even alongside centralized units. The slow build-up of fixed capital in worsted factories can best be understood in the context of the prevailing culture, labour- and capital-supply conditions of the worsted region. Labour in the area was plentiful and cheap, especially female labour, which continued to use the hand mule or throstle with great efficiency.[36] Opportunity costs were low as alternative occupations were few on the Pennine slopes and in the areas of spinning distribution in the Yorkshire Dales and east Lancashire. Population growth and migration added to the fluid supply of potential wage workers. Furthermore, the long period of fairly profitable putting out which had emerged to mesh neatly in with the social structure and labour supply of the rural worsted area can be seen as something of a hindrance to rapid centralization. Shifting from putting out to factory production required a major change in perceptions of risk in the nature of entrepreneurship and in the location of labour supplies. The dislocation of markets during the Napoleonic Wars, the extension of credit required by manufacturers to maintain sales and high entry thresholds militated against a rapid growth of fixed capital proportions, but notions of 'traditional' ways of organizing the industry and of local economic and social relationships proved very durable, as they also did in the woollen area.

Thus the development of both the woollen and worsted areas

in the transition from scattered to more centralized and capital-intensive forms of production manifested characteristics which it is helpful to consider in the context of agrarian and institutional developments over earlier centuries. Saying this is not to suggest a deterministic causal relationship between soil and society: clearly the picture was complex and varied, and involved dynamic and ever-changing relationships between agrarian legacies and evolving industrial structures. However, it does appear that in the West Riding, and presumably elsewhere, the structures of proto-industry and the nature and speed of industrial transformation can only be fully understood by referring to localized patterns of landholding, social structure, wealth distribution and customary practices. The comparative research on Sowerby and Calverley is beginning to reveal the many-sided nature and the full implications of these localized patterns.

NOTES

*An earlier version of this paper will appear in P. Swan (ed.), *Essays in Regional and Local History*, Hull, forthcoming. I wish to thank the Twenty-seven Foundation, the Leverhulme Trust, the Nuffield Foundation, the British Academy and the ESRC for financing various parts of the major project of which this study forms a part. My research assistant during the period 1986–7, Maria Davies, was responsible for much of the data inputting vital to the present paper and I am also most grateful for her assistance with the tabulations.

1 H. Heaton, *The Yorkshire Woollen and Worsted Industries from Earliest Times to the Industrial Revolution*, Oxford, 1920, 2nd edn Oxford, 1965; E. M. Sigsworth, *Black Dyke Mills: A History with Introductory Chapters on the Development of the Worsted Industry in the Nineteenth Century*, Liverpool, 1958; M. J. Dickenson, 'The West Riding woollen and worsted industries, 1689–1770: an analysis of probate inventories and insurance policies', unpublished Ph.D. thesis, Nottingham, 1974; D. T. Jenkins, *The West Riding Wool Textile Industry, 1770–1835: A Study of Fixed Capital Formation*, Edington, 1975.

2 This spatial organizational divide is discussed more fully in P. Hudson, 'Proto-industrialization: the case of the West Riding wool textile industry in the eighteenth and nineteenth centuries', *History Workshop Journal*, 12, 1981, and in P. Hudson, *The Genesis of Industrial Capital: A Study of the West Riding Wool Textile Industry. c. 1750–1850*, Cambridge, 1986.

3 Here we enter one of the most interesting debates to arise from the literature on proto-industrialization. For surveys and assessments of this literature with particular respect to the British case see L. A. Clarkson, *Proto-industrialization: The First Phase of Industrialization*, London, 1985; D. C. Coleman 'Proto-industrialization: a concept too

many?', *Economic History Review*, 36, 1983; R. Houston and K. D. M. Snell, 'Proto-industrialization: cottage industry, social change and industrial revolution', *Historical Journal*, 27, 1984; G. Eley, 'The social history of industrialization: proto-industry and the origins of capitalism', *Economy and Society*, 13, 1984. On the particular issue of the relationship between agriculture, landholding and the development and nature of proto-industrial forms see E. L. Jones, 'Agricultural origins of industry', *Past and Present*, 40, 1968; G. Gullickson, 'Agriculture and cottage industry: redefining the causes of proto-industrialization', *Journal of Economic History*, 43, 1983; F. F. Mendels, 'Seasons and regions in agriculture and industry during the process of industrialization' in S. Pollard (ed.), *Region und Industrialisierung*, Bielefeld, 1980; D. R. Mills, 'Proto-industrialization and social structure: the case of the hosiery industry in Leicestershire, England' in P. Deyon and F. F. Mendels (eds), *La protoindustrialisation: théorie et réalité*, Proceedings of the 8th International Economic History Conference, Budapest, 1982, 2 vols, Lille, 1982; I. D. Whyte, 'Proto-industrialization in Scotland' and L. A. Clarkson, 'The environment and dynamic of pre-factory industry in Northern Ireland', both in P. Hudson (ed.), *Regions and Industries: A Perspective on the Industrial Revolution in Britain*, Cambridge, 1989.

4 J. de L. Mann, *The Cloth Industry in the West of England from 1640 to 1880*, Oxford, 1971, 116.

5 Hudson, *Genesis*, op. cit., 26, 144.

6 This and the next paragraph summarize arguments to be found in Hudson, ibid., 61–70.

7 For some development of this argument see P. Hudson, 'From manor to mill: the West Riding in transition' in M. Berg, P. Hudson and M. Sonenscher (eds), *Manufacture in Town and Country Before the Factory*, Cambridge, 1983.

8 For a fuller account of the larger project on Sowerby and Calverley (of which this study forms a part) and the use of SQL, its facilities and drawbacks see M. Davies and P. Hudson, 'Two eighteenth-century locality studies and use of the SQL database' in *Computing and History Today*, 1987. Steven King is also currently doing Ph.D. research on the Calverley part of the database at the University of Liverpool.

9 Census abstracts, 1811. E179/210/393 16 Charles II Lady Day 1664, hearth tax returns, Public Record Office, Chancery Lane, London (henceforth PRO).

10 A total of 222 probate documents (the majority including inventories) covering the period from the 1690s to the 1760s were analysed for this study: Borthwick Institute, University of York.

11 ibid.

12 This is apparent where occupations of deceased females and of mothers of baptised (usually illegitimate) children are specified: Register of Sowerby St Peters, West Yorkshire Archive Service, Halifax. All the estimations of occupational structure for Sowerby and Calverley from the parish register data are adjusted for possible variations in occupation-specific fertility.

13 Based on analysis of register data 1812–20.

14 The three returns analysed for this study were 1664 (E179/210/393), 1666 (E179//210/394a), 1672 (E179/262/13), all PRO. The distributions of the hearths did not change markedly from one return to the next and only 1664 gives figures of households exempt by reason of poverty.

15 Discussion of the nature of the land tax and its usefulness and problems as a source for historians can be found in D. Mills and M. Turner (eds), *Land and Property: The English Land Tax, 1692–1832*, Gloucester, 1986, which has a comprehensive bibliography of earlier works.

16 Poor rate assessment, 1738, (SPL 46) and window tax, 1758–9, SPL 153, West Yorkshire Archive Service, Halifax.

17 Double Lay bill, 1694, Calverley; 'Tax assessment for carrying out a vigorous war with France', 1692, West Yorkshire Archive Service, Leeds.

18 See Table 11.2.

19 These were extracted from the collection in the Borthwick Institute, University of York (henceforth BI).

20 William Dawson, Probate Papers, 23 May 1693, BI.

21 Benjamin Sandall, Probate Papers, 3 September 1700, BI.

22 Jeremiah Riley, Probate Papers, 15 September 1715, BI.

23 Hudson, *Genesis*, op. cit., 86.

24 E. P. Thompson, 'The grid of inheritance: a comment' in J. Goody, J. Thirsk and E. P. Thompson (eds), *Family and Inheritance: Rural Society in Western Europe, 1200–1800*, Cambridge, 1976.

25 For a more pessimistic view of the effect of portions for female heirs on the viability of estates in part of a neighbouring township in the West Riding before the mid-eighteenth century see J. Harber *et al.*, *Shore in Stansfield: A Pennine Weaving Community 1660–1750*, Cornholme, Workers' Educational Association, 1986.

26 This aspect is an integral part of the comparative research project on the two townships. Both have good survival of township administrative records and these are currently undergoing analysis to discover the structure and change in township elites, the nature of poor relief and settlement policy, attitudes to expenditure and taxation at local level and the nature of other forms of communal activity. For details of the ethos of company mills see Hudson, 'From manor to mill', op. cit.

27 For a much fuller account of developments in technology and organization of the textile industries of West Yorkshire from the late eighteenth century see Hudson, *Genesis*, op. cit., 30–48, 70–84.

28 Hudson, 'From manor to mill', op. cit. 134–44.

29 See various witnesses in *Report from the Select Committee Appointed to Consider the State of the Woollen Manufacture of England*, 1806 (268) (168a), III. See also W. B. Crump and G. Ghorbal, *History of the Huddersfield Woollen Industry*, Huddersfield, 1935, 69.

30 *Report from the Select Committee Appointed to Inquire into the Present State of Manufacture, Commerce and Shipping in the United Kingdom*, 1833 (690), VI, 118, 646. *Reports of the Assistant Commissioner on the West Riding of Yorkshire and Ireland*, 1840 (43–11), XXIII, 527–63.

31 Statements as to the joint stock woollen mills in the West Riding of Yorkshire, 1844 (119), VII (House of Lords), 366.

32 See, for example, the evidence of Law Atkinson, clothier and merchant of Bradley Mills near Huddersfield, in *Report from the Select Committee on the Petitions of Merchants and Manufacturers Concerned in the Woollen Manufacture in the County of York and the Town of Halifax*, 1802–3 (71), v, 380. Also opinion of Thomas Bischoff, manager of the Leeds branch of the Bank of England, Leeds Branch Letters, 1832, Bank of England Archive.

33 Heaton, *Yorkshire Woollen and Worsted Industries*, op. cit., 418–21. The Worsted Committee had powerful rights of search and could call on heavy legal penalties, more so than any similar employer's organization before the late 1840s: Home Office Papers 45, item 1925, Public Record Office, Kew.

34 Hudson, *Genesis*, op. cit., 39, 75–6.

35 ibid., 39, 48

36 S. D. Chapman, 'The pioneers of worsted spinning by power', *Business History*, 7, 1, 1965, 116–17; Hudson, *Genesis*, op. cit., 43.

12

MARKETS IN CONTEXT: ARTISANS, PUTTING OUT AND SOCIAL DRINKING IN ESKILSTUNA, SWEDEN 1800–50

Lars Magnusson

I

Throughout Western Europe, preceding the period of factory industrialization, the putting-out or Verlag-system was characterized by the complex set of economical, social and cultural relationships which tied putting-out merchants, master artisans and workers close to each other. The complex and extensive ties of dependence which bound them together were in turn a consequence of the precarious nature of the system itself, especially its manifest inability to maintain control of the production process. This also helps to explain why debt relationships, 'the long pay', truck practices and customary arrangements of different kinds became such important factors of domination and dependence within this system. On the other hand, however, it is often held that the main reason why the putting-out system was able to persist for so long as a major form of industrial organization had to do with the vulnerability of the artisan or domestic producer in the market. Thus it is argued that their dependence was a consequence of the putting-out merchant's greater resources and his greater know-how regarding markets, especially more distant ones. It was the *raison d'être* of the putting-out merchant to extend the market – in Adam Smith's sense – and thus increase production.[1]

However, this does not, of course, exhaust the complex character of relationships prevailing between markets, artisans and putters out within this form of industrial organization. It might be that the artisan or domestic producer needed the putter out to market his products. However, this does not – which the recent heated but heavily functionalist and biased debate about the historical role of the putting-out system seems to have forgotten – exclude conflicting positions taken by the different agents, for example in the case of markets. Rather, as has been pointed out, the market was a main area of conflict during this period and served as a major nexus of industrial 'class struggle' before the factory.[2] Thus putting-out merchants condemned competition from the side by producers selling directly to customers as well as trying to criminalize practices like embezzlement and secret trading to pedlars, at fairs, in pubs, etc. As his profit really was an outcome of a zero-sum game, in which competition from underselling producers could be devastating, the Verlager was keen to uphold a form of monopoly in this sense. For the artisan producer selling directly to the customer, on the other hand, such practices could, of course, be a way of precluding an otherwise overwhelming dependence on the putting-out merchant or to bring in cash. During slack periods or business failures such a direct link to the market could obviously be crucial, and the only way to avoid economic and social disaster.[3]

It is the argument of this paper that custom and artisanal culture within the boundaries of systems of putting out – manifested in practices like embezzlement, and social drinking – are historically best understood in relation to such a web of social relationships, including conflicts regarding the market place. In most literature on artisan culture, however, such practices are mainly interpreted as means for social communication: through customary institutions artisans express their cherished 'honour' and draw up demarcating lines between themselves and others. The limitations of this view will hopefully be demonstrated later on.

Here I mainly deal with the institution of social drinking. To some extent this critically important practice in many craft communities can certainly be regarded as an institution for communication and self-expression. However, of itself it cannot be the only explanation for the special importance of social drinking and pub-going within the putting-out milieu – *within this special historical context*. I would argue that cultural practices in communities dominated by strong putting-out forms of organization were permeated by conflicts about markets and marketing, by the implication of credit dependence, by the struggle for control by putters out and the counter-strategies developed by the producers, by embezzlement

293

LARS MAGNUSSON

and selling on the side by artisans. Within this social and cultural context social drinking and the tavern – as well as other customs or cultural practices – served as such a counter-strategy or, even more profoundly, functioned as a cultural space where conflicts were expressed and made intelligible to members of craftsmen's communities entangled within the putting-out system.

It is further argued here that this is also the key to why drinking and tavern-going was such an important issue at the time, and so heavily condemned by the upper echelons of society. Without doubt the campaigns everywhere in Western Europe against artisan custom and culture, especially during the eighteenth and early nineteenth centuries, must be seen in a context which emphasizes custom as impregnated with social practices and conflict.[4] I begin the paper with a discussion of these matters and return later to the points stressed here, namely, how custom and cultural practices are linked to the social processes of production and appropriation, markets and trading in the case of the metal craft town of Eskilstuna in Sweden during the first half of the nineteenth century.

II

Governing elites in nineteenth-century industrializing Europe undoubtedly viewed with alarm what they believed to be the greatly increased alcohol consumption of the lower classes during this period. Widespread drunkenness was considered to be a part of 'the social question'. A long line of debators from the educated classes argued that hunger and poverty among the working classes was a direct function of alcohol consumption. The solution to the social question was, therefore, to reduce their dependence on alcohol. The French historian Louis Chevalier has coined the phrase 'classes dangereuses' to give some idea of how the upper echelons of society viewed the working classes during this period.[5]

Social historians have, over the past decades, put great effort into the task of describing how moral reformers, especially from the middle classes, tried to put forward the need for an increased control of the working classes in the period of the early Industrial Revolution. The growth of various bodies designed to reform and discipline the working classes such as Sunday schools, temperance leagues and workers' educational organizations has been studied. Newspapers, books, pamphlets and parliamentary reports from this period are full of descriptions of the social misery of the working classes, their bad conduct, loose morals, wild behaviour, uncivilized and distasteful pastimes and, last but not least, their substantial alcohol consumption.[6]

These observations, coloured by middle-class values from the last century, should not of course be automatically accepted by the historian who must maintain a healthy scepticism to the – in many cases undoubtedly highly exaggerated – descriptions of bad behaviour and other excesses from this era. This is also true of the type of social reporting carried out by radicals such as Friedrich Engels in his *Condition of the Working Classes in England*. Naturally this does not mean that historians should go to the other extreme and deny that alcohol consumption was very great during this period. On the contrary, many studies indicate that it was indeed very high, just before and in connection with the industrial breakthrough.[7] We should, however, be on our guard.

There is also another, probably more important, side to this. By the uncritical acceptance of the values espoused by an uneasy middle class in the middle of the nineteenth century the historian loses the ability to understand the essence of a culture which, viewed from above, was raw and uncivilized and in need of reform. It is the basis of my reasoning in this paper that at least some part of the *menue peuple* in this period had a pattern of behaviour which must be seen as part of an indigenous culture, and not just as evidence of degeneracy or as a feature of that breakdown of control which is so frequently emphasized by Parsonian sociology.[8]

This at least seems to be the case in Eskilstuna, a small Swedish city which, during the nineteenth century, was transformed from a proto-industrial centre of metal handicrafts to a busy factory town specializing in metal engineering. My discussion here is an interpretation of the craftsmen's drinking behaviour and drinking patterns in this locality at the beginning of the nineteenth century and is based on a wider study of this local community during the same period.[9]

Folk memory, narratives and autobiographies looking back to the middle of the nineteenth century often record and put great emphasis on the heavy consumption of aquavit, *brännvin*, in pre-industrial or industrializing Eskilstuna. 'One or two of the workmen did take care of themselves, but most of them used to drink like fury,' says Anna Holmberg (born 1855), for example.[10] Klara Atterberg relates, 'The old smiths . . . drank practically all the time. When they thought they had done enough work for the day they went to the tavern and drank or else brought spirits and drank out of doors.'[11]

In regard to what we have said about the middle classes and their reactions towards artisanal or working-class behaviour during this period, such statements must be regarded with some scepticism. However, it does seem clear that such recollections are not merely coloured by ideological attitudes from above: we must admit that they contain a grain of truth. Many independent sources describe the drunkenness prevalent at the time and give examples of chronic alcoholism. The medical officer for the area, P. C. Malm, states in his official report to the Royal College of Health in 1854 that the consumption of alcohol in Eskilstuna was enormous. He went so far as to write: 'There can scarcely be a place in the whole of Sweden which suffers so much from the adverse effects of alcohol as this town.' He calculated that the average consumption for the 1850s was one jug per registered male inhabitant per week. A jug contained 2.6 litres. He added, however:

> This might appear a moderate amount for someone used to spirits but there are, happily, very many men who drink not half this amount and some who consume not a quarter thereof. Each and every one of the heavy drinkers probably consumes one and a half jugs or more per week. To this can be added ale and cheap brandy.[12]

During this period the number of inhabitants of Eskilstuna never rose above 4,000. The number of taverns and bars licensed by the authorities was between ten and fifteen. There also existed several illegal bars which the authorities did their best to close down. The Census of 1831 shows, for example, that there were 2,768 people over the age of fifteen in Eskilstuna and twelve licensed taverns and bars. By 1838 there were 3,148 people and thirteen taverns and bars.[13]

Apart from Malm's statistics there is unfortunately not enough information available to make more than an educated guess at the level of alcohol consumption at the time. An investigation I have made of the records of Eskilstuna magistrates' court covering the period 1824–47 certainly shows a relatively stable number of convictions for drunkenness up to the middle of the 1840s. The records also show a probable subsequent increase. Whether or not this reflects a real increase in the level of alcohol abuse is difficult to say. An increase in the level of convictions can just as well be a reflection of the authorities' increasing concern with the problem. It is significant that the increase in convictions and the newspaper campaign (of *Eskilstuna Allehanda*) occur at approximately the same time. Various reports and investigations, however, give the impression that consumption began to decline somewhat from the end of the 1850s. At the beginning of the 1870s the medical officer's report to the College of Health states:

> Drunkenness has declined significantly over the past few years and continues to do so. This is probably a result of the lack of taverns and bars as much as a shortage of money. The monopolizing of the sale of spirits and the rapidly grow- ing workers' associations have also contributed much to this improvement.[14]

It was thus believed that restrictions from above as well as self-improvement from below had resulted in a decline in drunkenness.

We know very little, then, about how much the workers of Eskilstuna actually drank. One can also question the value of a figure (Malm's) said to represent that average consumption. Then, as now, the figure varied from person to person. A small group drank very large amounts and became social outcasts, while another group drank only moderate amounts. It is undoubtedly the case that many people in Eskilstuna drank so much that they were unable to function in society or perform any useful work. This type of heavy drinking requires its own explanation, but it was accompanied by the more moderate consumption practised by a much larger group of craftsmen and workers. The term 'moderate' is, of course, relative and its meaning tends to vary considerably depending on which historical period is being referred to. Court records and other material show clearly that it was far from being only the rougher elements of the community who frequented the taverns. On the contrary, they were popular among ordinary workers who functioned well in Eskilstuna handicraft society. This type of moderate drinking requires a different expla- nation from the first and it is this kind of 'social drinking' that interests us here. My intention is not to get involved in the dis- cussion of pre-industrial drinking and drinking behaviour as such and its multivarious roles and functions within different societies and communities.[15] Rather, my purpose here is only to place the drinking behaviour of the common Eskilstuna metal artisan within a specific cultural setting. That drinking was tied to other 'bad habits' and can only be seen in connection with those was also pointed out by the moral reformers themselves. It is to them that we now turn.

III

As implied above, during the 1840s many voices were raised against the drunkenness which it was believed characterized artisans, apprentices and labourers, the lower classes of Eskilstuna. In 1844 the minister, Rektor Ulrik Lundgren, set the tone. In an article in the newspaper *Aftonbladet* he describes the situation thus:

> What sorrowful reflections come to mind when one views the individuals who tramp the streets of this town. They seem more like a pack of downtrodden negro slaves than Nordic workers. The prime reason for this state of affairs is, I am convinced, the enormous quantities of strong spirits they consume.[16]

To combat this state of affairs Rektor Lundgren advocated preventive measures from the community in the form of restrictions on the sale of strong liquor, plus information and education. The latter, he considered, was especially important. The minister was the driving force behind the establishment of the Eskilstuna children's home and he organized musical evenings and popular lectures as well as founding reading and adult education classes. It was on his initiative that the Eskilstuna Women's Organization, a private charitable group, came into being.[17]

Rektor Lundgren was undoubtedly a man of his time. In Eskilstuna there were several initiatives to reduce drunkenness from about 1840 – thirty years before the foundation of the first voluntary temperance lodges.[18] Some of these initiatives were especially dear to Rektor Lundgren's heart: moral reform and education. Several societies and educational circles, having as their aim the reform of habits and customs, appeared at the end of the 1840s. In the local newspaper, *Eskilstuna Allehanda*, a steady stream of appeals and exhortations encouraging workers to take part in these activities appeared. As well as educational circles, musical activity was considered appropriate for the battle against drunkenness. In

1855 an advertisement for the Eskilstuna Musical Society, signed by several employers and other prominent citizens, began:

> For a number of years a musical society has existed here with the aim of encouraging a greater general interest in the true aesthetic pleasures and thereby avoiding the more raw and morally corrupting distractions which so easily tempt and lead astray the young.[19]

Practically all forms of social activity were mobilized in the battle against the demon drink. In 1848 an anonymous letter was published in the *Eskilstuna Allehanda* under the heading 'Long live the dance':

> Director Gahn has been active in Eskilstuna for three years and during that time has contributed much to the dissemination of culture to the artisan classes. One cannot but be amazed at the progress made by these workers during the past three years and this is in no small way due to the dance. It is generally believed that the dance contributes little to the advance of culture but this is far from being the case. One who claims to be cultured and cannot dance leaves himself open to ridicule. The difference between a worker who has learnt how to dance and one who cannot is immediately evident. As well as the self-assurance gained, the dance encourages moderation and temperance. Ashamed of his lack of accomplishment the worker saves the money which would otherwise have found its way into the tavern-owner's pocket, and purchases dancing lessons. The taste for spirits gradually disappears and nobler pleasures take its place. Associations with more cultivated individuals during the lessons has a greater effect on the promotion of culture than all the educational societies and their lecture circles can bring about.[20]

It is not unlikely that dancing teacher Gahn wrote the letter himself – the claims seem somewhat exaggerated, to say the least. It exemplifies drastically, however, the attitudes of the upper classes to the drunkenness of the workers and the desire to reform the individual working man's customs and ways of thinking.

There was, naturally, another side to these attitudes. As well as encouraging personal discipline and cultivation, reformers demanded restrictions on the selling of spirits and occasionally action on the part of the local police. In the autumn of 1853, for example, the *Eskilstuna Allehanda* advocated sterner measures from the police. 'Almost every Sunday one puts one's life in danger by walking past the taverns' began an editorial, and it finished with this salvo, directed at the police:

> To judge by the number of convictions for drunkenness during the last six months the consumption of alcohol has declined considerably . . . but when one almost daily meets inebriated persons on the streets one is little inclined to be convinced either of the extent of drunkenness or the control exercised by the police. We recognize, of course, that the police alone cannot be blamed when the employer himself cannot ensure the temperance, industry and good order of his workers. But so much the police can and should do, clear the streets of drunk and abusive individuals and ensure that the tavern owners keep to the law regarding the times of opening and closing their establishments.[21]

The *Eskilstuna Allehanda* began, during the 1850s, to press for the setting up of a public company to have a monopoly on the distribution of strong liquor. Following patterns set down in Jönköping and Falun, the company should be non-profit-making and the responsibility of the local council.[22] In 1858 such a company finally came into existence in Eskilstuna and the first paragraph of its prospectus stated clearly: 'The worst enemies of the moral tone and welfare of the working class are the taverns.'[23] The liquor distribution company was a suitable method of controlling the taverns. Those who failed to obey the rules and regulations or who kept disorderly houses had their licences revoked. This reform, together with the prohibition of the age-old practice of distilling spirits for 'household use' is generally considered to be the prime reason for the reduction in liquor consumption in Eskilstuna from the end of the 1850s.[24]

Which aspect of tavern culture did the authorities find most disquieting? That their concern was not restricted to the unhealthy effects of alcohol *per se* is apparent from the paragraph from the company prospectus cited above. It also added that:

> It is not only the excessive use of intoxicating liquors which creates this wretchedness, poverty and decline in moral behaviour. To this must be added the disorderly behaviour,

bad example and temptations of all kinds which are seldom absent from taverns and bars.[25]

From this and through extensive reading of court records, police reports, by-laws, sermons and newspaper articles of the period it seems clear that in the eyes of the educated classes drinking was seen as only a moment in a wider 'disorderly' culture that also included absenteeism from work, the celebration of traditional craft festivals, 'Blue Monday', fighting, cruelty to animals, 'defilation' (*katzen-Musik*), etc. In other words, it was the handicraft culture as such that was condemned. Most commonly it was criticized from the point of view of its effect on work discipline. In 1849 the *Eskilstuna Allehanda* complained: 'A large group of workers haunt these taverns, not only on Monday but several working days a week.'[26]

This becomes even clearer if one studies the resistance to the so-called Free market which was held every year at the beginning of October. A stream of peasants from the surrounding countryside flooded into the town to sell their products and animals and to buy the local merchandise. Metal products from Eskilstuna were on sale and many salesmen from Norrköping, Stockholm and other towns took the opportunity to sell their wares from hastily constructed barrows and stalls. The police viewed these affairs with some concern as scarcely an autumn market went by without considerable drunkenness, brawling and petty larceny. The local magistrate usually had an increased workload during October as a direct result of the market. More worrying was the fact that work in the forges and workshops tended to grind to a halt. The authorities had for many years tried to supress the market. A proclamation in 1798 regarding the St Michaelmas ox market, which was a forerunner of the Free market, ran thus:

> By reason of the fact that the Freetowns (e.g. Eskilstuna) trainees and apprentices on these occasions neglect their duties in the workshops and in the market practice diverse mischiefs and, for several days after, stroll and lounge about, it is hereby forbidden for all trainees and apprentices to frequent the market.[27]

This draconian law was probably not obeyed to the letter. Reports of negligent and lackadaisical trainees and apprentices are legion over the following decades. At the beginning of the 1850s criticism

LARS MAGNUSSON

became especially cutting. The *Eskilstuna Allehanda*, reporting in connection with the October market in the year 1851, states that:

> The market may very well be of some use to the community but it undoubtedly brings in its wake many inconveniences. Among these can be enumerated the unfortunate state of affairs whereby the majority of the local workpeople seem to regard the market days as a holiday and refuse to carry out their employment, spending their time in recreation and bacchanalian pleasures. Where it is possible to calculate these lost workdays they would undoubtedly amount to a considerable number.[28]

And again, in 1857:

> The market here has gone on, not for the originally planned two days, but for a whole week. This long extension has caused the community damage as regrettable as it is irreversible. We are constrained to remind those involved that Eskilstuna is a manufacturing town with at least 1,000 workers, of whom a large proportion have, on the day before the market, laid down their tools and left their workplaces . . . firmly decided not to start work again before the market was really over. The pecuniary, not to speak of the moral losses involved, strike a blow at the community all too great to be ignored.[29]

This time action was taken on the subject. The spring of 1858 saw an application being made to the local magistrate. Signed by numerous prominent citizens, among them many employers, it requested the abolition of the market in the following terms: 'Profit from the actual market to the townsfolk is non-existent. Losses, on the other hand, are considerable because of the thousands of working days wasted in more or less unedifying pursuits.'[30] This application was sent to the provincial government in Nyköping and the following year a regulation was passed abolishing the Free market in Eskilstuna and replacing it with a market for the sale of livestock to be held at the same time. According to the *Eskilstuna Allehanda*, this market was a much quieter affair, being held for only one day and attracting fewer people than an ordinary market day. It was the abolition of the Free market together with other attempts to reform the working class which induced an anonymous contributor to the newspaper to state – provoking the middle-

302

classes and also the editors of *Eskilstuna Allehanda*, who officially denounced him – 'Has experience shown that the abolition of public festivals and the closing down of gathering places can bring about a change for the better in the morals of the working people? I believe not.'[31]

We have seen so far that it was not only the consumption of strong liquor that influenced middle-class opinion in Eskilstuna. Tavern life and the consumption of alcohol were only part of a wider handicraft culture that employers and officials viewed with displeasure and finally tried to suppress. I also strongly believe that it is useful to view the drinking habits and tavern visits of the working classes in Eskilstuna during the nineteenth century as part of an extensive craft culture and as an important element in the social reproduction and sense of identity of its participants. A large and growing body of theories have been propounded in recent years regarding the historical background to the excessive consumption of strong spirits.[32] Without dismissing alternative interpretations, I shall here attempt to describe patterns of alcohol consumption and tavern culture in Eskilstuna during the first half of the nineteenth century. However, we first need more precise information on Eskilstuna itself and its characteristic features in the first half of the nineteenth century.

IV

Eskilstuna has been a town of iron working and smithery ever since the sixteenth century. There were blast furnaces and hammer works at Tunafors, immediately adjacent to Eskilstuna river, as early as the 1570s, and large-scale forging of nails and weapons to meet the needs of the Swedish army and navy was introduced there a couple of decades later. In the middle of the seventeenth century the *Karl Gustafs stads manufacture* was established, alongside the iron-working complex of Tunafors. It was under the direction of Reinhold Rademacher, a Dutchman. The result was a considerable production of fine smith work in the form of weapons, locks, nails, knives and so forth.[33]

Work in *Karl Gustafs stad* was located in a number of small smithies, each under a master smith assisted by his journeymen and apprentices. Rademacher himself functioned as putter out, and his successors did likewise. They distributed the raw materials, received the smiths' finished products and then sold them.

303

Production expanded during the course of the eighteenth century – but only slowly.

The Eskilstuna free city was established in 1771 in order to stimulate the smithing industry. Concretely, it meant that the crown bought out the old manufactures of *Karl Gustafs stad* and sold out its property to private smiths, while letting the new free city run some forges, hammers and grinding shops for the benefit of all. Production had hitherto been strictly regulated but it now became, in principle, open to anyone to settle in the town and practise the trade of smith. The 'only' limitation was of a financial nature: it was necessary to possess a certain amount of capital in order to buy oneself into one of the smithies provided by the crown.

The founding of the free city gave the old smithery town a shaking-up. In 1771 there had been only 27 masters and 37 journeymen in *Karl Gustafs stad*. Thirty years later there were already 137 masters and 252 journeymen and forge hands. The expansion continued into the early nineteenth century. The figures recorded for 1850 are 184 masters, 280 journeymen, 111 'smith workers' or forge hands and 481 apprentices. At this time production was still mainly located in the small smithies. Mechanical aids were sparse. Those few which were available, such as the so-called 'Eskilstuna lathe' (which was made of wood), were driven by hand power. However, there were a number of *sliphus*, or grinding shops along the Eskilstuna river, available for renting by individual 'manufacturers', and the grindstones here were driven by water power. It was not until the 1870s that the first true 'factories' appeared (apart from the *Gevärsfaktori*, a firearms factory owned by the crown, and *Munktells mekaniska verkstad*, the Munktell engineering works). From then on mechanization of production was introduced, and manufacturing was concentrated in larger workplaces. This was the setting for Eskilstuna's growth in the late nineteenth century into one of Sweden's most important industrial towns with an emphasis on engineering and smithery products.[34]

Up until the middle of the nineteenth century the smiths were bound by contract to individual *Verlag* capitalists, to whom they undertook to deliver certain quantities of smithery products. A large part of the payment was effected in kind. The smiths might, at best, have a provision inserted in their contracts to the effect that one-half (or some other fraction) of the payment was to be in cash. As a means of obtaining ready cash, therefore, many smiths tried to bypass their business with the *Verlag* capitalists by selling to buyers and dealers who travelled to Eskilstuna for the purpose. (See below.) On the whole, dependence on the *Verlag* capitalists was heavy. It is evident from surviving probate inventories and proceedings in bankruptcy that the smiths were heavily indebted to various *Verlag* capitalists.

If masters were thus closely tied to their *Verlag* capitalists, journeymen and forge hands were at least as tightly bound to their masters. Because a sum of capital was required in order to take over a smithy, the majority of journeymen were precluded in practice from becoming masters themselves – unless, of course, they could find an attractive marriage partner in the person of a smith's widow with her own workshop.[35] Journeymen still usually lived in with their masters in the middle of the nineteenth century. The relationship between the master and his workmen may perhaps be characterized as 'patriarchal' – provided it is remembered that 'patriarchy' was often no more than a screen concealing serious conflicts and creating frustration among journeymen and forge hands, who had to put up with being treated as minors even though they were, in fact, adults. Part of the workers' wages were paid in cash but most were in kind. They were often heavily in debt to their masters and for this reason found it hard to leave them. The only way of accomplishing a move was for the new master to pay off the journeyman's pre-existing debts. In these circumstances the only escape for many was to flee. The Eskilstuna press of the 1840s and 1850s contains reports of smiths and manufacturers seeking news of their runaway workers and even offering rewards for their return.[36]

In this way the *Verlag* system and the constant shortage of cash created a complex network of credit relationships between *Verlag* capitalists and masters and between masters and workers. However, a closer look at the probate inventories of craftsmen of different rank from this period suggests that such credit relationships functioned not only on the vertical but also on the horizontal plane. For example, in 1834–43 sixty-six masters in Eskilstuna had a total debt of *c.* 51,000 *riksdaler* of which sum 43 per cent originated from *Verlagers* or the state-owned *Manufakturdiskonten* which was established in the middle of the eighteenth century to provide credit to manufacturers and industrial establishments. The rest (57 per cent) was debts that masters had to other craftsmen, above all to other masters. To a large degree this was also the case with the journeymen: a great part of their debt, according to the probate records, originated from the lending out of other journeymen. This tangle of credit relationships undoubtedly created heavy dependence between individuals. One important cause behind all this was undoubtedly the shortage of cash, which forced many individuals to borrow money in order to make purchases or payments in ready cash. Because it was generally impossible in these circumstances to save cash for future needs – this is at least a hypothesis – a master would be unable, for example, to protect himself against downturns in business conditions but would have to borrow in order to get through the worst period. In such a situation he might prefer to borrow from someone of the same social level as himself rather than from a *Verlag* capitalist.[37]

V

To regard drinking and drinking behaviour among craftsmen as part of a wider craft culture is, of course, far from original. It is often stated that drinking, taking free Mondays, brawling, embezzling materials, etc. must be regarded as part of such an indigenous culture of work and leisure and was a characteristic feature of towns all over Europe in the pre-industrial era. Further, it is often stated that this culture served the purpose of self-identification for the craftsmen. Through a specific set of cultural practices they communicated their way of life and defined their place in a hierarchical society very much built on the status, rights and duties tied to certain estates. This 'code' is often described by German handicraft historians as an ethos of '*Ehre*'. It was through this code of 'honour' that the craftsmen defined themselves and their place in society. To be an 'honourable' artisan was to follow this ethos and the principles of craft life (the principle of '*Nahrung*', for example). It is also often suggested that this code had origins far back in history and was tied to customs by its almost mystical origin.[38]

However, culture cannot be regarded merely as a 'code' or a language – not even just as a 'repertory of languages', as David Hall defines it.[39] It is definitely used in practice and cannot be regarded exclusively as – as, for example, in much symbol-orientated and semiotically influenced historical anthropology at the moment – a set of signs used in communication. In accordance with historians and anthropologists like Gerald Sider, Marshall

Sahlins, Stanley Mintz, Isaac Rhys or Hans Medick I would rather see culture as historical practice, as a code summing up the historical and actual experience of a certain set of people, used in their daily practice.[40] Or, in Clifford Geertz's words:

> Culture is the fabric of meaning in terms of which human beings interpret their experience and guide their actions; social structure is the form that action takes, the actually existing networks of social relations. Culture and social structure are then but different abstractions from the same phenomena.[41]

From this point of view the historical origin of an ethos of *Ehre* becomes much less significant than the historical or daily struggles of the craftsmen themselves: the purposes for which they use their code or 'language'. In Hans Medick's words, 'What ought to be in the forefront of analysis is rather the process of production – the uses of culture – than the product itself, the specific custom or artefact.[42] Or to paraphrase Marshall Sahlins' dictum, that people use signs in action which are then consequently altered in action.[43] A certain defined system of signs – a culture – becomes in this way not only intimately connected with social and economic practice but in reality also defines and expresses this communal and social practice as it is experienced by those taking part in it. In opposition to the structuralist/semiotic model, Stanley Mintz emphasizes that:

> I don't think meanings inhere in substances naturally or inevitably. Rather, I believe that meaning arises out of use, as people use substances in social relationships. Outside forces often determine what is available to be endowed with meaning.[44]

It is rather in this context that I would like to see drinking and drinking behaviour in the *milieu* that I am studying here. Tavern life and the drinking patterns among the craftsmen in Eskilstuna can, of course, be seen as a set of signs within a whole system of symbols making the world intelligible for them. But which is the historical context of this world of symbols? If the core of a specific culture is, as Gerald Sider emphasizes, the historical 'form and manner in which people perceive, define, articulate and express their mutual relations' then we must know more about those historically shaped relations to be able to decode this culture and understand what it really signifies: at this time and in this special locality.[45]

To judge from the narrative sources available to us, and the reports of court proceedings and other documents used in this study, the tavern played a central role in the life and world of the craftsmen and their craft. Masters, journeymen and forge hands certainly did drink at their workplaces, and out of doors as well when occasion arose, but the tavern was undoubtedly an institution of central importance in this regard.[46]

However, the tavern did not function merely as a retail establishment for alcoholic beverages. Just as in the case of England, the tavern, in Keith Wrightson's words, 'was an institution of critical importance in popular culture'.[47] It was a place for enjoying oneself and meeting other people. The judgement books and records of court proceedings show clearly that the tavern had an important function in recreation and as a channel of popular cultural expression. Eskilstuna artisans appear to have been partial to games of various kinds and to physical sports. Card games were popular and people often seem to have played 'for the consumption of food and drink', as in January 1830 when eight journeymen and two masters were charged with having played cards within the confines of Carl Julin's house of refreshment.[48] Skittles was also a popular pastime in summer, and money or refreshments would often be at stake.[49] This was also the case with the physical sports in which they engaged: wrestling, pulling fingers, etc. Such games not infrequently ended up as furious battles involving many participants.[50]

However, being together in the tavern also had other important implications which are related more specifically to the social relations prevailing in Eskilstuna at the time: between *Verlagers* and masters; between masters and workers. In this respect it must be reckoned that the tavern was one of the few 'free' spaces where people could meet. Journeymen living in with their master had to go there to be able to free themselves from his direct influence, but the tavern could also cover up activities and confrontations of different kinds. The tavern was, then, a place where, for example, a journeyman could feel free but the tavern as a free space had other implications. One reason why craftsmen spent so much time at the tavern and why it was of such critical importance in their culture was that it served, for instance, as a selling place for embezzled and other goods. In this respect the tavern and its role

in the local culture expressed the social interactions and oppo-
sitions embedded in the economic and social milieu. As the market
was such an important social space in putting-out milieus it is
perhaps not so strange that an institution for selling embezzled
and secretly traded goods was invested with so much symbolic
importance, as was the case here. Without a doubt the function
of a tavern as a market place for such goods is an important
reason why its role was so hotly debated during this period – and
thus also why it was so frequented by the common artisans.

As we have seen, cash was a desirable object among Eskilstuna's
craftsmen. Since both smiths and workers received such a large
proportion of their remuneration in kind they had to look to other
ways of acquiring ready cash. Masters tried as far as possible to
circumvent the *Verlag* capitalists by selling to other buyers who
could offer cash. In the same way journeymen and apprentices,
having done their duty to their masters, would try to do some
manufacturing of their own so as to be able to sell the products.
They were entitled, by custom, to do this, though naturally on
condition that they paid for whatever raw materials and inputs
they utilized. The use of time was 'porous', however, and it is
very likely there were times when own-account manufacturing
took priority – while the master had to wait. The smiths and
manufacturers had very little scope, in practice, for supervising
and checking their workers. They had to leave the workplace
frequently – perhaps in order to negotiate with buyers at the
tavern. When journeymen and apprentices were manufacturing
articles 'on the side' in this manner they would, of course, be less
particular about paying the master for raw materials and other
inputs. 'Embezzled' manufactures were then sold to *smidesbetjänter*
('smithware touts') or other purchasers who either based themselves permanently in the city or else travelled around selling their
wares.[51] And much of this business seems to have been transacted
in the tavern: at any rate, the latter was where the contacts were
often made.

Records of magistrates court proceedings furnish a number of
examples of such activities. On 28 July 1824, for example, a
nailsmith named Sätterberg and his son were summoned before
the free city magistrates court to answer the charge that 'they
entered into trade with Petter Felldin, apprentice to master cutler
And. Broselius, concerning three pairs . . . of table knives'. Felldin
related:

that he did sell the knives which have now been exhibited and assessed at a value of One rix-dollar and 24 shillings Banco, to Sätterberg Senior, and in payment therefore did receive 1 rix-dollar *riksgälds*; that he, Felldin, did fabricate the knives from his master's materials after he had completed his work for his master, and Broselius has stated in this regard that he did give to Felldin and his other workers permission, after they should have completed their prescribed work for the day or week, to carry out so-called excess work using their master's materials, but nevertheless being bound to hand over these articles to him in return for reasonable payment and not, as now has occurred, to sell them to others.[52]

In the same way a Damask steel-maker named Heljestrand alleged of one of his apprentices, Carl Fredrik Bovin, aged nineteen, that he frequently 'without his master's knowledge and consent did take of these materials and fabricate scissors for himself, the which Bovin did sell, and did afterwards purchase *brännvin* for himself with the money'.[53]

Another method was simply to steal smithware from the master's stock and sell it. A manufacturer by the name of Vogel related such an incident to the magistrates court in January 1832:

that between 10 and 11 of the clock at last Saturday evening he did hear a rattling noise in the attic of his dwellinghouse and that Bergman (his journeyman) immediately thereafter did come down in holiday attire – and to the question whither he was bound so late in the evening he did reply with contumely that he intended to go out. Vogel did not then suspect that any theft was in question so did then go in and retire to bed, but the next morning Vogel had found the door to an attic lock-up broken open, and missing therefrom were a dozen dog-leads, 3 iron mousetraps and 4 cupboard locks, and a search then being carried out it was discovered that Lundström after having conferred with Bergman did carry out the burglary and theft, and that both Bergman and Bergstedt did afterwards endeavour to dispose of the stolen articles (these were all journeymen).[54]

All the indications are that embezzlement and linked activities were extremely common. Those who committed such 'crimes' were

310

sometimes journeymen, sometimes apprentices. When they were caught they were usually 'under the influence of drink', having disposed of their booty and then drunk all or part of the money away in some tavern, often the very one in which they had sold the articles in the manner already described. For it was in the taverns that all those gathered who might conceivably be interested in buying – the 'smithware touts', the *dalkarlar* (itinerant pedlars from Dalarna county) and the rest. The court records show that in 1828, for example, two apprentices named Adam and Per Olof Westlander (they were brothers, aged twenty and twenty-three years respectively) had 'sold diverse smithware to men of Dalarna and other persons', having stolen it from a *Verlag* capitalist by the name of Moback. Public prosecutor Nibelius described the situation thus:

that Adam Westlander on Thursday evening last did enter Hellberg's house of refreshment and did offer for sale to men of Dalarna there present clasp knives of many kinds and thereof did sell several dozen.[55]

Since the selling of goods in taverns by journeymen and apprentices frequently followed upon criminal acts these are the sales which we mainly find recorded in the judgement books. Now and then it also emerges that master smiths met 'smithware touts' and other buyers in taverns and negotiated sales to them. On 4 September 1822, for example, a forge hand named J. P. Moberg was summoned before the magistrates court charged with 'having been under the influence of drink' and with having 'assaulted and beaten' A. O. Hagberg, a cutler. The latter related that 'after he had sold one dozen pocket knives and as agreed was to treat him to *brännvin* . . . Moberg after having drunk up, had struck him a blow on the shoulder'. The incident had occurred at Carl Julin's house of refreshment and Moberg had pleaded as his excuse that he had been trying to keep Hagberg where he was because he was 'intoxicated by strong drink and incapable of going home'.[56]

As well as functioning as points of sale, taverns could also sometimes act as places of assembly for secret journeymen associations, and these sometimes become the object of legal proceedings. Immediately after New Year 1829, for example, the journeymen hatters had assembled at the house of refreshment of John Törngren, engraver, although this was prohibited. Nibelius, the public prosecutor, and two municipal officers named Nygren and Ramström related:

> that those who received instructions to ensure that no illegal gatherings took place in houses of refreshment had last Monday evening at Törngren's tavern had it in view to instruct Törngren to stop the meeting which the journeymen hatters were then holding at Törngren's without due permission, whereupon after they had ordered a tot of *brännvin* each, Törngren's wife refused to allow Nygren and Ramström to stay in the room, and when they explained that they were entitled like all others to enter a public house of refreshment, especially since they were charged with ensuring that no disorder or misbehaviour took place there, they were assaulted with blows to the face, first by Törngren's wife and subsequently by her husband, who had come forth immediately thereafter, so that they were compelled to depart thence, and Nygren and Ramström demanded that in such an affair Törngren and his wife must answer before the law.

Törngren and his wife admitted in principle that the incident had occurred as stated but declared that they had had to protect themselves in the face of the municipal officers' 'belligerence and disturbance of the domestic peace'. The court in its turn took the view that the Törngrens had been wrong to turn away the two officials and that the hatters 'had without due permission and in breach of the guild rules been allowed to hold meetings' in their premises. However, at the same time they felt that the offence was trivial and therefore urged the municipal officers and the Törngrens to 'seek an amicable reconciliation'.[57]

VI

However, I think it is possible to go a step further. It was not only that the tavern played an important role in the journeymen's, and even the masters', 'material' well-being, in the way just described; Hugh Cunningham made the point that 'leisure activities were infused with the experience of work' or that leisure and work at this point were fused together into a single whole.[58] The tavern and its social life had an even more profound role, related to what was said above about credit relationships and how people were involved in a complex net of such relations both on a vertical but even more profoundly on a horizontal plane.

Social anthropologists have long been telling us that the consumption of various products helps to create and maintain social relationships.[59] In their '*The World of Goods: Towards an Anthropology of Consumption*, Mary Douglas and Baron Isherwood develop one aspect of this point of view. They explain, above all, the communicative aspects of consumption. By consuming certain products people confirm both their identities and their membership of a particular social group. Douglas and Isherwood want us to forget, for the moment, that products satisfy what we believe are our needs. We should, instead, they believe, view the consumption of goods as part of the flow of information. Products make it possible for us to communicate with others. To be rich, that is to say, to have access to a large amount of goods, is the same as having the possibility of communicating with a larger number of people. To be poor, by the same token, is to be deprived of the possibility of communicating with others, to be poorly informed and deprived of the chances and opportunities which life offers. In a class-structured society or a society consisting of several cultures – as Douglas and Isherwood describe – consumption habits are as natural as our skin: they become a criterion for membership and are used as a means of exclusion. Through goods, our power and class membership are expressed. To be denied access to certain types of goods is synonymous with being excluded from the social group or class.

This way of describing the role of consumption as a system of communication goes far beyond a semiotic approach to culture as a system of signs. Douglas and Isherwood point out how important it can be – given a certain social setting and society – to express allegiance to a social group perhaps, as in this example, by going to the tavern and buying each other drinks. A certain pattern of consumption signifies our membership of a certain social group and plays the part of a sort of admission ticket. To stand on one side results, as Douglas and Isherwood express it, in being unable to make one's voice heard, in being ignored, oppressed and pushed to one side.[60] Instead, to participate is to become part of a social infrastructure of great importance for the individual.

There were several reasons why drinking and tavern-going were picked out as of strategic importance in this connection. First, beer and spirits were the only products, apart from basic necessities,

313

which were generally available for social consumption.[61] Secondly, as we saw, because of the general lack of living space in Eskilstuna at the time, coupled with the fact that owners and wholesalers would not allow public meetings on their property, the tavern was one of the few places where ordinary working men could meet. Third, the exchange of drinks has traditionally had a strong symbolic value. Anthropologists have shown that many cultures outside Europe had clearly defined food or drinking rituals to be performed in the exchange of contracts, business agreements and the like. This was also the case in nineteenth-century Eskilstuna where contracts between craftsmen were exchanged after a ritual in which the exchange of drinks played a part.[62] All this meant that drinking and taverns played an important role in the culture of the Eskilstuna craftworkers and were invested with much symbolic power.

By taking part in the life of the local tavern one became an active participant in the life of the local community. One could establish important contacts; as I have pointed out, the lack of money and the extensive networks of debts resulting from this made the inhabitants of Eskilstuna strongly dependent on one another. By buying someone a drink one could perhaps ensure, or at least make more likely, his assistance on some future occasion. To have access to a wide circle of social contacts meant that there was a greater likelihood of being able to borrow money if the need arose, in the event of sickness, unemployment, etc. Also, mortality for men was high in the Eskilstuna of the early 1800s[63] and widows needed help even to the extent of board and lodging in order to avoid the workhouse. This was, at least in some cases, provided by the dead husband's former workmates. Social contacts at the local tavern also came in useful in other ways. An artisan with many sons must secure their future by attempting to place them with other craftsmasters. Tavern life became something of a necessity for the smiths and other workers.

For the historian it is, of course, very difficult empirically to verify these informal aspects of the social security net and the role of, for example, social drinking in this respect. In a general sense, it seems clear that such an informal net was of acute importance in Eskilstuna where, for instance, the complex credit relationships expressed how closely people were knitted together. More specifically, there are many instances in our source-material which indicate that buying drinks served as a way of creating relationships.

Among reformers from the middle classes this social aspect of drinking was also looked upon as one of the main factors behind why the tavern was of such importance for craftsmen at the time.[64] What could happen when someone refused to pay or repay a drink and thus refused to establish a relationship is shown in the court case between Olof Jädercrantz, a journeyman cutler, and Olof Eriksson, an apprentice grinder. Here the offence was even more severe, because it was an apprentice who refused to make friends with a journeyman:

> that (Eriksson) he last Saturday afternoon did enter the widow Öhman's house of refreshment and did order a tot of *brännvin* for himself, but when the seller ... did refuse to supply *brännvin* unless food was ordered as well, Eriksson had also ordered a small portion of sparling (a type of fish). After he had partaken thereof ... Jädercrantz did approach him and did declare that Eriksson should treat him to a tot of *brännvin*, which Eriksson refused, when Jädercrantz did assault him and deliver him a blow. After Eriksson had departed, Jädercrantz, having gone out before him, did approach him and ... did put his hand into Eriksson's coat-pocket and purloin the money which he had kept therein ... and when Eriksson did demand the money back then did Jädercrantz assault Eriksson and did knock him down and retain the money himself.[65]

At the trial Jädercrantz was unable to give any satisfactory explanation of his conduct. There is nothing to suggest that Eriksson may have owed Jädercrantz's money, for example. It appears that he simply took offence because Eriksson refused to treat him to a drink. We should once again bear in mind that Eriksson was an apprentice and Jädercrantz a journeyman. Jädercrantz had extended a hand to Eriksson – initiated a move towards social contact – and Eriksson ought to have been honoured. But the latter declined the invitation and Jädercrantz accordingly felt deeply affronted.

This is also what Marcel Mauss emphasized in his discussion of the symbolic aspect of gifts: 'To refuse to give, or fail to invite is – like refusing to accept – the equivalent of a declaration of war; it is a refusal of friendship and intercourse.'[66] However, buying someone a round was probably even more than a token of friendship. According to Mauss, a gift creates a basic credit relationship where the person who initially receives the gift is placed in a position of debt in relation to the gift-giver. Thus, in accordance with this reasoning, to buy someone a drink was an act of opening up a credit relationship that might involve – this is at least a highly possible hypothesis – much more than just buying drinks for each other.

That some men – against this background – would do almost anything in order to obtain money for visits to the tavern is apparent from the concise references in the court records. There are numerous petty thefts recorded where the perpetrator was subsequently discovered in one of the local taverns or bars 'heavily under the influence of intoxicating liquor'. As we saw, cases of workers stealing from their employer's store of material were commonplace and embezzlement and petty thefts were pointed out as a major problem for the masters. In 1820 several apprentices appeared before the court for, despite several warnings, selling their clothes and using the proceeds to buy drink. The impecunious who were unwilling to commit such 'crimes' were forced to stay away from the tavern and all that this entailed.[67]

To refrain from taking part in the life of the local tavern and to refuse to buy rounds of drinks was in a way tantamount to putting oneself outside the community and the social net which undoubtedly existed. For the master it might mean that he received no help in a period of slump or when he was sick and unable to work. For the journeymen it might mean that he could not find any work and never be able – in a situation where only a minority could reach so far – to establish himself as a master in his own right.[68]

NOTES

1 For a general account of the putting-out industry see, for example, G. Schmoller, *Grundriss der Allgemeinen Volkwirtschaftslehre* I, Leipzig, 1908, 481 ff; E. Lipson, *The Economic History of England*, II, London, 1931, 1 ff; W. Sombart (*Verlag* system), *Handwörterbuch der Staatswissenschaften*, Bd VIII, Jena, 1911; P. Kriedte, H. Medick and J. Schlumbohm, *Industrialization before Industrialization*, Cambridge, 1981; L. A Clarkson, *The Pre-industrial Economy in England 1500–1700*, London, 1971; and T. S. Ashton, *An Economic History of England: The Eighteenth Century*, London, 1964. Among monographs see, for example, A. Wadsworth and J. de Lacy Mann, *The Cotton Trade and Industrial Lancashire 1600–1780*, Manchester, 1965; W. Reddy, *The Rise of Market Culture.*

The Textile Trade and French Society 1750–1900, Cambridge, 1984; and L. Magnusson, *Den bråkiga kulturen*, Stockholm, 1988.

2 J. Styles, 'Embezzlement, industry and the law in England 1500–1800' in M. Berg, P. Hudson and M. Sonenscher (eds), *Manufacture in Town and Country Before the Factory*, Cambridge, 1983. See also the debate between S. Marglin, 'What do bosses do?', *Review of Radical Political Economy*, 6, 1974, and D. Landes, 'What do bosses really do?', *Journal of Economic History*, XLVA, 1986.

3 I deal more directly with this aspect in L. Magnusson, 'Embezzlement, theft and secret trading', forthcoming.

4 For example in H. U. Thamer, 'On the use and abuse of handicraft: journeymen culture and enlightened public opinion in eighteenth- and nineteenth-century Germany' in S. L. Kaplan (ed.), *Understanding Popular Culture*, Berlin, 1984.

5 L. Chevalier, *Laboring Classes and Dangerous Classes in Paris During the First Half of the Nineteenth Century*, Princeton, 1973.

6 See, for example, the essays in A. D. Donajgrodzki (ed.), *Social Control in Nineteenth-Century Britain*, London, 1977. For a critical review of such studies see G. Stedman Jones, 'Class expression versus social control? A critique of recent trends in the social history of leisure', reprinted in the same author's volume *Languages of Class*, Cambridge, 1983. On the 'drinking problem' see especially B. Harrison, *Drink and the Victorians*, London, 1971. See also R. W. Malcolmson, *Popular Recreations in English Society*, Cambridge, 1973, 118 ff.; E. Weber, *Peasants into Frenchmen: The Modernization of Rural France 1870–1914*, Stanford, 1976; D. A. Reid, 'The decline of saint Monday', *Past and Present*, 71, 1976; R. D. Storch, 'Introduction' in his *Popular Culture and Customs in Nineteenth-Century England*, London, 1982.

7 See W. J. Rorabaugh, *The Alcoholic Republic*, Oxford, 1979 and J. Roberts, *Drink, Temperance and the Working Class in Nineteenth-Century Germany*, Winchester, Mass., 1984.

8 On 'social drinking' see M. Roberts, *Drink, Temperance and the Working Class in Nineteenth-Century Germany*, Boston, 1984, 107 ff.; B. Harrison, 'Pubs' in H. J. Dyos and M. Wolf, *The Victorian City*, I, London, 1973. A more purely sociological perspective can be found in C. MacAndrew and R. Edgerton, *Drunken Compartment*, Chicago, 1969. On the 'breakdown of control', see A. D. Donajgrodzki, op. cit., 9 ff.

9 L. Magnusson, *Den bråkiga kulturen: smideshantverkare i Eskilstuna 1800–1850*, Stockholm, 1988. See also my 'Drinking and the *Verlag*-system 1820–1850: the significance of taverns and drink in Eskilstuna before industrialization', *Scandinavian Economic History Review*, XXXIV, 1, 1986.

10 Anna Holmberg b. 1855. Folkminnesuppteckning, Eskilstuna. ULMA.

11 Klara Atterberg b. 1873. Folkminnesuppteckning, Eskilstuna. ULMA.

12 Sundhets-Collegii underdåniga berättelse om medicalverket i riket 1851, Stockholm, 1853, 84 ff.

13 Mantalslängder. Eskilstuna stads arkiv: Rådhusrättens och magistratens arkiv. ULA.

14 The number of convictions is gathered from Saköreslängder. Eskilstuna

LARS MAGNUSSON

stads arkiv: Rådhusrättens och magistratens arkiv. ULA. The citation from G. Silfverstolpe 'Den månghamrande staden', Eskilstuna, 1962.

15 For a survey see D. J. Pittman and C. R. Snyder (eds), *Society, Culture and Drinking Patterns*, New York, 1962; M. W. Ewerett *et al.*, *Cross-Cultural Approaches to the Study of Alcohol: An Interdisciplinary Perspective*, The Hague, 1976; M. Marshall (ed.), *Beliefs, Behavior and Alcoholic Beverages: A Cross-Cultural Survey*, Ann Arbor, Michigan, 1979. For historical interpretations of the situation in Germany, see M. Roberts, *Drink, Temperance and the Working Class in Nineteenth-Century Germany*, Boston, 1984; for France, M. R. Marrus, 'Social drinking in the belle époque, *Journal of Social History*, 7, 2, 1974; for England, B. Harrison, *Drink and the Victorians*, London, 1974; for the USA, W. J. Rorabaugh, *The Alcoholic Republic*, Oxford, 1979.

16 Cit. after K. Hellberg, *Järnet och smedernas Eskilstuna*, II, Katrineholm, 1938, 154.

17 See Hellberg, op. cit., 156. See also G. Nyman, *Bibliotek i Eskilstuna intill 1938*, Eskilstuna, 1975.

18 For the introduction of temperance lodges in Eskilstuna see, for example, B. Öhngren, *Folk i rörelse: Samhällsutveckling, flyttningsmönster och folkrörelser i Eskilstuna 1870–1900*, Uppsala, 1974, 180 ff.

19 *Eskilstuna Allehanda*, 19 December 1855.

20 *Eskilstuna Allehanda*, 15 July 1848.

21 *Eskilstuna Allehanda*, 9 November 1853.

22 See, for example, *Eskilstuna Allehanda*, 1 May 1852, 16 April 1853 and other dates.

23 *Eskilstuna Allehanda*, 24 April 1858.

24 G. Silfverstolpe, *Den månghamrande staden*, Eskilstuna, 1962, 38.

25 *Eskilstuna Allehanda*, 24 April 1858.

26 *Eskilstuna Allehanda*, 12 September 1849. For English comparisons see Reid, op. cit.

27 Regulation 22 September 1798. Eskilstuna stads arkiv. Fristadssamhällets och ordningsrättens arkiv, vol. BII:1. ESA.

28 *Eskilstuna Allehanda*, 8 October 1851.

29 *Eskilstuna Allehanda*, 10 October 1857.

30 *Eskilstuna Allehanda*, 22 May 1858.

31 *Eskilstuna Allehanda*, 3 August 1859.

32 For a presentation see, for example, Harrison, op. cit. and Roberts, op. cit.

33 For a general history, see Hellberg, op. cit. and M. Isacson and L. Magnusson, *Protoindustrialization in Scandinavia*, Leamington Spa, 1987. Cf. also B.-E. Ohlsson, *Eskilstuna Fristad*, Eskilstuna, 1971.

34 Isacson and Magnusson, op. cit.; L. Magnusson, *Arbetet vid en svensk verkstad: Munktells 1900–1920*, Lund, 1987.

35 A. Hörsell, *Borgare, smeder och änkor: Ekonomi och befolkning i Eskilstuna gamla stad och fristad 1750–1850*, Uppsala, 1983, 103.

36 L. Magnusson, *Den bråkiga kulturen: smideshantverkare i Eskilstuna 1800–1850*, Stockholm, 1988.

37 ibid.

38 R. Stadelman and W. Fischer, *Die Bildungswelt der deutschen Handwerker*

um 1800, Berlin, 1955, 67 ff.; J. Bergmann, *Das Berliner Handwerk in der Frühphasen der Industrialisierung*, Berlin, 1973, 16 ff.; R. Wissel, *Des Alten Handwerks Recht und Gewohnheit*, I, Berlin, 1971, 145 ff. See also A. Griessinger, *Das Symbolische Kapital der Ehre*, Frankfurt, 1981, chap. 8.

39 D. Hall in S. Kaplan (ed.), *Understanding Popular Culture*, Berlin, 1984, 14 ff.

40 See M. Sahlins, *Culture and Practical Reason*, Chicago and London, 1976 and *Islands of History*, Chicago and London, 1985, chap. 1. S. Ortner, 'Theory in anthropology since the sixties', *Comparative Studies in Society and History*, 26, 1984; E. Wolf, *Anthropology*, New York, 1974. 38 ff. See also H. Medick, 'Missionare im Ruderboot? Ethnologische Erkenntnis-weisen als Herausforderung an die Sozialgeschichte', *Geschichte und Gesellschaft*, 10, 1984 and the Introduction by Medick and Sabean in H. Medick and D. Sabean (eds), *Interests and Emotions*, Cambridge, 1984. Of interest also is G. Sider, *Culture and Class in Anthropology and History: A Newfoundland Illustration*, Cambridge, 1986; G. Sider, 'Family fun in Starve Harbor: Newfoundland' in Medick and Sabean, op. cit.; G. Sider 'Christmas mumming and the New Year in Outport Newfoundland', *Past and Present*, 71, 1976; M. Sahlins, *Islands of History*, Chicago, 1985; M. Sahlins, *Historical Metaphors and Mythical Realities: Structure in the Early History of the Sandwich Island Kingdoms*, Ann Arbor, 1981; S. Mintz, *Sweetness and Power: The Place of Sugar in Modern History*, New York, 1985; R. Isaac, *The Transformation of Virginia 1740–1790*, Chapel Hill, 1982, 323.

41 C. Geertz, 'Ritual and social change: a Javanese example' in his *The Interpretation of Cultures*, New York, 1973, 145.

42 Medick, op. cit.

43 M. Sahlins, *Islands of History*, op. cit., vii.

44 Mintz, op. cit., xxix.

45 G. Sider, 'The ties that bind: culture and agriculture, property and propriety in the Newfoundland village fishery', *Social History*, 1980, 24.

46 Magnusson, op. cit.

47 K. Wrightson, 'Alehouses, order and reformation in rural England 1590–1660' in E. and S. Yeo (eds), *Popular Culture and Class Conflict 1690–1914: Explorations in the History of Labour and Leisure*, Sussex, 1981. See also P. Clark, 'The alehouse and the alternative society' in D. Pennington and K. Thomas (eds), *Puritans and Revolutionaries: Essays in Seventeenth-Century History Presented to Christopher Hill*, Oxford, 1978, and Harrison, op. cit., 175 ff.

48 20 January 1830. 'Dombōcker.' Eskilstuna stad. Rådhusrättens och magistratens arkiv. ULA.

49 See e.g. 18 June 1828 and 9 July 1832. 'Dombōcker.' Eskilstuna stad. Rådhusrättens och magistratens arkiv. ULA.

50 See 26 May 1823, 9 February 1824, 6 February 1824. 'Dombōcker.' Eskilstuna stad. Rådhusrättens och magistratens arkiv. ULA.

51 An account of these buyers is given by B. Rosander 'Smidesbetjänter: Eskilstunasmidets avsättning genom kringvandrande dalfolk', Eskilstuna Museers Årsbok, 1965. See also Magnusson, op. cit.

52 28 July 1824. 'Domböcker.' Eskilstuna stad. Rådhusrättens och magi-
    stratens arkiv. ULA.
53 ibid.
54 30 January 1832. 'Domböcker.' Eskilstuna stad. Rådhusrättens och
    magistratens arkiv. ULA.
55 12 January 1828. 'Domböcker.' Eskilstuna stad. Rådhusrättens och
    magistratens arkiv. ULA.
56 4 September 1822. 'Domböcker.' Eskilstuna stad. Rådhusrättens och
    magistratens arkiv. ULA.
57 14 January 1829. 'Domböcker.' Eskilstuna stad. Rådhusrättens och
    magistratens arkiv. ULA.
58 H. Cunningham, *Leisure in the Industrial Revolution*, London 1980, 68.
    For a discussion of the relation between work and leisure see also G.
    Huck (ed.), *Sozialgeschichte der Freizeit*, Bielefeld, 1980, 12. Cf. also
    Cunningham, op. cit., 57 ff.; K. Hammerich and M. Klein (eds),
    Materialien zur Soziologie des Alltags, Opladen, 1978; M. Marrus (ed.),
    The Emergence of Leisure, New York, 1975; and G. Stedman Jones, op.
    cit.
59 See e.g. R. Firth, *Symbols Public and Private*, London, 1975, chap. 7, for
    a survey, and R. Finnegan, *The Limba of Sierra Leone*, Oxford, 1963,
    324 ff. for a discussion of 'exchange of drinks'. Here, of course, mention
    must also be made of C. Lévi-Strauss's works (even though their
    starting-point is different), e.g. *Mythologiques I: Le cru et le cuit*, Paris,
    1964 (English-language version *The Raw and the Cooked*, New York,
    1969). Cf. also M. Mauss, *The Gift*, London, 1954; M. Sahlins, *Stone
    Age Economics*, Chicago, 1972; and C. Geertz, H. Geertz and L. Rosen,
    Meaning and Order in Moroccan Society, Cambridge, 1979, 123 ff.
60 M. Douglas and B. Isherwood, *The World of Goods: Towards an Anthro-
    pology of Consumption*, Harmondsworth, 1980, 85, 92, etc.
61 See Roberts, op. cit., 42; Rorabaugh, op. cit., chap. 3; and also H.
    Medick, 'Plebeian culture and the transition to capitalism' in R.
    Samuel and G. Stedman Jones (eds), *Culture, Ideology and Politics: Essays
    for Eric Hobsbawm*, London, 1983.
62 Magnusson, op. cit.
63 See, for example, Hörsell, op. cit.
64 Magnusson, op. cit.
65 3 May 1830. 'Domböcker'. Eskilstuna stad. Rådhusrättens och magi-
    stratens arkiv. ULA.
66 Mauss, op. cit.
67 Example in Ordningsrättens prootkoll 17 May 1820. Eskilstuna stads
    arkiv. Ordningsrättens och fristadssamhällets arkiv. ULA.
68 Hörsell, op cit.; Ohlsson, op. cit.; Magnusson, op. cit.

CONTRIBUTORS

MAXINE BERG is Senior Lecturer in Economic History at the University of Warwick.

BRENDA COLLINS researches at the Institute of Irish Studies, Queen's University Belfast and teaches for the Open University.

GAY L. GULLICKSON is Associate Professor of History, University of Maryland.

PAUL M. HOHENBERG is Professor of Economics, Renssalaer Polytechnic Institute, Troy, New York.

PAT HUDSON is Senior Lecturer in Economic History, University of Liverpool.

TOSHIO KUSAMITSU is Lecturer in History, Tokyo Women's University.

LARS MAGNUSSON is Reader in Economic History, Uppsala University, Uppsala, Sweden.

SIDNEY POLLARD is Professor of History, Fakultät für Geschichtswissenschaft und Philosophie, University of Bielefeld.

DEBORAH SIMONTON is Lecturer in History, Hillcroft College, Surbiton, Surrey.

J. K. J. THOMSON is Lecturer in History, University of Sussex.

JAUME TORRAS is Professor of History, Universidad Autonoma, Barcelona, Spain.

INDEX

agencies/agency system 142, 146–7, 150

agent(s) 20, 21, 79, 100–1, 114–38; *see also* factors; fashion; middlemen

aggregate growth 173, 174, 175, 198

agrarian: change 7, 22; environment 7, 265; occupations 268, 269; and proto-industry 7, 22, 31; resources 43; structures 22

agricultural: change 4; demands 145; labour 160, 161; productivity 12–13, 177; resources 36; technique 36

agriculture 3, 4, 6, 46, 173, 264; and apprenticeships 240, 252; commercialized 94, 159; and domestic industry 9, 208; *see also* seasonality

Allen, R.A.C. (forthcoming) 13, 24n

American: colonies, trade with 19, 182; demand 143; market 68, 121; trade 65; *see also* Spanish America

Americas, European trade with 15, 16, 82, 165

apprenticeship 161: aims of 253–5; female 233, 234, 243–53; functions of 252; and gender 227–58; legislation on 228–9, 231, 234, 235–6, 255–6n, 257n;

'outdoor' 232, 256n; records and registration 232–4, 256–7; as restricted practice 23; social or class distinctions 249; *see also* parish

Ariès, P. (1974) 228, 230, 255n, 256n

artisan(s) 95, 98, 108, 175, 284; independent 22, 263; and property 190–6, 197; skills 10, 107; structure, organizational forms 262, 263, 264, 285–6

Asia, European trade with 16, 19, 65, 164

Bairoch, Paul (1988) 6–7, 9, 23n, 24n

Barcelona 64, 70, 76–9, 95, 97, 113n *see also franquicias*

Belfast 141, 142, 143, 144–5, 150, 151, 152

Berg, Maxine 3–26, 173–201; (1985) 24n, 49n; (1987) 22, 25n

Birmingham 11, 173–201; and Black Country 179, 181; character of 180–3; economy 184; hinterland 197; markets/ marketing 20, 21, 181; compare Manchester 174, 175, 176; and tradition 174; *see also* commerce; creativity

Black Country 180, 181, 183, 236

Boulton, Matthew 14, 21, 181, 184, 185–6, 187–8, 189, 201n

bourgeoisie: demands for quality
164
Braudel, F. 41, 160, 171n; (1973)
38, 52n; (1984) 21, 25n
Braun, Rudolf (1966) 214, 217,
220, 225n
Briggs, Asa 174, 199n; (1950) 176
Bristol 19, 176, 180
Britain 9, 10, 15, 60–1, 66–7, 68,
121
British exports/foreign trade 16,
110

calico-printing industry 57–89,
94–5, 164; British 60, 118, 132,
134; in Europe 57, 58, 59, 60–4,
75–6, 84n; in Spain 64–70; see
also Catalan
Calverley: textile study 266–84, 288
Campbell, R. (1747, 1969) 237,
249, 257n, 258n
canal system networks; regional
basis 20–1, 182–3
capital 41, 148, 162, 168, 195, 262,
168, 262, 287, 304; -intensive
production 167, 262;
merchant/mercantile 5, 108, 120,
123, 175; see also calico-printing;
Spain
capitalism 4, 29, 30, 37–8, 108, 160
Cappe, Catherine (1805) 235, 257n
Caspard, Pierre 62, 85n
Catalan: calico-printing industry:
state intervention 57–89; cloth
manufacturing industry 95;
workers/merchants outside
Catalonia 103–4
Catalonia 95–108
Caux: proto-industrial work and
women's status 207–26
centralization of manufacturing 75,
262, 287
change: industrial 44; resistance to
161; urban–rural 160–3; see also
technical
Chapman, S.J. (1979) 120, 123,
137n
Chassagne, Serge 63, 84n, 86n
Chevalier, Louis (1973) 294, 317n

child labour 142, 150, 161
Clark, Alice (1919) 206, 223n, 244,
258n
class: conflict 174; distinctions
253–4; struggle 293
cloth: halls 120, 124–7, 263;
manufacturing 95–108, 264
clothier(s) 271, 287
coal 176, 180
Coleman, D.C. (1969) 31, 48n, 116,
120, 136n; (1973) 116, 136n
Collins, Brenda 9, 12, 20, 139–56,
216; (1982) 154n, 214, 225n;
(1988) 154n
colonial markets 5, 10, 19, 106, 108,
109n, 164, 176, 181
commerce 5–9, 17, 18, 22–3,
159–72, 173–201, 259–320
commercial: agriculture 159;
capitalism 30; expansion 3, 22;
functions, urban 6, 7, 177;
independence 107; information
103; intermediaries 102; –urban
networks 6; organization 7,
114–15; relationships 147
communication 40, 313–16
community 22, 185, 316
companies/units, large enterprise
34
competition 30, 32, 118, 121, 123,
236–7, 293; Birmingham 185,
197; calico-printing 64, 83, 95,
96, 104; urban resistance to 166,
167, 171
consumer: choice 139, 143; demand
117, 171; industries 5, 11, 34, 38,
45, 115, 176; market 10, 11, 57–8,
164; orientation 116; see also
mass production
consumption 6, 10–11, 12–15, 21,
114, 117; patterns 3, 11–12; see
also drinking
co-operation/competition 185n,
197
corporate order/structure,
traditional: Birmingham 188–9,
195
corporative: regulations 83–4;

323

shirt/underclothing industry
139–40, 147–52
Sider, Gerald (1986) 306, 307–8,
319n
Sigsworth, E.M. (1958) 130, 138n,
262, 288n
silk 60, 61, 63, 65, 122
Simonton, Deborah 22, 227–58;
(1988) 256n, 258n
skill(s) 41, 107, 164, 167; through
apprenticeship 161, 227, 230,
242, 243, 251–2, 253, 254;
Birmingham 174, 185
skilled labour/workers 10, 11, 41,
126
small/large-scale industry 43, 264
small-scale manufacturers 42–4,
107, 108, 123, 174, 262; and
innovation/creativity 184;
technology 175
Smith, Adam (1776, 1976) 229–30,
233, 236–7, 256n, 257n, 292
Snell, K.D.M (1985) 22, 25n
social aspects 4, 43, 46, 174, 195,
265, 294: of apprenticeship 228,
230, 231, 239, 243, 247, 249, 253,
255; of economy 3, 94, 147; of
putting out system 30, 292–320
social: institutions 22–3, 139–40,
259–320; position 245;
relationships 151, 239, 313–16;
structure 174, 185, 190, 261–91
society, organization of 117; and
regionality of industries 35
socio-economic: history 3, 5, 114;
relationships of industrial
localities 37, 266
Sonenscher, M., Berg, M. and
Hudson, P. (eds) 47n, 48n, 49n,
153n, 171n, 289n
Sowerby: textile study 266–84, 288
Spain 20, 21, 64–70, 93–113, 165
Spanish America, trade with 66
specialisms, European industrial
19–20
specialization 20, 21, 32, 35, 43,
164: Birmingham as centre for
174 Catalan 96, 103; export
industries 17, 36; flexible 10–12;

regional 41, 44, 77; in Yorkshire
woollen industry 121, 262, 263
spinning 139, 140, 208, 209, 216,
217
stability 160, 167, 169, 171
stagnation blocking development
40
state, the: and concentration of
industry 37–40; intervention
57–89, 95, 107; and the market
27–89; policies 23, 38, 64, 82; *see
also* Donegal; power; protection;
restrictions; royal interest
status, social 206, 207, 218–22; and
apprenticeship 233, 237, 241,
243; female 206, 207, 213,
218–22, 244, 247, 249, 251–2,
253–4, 255
Statute of Artificers (1563) 228–9,
233, 235–6, 237, 244
structural change 9
Sweden 292–320
Switzerland 60, 61, 62, 68
subsidization, state: for industries
38–9
supply and demand 3, 15, 144–5

tariffs, protective 40, 95, 145
taste(s) 3, 10, 11, 13; and fashion
20, 135
tavern, functions of 308–16
taxes 60, 162, 273–80, 290n
technical: ability 66; change 197;
considerations 59; expertise 68;
innovation 35–6; requirements
34, 79
technique(s) 10–11, 36, 171, 197
technological innovation and
change 46, 116, 135, 162, 168,
173, 184,
technology 3, 10, 116, 173, 175,
286–7; calico-printing processes
57, 62, 72–3, 76–7; machine
(shirt industry) 148, 149, 151–2
Tennent, J.E. (1841) 118, 119,
136n
textile(s): growth 93–113, 120;
industries 36, 45–6, 116, 118–20,
135; manufacture 33, 96, 261–90;

printing 66; proto-industrial 7,
32, 219–20; spinning 159; trade
66, 120, 248–9
Thirsk, Joan (1973) 115, 116, 117,
119, 136n
Thompson, E.P. (1976) 282, 290n
Thomson, J.K.L. 9, 57–89, 95, 107;
(1982) 110n, 113n; (1989) 84n
Torelló, Josep 97–107
Torras, Jaume 9, 20, 58, 89n,
93–113; (1984) 110n
town and country 8, 107, 160–3,
177
trade/trading 6, 8, 40–1, 82, 190,
294; and apprenticeship 229,
235–7; classification 240–3, 244,
247–8, 250–1, 254; commercial
capitalism 30; cycle 286;
'diasporas' 94, 95, 104, 107;
interrelationships, European
15–20, 65; markets 3–26;
networks 142, 169–70; overseas
3, 119, 182: see also free; guilds;
international; population
expansion; restrictions; retail
tradesmen, small 13
trades unions 167, 174
tradition 106, 107–8, 161, 166, 287
traditional corporate structure
188–9
training: and apprenticeship 228,
231, 232, 254–5; commercial 81;
and gender 227–58; industrial
81, 232; moral 231; as social
institution 22; systems 38;
vocational 228, 231
transport 20–1, 33, 36, 40, 162,
182–3
Truck Acts 147
truck practices 292

Ulster: sewing industry 139–56
unskilled labour 163
United States of America, trade
with 11, 121, 142, 145
upper-class demand 14
urban: commercial and service
functions 6, 177; cultures 160;
decline 6, 9; economics/economy

6, 9, 159–72; employment 7, 77;
growth 6, 7–8, 16, 165, 173;
industries/industrialization 6, 7,
8, 58, 59, 161, 166, 170, 177; 'lag'
165; manufacture 6, 97,
157–258; merchants 4, 177;
production costs 167; resistance
to change 169; –rural society 7;
–rural shift 159, 161
urbanization of industry 6–7, 10,
13, 170, 196, 197–8
USA see United States of America

Verlag: capitalists 304–5, 306, 309
system 292; see also domestic
industries; outwork; putting out
Vicens Vivas, J. (1972) 65, 86n
Vilar, P. (1962) 65, 86n

Wadsworth, A.P. and Mann, J.L.
(1931) 82, 85n
wage goods 164, 165, 166
wages 12, 15, 166, 171n, 211–16,
304, 305, 309
water-power as resource 36, 181,
304
wealth, distribution of 190–6
weaver-farmers 277
weavers as mobile group 270
weaving 104, 105–6, 139, 140,
209–17, 218–19
Wedgwood, Josiah 21, 114, 134n
West Midlands: overseas trade 181,
182
Wilson, R.G. (1971) 120, 136–7n
world system 5
Wrightson, Keith 308, 319n
Wrigley, E.A. (1987) 6, 9, 23n, 24n
women 22, 203–58, 280–2: status
206
woollen industry 18, 19, 22, 31, 43,
63, 64: British 60, 61, 110n;
French 208; Spanish 65, 68, 80,
95, 96–108; Yorkshire 120–2,
261, 262–3, 264, 265, 285–8n; see
also spinning; weaving
work: culture 306–16; organization
20–1, 22, 116
workers 174, 292, 294, 297, 305

workforce 43, 174
workshops 33–4, 36, 176, 195, 262
worsted industry 18, 19, 104, 121,
 122; Yorkshire 262, 263, 264–6,
 285, 286–8

Young, Arthur (1969) 208, 211
youth, concept of 228
Yorkshire manufacturing
 industries 21, 45, 261–91; *see also*
 woollen/worsted industries